Masculinities and the Law

A Multidimensional Approach

Edited by Frank Rudy Cooper and Ann C. McGinley

Foreword by Michael Kimmel

If women default c at, then disguises both power and subjugation of diff't grps of men.

D1500748

NEW YORK UNIVERSITY PRESS
New York and London

NEW YORK UNIVERSITY PRESS
New York and London
www.nyupress.org

References to Internet websites (URLs) were accurate at the time of writing.
Neither the editors nor authors nor New York University Press are responsible for URLs that
may have expired or changed since the manuscript was prepared.

Library of Congress Cataloging-in-Publication Data

Masculinities and the law : a multidimensional approach / edited by Frank Rudy Cooper and
Ann C. McGinley ; foreword by Michael Kimmel.
    p. cm.
Includes bibliographical references and index.
ISBN 978-0-8147-6403-9 (cl : alk. paper)
ISBN 978-0-8147-6969-0 (pbk. : alk. paper)
ISBN 978-0-8147-6404-6 (ebook)
ISBN 978-0-8147-2350-0 (ebook)
    1. Masculinity. 2. Feminist theory. 3. Race. I. Cooper, Frank Rudy. II. McGinley, Ann C.
HQ1088.M85 2012
305.31--dc23   2012009363

New York University Press books are printed on acid-free paper,
and their binding materials are chosen for strength and durability.
We strive to use environmentally responsible suppliers and materials
to the greatest extent possible in publishing our books.

Manufactured in the United States of America
c 10 9 8 7 6 5 4 3 2 1
p 10 9 8 7 6 5 4 3 2 1

To my children, Ryan, Shanen, and Reed McGinley-Stempel, and to my husband and colleague, Jeff Stempel
Ann

To my son, Thelonious Abraham Cooper
Frank

CONTENTS

ACKNOWLEDGMENTS

First of all, we wish to acknowledge our extreme gratitude for the work of Rick Buckingham. The Suffolk University Law School Moakley Law Library Electronic Services/Legal Reference Librarian, Rick served as the Citation and Formatting Czar for this whole book. His fingerprints are on every chapter. His attention to detail, insightfulness, and patience were invaluable. Thank you, Rick. Thanks as well to Suffolk University Law School Moakley Law Library Director and Professor of Law Elizabeth McKenzie for loaning Rick to us.

The Wiener-Rogers Law Library at UNLV Boyd School of Law has been extremely helpful. In particular, the Library Director and Associate Professor of Law, Jeanne Price, has been wonderful in supporting the project. She amassed a comprehensive collection on masculinities, created an excellent bibliography on masculinities, and presented an inspiring book display for our conference on masculinities held at UNLV Boyd School of Law in February 2011: *Multidimensional Masculinities and Law: A Colloquium*. Boyd law students Erica Bouttee, Derek Marr, and Elizabeth Ellison have compiled and updated the bibliography. The colloquium presentations can be found at UNLV Law School's institutional repository: Scholarly Commons @UNLV Law. It appears at http://scholars.law.unlv.edu/mml/2011. UNLV Boyd School of Law IT head Don Castle and his student helpers were also particularly helpful at the colloquium. Throughout the entire book project, David McClure, head of research and curriculum services at the law library, never failed to find what we needed in a timely fashion.

Suffolk University Law School, especially through Dean Camille A. Nelson, has provided both material and emotional support for this project from the start. Many of Frank's colleagues deserve "shout-outs" for assistance and support, not least of which, the following: Andrew Beckerman-Rodau, Christopher Dearborn, Kathleen Engel, Diane Juliar, Kim McLaurin, Andrew Perlman, Jeff Pokorak, Ann McGonigle Santos, Miguel Schor, Ilene Seidman, Ragini Shah, Patrick Shin, Jessica Silbey, Linda Simard, Gabe Teninbaum, and Elizabeth Trujillo. Reference librarian Diane D'Angelo has also been especially helpful.

UNLV William S. Boyd School of Law has been extremely helpful. Dean John V. White has been supportive throughout and sponsored a wonderful conference with authors from this book and other masculinities scholars as we were editing the book. That conference was invaluable to our improved understanding of the endeavor. Faculty members at UNLV Boyd School of Law were also very supportive. Particular thanks go to Rachel Anderson, Ann Cammett, Linda Edwards, Sylvia Lazos, Elizabeth MacDowell, Fatma Marouf, Jay Mootz, Terry Pollman, and Elaine Shoben. The staff at UNLV was also extremely helpful in assuring the success of the conference, especially Annette Mann, Elaina Bhatttacharyya, Kelli Bonds, Maria Campos, and Sandra Rodriguez. In particular, Associate Dean Christine Smith's work was invaluable. Special thanks go to student fellows Debra Amens and Jill Koloske for the work they did on the conference.

We wish to acknowledge Deborah Gershenowitz, Senior Editor for New York University Press, who championed this project from the beginning and provided valuable advice at every stage. Also helpful were Gabrielle Begue, Despina P. Gimbel, Constance Grady, and Alexia Traganas of NYU Press.

The work and advice of many scholars has inspired and aided us. Among them, we wish to single out Nancy Dowd for her book, *The Man Question: Male Subordination and Privilege* (NYU Press, 2010). Also particularly helpful were the work and comments of Christine Beasley, Devon Carbado, Martha Chamallas, David Cohen, Richard Collier, R. W. Connell, Jerome McCristal Culp, Richard Delgado, Angela Harris, Joan Howarth, Darren Hutchinson, Michael Kimmel, Cynthia Lee, Nancy Levit, Eric Miller, Athena Mutua, Marc Poirier, Jean Stefancic, Song Richardson, Russell Robinson, Michael Thomson, Frank Valdes, Valorie Vojdik, Juliet Williams, and Verna Williams. Martha Fineman's work and the workshop on masculinities and law that she and Michael Thomson conducted at Emory Law School were especially helpful.

Frank wishes to acknowledge the great support of his wife, Daniella Etel Courban. A doctor, an artist, an avid reader of contemporary literature, and an excellent mother, Daniella's suggestions and patience have been sustaining throughout this process. Frank also wishes to acknowledge the support of some of his family members: daughters Kalila Courban and Sage Shavers; parents Clarence and Fran Cooper; brother Seth Martin Cooper; and sisters Autumn Cooper McDonald and Sarah Lynne Cooper Lundell.

Ann wishes to thank her husband and colleague, Jeff Stempel, who spent hours discussing masculinities and how they affect men, women, and the law. She also thanks her mother, Mary McGinley, who even in her tenth decade is supportive and interested, and her sisters and brother, Ellin Daum, Laurie McGinley, and Paul McGinley, for their support. Last, but not least, Ann thanks her children, Ryan, Shanen, and Reed McGinley-Stempel, all of whom probably have heard more than they would like about men and masculinity.

MICHAEL KIMMEL

Not so long ago, a volume on "Masculinities and Law" would have been a non sequiter. It wasn't really until the 1960s that feminists began to question the exclusion of actual, real, corporeal women from the legal profession, and it took another decade until feminist legal theorists revealed that the relationship of gender and law was not merely a simple dynamic of discrimination or exclusion. Those earlier scholars had often assumed that gender was like property—a possession, something one either "had" or "acquired" through some mystical process called socialization, by which the values and norms of society were inscribed onto a black slate creature, much as the crimes of Kafka's penal colony inhabitants had their crimes inscribed upon their skin.

And still, when one said "gender," one meant women. A course on Gender and Law in the late 1980s would have largely centered on discrimination against women—workplace discrimination, sex-typing of jobs, sex segregation—and the exclusion of women from various institutions, such as the military or fire departments. By the end of that decade, such a course would have added "sexuality" issues, such as prostitution, pornography, and sexual assault.

By the mid-1990s, scholars began to recognize not only that "men have gender too," in that infelicitous formulation, and that, more accurately, the term "gender" included men. What's more, politically, the failure to include men-as-gendered in our work meant that men remained the unexamined center, the invisible pole around which gender dynamics revolved. Not "naming" men and masculinity reinscribed their dominance.

Not only were men gendered, but institutional practices, discourses, were gendered. In the workplace, the emphasis on the ideal worker as an unencumbered worker made women's experiences inevitably problematic, given traditional family arrangements. Institutional practices, such as front-loading the heaviest workloads on professionals in their first years of their careers, ages 25–40, were gendered, meaning that women, more often than men, had to choose between work advancement and family lives—a choice their partners rarely seem to have been asked to make. Indeed, the law itself—with its over-emphasis on the autonomy of the individual actor over his or her embeddedness in webs of connections—was a gendered discourse. Institutional frameworks such as the market and the state, framed by rationality and the sanctity of the individual, are likewise gendered as masculine.

Thus, it turned out that gender equality would entail more than simply removing institutional barriers to women's entry, but would require also a reformulation of the organizing normative principles of those institutions. Gender equality was not simply adding women as narrators of their own lives (the old "add women and stir" model); it also required a reframing of the story itself.

This reframing could get very depressing, as researchers and activists suddenly faced the enormity of the task of substantive gender equality. It seemed that, armed with the ideas of Foucault and other postmodernists, scholars had stumbled on the depressing conclusion that power was embedded in the discursive arrangements of society, and that even resistance was subject to the same discursive practices, and that, therefore, even resistance reinscribed the legitimacy of the normative discursive arrangements. And, for a time, postmodernists did become politically depressed; struggles over power became depoliticized contestations over texts. Someone took the politics out of political struggle.

Not so, however, in the law. Or at least it seemed that way to this outsider. Just as the social sciences and humanities turned inward, gender equality made enormous advances in the legal arena. Landmark cases, from *Price Waterhouse v. Hopkins*[1] to *U.S. v. Virginia*,[2] and new legal instruments, such as Title IX, removed obstacles to women's entry and insisted that, once admitted, the playing field be leveled.

But something happened during those legal struggles for the inclusion of women. The "question" of masculinity suddenly became obvious—not simply as the disembodied norm against which women were always to be measured. At Virginia Military Institute, for example, as in the entry of women into fire departments and the military more generally, the question was framed as "can women do what men do—that is, are they as 'competent' for military training as men are?" To several pioneering legal scholars of masculinity that was the wrong question—or at least only one question on offer. What does it say about masculinity? What does it say about men who do not choose to go to Virginia Military Institute? What about differences among men?

This pioneering group of scholars, including several who are represented in this collection—such as Ann McGinley, Deborah Brake, Nancy Levit, Athena Mutua, Nancy Dowd, and Val Vojdik—mobilized multicultural feminist theory to push beyond the notion of women being measured by male standards (and thus put in the strange position of having to assert that they were just as good at masculinity as men were), to decentering masculinity as the norm against which all behaviors were to be measured, and thus to deconstructing masculinities (note the plural).

As a social scientist, but an outsider to legal scholarship, that has been my reading of the dominant trajectory of legal research—this disaggregating of masculinity into multiple iterations and exploring the normative relations among masculinities. And it's been remarkably fruitful—as in the work on men as victims of sexual harassment (as in *Oncale v. Sundowner Offshore Services, Inc.*),[3] bullying, fatherhood, and even Don't Ask, Don't Tell and gay marriage. Seeing male-male interactions as equally constitutive of the normative construction of gender, and the consequent gender policing of some men by other men—that is, the focus on the specifically *homosocial* nature of much of masculinity construction—has been enormously generative of insight.

Some have even said that this line of research has gone too far, as if the focus on the homosocial has come dangerously close to writing women out of the social construction of masculinity altogether. However, making this homosocial foundation visible in gender dynamics does not mean ignoring the important role of relations between women and men; it means understanding precisely the dynamic interaction between heterosocial and homosocial interactions in the construction of both masculinities and femininities. Men and women are both policed by both men and women—and the social institutions that express and solidify these interactions legitimate this policing.

The chapters in this collection take us beyond this conversation and herald a new generation of legal scholarship on masculinities. These chapters take variations among men as a given, not as a problem to be explained. They assume the homosocial policing as well as the dynamics of inequality between women and men.

Some essays, particularly those in part I, establish what is now a two-decades-long legal tradition of using feminist theory, queer theory, and multicultural theory to explore variations and dynamics among masculinities. Subsequent parts examine the legal implications of the inequalities among men and the relations among different groups of men. And they represent the three most critical directions that masculinities research is today heading.

The chapters in part II are more personal than those in the preceding group, but no less theoretical. Discussing gender in law requires that we take account of people's stories, their own experiences. In a legal apparatus that often disaggregates to protect individuals (a gendered move itself), these stories suggest both the limits of traditional constructions of masculinity and the promise of embracing difference. It's not just those on the margins who benefit from these inclusive efforts; it's the center itself, and the relationship between center and margin which are challenged and often upended.

The chapters in part III explore more literally embodied masculinities, as contrasted with either theoretical constructions in law or in media representations like television shows. Dealing with gender nonconformity and gender variance, as David Cohen does, exposes the fictions of a biologically based binary that is the foundation of legal gender theory. Seeing prison rape as a racial issue as well as a gender issue, and re-examining the taken for granted equation of sports and masculinity through looking at Title IX, both expand the theoretical conversation and ground it in corporeality.

Finally, masculinity studies has taken a global turn—seeing local constructions as illustrative of the social foundation of gender ideologies, as well as the ways in which those local constructions influence, and are influenced by, global processes of gender arrangements (such as global flows of labor). The chapters in part IV amply illustrate the promise of this global turn—whether in debates about appropriate local gender arrangements (the head scarf), the mobilization of children into masculinity-producing behaviors (child soldiers), or in the ways that local cultural expressions articulate with global sexual relations.

Masculinities and the Law: A Multidimensional Approach thus inherits a rich intellectual legacy framed over the past few decades as masculinity has been examined through various legal theoretical lenses. These chapters do not rest on that legacy, but rather rest uneasily with it, pushing at its seams, exploring its crevices. And by focusing on the three most generative substantive areas of research—the body, the global, and the self-reflectively individual—these chapters both express the richness of the current state of the field and offer the promise of what that field may offer in the future.

NOTES

1. 490 U.S. 228 (1989).
2. 518 U.S. 515 (1996).
3. 523 U.S. 75 (1998).

INTRODUCTION

Masculinities, Multidimensionality, and Law: Why They Need One Another

ANN C. MCGINLEY AND FRANK RUDY COOPER

This book engages the emergence of a new school of legal thought: multidimensional masculinities theory. As a critical theory of law, multidimensional masculinities theory assumes that law distributes power by relying upon assumptions about human behavior that reproduce preexisting social relations. Law and culture are co-constitutive (Nice 2000): cultural norms influence law and legal norms simultaneously influence culture. This book seeks to expand critical legal theory by considering a set of cultural and legal norms that have been under-explored: masculinities.

Masculinities theory has already established itself in the social sciences (Connell 1995), and posits that "assumptions about the meaning of manhood influence behaviors, ideologies, and institutions" (Cooper 2009, 635). Masculinities scholars analyze "how societal norms shape behavior of individual men and women, how masculinities are imbedded in the structure of institutions, and how individuals and groups perform masculinities within those institutions" (McGinley 2010, 720). Masculinities scholars thus evaluate the ways that concepts of masculinity are used to produce power.

The purpose of multidimensional masculinities theory is to investigate how concepts of masculinity interact with other categories of identity in varied legal contexts. Multidimensionality theory holds that categories of identity are (1) always intertwined with one another and (2) experienced and interpreted differently in different contexts (Cooper 2010). We apply multidimensionality theory to masculinities theory because it helps show that masculinities differ depending on the context and the other categories of identity with which they overlap. We bring masculinities theory to multidimensionality theory because too few scholars have focused multidimensionality theory on the often-invisible category of masculinity.[1]

Multidimensional masculinities theory has a number of theoretical foundations. It derives from feminist theory, feminist legal theory, and critical race theory (especially critical race feminism, as influenced by queer theory), which together spawned multidimensionality theory. This book attempts to expand masculinities theory by viewing it through a multidimensional lens in order to examine legal issues in new ways. To convey this approach, we begin with a short explanation of how multidimensional masculinities theory has emerged and where we hope the new discipline of Multidimensional Masculinities and Law will go.

Historical Development of Underlying Theories

When looking at feminist legal theory and critical race theory as the foundations of multidimensional masculinities theory, we see contrasting trajectories. In both the social sciences and law, feminist theory, in large part, birthed masculinities theory. In this book we intentionally intervene in masculinities theory in order to bring critical race and feminist theories to masculinities theory and apply the result to law.

Feminist Theory and Feminist Legal Theory

Masculinities theory is an outgrowth of the feminist theorizing that developed as a response to the "feminist movement" of the late 1960s and early 1970s. Those feminists posited that patriarchal systems allowed men as a group to exercise power over women as a group. Soon thereafter, feminist legal theory developed. As the numbers of women in the legal academy grew, they began to challenge the male-oriented foundations of the law. Feminist legal theory, "as an approach ... describes and analyzes the law's impact on women, particularly focusing on how law subordinates women" (Perry 2011, 244).

Similarly, the number of law professors of color increased significantly in the late 1980s, and some of these professors began to write about race in new ways, challenging the neutrality of the law (ibid.). These scholars focused on the invisible racial biases contained in the law. They would ultimately create the critical race theory movement. In the late 1980s and early 1990s, Kimberlé Crenshaw and Angela Harris, two black female law professors, wrote influential articles criticizing white feminist legal theorists for their failure to recognize that women of color experience law and culture differently than white women do (ibid. 244–45).

Simultaneously, postmodernism began to take hold in feminist thought, especially in the social sciences, emphasizing that there is no one truth and questioning the power of law to find one solution to a common problem among women (Vicente 1997). Recently, feminist legal theorists like Martha Fineman do not focus on gender. Rather, they address what they perceive to be all people's common vulnerability (Fineman 2008). Nonetheless, it is fair to say that feminist theory originally focused on women and that many, if not most, feminist legal theorists continue to do so.

As feminist legal theory took hold in the legal academy, masculinities theory was emerging in the social sciences in response to the women's movement of the 1970s. Masculinities theorists would agree with feminists that men as a group have power over women as a group, but they tend to complicate the situation. Peter F. Murphy explains that by the late 1970s, for the first time, men began to examine the effects of the social construction of the roles of men. In essence, men started using feminist methodology to "turn the feminist lens upon themselves as men" (Murphy 2004, 9). He states, "feminism became more a critical perspective through which men could scrutinize masculinity, and less a call for men to act solely as advocates for women's causes" (ibid.).

Whereas feminist theory focuses on women as the subject, masculinities theorists focus on men. Both theories see much of gender as socially constructed, but feminist theory, in its focus on women, tends to see men in essentialist ways (Dowd 2010). Feminist theory has tended to analyze all men as fundamentally and equally oppressors of women. Thus, while feminist theory does the important work of analyzing the power that men have as a group over women as a group, it does not always consider how men achieve power and retain power, power differentials among men, and how those power differentials harm not only women as a group but also some men. In contrast, masculinities theorists see masculinity as a social construct that encourages men to compete with one another in order to prove their masculinity to each other. Those behaviors, in turn, harm women because as men anxiously compete to prove their masculinity to one another, they often use women as pawns or props in the competition (Kimmel 2005). Moreover, segregation of the sexes and differentiation from women and all things "feminine" enhances the masculinity of men, leading to the false impression that women are inferior (Cohen, this volume).

The masculinities theorists whose work we develop in the legal context are feminists, and the theory derives from feminism, but, unlike feminist theory, much of this work describes the harm that our gendered culture does to men. In joining this discussion of harms to men, we feel the need to emphatically distance ourselves from certain work on men. There is another branch of theorists who engage in male studies who agree that culture harms men, but who see feminism as one of the culprits. This group sees feminism as placing a restriction on men's true nature and encourages men to "be men" by engaging in hypermasculine behaviors. The classic statement of that approach is Robert Bly's *Iron John: A Book about Men* (1992). Groups of mostly white, mostly older men meet to bemoan their position in the world vis-à-vis women (Liu 2011). We see that work as unsophisticated in its understanding of the nature of the gender system and the harm it does to men, and downright puerile in its depiction of women and suggestion that the answer is to be more manly (defined as aggressive). There exists another branch of writings on men that might be called "collaborator 'feminism.'" Here we are thinking of publications, mostly by women, that claim there is a "War on Boys." An example is Christina Hoff Sommers, *The War against Boys: How Misguided Feminism Is Harming Our Young Men* (2001). These texts seem to be aligned with groups like the anti-choice Susan B. Anthony List and the "mama grizzly" politicians. Such claims to feminism would be laughable if they were not so dangerous.

Feminist legal theorists who engage with masculinities theory not only analyze the ways masculinities harm men but also ask how we might break down gender segregation and social gender barriers to the benefit of both men and women. In this collection, for example, Nancy Dowd, Nancy Levit, and Ann McGinley use masculinities theory not only to understand the male subject better, but also to return to the question of how societal constructions of men's roles create difficulties for women who seek equality. It is necessary, they assert, to understand masculinities theory and the pressure that the gender order places on men in order to consider how feminism should respond. Moreover, Dowd, Levit, and McGinley explain that it is often important to shift lenses in order to see what is in front of you. For example, a study of boys in prisons requires us to shift the primary lens of analysis from gender to race in order to understand the simultaneously gendered and raced issues prevalent in the juvenile justice system.

This book engages in such lens-shifting in order to merge masculinities theory with feminist and critical race theories, and in some instances, queer theory, to achieve an understanding of why masculinity in general is such an enduring social value and how masculinities combine with race, sexual orientation, class, and other identities in different contexts. Furthermore, it uses multiple lenses to show both how identity concepts are embedded in the law and how the law furthers gendered, racial, classed, and other hierarchies.

In pursuing this project, we note that although masculinities theory begins with feminism, it sometimes becomes so absorbed with its analysis of the harm that socially constructed masculinity does to men that it appears to forget that, as a group, men have power over women as a group. Thus, some masculinities theorists have responded to this weakness by moving from the concept of hegemonic masculinity, the view that there is a form of masculinity that is most powerful, to the concept of the hegemony of men, the view that men as a group have significant power even though individual men do not always experience that power because of their race, class, or other characteristics (Beasley 2008; Hearn 2004).[2] We do not see the concepts of hegemonic masculinity and the hegemony of men as mutually exclusive. We endorse an approach that uses the idea of hegemonic (norm-setting) masculinity to explain why women and some men are disadvantaged in a given cultural context but also remains vigilant about remembering the overall dominance of men over women. We use the term "hegemonic masculinity" more broadly here to mean any form of masculinity that has power over others in a particular place at a particular time. Thus, although many regard the upper-middle-class white male's form of masculinity as hegemonic, that type of masculinity is most powerful in many settings, but not in all. Other forms of masculinities that are often characterized as reactive to the hegemonic masculinity may actually become hegemonic (in the sense of being norm-setting) in certain local settings (Demetriou 2001). For example, while the white upper-middle-class type of masculinity may reign in board rooms and may have more power socially because of its access to capital, hypermasculinities may be hegemonic when they govern in blue collar workplaces or inner-cities (Cooper, this volume; McGinley 2008). And, even these two types of hypermasculinity, both hegemonic in their own local economies, will manifest themselves differently depending on the other identities in play and the context of the situation.

Critical Race Theory

Multidimensional masculinities theory argues that we will best understand the significance of the multiplicity of identities and the difference context makes by linking feminist theory with a multi-lensed version of critical race theory. Critical race theory is fundamentally about investigating the paradox that race is simultaneously socially constructed and materially crucial (Cooper 2006b). One of the major tenets of critical race theory is that identities are "socially constructed." The meanings of race do not derive from nature, but nurture; people are trained to associate particular characteristics with particular phenotypes (Onwuachi-Willig and Barnes 2005). Second, there are hierarchies among and within categories of identity (Cooper 2006a). Third, the material consequences of the hierarchization of identities include the skewed distribution of goods ranging from money to social capital (ibid.). Fourth, the skewing of the distribution of goods, previously accomplished by de jure and de facto regimes of intentional discrimination, is now most often accomplished by means of implicit bias (Kang 2005). Fifth, identities are intersectional. This means that people's identities intersect; we are simultaneously raced, gendered, sex-oriented, classed, and so on (Crenshaw 1991; Harris 1990).[3]

This book's multidimensional approach works within and also seeks to extend the intersectionality school of critical race theory. In a nutshell, intersectionality is the concept that unique identities are formed at the places where categories of identity intersect (Crenshaw 1991). For example, critical race feminism (Wing 2003) is premised on the notion that black women have identities that are not reducible to the sum of the lowest common denominator of racial identity plus the lowest common denominator of female identity. Black women's senses of self and the traits externally attributed to them are distinct from those associated with black men and white women. Intersectionality theory is thus antiessentialist in its rejection of the tendency to identify the needs or goals of black women in light of what is deemed generally important to groups with which they overlap (Harris 1990).

Multidimensionality theory stems from intersectionality theory and was developed by critical race theorists who were also concerned with queer theory (Hutchinson 2000; Kwan 1997; Valdes 1998). Multidimensionality theory can be broken down into at least five insights that are well-identified by Athena Mutua (this volume). As a general matter, these boil down to two principles: (1) identities are co-constituted and (2) identities are context-dependent. A multidimensional approach argues that since identities are co-constituted, race, gender, class, sexual orientation, and other discrete identities are actually imbricated within one another and cannot be understood in isolation. For example, assumptions about the gender characteristics (e.g., overly masculine) and sexual proclivities (e.g., excessive) of blacks are themselves part of the meanings of blackness (Williams 1998). A multidimensional approach also argues that the meanings of discrete identities, even when understood in light of their co-constituted nature, interact differently in different settings. For example, the self identities and attributed identities of black men are generally different in the U.S. South than the North (Richardson 2007). Moreover, the same individual may find different aspects of his identity to be more or less salient over time, in different settings, and depending on what other identities are in the mix. Consequently, an individual with the same combination of identities might be treated very differently depending on the cultural context (Ehrenreich 2002).

With that focus on context in mind, it will be helpful to describe how these multidimensionality insights relate to intersectionality theory.[4] Multidimensionality theory makes the most sense when it is explained in light of its roots in intersectionality theory. We switch terms simply to focus the mind on the broader context in which overlapping identities interact. The metaphor of intersectionality suggests two cars traveling down roads that collide at an intersection (Crenshaw 1989). The metaphor of multidimensionality more readily suggests a world that exists at many levels, with trains underground, planes above, and other automobiles on the roads. At the level of metaphor, while intersectionality theory might be understood as two-dimensional, multidimensionality theory clearly encompasses three or more dimensions. It is not that one cannot read the original intersectionality articles to imply multiple dimensions, but we think one is more likely to consider multiple identities and contexts when thinking about the multidimensionality of identities. As we discuss in the next part of this introduction, legal interpretation needs masculinities theory, and a masculinities theory of law needs multidimensional theory.

Themes of This Collection

In this collection we attempt to demonstrate that a multidimensional approach to masculinities theory allows us to capture human experience more accurately and richly. Because much legal interpretation is based on concepts of how and why people behave in certain ways in particular contexts, a more multidimensional understanding of this behavior should affect how law is interpreted. We therefore pose two questions that we briefly answer in this part of the introduction: (1) Why does law need masculinities theory? (2) Why does a masculinities theory of law need multidimensionality theory?

Why Does Law Need Masculinities Theory?

Much of law is based on untested implicit and explicit assumptions about human behavior. Many of those assumptions include dated views of motivations for behavior that judges and the law ascribe to actors in particular contexts. Masculinities theory can be used to push the law to interpret behavior differently in certain situations.

Law is a discipline that relies on other disciplines to give it content. (Or, at least it should do so more often than it does.) While laws and regulations can be found in law books or on the Internet, the laws themselves do not answer most of the important questions regarding interpretation and application. Most law, be it statutory or common law, needs interpretation so that it can be applied to the circumstances before the decision maker—judge, jury, legal counsel, or citizen—who is governed by the law. This interpretation is largely based on the decision maker's experience, especially his or her understanding of how "reasonable" people act in given circumstances. But often a decision maker is incapable of intuiting whether a person's behavior is proper or reasonable because the decision maker, perhaps unconsciously, employs stereotypes and cognitive biases as a screen through which she or he processes information. The Implicit Association Test, which grades the subject's automatic preference for black or white faces, for old or young, for the disabled or the able-bodied, for women or men in careers, demonstrates that even though people believe that they do not hold preferences for one group or another, they respond differently to prompts identified with one group or the other (Kang 2005). If people are still pervasively implicitly biased, and research confirms that we are, law's supposedly objective search for the perspective of "the reasonable man" or even "the reasonable person" is doomed (Lee 2003). The problem is not just that stereotyping prevents most people from acting reasonably, but also that stereotyping prevents us from attaining objectivity in our interpretations of behavior.

A powerful example of how stereotypical beliefs may affect law is the idea embodied in the saying, "boys will be boys." What does this aphorism say about masculinity? First, it assumes that all boys are the same, at least in the essence of what makes them male. Thus, their behavior is biologically related and not a product of social construction. Second, it assumes that it is natural for boys to act aggressively and wildly (Cohen 2009). This saying is used ordinarily to excuse behavior that is somewhat antisocial or wild, even illegal. It protects boys who have engaged in behavior such as drunkenness, destruction of property, or assaultive offenses against girls or less masculine boys. It presumes that this behavior is natural, a result of male hormones, and that the boys will outgrow it. It ordinarily applies to boys who, when acting in groups, engage in this destructive behavior. Because this behavior results from biology, the saying seems to assume, we should forgive boys for their behavior. They cannot help it. Nor can we help it through any intervention.

Masculinities theorists have a different view of the behavior. We do not agree that boys' behavior is controlled by biology. Society encourages and pressures boys to compete with one another to prove their masculinity. These pressures create relentless competition among boys, and they engage in a homosocial (intra-gender) battle to prove themselves (Kimmel 2005; Sedgewick 1985). Thus, a boy proves his masculinity by engaging in reckless, destructive behavior that often constructs women or girls as objects to be used to prove the boys' masculinity to other boys.

An example of this type of behavior and community response is illustrated in *Our Guys* (Lefkowitz 1998), the true story of a group of high school football players in a middle-class New Jersey town who raped a mentally impaired teenage girl. The boys involved had for a number of years engaged in destructive, disrespectful, and at times criminal behavior, all of which was excused or ignored by their families and the community. When the rape occurred, the town closed ranks around the boys and blamed the victim, the press, and the justice system, but few believed that the boys themselves or their families were responsible for the behavior. This reaction was harmful to the young woman and her family, to other girls in the town, to the community as a whole, to the other boys who did not engage in such behavior, and even to the very boys who raped the girl because, even despite the criminal prosecutions, they learned from their parents and the community that their behavior was acceptable.

This "boys will be boys" attitude is apparent in hostile work environment law under Title VII of the 1964 Civil Rights Act as well. A victim must prove by an objective standard that the harassing behavior was severe or pervasive, that it was unwelcome, and that it occurred "because of sex." This standard, which the courts interpret as being difficult to meet, doubts the veracity of the victim, assumes that the encounter was welcome, and then concludes that without severity or pervasiveness the behavior is not actionable. Moreover, when a man is the victim, especially when a group of men are engaged in the harassment, he often loses his lawsuit because the courts consider the behavior to be mere "hazing" or insufficiently severe or pervasive

(McGinley 2008). Masculinities theorists understand that these behaviors occur as homosocial testing grounds. Members of the group harass the victim to prove their masculinity to one another and to prove the masculinity of the group. They select their male victim because of his failure to conform to masculinity norms, and dominating him demonstrates to the group that he is not one of them. This harassment thereby preserves the masculinity of the group and its members.

In light of the "boys will be boys" attitude, consider an example of how masculinity plays out in the criminal law. When killers seek to mitigate their culpability from the crime of murder down to that of manslaughter, which significantly reduces the sentence, courts look for evidence that they acted in the "heat of passion" and with "sudden, adequate provocation." The crucial question of whether what provoked the killer was adequate is answered by asking how the "reasonable person" would act in the circumstances. This used to be called the "reasonable man" test. It turns out that many of the cases taught to law students in order to demonstrate the standard involve men killing women who have bruised their masculine esteem by denigrating their sexual prowess or becoming involved with other partners (Harris 2000). It seems that defending one's masculinity against women is reasonable enough to cut years off your sentence. Here, then, is an example of law mirroring, if not reinforcing or even creating, a culture in which we assume "boys will be boys."

But the boys in Our Guys did not merely enjoy the privilege of their gender. It also seems clear that they enjoyed privilege along lines of race, sexual orientation, class, and geography. How should we analyze the difference those privileges made?

Why Does a Masculinities Theory of Law Need Multidimensionality Theory?

A multidimensional masculinities analysis begins by noting that the "boys will be boys" slogan does not protect all boys. A large percentage of boys engage in lawbreaking behavior, but a much smaller percentage of them are prosecuted for it (Dowd 2010). While many believe that the law responds neutrally to criminal behavior by boys, social forces excuse some boys while punishing others for similar behavior. "Boys will be boys" shields only boys who are members of privileged classes—primarily white, "straight," upper-middle-class, Christian boys. Black boys, especially those in lower socioeconomic classes, do not enjoy the protection of the mantra. Rather, black boys are criminalized at younger and younger ages, often arrested and tried as adults for their violations. Black masculinity, an alternative (and assertedly subversive) form of masculinity, is dangerous and frightening to the white community, and the law presumes that it must be contained (ibid.).

Here we see that identities are co-constituted because masculinity does not mean just one thing even when we consider only the context of the juvenile justice system. Young black masculinity means "punish" while young white masculinity means "rehabilitate" (Goel 2009). Simultaneously, the differential meanings of young black and white masculinities demonstrate the contextual nature of the "boys will be boys" narrative. Because concepts such as "boys will be boys" are embedded into law, there will be unequal prosecution and treatment of boys, depending on their social class and race. Moreover, boys who are accused of crimes will be treated differently from girls who engage in similar behavior.

The topic of crime provides another example: the disturbing phenomenon of hyper-incarceration. You will note that we do not refer to the explosion in incarceration over the past 40 years as "mass incarceration." Instead, we use the term "hyper-incarceration" to capture the targeted nature of punishment in the United States. Mass incarceration would be either truly a general phenomenon or *deservedly* focused on certain populations requiring social control. The Nixon-era reframing of the government as the enemy, which was greatly accelerated by the Reagan Revolution, is the real reason we have seen the explosive growth of the prison industry. The current anti-government discourse suggests that helping the poor is insensible and warehousing the poor in prison is responsible.

Sociologist Loïc Wacquant reveals that this hyper-incarceration is a multidimensional attack on a specific group of people (Wacquant 2008). He argues that hyper-incarceration "[has] been finely targeted, first by class, second by that disguised brand of ethnicity called race, and third by place" (ibid. 59). That is, the poor are the targets. But not just any poor people: blacks and Latina/os. Further, it is important to note that hyper-incarceration consists mostly of inner-city residents. Moreover, there is a gender element, as it is the men who are most targeted for incarceration, while poor racial minority women in the inner city are "inculcat[ed with] the duty of working for work's sake" (ibid. 68). A straightforward masculinities approach to law might note hyper-incarceration's targeting of racial minority males, but needs multidimensionality theory to explain how all of the pieces of this puzzle fit together. The chapters in this book demonstrate the various ways that a multidimensional masculinities approach helps us better understand the inequalities built into the cultural narratives that affect and are affected by law.

This Collection of Chapters
Part I: Theorizing Multidimensional Masculinities

In chapter 1, Feminist Legal Theory Meets Masculinities Theory, Nancy Dowd, Nancy Levit, and Ann McGinley introduce the reader to masculinities theory. The authors argue that masculinities and feminist theories can aid one another in understanding gender. As with the physical sex segregation in education, work, and other areas, the theories themselves are ordinarily segregated by sex: feminist theory for women and masculinities theory for men. The chapter urges both feminists and masculinities theorists to learn from one another and to incorporate concepts from the other theory to gain a more complicated understanding of gender. It explains that masculinities theory, while derivative of feminist theory, often describes the circumstances of men only and focuses on men's identity without acknowledging male power, whereas feminist theory tends to focus on women and to see men as powerful in an essentialist way that disregards partly subordinated alternatives to the generally hegemonic masculinity. Masculinities theory can benefit from feminist theory by studying the power of men as a group. Feminists can learn from masculinities theorists that although men as a group are more powerful than women as a group, different circumstances may make individual men feel, and be, powerless.

Dowd, Levit, and McGinley also encourage the use of masculinities theory to reveal race to be a gender issue. They propose using complexity theory, of which multidimensionality theory is a form, to go beyond the intersection of race and gender to examine the myriad identity categories, experiences, and environments in which individuals are located. Masculinities theory, as these authors interpret it, would encourage a shifting of lenses when analyzing a legal problem. This lens-shifting allows the theorist to understand the problem from a more nuanced perspective. The chapter demonstrates how to shift the lens in various ways, by discussing the juvenile justice system as not only racially segregated, but also segregated by gender, and the implications that lens shift raises; by considering sex-segregated education through a racial lens, which allows a more nuanced understanding of the problems of segregating students by sex; and by analyzing *Ricci v. De Stefano*, a race discrimination suit, using a gender and class lens because of the gendered, classed, and racial history of firefighting.

Devon Carbado's chapter, Masculinity by Law, also shifts lenses. He starts with a feminist critique of the *Jespersen v. Harrah's Operating Co.* (9th Cir. 2004) case, in which a female casino bartender was fired for not wearing makeup, as an example of how women are not allowed to be masculine. He then analyzes the mainstream campaign against the anti-gay Don't Ask Don't Tell military policy in order to show that it normalized gays as white and blacks as heterosexual by presenting the sympathetic gay soldier as a hegemonic white man but for his sexual orientation. Carbado switches lenses again to show how both the ACLU's anti-racial profiling campaign and criticism of Sergeant Crowley for arresting Henry Louis Gates utilize a similar mechanism to make the paradigmatic victim normatively masculine in contrast to the presumed hypermasculinity of racial minority men. Carbado ties this all together by putting on the lens of Marlon Riggs' assertion that black-gay-masculinity is a "triple negation," which helps demonstrate that there are multiple normative masculinities. He thus concludes that we might employ the term "palatable masculinities" rather than "hegemonic masculinities."

Athena Mutua's chapter, The Multidimensional Turn: Revisiting Progressive Black Masculinities, picks up on the multiplicity of masculinities to argue for utilizing multidimensionality theory to analyze masculinities. Mutua's goal is to promote progressive black masculinities (Mutua 2006). That project would combine progressive blackness—the disruption of white supremacy—and progressive masculinities—the disruption of patriarchy. To describe the project, Mutua explicates multidimensionality theory. Multidimensionality has its roots in the related concepts of antiessentialism—the idea that there is no lowest common denominator experience of any identity group—and intersectionality theory, which analyzes the effects of the above-noted fact that every individual is the product of intersecting identities. Together, antiessentialism and intersectionality generate five tenets of multidimensionality. First, individuals have many dimensions of identity, ranging from gender to pet ownership. Second, groups are multidimensional, including male and female individuals, gay and straight individuals, and myriad other variations of the shared quality of, say, being black. Third, societies distribute resources based on hierarchies within and among identities. Fourth, those systems of allocation interact with one another in shifting ways. Fifth, the context in which the systems interact affects how particular individuals are seen and see themselves. Mutua ties those insights together by arguing that black men should pursue progressive black masculinities because, having seen the way white supremacy oppresses racial minorities (and patriarchy oppresses both women and men), it is both ethical and strategically necessary to seek to disrupt all forms of oppression at once.

Frank Rudy Cooper's chapter, The King Stay the King: Multidimensional Masculinities and Capitalism in The Wire, picks up on and applies Mutua's argument for multidimensionality. He looks at the critically acclaimed HBO police drama The Wire's metaphor of the drug game as a chess game. This analogy is also a metaphor for the way the hierarchy of identities reproduces itself. He argues that "the king stay the king," in chess and in the game of real life identities, because we tend to accept the fundamental principle that there will always be some form of hierarchy. Addressing the hegemonic masculinity versus hegemony of men debate within masculinities studies, Cooper argues that multidimensionality theory helps provide an answer by showing that there is simultaneously a general but diffuse hegemonic masculinity and a variety of alternative masculinities that are sometimes hegemonic in particular contexts. In the context of *The Wire*, that simultaneity is reflected in the fact that the drug dealers who are so well-depicted in the show aspire to succeed under both the general society's definition of success and their own inner-city codes. Highlighting the class dynamics that travel along with racial and gender dynamics in the show, Cooper calls for a multidimensional masculinities theory that incorporates a critique of capitalism.

Part II: Telling Stories about (Heroic) Masculinities

In Rescue Me, Robert Chang discusses the absence of Asian Americans as firefighters in fire departments nationwide. Chang uses illustrations from popular culture to demonstrate that the common stereotype of Asian American men does not conform to masculine norms generally accepted as necessary for firefighters. For example, in the cable television program, *Rescue Me*, the firefighters are predominantly white men with an occasional black or Latino male and one woman. There are no Asian American firefighters. Their absence, moreover, is invisible, just like that of their non-existent female firefighter colleagues discussed in Dowd, Levit, and McGinley's chapter in this volume. Chang also describes the exaggerated homophobia and misogyny that is represented in *Rescue Me*. For example, in a speech to probationary officers, the main character brags about the size of his "balls," calls the cadets "pussies," and tells them that the fire department is in the business of discovering cowards. Thus, male firefighters reinforce their own masculinity by differentiating themselves from women and gays. And, because Asian Americans are considered effeminate and unmanly, they cannot be successful firefighters. Specifically, white men use firefighting to distance themselves from these "others" in order to assure their own manliness. Ultimately, the invisible absence of Asian American male firefighters exists not only in *Rescue Me*, but also in race discrimination lawsuits brought to equalize opportunities in fire departments. These suits, while important in gaining rights for some racial minorities, lionize the black/white racial paradigm and often neglect other racial minority groups.

The policing of the boundaries of masculinity, such as that occurring in firefighting, produces a fear that John Kang describes in the next chapter, Manliness's Paradox—the fear of being called a coward. Kang discusses soldiers in combat to demonstrate that not only women, but also men—even those who appear particularly masculine—are oppressed by the requirements of manliness. Kang demonstrates that courage, a virtue associated with and required of men by society to the extent that a lack of it is unmanly, actually results from men's fear (a woman's vice) of being considered a coward. He demonstrates through letters of Civil War soldiers as well as soldiers fighting in Vietnam and other wars that the same concern has existed among male soldiers for more than a century. Men who are soldiers demonstrate through their own words that their most haunting fear is that of being considered afraid. This fear propels them to go to war and to act bravely in battle. Thus, the paradox of manliness is that fear itself is what motivates fearlessness. Men, Kang notes, unlike women, do not have a choice to be courageous or not, if they are to be considered manly by society. He notes that being a man can thus be "appallingly oppressive." This oppression is regulated by law, which requires men, and not women, to register for the draft and which prohibits women, but not men, from engaging in combat.

Like Chang's firefighters and Kang's soldiers, undocumented male workers seek masculinity in their work. In Border-Crossing Stories and Masculinities, Leticia Saucedo analyzes interviews she conducted with men from Hidalgo, Mexico, who immigrated illegally to the United States to work and then returned to Mexico. Saucedo identifies three masculinity narratives that she coins the "endurance" narrative, the "family provider" narrative, and the "family order" narrative. The endurance narrative emphasizes the difficulty of passing into the United States illegally and the strength and honor that men who make the passage must have in order to cross the border; strength that is necessary to do the difficult and dirty work that the undocumented workers find when they get to the United States. The family provider narrative focuses on the men's sacrifice in order to provide for their families back home in Mexico and bestows honor and dignity on the men who agree to make the sacrifice. The family order narrative helps the men to deny the effect of the American economy on their job prospects in the United States and claims instead that the men return to Mexico in order to assure that their children are receiving the proper discipline that only a man can bestow. All of these narratives allow men who work in the most menial jobs in the United States, and who are sometimes intensely disliked by U.S. citizens, to enhance their masculinity and their dignity in their own eyes and in the eyes of their families and their communities. The narratives explain why changes in the immigration laws that make it more difficult and more dangerous to enter the United States actually serve to enhance the masculinity of the men who cross the border and therefore make border crossing attractive to them.

Part III: Questioning Segregation in Masculine Spaces

David Cohen's chapter, Sex Segregation, Masculinities, and Gender-Variant Individuals, leads off Part III by arguing that sex segregation harms women by reinforcing the power of men as a superior group and subordinates individuals whose biological sex and/or gender do not conform to societal ideals (gender variants) by promoting assimilation to essentialist notions of gender. For Cohen, sex segregation, whether required or merely tolerated by law, reproduces the essentialist idea that there are only two sexes and that those sexes determine whether a person is and should be masculine or feminine. The tendency of the law and society to sex segregate reinforces both hegemonic masculinity and the hegemony of men. It is not only restrictive but also dangerous for gender variants because it forces people to conform to the expectations that society places on them.

Kim Shayo Buchanan's chapter, E-race-ing Gender: The Racial Construction of Prison Rape, shifts the lens when she analyzes another sex-segregated environment: prisons. She explains that the empirical research concerning prison rape in male prisons has largely been ignored by those telling the story of prison rape. Although the race rape myth about prisons posits that black men subject white men to rape in prisons more frequently, the empirical data do not support this conclusion. Rather, it is interracial men who are raped more often by fellow prisoners, and black men who are raped more frequently by staff. More importantly, rape in prison depends on gender—masculinity—rather than race. As Buchanan notes, the prison rapist "is commonly described in hypermasculine terms" while his victim is often described as a "fag" or a "queen" (Buchanan, this volume). Prison rape is, therefore, a "practice of gender enforcement that enhances the perpetrator's masculinity while emasculating his target" (ibid.).

Buchanan's chapter further demonstrates that the race rape myth is enduring despite its falsity. Academic commentators and policymakers uncritically assert and rely on it when making policy prescriptions. The danger in this response, according to Buchanan, is that the uncritical acceptance of the myth affects whether a particular inmate is believed when he reports rape. It also leads to bad policy, as it has encouraged the current call by some policymakers for racial segregation in the prisons.

Deborah Brake's chapter, Sport and Masculinity: The Promise and Limits of Title IX, also tells the story of a particularly valorized masculinity, that of athletes. She starts by noting the successes of Title IX's development of women's sports. Unfortunately, that success has not de-gendered sports. Certain sports provide a celebrated, traditional masculinity that privileges heterosexuality and confers access to women, though the valorization varies somewhat along lines of race and class. In order to explore that valorized masculinity, Brake considers legal opinions about claims that male athletes sexually assaulted women or male teammates. She finds some hope in courts' increasing ability to see the gendered nature of actions such as hazing. She argues that we need to encourage this increasing sensitivity of the courts because male as well as female athletes pay a price for the valorization of sports masculinity, especially in the form of educational neglect.

Part IV: Constructing Masculinities in the Global Context

In Masculinities and Child Soldiers in Post-Conflict Societies, Fionnuala Ní Aoláin, Naomi Cahn, and Dina Haynes explore the importance of masculinities in the rehabilitation of child soldiers in post-conflict societies. They explain that conflict does not end automatically with the formal end of hostilities. Post-conflict societies experience numerous problems related to gender. War, violence, and masculinity are inextricably related, and peacekeepers must understand that the formal end of public hostilities does not mean that hostilities have ended in the private sphere. Boy soldiers are both perpetrators and victims of the conflict and have been trained in a hypermasculine method of fighting. This training, along with the child soldiers' failure to attend school and inability to provide for themselves and their families economically in nonviolent ways, can cause serious problems. Moreover, there are intergenerational pressures on boys and girls that entrench stratified gender roles. As the authors state, "The core point is that conflicted societies can mummify highly gendered role expectations for men and for women from early childhood in ways that are quantifiably more intense than in societies not experiencing communal violence" (Ní Aoláin, Cahn, and Haynes, this volume). The authors thus argue that DDR programs (disarmament, demobilization, and reintegration) should take into account the problematic transfer of masculinity norms and their contribution to conflict. These programs need to develop counseling and training that addresses the harms experienced by child soldiers and the community.

In Sexuality without Borders: Exploring the Paradoxical Connection between Dancehall and Colonial Law in Jamaica, Camille Nelson interrogates the hypermasculine, homophobic lyrics of dancehall music in Jamaica. Explaining that dancehall music is wildly popular in Jamaica and important in defining the identity of Jamaicans, Nelson resists the calls to ban the music. Musicians engaged in dancehall argue that by condemning homosexuality they are resisting white colonial power. They link colonial power to homosexuality, and express their own identities as African and heterosexual. Ironically, Nelson demonstrates, the Jamaican statute criminalizing homosexuality was created by the English colonizers. Moreover, Nelson demonstrates that the law is based in masculinity in that it forbids male penetration of other men but does not equally condemn women engaging in same-sex acts. Finally, she notes with irony that contemporary Jamaican leaders forbid homosexuals in their cabinets. Thus, these contemporary leaders are aligned with the Jamaican dancehall artists who assert that they create an authentic Jamaican voice by condemning homosexuality. While not supporting the under-theorized proposals for external boycotts of Jamaica, Nelson concludes that Jamaicans should recognize the colonial roots of laws banning homosexual acts and revise the culture and music they have inspired.

Valorie K. Vojdik's chapter, Masculinities, Feminism, and the Turkish Headscarf Ban:Revisiting *Şahin v. Turkey*, reveals how masculinities are at stake in the debate over banning the Islamic headscarf. She reviews a legal case before the European Court of Human Rights (ECHR) that was brought by a female Turkish student who was suspended from her university for wearing the headscarf in contravention of the state's enforcement of secularism. The court held the ban was justified in order to prevent the threat posed by Islamic fundamentalism. Vojdik reveals that the headscarf ban was part of a narrative situating the state as the masculine protector of women from the excessive and restrictive masculinity of Islamic fundamentalists. Vojdik complicates Turkey's presentation as enlightened by showing that the women now challenging the ban are using the headscarf as a political act, challenging the secularism of the state while not accepting some tenets of Islamic fundamentalism. The ECHR's ruling against the headscarf thus reproduces a masculinist narrative in the face of certain women's attempts to exercise their agency.

Conclusion

In the proverbial nutshell, this book attempts to unify three different areas of inquiry—masculinities theory, multidimensionality theory, and law—to arrive at a deeper understanding of how gender, race, national origin, religion, sexual orientation, class, and other identity factors are present yet often invisible in legal theory and doctrine. Multidimensional masculinities theory of law argues that we must always simultaneously consider gender, race, class, and other identities, but we must also often shift lenses to put the primary focus on a particular identity that is foregrounded in that cultural context. Multidimensional masculinities theory thus explores how particular concepts of masculinity are used to produce power in ways that differ depending on what other categories of identity they interact with, and in what cultural context. Using that approach, this book reveals how individual men and groups of men achieve and retain power, that there are differentials among men, and how these differentials harm both women as a group and some men. Because much legal analysis is based on narrow conceptions of how and why people act in certain ways in particular situations, multidimensional masculinities theory can change how law is interpreted and applied. We believe that these changes would result in a more just society.

NOTES

1. Of course forerunners exist (Carbado 1999; Harris 2000; Hutchinson 2000; Valdes 1998).
2. At the University of Nevada,Las Vegas Boyd School of Law February 18–19, 2011, conference celebrating the completion of the chapters in this book, *Multidimensional Masculinities and Law: A Colloquium*, Russell Robinson pointed out that the term "hegemony of men" risks erasing female masculinities.
3. For analysis of other tenets of critical race theory, see especially the three predominant volumes on the subject (Crenshaw et al. 1995; Delgado and Stefancic 2000; Perea et al. 2007).
4. At the aforementioned conference celebrating the completion of the chapters in this book, Devon Carbado emphasized that multidimensionality is not "post-intersectionality," but implicit within a proper reading of some of the original works. We agree, but use the term multidimensionality because we think its use tends to focus people on the influence of cultural context. At the same conference, Juliet Williams pointed out that there are political reasons for making people aware of the intersectional roots of multidimensionality, not least of which is to avoid displacement of the critical race feminist roots of intersectionality.

REFERENCES

Beasley, Christine. 2008. Rethinking Hegemonic Masculinity in a Globalizing World. *Men and Masculinities* 11:86–103.

Bly, Robert. 1992. *Iron John: A Book about Men*. New York: Vintage Books.

Carbado, Devon, ed. 1999. *Black Men on Race, Gender, and Sexuality*. New York: New York University Press.

Cohen, David. 2009. No Boy Left Behind? Single-Sex Education and the Essentialist Myth of Masculinity. *Indiana Law Journal* 84:135–88.

Connell, R. W. 1995. *Masculinities*. Berkeley: University of California Press.

Cooper, Frank Rudy. 2010. Masculinities, Post-Racialism, and the Gates Controversy: The False Equivalence between Officer and Civilian. *Nevada Law Journal* 11:1–43.

———. 2009. Our First Unisex President? Black Masculinity and Obama's Feminine Side. *Denver University Law Review* 86:633–61.

———. 2006a. Against Bipolar Black Masculinity: Intersectionality, Assimilation, Identity Performance, and Hierarchy. *U. C. Davis Law Review* 39: 853–903.

———. 2006b. The "Seesaw Effect" from Racial Profiling to Depolicing: Toward a Critical Cultural Theory. In *The New Civil Rights Research: A Constitutive Approach*, edited by Benjamin Fleury-Steiner and Laura Beth Nielsen. Burlington, VT: Ashgate, 139–55.

Crenshaw, Kimberlé W. 1991. Mapping the Margins: Intersectionality, Identity Politics, and Violence against Women of Color. *Stanford Law Review* 43:1241–99.

———. 1989. Demarginalizing the Intersection of Race and Sex: A Black Feminist Critique of Antidiscrimination Doctrine, Feminist Theory and Antiracist Politics. *University of Chicago Legal Forum* 1989:139—67.

Crenshaw, Kimberlé, Neil Gotanda, Gary Peller, and Kendall Thomas, eds. 1995. *Critical Race Theory: The Key Writings that Formed the Movement*. New York: New Press.

Delgado, Richard and Jean Stefancic, eds. 2000. *Critical Race Theory: The Cutting Edge*, 2nd ed. Philadelphia: Temple University Press.

Demetriou, Demetrakis Z. 2001. Connell's Concept of Hegemonic Masculinity: A Critique. *Theory and Society* 30(3):337–61.

Dowd, Nancy E. 2010. *The Man Question: Male Subordination and Privilege*. New York: New York University Press.

Ehrenreich, Nancy. 2002. Subordination and Symbiosis: Mechanisms of Mutual Support between Subordinating Systems. *University of Missouri-Kansas City Law Review* 71:251–79.

Fineman, Martha Albert. 2008. The Vulnerable Subject: Anchoring Equality in the Human Condition. *Yale Journal of Law and Feminism* 20:1-23.

Goel, Rashmi. 2009. Delinquent or Distracted?: Attention Deficit Disorder and the Construction of the Juvenile Offender. *Law and Inequality: A Journal of Theory and Practice* 27:1–52.

Harris, Angela P. 2000. Gender, Violence, Race, and Criminal Justice. *Stanford Law Review* 52:777–807.

———. 1990. Race and Essentialism in Feminist Legal Theory. *Stanford Law Review* 42:581–616.

Hearn, Jeff. 2004. From Hegemonic Masculinity to the Hegemony of Men. *Feminist Theory* 5(1):49–72.

Hutchinson, Darren Lenard. 2000. "Gay Rights" for "Gay Whites"?: Race, Sexual Identity, and Equal Protection Discourse. *Cornell Law Review* 85:1358–91.

Jespersen v. Harrah's Operating Co., Inc., 444 F.3d 1104 (9th Cir. 2004).

Kang, Jerry. 2005. Trojan Horses of Race. *Harvard Law Review* 118:1489–593.

Kimmel, Michael. 2005. *The Gender of Desire: Essays on Male Sexuality*. Albany: State University of New York Press.

Kwan, Peter. 1997. Jeffrey Dahmer and the Cosynthesis of Categories. *Hastings Law Journal* 48:1257–92.

Lee, Cynthia. 2003. *Murder and the Reasonable Man: Passion and Fear in the Criminal Courtroom*. New York: New York University Press.

Lefkowitz, Bernard. 1998. *Our Guys: The Glen Ridge Rape and the Secret Life of the Perfect Suburb*. New York: Vintage Books.

Liu, Jonathan. 2011. It's Raining on Men: Balls Deep at the Conference on Male Studies. New York Observer, http://www.observer.com/print/141414, April 12.

McGinley, Ann C. 2010. Erasing Boundaries: Masculinities, Sexual Minorities, and Employment Discrimination. *University of Michigan Journal of Law Reform* 53: 713–71.

———. 2008. Creating Masculine Identities: Bullying and Harassment "Because of Sex." *University of Colorado Law Review* 79:1151–241.

Murphy, Peter F., ed. 2004. *Feminism and Masculinities.* Oxford: Oxford University Press.

Mutua, Athena D. 2006. Theorizing Progressive Black Masculinities. In *Progressive Black Masculinities*, edited by Athena D. Mutua. New York: Routledge, 3–42.

Nice, Julie A. 2000. Equal Protection's Antinomies and the Promise of a Co-Constitutive Approach. *Cornell Law Review* 85:1392–425.

Onwuachi-Willig, Angela, and Mario L. Barnes. 2005. By Any Other Name?: On Being "Regarded as" Black, and Why Title VII Should Apply Even If Lakisha and Jamal Are White. *Wisconsin Law Review* 2005:1283–1343.

Perea, Juan, Richard Delgado, Angela Harris, Jean Stefancic, and Stephanie Wildman. 2007. *Race and Races: Cases and Resources for a Diverse America*, 2d ed. St. Paul, MN: Thomson/West.

Perry, Twila L. 2011. Family Law, Feminist Legal Theory, and the Problem of Racial Hierarchy. In *Transcending the Boundaries of Law: Generations of Feminism and Legal Theory*, edited by Martha Albertson Fineman. New York: Routledge, 244–57.

Richardson, Riché. 2007. *Black Masculinity and the U.S. South: From Uncle Tom to Gangsta.* Athens: University of Georgia Press.

Sedgwick, Eve Kosofsky. 1985. *Between Men: English Literature and Male Homosocial Desire.* New York: Columbia University Press.

Sommers, Christina Hoff. 2001. *The War against Boys: How Misguided Feminism Is Harming Our Young Men.* New York: Simon & Schuster.

Valdes, Francisco. 1998. Beyond Sexual Orientation in Queer Legal Theory: Majoritarianism, Multidimensionality, and Responsibility in Social Justice Scholarship or Legal Scholars as Cultural Warriors. *Denver University Law Review* 75:1409–64.

Vicente, Esther 1997. Feminist Legal Theories: My Own View from a Window in the Caribbean. *Revista Jurídica: Universidad de Puerto Rico* 66:211–68.

Wacquant, Loïc. 2008. Racial Stigma in the Making of America's Punitive State. In *Race, Incarceration, and American Values*, edited by Glen C. Loury; with Pamela Karlan, Loïc Wacquant, and Tommie Shelby. Cambridge, MA: MIT Press.

Williams, Rhonda M. 1998. Living at the Crossroads: Explorations in Race, Nationality, Sexuality, and Gender. In *The House That Race Built: Original Essays by Toni Morrison, Angela Y. Davis, Cornell West, and Others on Black Americans and Politics in America Today*, edited by Wahneema Lubiano. New York: Vintage.

Wing, Adrien Katherine, ed. 2003. *Critical Race Feminism: A Reader.* New York: New York University Press.

PART I

Theorizing Multidimensional Masculinities

1

Feminist Legal Theory Meets Masculinities Theory

NANCY E. DOWD, NANCY LEVIT, AND ANN C. MCGINLEY

Men and boys are gendered beings who operate in a gendered context and collectively experience both privilege and harm as a result of the social construction of what it means to be a boy or a man. Their collective privilege puts men as a group above women as a group, and infuses structures, culture, and policy with masculinities because men have historically held positions of power. At the same time, gender for men and boys does not operate uniformly, and is particularly affected by intersections with race, class, and sexual orientation. Within the collective of men and boys, there are hierarchies that reserve the highest privileges to only certain men and boys, and sometimes outweigh the benefits of manhood (Connell 2005; Dowd 2010).

"Masculinities" has multiple meanings. First, it is a structure that gives men as a group power over women as a group. Second, it is a set of practices, designed to maintain group power, that are considered "masculine." Third, it is the engagement in or the "doing" of these masculine practices by men or women. Finally, the term refers to a body of theory and scholarship by gender experts in various fields of social science.

Understanding and examining masculinities is a relatively recent area of scholarship. "Gender" is more frequently associated with girls and women, while boys and men are often treated as if they are gender-less. This everyday, taken-for-granted quality of masculinities perpetuates inequality behind either a façade of universality and neutrality or a myth of gender difference (Kimmel 2004a).

In this chapter we explore the theoretical scope of masculinities scholarship, and suggest some of the ways it can contribute to the project of equality and justice. First, we discuss the history and development of masculinities scholarship. Although derivative of feminist theory, masculinities scholarship has largely evolved separately from feminist theory. Second, we summarize the core theoretical contributions of masculinities scholarship. Primarily derived from sociology and psychology, this scholarship suggests a series of insights for gender analysis. Third, we explore the relationship between feminist theory and masculinities scholarship. The pattern of separate evolution of these two areas creates challenges. In addition, at the point of convergence, it raises the question of whether the future direction of the field should be in creating integrated theory or ongoing separate development with interchange and coalition but not a singular grand theory. At a minimum, we suggest some ways that feminism can benefit from masculinities scholarship and that masculinities scholarship can benefit from feminist insights. Fourth, we examine the interrelations among multiple identity categories by considering the racialization of gender issues. Here we look through the lens of masculinities theory at the construction of gender hierarchy through race, and conclude that this focus requires that race be addressed as a feminist and masculinities issue. Finally, we engage in demonstrating how masculinities are practiced by exploring two substantive areas: education and work. The education example is a powerful reminder of the harm of separate theorizing and the benefits of convergence and complexity. The work example exposes how gender policing occurs in the context of a male-dominant occupation—firefighting—and suggests how a gender-informed analysis can point the way to reform.

History and Development

Different strands of feminist legal theory, such as inequality theory or special treatment theory or postmodern feminism, have, respectively, treated men as oppressors, or as "other" or have simply omitted attention to the situations of men (Levit 1996). The result is to essentialize men: "Feminist theory has examined men, patriarchy, and masculine characteristics predominantly as sources of power, domination, inequality, and subordination . . . In much feminist analysis, men as a group largely have been undifferentiated" (Dowd 2008, 201–4). One unintended consequence of this neglect of men and masculinities is that it implicitly presumes that the lives of men are the standard default position. This presumption "inadvertently re-enshrine[s] men as the neutral yardstick by which to measure women's achievements" (Batlan et al. 2009, 127).

Early works in men's studies owed inspiration to feminist theorizing. When contemporary feminism pointed out that the characteristics of men were the unexamined norm, this prompted interest in "men's and boys' identities, conduct, and problems" (Connell, Hearn, and Kimmel 2005, 1). Masculinities studies are expressly about "understanding how male identity is constructed and sustained" and exposing the ways in which "structures and cultures are gendered male" (Dowd 2008, 231, 233). As a fledgling discipline, most of the early literature in men's studies was preoccupied with upper middle-class, white, professional men and heterosexual masculinity (Stoltenberg 1999, xii; Tolson 1977, 112, 143). Later constructions of masculinities recognized multiple different masculinities, shaped by different political and cultural circumstances, age, race, class, and sexuality. In both law and the social sciences, theorists have recognized that gender interacts and intersects with other identity characteristics and personal situations (Levit 2002).

Works in masculinities studies have examined how laws and institutions marginalize men who are battered, raped, or sexually harassed, men who want to be family caregivers, gender nonconforming men, and men of color in realms from the workplace to the criminal justice system. But masculinities studies show little interest in the female subject. While works in masculinities studies give somewhat more attention to feminist theory than to the contemporary situations of women, it is often primarily as an historical progenitor or source of methodology. Among the relatively few areas of intersection between masculinities studies and feminist theory have been issues regarding social constructivism, gender nonconformity, and LGBT (lesbian, gay, bisexual, and transgender) rights (Valdes 1995).

Core Contributions of Masculinities Scholarship

Masculinities scholarship, centered in sociology and psychology, has developed a rich body of work on gender theory (Connell 2005; Hearn 2004;

Kimmel 2004a; Messerschmidt 2001; Pleck 1995). In this scholarship there is a core set of understandings, which can be summarized as follows:

1. Men are not universal or undifferentiated. . . .
2. Men pay a price for privilege. . . .
3. Intersections of manhood particularly with race, class, and sexual orientation are critical to the interplay of privilege and disadvantage, to hierarchies among men, and to factors that may entirely trump male gender privilege. . . .
4. Masculinity is a social construction, not a biological given. . . .
5. Hegemonic masculinity recognizes that one masculinity norm dominates multiple masculinities. . . .
6. The patriarchal dividend is the benefit that all men have from the dominance of men in the overall gender order. . . .
7. The two most common pieces defining masculinity are, at all costs, not to be like a woman and not to be gay. . . .
8. Masculinity is as much about relation to other men as it is about relation to women. . .
9. Men, although powerful, feel powerless. . . .
10. Masculinities study exposes how structures and cultures are gendered male. . . .
11. The spaces and places that men and women daily inhabit and work within are remarkably different. . . .
12. The role of men in achieving feminist goals is uncertain and unclear. . . .
13. The asymmetry of masculinities scholarship and feminist theory reflects the differences in the general position of men and women. (Dowd 2010, 57–65)

Seeing men in a non-essentialist way is a critical insight of this work. The naming of this scholarship as *masculinities*, plural, reflects the insight that gender is not constructed as a universal and does not operate in an undifferentiated way. Masculinities studies expose the hierarchies among men and the importance of men's relationship to each other as a critical piece of the construction of gender (Dowd 2010). Much prior gender analysis, particularly feminist analysis, has assumed the primacy of male/female relationships, but masculinities scholarship exposes the coequal or even arguably greater significance of men's relationship to other men, and that the relationship generally is characterized by hierarchy, not collaboration. That core understanding explains what might at first glance seem counterintuitive, that despite the attributes of power that adhere to men as a group, as individuals they frequently feel power*less* (Kimmel 2004a, 2004b). The experience of powerlessness reflects the primacy of men's relationship to each other.

Men's relationship to each other is not stable. That is, men perform their gender daily, in countless encounters where their place vis-à-vis other men must be established (Pleck 1995). In the demonstration of manhood, the negative commands to not be like women and to not be gay are primary. These primary negative orientations, and the limits they impose, are the opposite of much popular culture that associates only positive qualities with manhood, such as strength, leadership, and courage. The negatives remain powerful, however, and men's resistance to or attempts at redefining masculinity face strong limits because of these negatives (Gilmore 1990). They also operate to feed patriarchy, misogyny, racism, and homophobia (Hearn 2004).

There is a dominant masculinity functioning in male hierarchy that scholars have named hegemonic masculinity (Connell 2005). Consistent with the hierarchical relationships among men and the general dominance of men over women, there is a dominant masculinity that reinforces who is at the top of the masculine heap. As articulated by masculinities scholars, this embraces many familiar male stereotypes. What is most fascinating is how this hegemony functions. By its terms, it is supported by men who do not achieve it, and by women who are subordinated by it (ibid.). This is an essential characteristic of hegemony: it exists by virtue of the support of the dominated and subordinated, not by sheer force. It also changes over time, exposing its social construction. This dominant masculinity assures what masculinities scholars identify as the patriarchal dividend, how all men benefit from the reinforcement, central to hegemonic masculinity, of male dominance (ibid.). At the same time, the preferential place given to one form of masculinity exposes that masculinity, again, is not singular or universal. Race is perhaps the most powerful determinant of place in the hierarchy, in addition to sexual orientation and class. Race may nearly completely obliterate gender advantage, so that some men in reality do not exercise dominance in many, if any, contexts. Alternative, and subversive, masculinities exist based on these characteristics.

Masculinities sustain themselves through the dominance of men over men, but also, critically, they continue to construct themselves in a way that incorporates dominance over women (Hearn 2004). Because male norms infuse structures, culture, and policy, this continues to disadvantage women and certain men. Masculinities scholarship unpeels the layers and makes it easier to see the ways in which things are gendered male. Ironically, some of that structuring creates a price, not a privilege; it creates harm, not benefit (Dowd 2010). For instance, men and boys are the primary targets of male violence. Men's socialization to deny emotions has a lifelong negative impact on relationships. Men's role as breadwinners leaves them ill-equipped to be fathers that nurture their children. Harm is frequently translated into sacrifice that constructs negatives as positives, as signs of masculinity, thereby reinforcing the price paid as worthwhile (Kang, this volume). Part of that worth is the claim of superiority. Feminists have tended to focus on male privilege; masculinities scholarship reminds us that a price may be attached to that privilege; comprehending these costs will help us better understand how to dismantle inequality.

Gender for men is therefore constructed, not inherent, an insight that has been recognized for women as well. But it is constructed differently, asymmetrically, and thus men as a group find themselves as a group differently situated than do women in relation to equality. Men's relationship to equality is different because they hold so much advantage as a group (Segal 1990). This is particularly evident in the patterns masculinities scholars have exposed in everyday life, including the different ways men and women inhabit space, whether in homosocial, single gender dominant, or mixed settings (Spain 1993). In order to achieve equality, the task of boys and men is different, including how they imagine their role in achieving equality for girls and women.

The value of these core insights is to expose the reality that boys and men suffer gender harms in addition to gender privilege, and that those harms should be addressed. The construction of masculinities brings a much richer picture of privilege, and therefore additional means to achieve long-held feminist goals. The presence of gender harms for boys and men suggests openings for collaboration rather than the persistence of presumed opposition. Nevertheless, since changing masculinities means relinquishing privilege, the task is more difficult in many respects than opening doors to attain equal freedom or personhood.

Finally, masculinities scholarship reinforces the antiessentialist reminder that inequalities are complex and interlocking. The hierarchical pattern of masculinities falls along a number of fault lines, but race is perhaps the strongest. Race arguably sometimes trumps the patriarchal dividend (Dowd 2010). Masculinities analysis has explored black masculinities as a subversive, alternative masculinity in response to white middle-class hegemonic masculinity. Feminist analysis has also grappled with the intersections of race and gender, with the critique of dominant theory as reflective of white women. This questioning has led to antiessentialism as a core tenet of feminist theory (Crenshaw 1989). The combination of these two approaches reminds us that masculine privilege is neither absolute nor universal, and gender subordination for women is differentiated along racial lines (Harris 1990). The exposure of race as a means to define patriarchy is not new, but the perspective and operation of race for men as well is a powerful reminder of the interlocking use of race as a component of gender subordination, a tool of hegemonic compliance and complicity. It also suggests that gender analysis should ask the race question; that is, it should look for and examine the operation of race in connection with gender, as well as asking whether race subordination is functioning in a primary way that requires that it be addressed as the core axis of inequality.

An example of this analysis is the juvenile justice system. The juvenile justice system, like the adult criminal justice system, has rarely been analyzed as a gender system. Yet clearly it is, as the juvenile justice system more accurately could be called the "boys'" justice system (or, depending on the analysis, the boys' *in*justice system) (Dowd 2010). Most of the juveniles in the system are boys. Boys constitute roughly three-quarters of all arrests and convictions, and an even higher rate of residential placements. They stay in those placements nearly twice as long as girls. Overwhelmingly, the boys in the system are black, disproportionately so at both the arrest and conviction stages. *One in three young black males is in the juvenile system in some form* (ibid.).

Masculinities analysis is critical to understanding why boys commit more juvenile crime, and how they are treated in the system. It is also important in evaluating the goals of the system and, particularly, the consequences of the system. We evaluate the conduct of boys and girls differently, and charge and convict them differently. Boys are viewed through a lens that sees them as dangerous and scary—and because they are predominantly black boys, racialized masculinities affect how they live in a racialized system of policing and justice, as well as society's goals for them (Messerschmidt 2001). The movement toward being "tough" on crime and imposing harsh sentences, such as "adult time for adult crime," is largely a hybrid gendered and raced judgment. As explained below, this treatment is contrary to developmental data, and imposes outcomes that lack empirical effectiveness but feed social constructions (Scott and Steinberg 2008).

Boys' masculinities include a process of shutting down emotion and taking risks in order to prove manhood. In adolescence, the traditional norms of manhood are at their peak, and alternative masculinities go underground. "A boy lives in a narrowly defined world of developing masculinity in which everything he does or thinks is judged on the basis of the strength or weakness it represents: you are either strong and worthwhile, or weak and worthless" (Kindlon and Thompson 1999, 78). The masculinity norms of violence, toughness, and risk all conspire to make it very likely that teenage boys will commit a crime, and many do. The developmental norms suggest that they will mature beyond this behavior and can move in an affirmative direction with the right guidance. Too many of the programs to which they are committed, however, reinforce traditional masculinity as the norm, which leaves boys no better equipped to manage their lives (Dowd 2010).

The gender analysis of the juvenile justice system inexorably exposes the race issue intertwined with gender. Because more offenders are boys and because those brought into the system are disproportionately black, the system is poised to punish and destroy rather than to build and support. Who is served by this? The masculinities answer is that all men and boys on the outside benefit from the perception that all men are dangerous. And yet, men and boys who are not incarcerated do not pay the price of dangerousness that is paid by those in the juvenile and adult criminal systems. White males, especially middle- and upper-class white males, benefit from the juvenile justice system's construction of dangerousness in a way that retains their gender privilege while sustaining their race privilege in the gender hierarchy.

Masculinities analysis requires that we ask the man question, as explained below, and that we further ask whether it is the same for all men. That may lead us, in gender analysis, to ask the race question and take on race as a gender issue. Privilege analysis should also ask questions about the interplay of other facets of identity, such as class, sexual orientation, or religion, along with race and class. We touch on class later in our discussions.

Masculinities and Feminist Theory

The multiplicity of masculinities has an analogue in the multiplicity of identity theories. Masculinities scholarship has implications for many areas of critical scholarship, including critical race theory, gay and lesbian rights/queer theory, post-colonial/human rights, and feminist theory. In this section we limit ourselves to considering the implications of masculinities scholarship for feminist theory.

Separate Development

Of necessity, in the early years, the subject of inquiry was particular: masculinities studies centered on the situations of men. In legal theory, analyses of the gender implications of various laws or legal concepts typically focused on relative victimization—how men were harmed disproportionately by particular laws (Williams 2004). Yet even in relatively recent years, with recognition that gender relations are a continually shifting, interactive process, and that gender identity is interactional and dynamic, masculinities studies shows a sharp disinterest in the female subject. Separatism is a hallmark, then, of much of masculinities scholarship.

Only in very recent years have theorists from law and the social sciences worked to integrate understandings from masculinities studies and feminist theory (Gardiner 2002). These integrations consist of several different theoretical directions. Some feminists have emphasized the importance of evaluating gendered harms to men (Harris 2000). Some masculinities studies theorists look for connections between feminist legal theory, masculinities studies, and critical race theory (Cooper 2009a). Others have examined the political interactions of the different movements—engaging, for example, in very thoughtful analysis of whether the fathers' rights movement represents a backlash against feminism and yet still raises valid concerns about the politics of fatherhood (Collier 2009). Theorists working in both feminist studies and masculinities studies have cultivated the concept of intersectionality—which explicitly rejects gender, or any other identity characteristic, as an isolated or discrete category (Case 1995; Cooper 2006). A very few scholars have used the specific methods of one set of theories to analytically evaluate gender problems for both sexes (McGinley 2010, 2008). Although there are some exceptional thinkers and promising directions, the overwhelming majority of scholarly projects in masculinities studies and feminist theory are occurring in separate bunkers.

This singular focus on one sex at a time is not unique to law, but is emblematic of other disciplines as well. What this single-sex focus has led to in other disciplines is pockets of ignorance about the "other" sex. For example, the fastest growing segment of prison populations is women. Female inmates have extremely high rates of mental illness, but the same mental illness may have different presentations in women as compared to men, and result in different diagnoses. Yet in research at the intersection of penology and psychology, women are not studied, and the different presentations of mental illness in this sub-population may be misdiagnosed (Woods 2009). Similarly, the prevalence and symptoms of ADHD in girls remains largely unexplored (Rabiner 2009). Regarding men, the medical community has only recently addressed the phenomenon of "male menopause." Preliminary research indicates that andropause (a decrease in testosterone related to aging) is a common, but rarely treated, medical condition, and one that is woefully under-explored (Hollander and Samons 2003).

In international relations, until just the past decade, men were missing from discussions of gender and development policy. Perhaps understandably, the thought was that men in developing countries possessed the power and the wealth and that a focus on promoting gender equality necessitated attention primarily to the situations of women in poverty. New research has moved from simple evaluations of ways men could change to give up power to women to broader theorizing of the ways sociopolitical obligations trap men. It also addresses how violence affects developing masculinities, and encourages male involvement in development policies. Moreover, it suggests ways of incorporating men in development practices to ensure more sustained gender equality over time (Men, Masculinities and Gender Relations in Development: Seminars 1998–2000).

Depolarizing Gender Discourse

Given this pattern of separate development, and the problems that it creates, the question arises whether masculinities scholarship and particularly theoretical work should be merged with feminist theory to create a unified gender theory. Our tentative answer is in the negative: the two theoretical frameworks are so distinctive, generated by the different position of men as a group as compared to women as a group, that it makes more sense to incorporate certain insights but not attempt "grand theory." What is essential is that neither discipline lose sight of the other, and at the same time, that collaboration and growth continue. The downside of this approach is that the pull of separation and difference might result in momentary acknowledgment rather than sustained collaboration or incorporation. For example, feminist theory continues to be challenged to meaningfully incorporate the critiques and insights of critical race theory as well as lesbian and queer theory. What needs to be created is greater dialogue and more of what Martha Fineman calls "uncomfortable conversations" (2009, 1).

At the same time, theorists might move toward ways of analyzing gender that are more exploratory and collaborative. Gender discourse has traditionally developed harms to men and harms to women as pairs of warring opposites. Claude Lévi-Strauss points out that we envision the world as a series of antinomals—matched pairs of opposites, such as hot and cold, wet and dry, or raw and cooked (1969). When the matched pairs do not present themselves, we have become so accustomed to antinomal thinking that we tend to create the pairs of opposites. We do not see the gray or look for the continuum. In contrast, masculinities and feminist theorists should search for intersections, commonalities, and mutually beneficial understandings between their disciplines.

Another technique that can depolarize gender discourse is to look through the lens of other identity categories or social practices. One way of changing polarized thinking about gender is to examine a shared identity category or status that transcends gender. For example, parenthood can be used instead of comparing mothers and fathers. Findings in masculinities studies, sociology, demography, and family relations document convergences in familial roles and ever-greater decision-making equality between men and women within marriage (Amato 2007). Increasing rates of employment among women with school-age children have been matched by fathers participating to a much greater extent in primary childcare (Monahan and Risman 2006). To the extent that couples are sharing childcare more, they are sharing the social problem of balancing work and family responsibilities. One of the fastest growing employment discrimination theories is that of family responsibilities discrimination (Williams and Bornstein 2008). If the lens is altered—and theorists begin to examine gender inequalities through the perspective of a different category that embraces both sexes, such as parenthood or familial caregiver—this may create a more robust theory to combat discrimination. It may also solidify greater political and social support for an activity, familial caregiving, that has been dramatically gendered throughout history. At the same time, this approach does not mean hiding differences in the relative positions of most fathers and most mothers, even while searching for common ground.

Another approach is to use the insights of both feminist and masculinities theories to "ask the other question," that is, to ask what else is going on beneath an assumed explanation for inequality. We draw on this related technique of changing the perspective below in our examples about education and work: we will look through the lens of race when gender is the dominant narrative, as it is with single-sex schools; we will look through the lens of gender in a discussion of race discrimination in employment.

An additional way of seeing connections, overlaps, and exchanges is to tap empirical understandings of the ways gender is constructed. Returning to first principles, "asking the woman question" was in no small part an empirical assessment—using data to reveal how seemingly neutral laws contain a gender bias (Levit and Verchick 2006, 46). A more contemporary search for the explanatory mechanisms of prejudice should use methods developed in other disciplines.

One of those methods from the sciences is complexity theory. The science of complexity looks at the various relations among parts of systems and evaluates the collective behaviors of that system. Applied to the social sciences, complexity theory looks at complex dynamics of relationships and their interactions with institutions. Multiple strands of social inequality occur simultaneously and have to do with systems and institutions beyond facets of identity—with religion, nations, and economic and political systems. Identity categories are not static, but interact with all of these systems (Walby 2007, 2009). The science of complexity tries to move away from incomplete or fractional perspectives and fixed understandings. As Cass Sunstein says, what tends to "emerge from close attention to mere pieces of complex problems" are, quite simply, only "partial perspectives" (1996, 261–62).

Consider a concrete example of the ways in which complexity theory might change thinking about gender studies. Social organization theorists have demonstrated that various types of gender bias affect promotion of leaders in an organization. This phenomenon is known colloquially as "the glass ceiling" (Jolls 2002, 1). Mary Hogue and Robert G. Lord have applied complexity theory to this idea. They argue that gender bias in organizations functions as a complex system of behaviors at various organizational levels with numerous different units, occupations, and processes (2007). They maintain that an understanding of how gender bias occurs at various levels and in different relationships requires more than simple unidimensional explanations. It is a conceptual error to generalize that prejudice at one level—which may result, for instance, from a female leader displaying characteristics that are not typical either for her gender or for the typical occupant of the role—works the same as prejudice at other levels. Many different types of prejudice (such as lower evaluations of competence of women than men in leadership roles or reluctance among women in mixed-sex groups to seek leadership positions) can work simultaneously to make identification of the sources of prejudice difficult (ibid.).

The science of complexity, which understands organizations such as places of employment as complex systems, would suggest looking for interconnections among different types of prejudice and aggregation of multiple types of bias occurring in different ways at various levels. A more sophisticated understanding of the different currents of prejudice, stereotyping, and relational disadvantage poses a challenge for current antidiscrimination law, which often impels an unrealistic search for unicausal channels of discrimination (Harper 2010). A complex understanding of the relational nature of the ways leaders emerge might nudge theories of employment discrimination away from simple causal explanations.

In the late 1980s, critical theorists pushed identity theories such as feminism toward antiessentialist understandings by pointing out that discrimination occurred at the intersection of identity categories (Crenshaw 1989; Harris 1990). For instance, a black woman "experiences not just racism and sexism, but the greater-than-double burden of intertwined racism and sexism, which is its own unique (and perhaps particularly virulent) form of discrimination" (Levit 2002, 228). Since then feminists and critical race theorists have built on intersectionality ideas that discrimination based on a single identity characteristic can be compounded by discrimination based on other facets of identity. They are adding to ideas of intersectionality (as discrimination based on intersecting aspects of identity) by using concepts from complexity theory. Intersectionality examines the interrelations of various facets of identity, such as gender, race, ethnicity, and class; complexity moves to a more four-dimensional model that considers individuals and their identity characteristics, their environments, and normative practices and institutions, across time and cultures.

Darren Lenard Hutchinson calls these new understandings "multidimensionality" and suggests going beyond intersectionality by understanding invisible privileges, such as whiteness and the benefits of class standing (2002). He urges an understanding of how privileges operate in tandem with staid institutions, governmental policies, and public discourse to shape legal doctrines. Nancy Ehrenreich's "symbiotic" approach is another example of the use of complexity theory in legal analysis. She urges evaluations of doctrines and discourse "by focusing attention on the multiplicity of oppressions and the complex mechanisms by which subordinated statuses interact" (2002, 322).

Complexity theory says humans are complex organisms, adapting to life around them, but not in a linear way (Kauffman 1993; Lewin 1992; Waldrop 1992). Similarly, law is an adaptive institution—evolving and becoming more organized (Ruhl 1996). Applying these understandings to gender theory, complexity theory would recognize that the gendered subject is complex: family circumstances, sexuality, race, class, age, and other characteristics matter to everyday interactions. Gender relations occur in various different networks and gender is constructed in multiple dynamic processes. This is in part what Raewyn Connell suggests when she urges consideration of multiple masculinities, encompassing varying presentations of masculinity even for a single individual in different circumstances such as at home, at the office, or in sports (2002). What all of this implies is that understandings of gender solely through feminist theory or masculinities studies are relatively unidimensional, while gendering is a multidimensional, dynamic, and relational process.

A critique of the idea of using complexity theory is that when it insists on multiple, incommensurable factors and the adaptive properties of complex systems, complexity sounds like classic relativism—it is hard to say anything certain about much of anything, but we know it's complicated. This poses difficulties in the practical application of the theory as a matter of methodology. Gender theory can certainly tap the understandings of the science of complexity, while also using models developed in other disciplines to break down disciplinary walls and encourage recognition that gender inequalities are interrelated, path-dependent, and constructed in multiple dynamic processes.

Nevertheless, even as there are interconnections, there are places where the fields benefit from separate inquiry and have specific benefits to be gained from the other. It is well to begin with what each may incorporate from the other.

What Feminism Has to Gain from Masculinities Theory

Feminism has much to gain from exploring the understandings of masculinities theory. Most fundamentally, masculinities scholarship requires that we ask the man question (Dowd 2010). That means that in situations where we are conscious of inequality, discrimination, or injustice, and have framed issues in a particular way, as a race or class or women's issue, for example, that we should ask, "What about the boys? What about the men?" In addition, it means that we should go on to ask, "Are all men situated the same, or are different men situated differently?" Finally, we should be conscious when the question suggests we should be asking yet more questions—as, for example, when the gender questions lead us to ask race questions.

The man question must be asked carefully, so as not to shift focus away from women or feed into misogyny. The asymmetry of men's and women's positions as a group must be kept in view, but their differences also argue that we consider gender-specific approaches in order to move more meaningfully toward equality. This means resisting either/or thinking, or false equivalences, and instead embracing both/and approaches, accepting the interconnected aspects of inequalities. Differences in the general position of men as a group and women as a group may argue for the necessity of gender-specific approaches to achieve equality.

Masculinities theory also reinforces feminist antiessentialism by exposing differences among men and the powerful role of race in constructing gender. This should lead to reinforcing antiessentialist approaches among feminists, as well as taking on race as a feminist issue.

What Masculinities Has to Gain from Feminist Theory

Just as feminists must ask the man question, masculinities scholars must ask the woman question. But it is a different question, with different implications. The reason that masculinities scholars must persistently ask this question is that otherwise women become invisible in the masculinities project. Most important, then, masculinities scholars need to unearth and dissect male power and how it can be dismantled where it functions as power-over rather than empowering.

Women have good reason to be uneasy about masculinities scholarship to the extent that it loses sight of the subordination of women, or implies that men are equally subordinated or that it is their "turn" for analysis. Although there is widespread lack of agreement among feminists about how to analyze and approach inequality, or alternatively, multiple ways of approaching inequalities, it is fair to say that a power analysis holds wide credibility.

A second contribution from feminist theory to masculinities studies would be to reinforce the importance of continuing to identify material differences and conditions. Jeff Hearn has been most vocal that the focus should be on the material conditions of men as a group, not how they define their identities (Hearn 2004).

Substantive Applications of Collaborative Masculinities and Feminist Theorizing

The suggestion of cross-fertilization of understandings between masculinities studies and feminist theory works well on a theoretical level. In this section we aim to show how this might be accomplished on a practical level, and thereby suggest the potential for masculinities scholarship in a range of settings.

Education

One example of segregative thinking—thinking about legal problems as affecting a single sex and requiring a sex-specific remedy—has occurred in the realm of education. Two decades ago, when evidence showed that girls were being shortchanged in the classroom, legal commentators touted single-sex schools as a remedy (Salamone 2003). In the past several years, parallel arguments have emerged that a relatively recent "boy crisis" in education justifies single-sex education (Cohen 2009; Kisthardt 2007). In 2006, the Department of Education released new regulations expanding the opportunities for single-sex classes, schools, and extracurricular activities (34 C.F.R. § 106.34(b) (2010)). These regulations fueled an explosive increase in single-sex public schools and classes. In 1995, only three public schools in the country offered single-sex options for students; in 2010, 540 public schools were either entirely single-sex or offered all boys' and all girls' classes (Kisthardt 2007; National Association for Single Sex Public Education 2010).

Interestingly, both waves promoting single-sex education were prompted by concerns about a single sex. Proponents selectively culled favorable studies and overlooked the wealth of data that showed—once conflating variables were controlled—no academic advantages of single-sex over mixed-sex education (Levit 1999). Is it any wonder that when researchers begin with the assumption of gender differences and look for them and find some that the end recommendation is a sex-segregative remedy?

Omitted by the promoters of single-sex schools and classes was consideration of the interrelated effects on the other sex from the creation of all boys' or all girls' preserves. Research showed, for example, that creating all girls' classes had deleterious effects on the boys left behind (Levit 1999). Also neglected was the larger social picture: the protectionist model of the single-sex remedy does nothing to improve coeducation, nor does it teach boys and girls how to interact in coeducational settings. Furthermore, sex exclusivity often leads to regressive forms of gender-differentiated treatment:

> The concern that segregation based on sex can reinforce gender stereotypes is supported by a study of the experimental California academies. In 1997, as a pilot project, California provided five million dollars to institute ten public single-sex academies, equal down to the number of pencils. A study conducted by researchers from the University of Toronto and the University of California at San Diego, and sponsored by both the Ford and Spencer Foundations, evaluated the academies between 1998 and 2000, interviewing over 300 students, parents, teachers, and administrators, and observing classes. An important finding was that although the California administrators insisted on equal resources, assumptions about the different educational needs of boys and girls caused the educators to explicitly reinforce traditional gender stereotypes. As one example, during a unit on frontier exploration, the boys' schools learned survival skills, and the girls' schools learned how to quilt and sew. (Levit 2005, 487)

Finally, state sponsorship of sex segregation stigmatizes—"it explicitly states and physically embodies, that the problem is the presence of the opposite sex" (Levit 1999, 517). In short, gender equality in schools is treated as a "zero sum game" (Dowd 2008, 247).

One of our overarching suggestions in this chapter is to alter the lens—to view issues through the perspective of different identity categories. Historically, single-sex education has been considered, not surprisingly, a gender issue. Let's shift the lens for a moment and consider the racial overlay.

In the early 1990s, some black families and some policymakers were in favor of single-sex schools as a way to address high dropout rates, teen pregnancies, and low morale. They thought, for example, that the construction of several all-male academies in Detroit might create an "elite institution" for an "'endangered species'" (Williams 2004, 16, 21). The federal district court that heard the case challenging the creation of the academies ruled that these schools violated the equal protection rights of young girls of color, who were not flourishing in the city schools either (*Garrett v. Board of Education* 1991). These impulses toward reform—well-intended as they were—ignored both history and consequences.

They overlooked the racially charged history of single-sex schools—created in the south to avoid racial mixing, promiscuity, and, in the words of segregationist Virginia Governor J. Lindsay Almond, the "'livid stench of sadism, sex immorality, and juvenile pregnancy' [that] was 'infesting the mixed schools'" (Mayeri 2006, 198–200). Sex-segregated schools, within already racially segregated communities, did more than reinforce historical racism; they promoted some of the worst gender stereotypes at the intersection of sex and race: "So much of the rhetoric regarding Black girls in education is about their sexuality, suggesting that just by sitting in the same classroom with male students, there is a risk of pregnancy" (Williams 2004, 24). The important thing was to ask the questions whether the sex-segregated schools promoted "racialized gender roles" or "contribute[d] to sexualizing race" (ibid. 75).

Informed by both feminist theory and masculinities analysis, and considering the layers of racial as well as gender hierarchies, the problems experienced by minority males in schools should not lead in the direction of segregation. Masculinities analysis rightly identifies the problems of boys, but that does not lead ineluctably to separatism: "While some researchers have found that single-sex education may have some advantages for minority-race boys, the general consensus is that males do not flourish in single-sex environments. Providing separate classes for boys is either a neutral or negative along dimensions of socialization and academic qualities" (Levit 2005, 486). Masculinities and feminist theories point instead to a both/and approach that looks at gender-specific issues as well as their interaction. It is not the coeducational aspect of schools that is failing either minority males or females; it is more likely the issues of class and resources. Educators should consider the quality of the educational experiences for both sexes—including the student-teacher ratios, percentage of teachers with advanced degrees and years of experienced teaching, financial contributions, and curricula (Parker 2008).

Shifting the perspective about what have been viewed as "gender issues" to ask about the intersection of sex and other identity categories such as race is critically important for masculinities and feminist theories as they move forward. The reminder of race as an essential gender issue here leads to noticing that gender is used racially and that race differentials are even worse than gender differentials in schools—that recognition is critical to preventing gender consciousness from being used in a way that ultimately has negative race consequences. The next section applies both masculinities and feminist theories to the world of work. It also performs another shift in perspective by examining the controversial *Ricci v. DeStefano* case—considered a paradigm race discrimination case—through the lens of gender.

Work

Work is an important site of masculinity construction. Through work behaviors and relationships, men create their masculine identities. Often they engage in competitive behaviors in order to prove their masculinity to other men in the workplace (Collinson 1988). This behavior occurs in different ways in different types of jobs depending on the race and class of the men occupying the jobs (Saucedo and Morales 2010). Moreover, racial, class, and gender hierarchies are reinforced through behavior.

Firefighting is a classic workplace of male identity construction in a job traditionally passed down from father to son in white ethnic communities (McGinley 2010). Firefighters engage in a variety of masculine performances including harassing and hazing probationary firefighters and using humor to relieve tension, gauge other men's ability to do the job, and form bonds with other men (Chetkovich 1997). This homosocial behavior permits masculine firefighters to express emotion toward one another without fear of being labeled homosexual. In the firehouse, emotions are close to the surface because of the danger and difficulty of the job and the amount of time that firefighters spend with each other in a family-like community (Halberstam 2002; Picciotto 2003).

Male firefighters construct masculinity through sexualization of the job. The equipment enhances heterosexual masculinity; the fire hose that emits a gush of water is reminiscent of the ejaculating penis (McGinley 2010). Firefighters also emphasize their sexuality in order to de-emphasize the "dirty work" of firefighting (Tracy and Scott 2006, 16). The "dirty work" includes the more feminine, care-taking aspects of the job relating to emergency medical services, especially those administered to indigents (ibid.).

Finally, firefighters construct their masculinity by treating their female colleagues as inferior, through sexual harassment and derogation of the women's abilities (Hulett et al. 2008). This harassment is also racialized. While studies demonstrate that both black and white female firefighters suffer from discrimination, black women generally continue to suffer rejection throughout their tenure at the firehouse, whereas discriminatory behaviors are less problematic over time in the careers of white women (Yoder and Berendsen 2001; Yoder and Aniakudo 1997).

RICCI V. DESTEFANO

With this understanding of the gendered nature of firefighting in mind, a case study of *Ricci v. DeStefano* demonstrates that masculinities theory can provide another perspective on a case that is typically characterized as purely a race discrimination case.[1] In *Ricci*, one Hispanic and seventeen white male firefighters sued the City of New Haven alleging that the city's failure to certify the results of promotional exams was illegal race discrimination in violation of Title VII of the 1964 Civil Rights Act (Title VII). The City refused to certify the exam results because doing so would have had a disparate impact on African Americans and Latinos. Reversing lower courts that ruled in favor of the City, the Supreme Court held that an employer is liable under Title VII if it overturns test results because of race unless the employer can demonstrate that it has a strong basis in evidence that it would lose a disparate impact suit (*Ricci v. DeStefano* 2009). The Court concluded that the City could not meet this standard (ibid.).

Ricci gained unprecedented notoriety when it became entangled in the Supreme Court nomination of then-Judge Sonia Sotomayor, who was the first Latina nominated to the Court. Judge Sotomayor was a member of the Second Circuit panel on the *Ricci* case (Baker and Zeleny 2009). The hearings on her nomination became a battleground for issues of race; behind that story, however, a masculinities story was told as well.[2]

Republicans on the Senate Judiciary Committee invited plaintiffs Frank Ricci and Ben Vargas to testify on a panel on Minority Issues at the Senate Judiciary Committee's hearings on Judge Sotomayor's nomination. Their testimony was compelling, and they were treated as heroes not only because they saved lives in their work, but also because they represented right against wrong in the lawsuit. Both Ricci and Vargas highlighted their strong belief in the American Dream. They tapped into the "man as breadwinner" concept of masculinity which views the man as the head of the family whose main responsibility is to provide for his family. While Ricci had worked diligently to overcome an obvious reading disability to study for the test, Vargas had worked equally hard to overcome his Puerto Rican background and to assure a future in "the greatest country in the world." Their wives' roles were subordinate to and supportive of their husbands'.

Feminist and critical race theory might view these narratives with suspicion. Feminists might argue that Ricci belongs to the group that historically has used its power to the detriment of women and persons of color. Critical race theorists might argue Vargas was a "sellout," because Vargas belongs to a group historically victimized by discrimination.

Masculinity theory adds another dimension to the analysis. It reminds us that although men as a group are powerful, and have historically oppressed outsiders, individual men do not always feel powerful (Kimmel 2004b). This feeling of powerlessness derives from competition among men to conform to an ideal of the hegemonic masculinity, an ideal that most men cannot achieve because of their class, race, age, sexual orientation, or other failure to conform (ibid.).

Ricci's testimony illustrates this concept well. Although he belongs to a group that historically has exercised its power over others, Ricci's dyslexia makes him vulnerable. While his disability might diminish the masculinity of an ordinary man, it did not diminish his masculinity because he daily risks his life for others in one of the toughest and most dangerous jobs on the planet. Ricci stressed the danger—the more masculine part—of the job by testifying that 100 firefighters die every year battling fires. The combination of the masculinity of the job of firefighter and the courage that it took for Ricci to pursue the lawsuit confirmed his masculinity despite the feminine vulnerability that his reading disability displayed.

Vargas, too, presented as a "real man." He was born in Puerto Rico, but had come to the United States as a child and had worked his way up in the fire department. Because he worked and studied hard for the captain's exam, he earned the promotion. He was thankful that his hard work paid off, and he wanted his three sons to learn that this is possible in the "greatest country in the world." He was proud of his heritage, but he wanted to be rewarded for his merit and hard work, not his ethnicity.

From *Ricci*, it is clear that the image of a firefighter who is worthy of promotion to lieutenant or captain is male, heterosexual, white or, on occasion, Hispanic. The case, the testimony, and the Senate Judiciary Committee's reaction to the testimony rendered black male and all female firefighters invisible. No one questioned why there were no women on either side of the case. No one asked why there was only one woman lieutenant and no women captains. No one asked why the black men who took the test scored significantly better on the oral part of the test than on the written portion. No one wondered why the union, which should represent all firefighters, sought to join the lawsuit on behalf of the white male plaintiffs (Allen and Bazelon 2009).

The fact that Ricci's and Vargas's testimony lionized a particularly traditional form of heterosexual masculinity was also invisible. Masculinity research explains that the practice of masculinity is often invisible. As the national audience viewed the hearings, it generally approved of the narratives of Ricci and Vargas. Those narratives placed men at the head of their families, in the traditional role as breadwinner and protector, doing men's work.

LEARNING FROM *RICCI* AND MASCULINITIES THEORY

Beyond unraveling the narratives in the case, masculinities theory can suggest how to eliminate bias. In *Ricci*, Dr. Christopher Hornick, an industrial/organizational consultant with 25 years' experience in police and firefighting testing, testified that many fire departments across the country use assessment centers to gauge who should be promoted (*Ricci* 2009, Ginsburg, J. dissenting). Assessment centers allow those grading the applicants to measure important intangibles such as leadership and command presence that are necessary to successful completion of the job (ibid.)

Assessment mechanisms must be carefully examined, however, to assure that they do not incorporate a bias toward "the masculine." Centers have been successfully used to promote racial diversity, but may still incorporate a masculine definition of leadership and command presence. If this is the case, then they may undervalue the applications of women or men who do not conform to gender norms.

Leadership studies demonstrate that female leaders are judged adversely because most people identify leadership with masculine qualities (Eagly and Karau 2002). Even when a woman's work performance is equal to that of her male colleagues, male group members evaluate the woman's work as less competent (Foschi et al. 1994). And in jobs that have traditionally been held by men, both men and women judge a woman as less likeable than an equally competent man (Eagly and Karau 2002). Female leaders face a dilemma: they can be either competent or likeable, but not both (Heilman et al. 2004). This research suggests that fairly judging women's leadership performance in an assessment center is feasible only with awareness of these issues and a plan for overcoming the inherent biases in the measure.

Command presence similarly is often interpreted to require masculine traits (Cooper 2009b). Frank Rudy Cooper explains, however, that proper command presence requires police to eschew hypermasculine behavior by acting with restraint when their authority is questioned (ibid.). He advocates training that develops "calmness, self-respect, the ability to tolerate ambiguous situations, and the ability to apply legal concepts in concrete situations so that the officer can respond flexibly in the field" (ibid.). These recommendations dispute the hypermasculine, violent interpretation of the term "command presence" that is accepted in some police departments. Cooper's insight enables employers to make visible the invisible race and gender biases in assessments that assume that command presence and leadership skills describe a particular masculinity.

Finally, *Ricci* suggests that assessment should consider the history of firefighting and traditional routes into the department. Assessment should be tailored to reward job-related characteristics and qualifications while taking into account the differential burdens the assessment mechanisms place on all groups.

Conclusion

In this chapter, we have encouraged greater discourse between those working in masculinities studies and those working in feminist theory. We urge masculinities and feminist theorists to look for collaborative theoretical prospects, as well as political alliances. We have proposed a variety of different ways to move toward at least some integrated explorations. Theorists should try to alter their perspectives—change the lens by looking at situations through different identity filters. We offered two examples here—viewing single-sex education as, in some circumstances, a racialized gender issue, with both historical and contemporary racial markers interacting with those of gender, and examining the *Ricci* "race discrimination" case as also being about the construction of gender.

More broadly, we urge those engaged in masculinities and feminist theories to draw lessons from emerging complexity theory (Farber 2003). This entails examining how the complex structures of race, class, and other facets of identity interact with gender and looking for multiple different ways that various hierarchies and patterns of social inequality operate simultaneously and inextricably.

NOTES

1. 129 S.Ct. 2658 (2009). This discussion is derived in large part from Ann C. McGinley, *Ricci v. DeStefano*: A Masculinities Theory Analysis, 33 *Harvard Journal of Law & Gender* 581 (2010).

2. The following discussion is based on the videotape of the Senate Judiciary Hearings, Day 4, Minority Issues Panel of the Sotomayor Hearings before the Senate Judiciary Committee. Ricci, Vargas and others testified. *Sotomayor Confirmation Hearing, Day*

4, Minority Issues Panel (CSPAN television broadcast July 16, 2009), available at http://www.c-spanarchives.org/program/287762-104.

REFERENCES

Allen, Nicole, and Emily Bazelon. June 25, 2009. The Ladder: Part 4: Is There a Better Way to Decide Who Gets Promoted? *Slate.* http://www.slate.com/id/2221250/entry/2221298/.

Amato, Paul R. 2007. *Alone Together: How Marriage in America Is Changing.* Cambridge, MA: Harvard University Press.

Baker, Peter, and Jeff Zeleny. May 27, 2009. Obama Chooses Hispanic Judge for Supreme Court Seat. *New York Times,* p. A1.

Batlan, Felice, Kelly Hradsky, Kristen Jeschke, LaVonne Meyer, and Jill Roberts. 2009. Not Our Mother's Law School: A Third Wave Feminist Study of Women's Experiences in Law School. *University of Baltimore Law Forum* 39:124–51.

Case, Mary Anne C. 1995. Disaggregating Gender from Sex and Sexual Orientation: The Effeminate Man in the Law and Feminist Jurisprudence. *Yale Law Journal* 105:1–105.

Chetkovich, Carol. 1997. *Real Heat: Gender and Race in the Urban Fire Service.* New Brunswick, NJ: Rutgers University Press.

Cohen, David S. 2009. No Boy Left Behind? Single-Sex Education and the Essentialist Myth of Masculinity. *Indiana Law Journal* 84:135–88.

Collier, Richard S. 2009. The Fathers' Rights Movement, Law Reform, and the New Politics of Fatherhood: Some Reflections on the UK Experience. *University of Florida Journal of Law and Public Policy* 20:65–111.

Collinson, David L. 1988. "Engineering Humor": Masculinity, Joking and Conflict in Shop-Floor Relations. *Organization Studies* 9:181–99.

Connell, R. W. 2005. *Masculinities,* 2d ed. Berkeley: University of California Press.

———. 2002. *Gender.* London: Polity Press.

Connell, R.W., Jeff Hearn, and Michael S. Kimmel. 2005. Introduction. In *Handbook of Studies on Men and Masculinities,* edited by Michael S. Kimmel, Jeff Hearn, and R. W. Connell. Thousand Oaks, CA: Sage, 1–34.

Cooper, Frank Rudy. 2009a. Our First Unisex President?: Black Masculinity and Obama's Feminine Side. *Denver University Law Review* 86:633–61.

———. 2009b. "Who's the Man?": Masculinities Studies, Terry Stops, and Police Training. *Columbia Journal of Gender and Law* 18:671–742.

———. 2006. Against Bipolar Black Masculinity: Intersectionality, Assimilation, Identity Performance, and Hierarchy. *U.C. Davis Law Review* 39:853–903.

Crenshaw, Kimberlé. 1989. Demarginalizing the Intersection of Race and Sex: A Black Feminist Critique of Antidiscrimination Doctrine, Feminist Theory, and Antiracist Politics. *University of Chicago Legal Forum* 1989:139–67.

Dowd, Nancy E. 2010. *The Man Question: Male Subordination and Privilege.* New York: New York University Press.

———. 2008. Masculinities and Feminist Legal Theory. *Wisconsin Journal of Law, Gender and Society* 23:201–48.

Eagly, Alice H., and Steven J. Karau. 2002. Role Congruity Theory of Prejudice toward Female Leaders. *Psychological Review* 109:573–98.

Ehrenreich, Nancy. 2002. Subordination and Symbiosis: Mechanisms of Mutual Support between Subordinating Systems. *University of Missouri-Kansas City Law Review* 71:251–324.

Farber, Daniel A. 2003. Probabilities Behaving Badly: Complexity Theory and Environmental Uncertainty. *U.E. Law Review* 37:145–73.

Fineman, Martha Albertson. 2009. Introduction: Feminist and Queer Legal Theory. In *Feminist and Queer Legal Theory: Intimate Encounters, Uncomfortable Conversations*, edited by Martha Albertson Fineman, Jack E. Jackson, and Adam P. Romero. Surrey, UK: Ashgate, 1–6.

Foschi, Martha, Aaron S. Wallen, Daniella Fuchs, and Melina M. Tamkins. 1994. Gender and Double Standards in the Assessment of Job Applicants. *Social Psychology Quarterly* 57(4):326–39.

Gardiner, Judith Kegan, ed. 2002. *Masculinity Studies and Feminist Theory: New Directions*. New York: Columbia University Press.

Garrett v. Board of Education, 775 F. Supp. 1004 (E.D. Mich. 1991).

Gilmore, David. 1990. *Manhood in the Making: Cultural Concepts of Masculinity*. New Haven, CT: Yale University Press.

Halberstam, David. 2002. *Firehouse*. New York: Hyperion.

Harper, Michael C. 2010. The Causation Standard in Federal Employment Law: *Gross v. FBL Financial Services, Inc.*, and the Unfulfilled Promise of the Civil Rights Act of 1991. *Buffalo Law Review* 58:69–145.

Harris, Angela P. 2000. Gender, Violence, Race, and Criminal Justice. *Stanford Law Review* 52: 777–807.

———. 1990. Race and Essentialism in Feminist Legal Theory. *Stanford Law Review* 42:581–616.

Hearn, Jeff. 2004. From Hegemonic Masculinity to the Hegemony of Men. *Feminist Theory* 5(1):49–72.

Heilman, Madeline E., Aaron S. Wallen, Daniella Fuchs, and Melina M. Tamkins. 2004. Penalties for Success: Reactions to Women Who Succeed at Male Gender-Typed Tasks. *Journal of Applied Psychology* 89:416–27.

Hogue, Mary, and Robert G. Lord. 2007. A Multilevel, Complexity Theory Approach to Understanding Gender Bias in Leadership. *Leadership Quarterly* 18(4):370–90.

Hollander, Eric, and Daniel M. Samons. 2003. Male Menopause: An Unexplored Area of Men's Health. *Psychiatric Annals* 33:497–500.

Hulett, Denise M., Marc Bendick, Sheila Y. Thomas, and Francine Moccio. April 2008. *A National Report Card on Women in Firefighting*. http://www.i-women.org/images/pdf-files/35827WSP.pdf.

Hutchinson, Darren Lenard. 2002. New Complexity Theories: From Theoretical Innovation to Doctrinal Reform. *University of Missouri-Kansas City Law Review* 71:431–45.

Jolls, Christine. 2002. Is There a Glass Ceiling? *Harvard Women's Law Journal* 25:1–18.

Kauffman, Stuart A. 1993. *The Origins of Order: Self-Organization and Selection in Evolution*. New York: Oxford University Press.

Kimmel, Michael S. 2004a. *The Gendered Society*. New York: Oxford University Press.

———. 2004b. Masculinity as Homophobia. In *Feminism & Masculinities*, edited by Peter F. Murphy. Oxford: Oxford University Press, 182–99.

Kindlon, Dan, and Michael Thompson, with Teresa Barker. 1999. *Raising Cain: Protecting the Emotional Life of Boys*. New York: Ballantine Books.

Kisthardt, Elizabeth S. 2007. Singling Them Out: The Influence of the "Boy Crisis" on the New Title IX Regulations. *Wisconsin Women's Law Journal* 22:313–37.

Lévi-Strauss, Claude. 1969. *The Raw and the Cooked: Mythologiques*. Chicago: University of Chicago Press.

Levit, Nancy. 2005. Embracing Segregation: The Jurisprudence of Choice and Diversity in Race and Sex Separatism in Schools. *University of Illinois Law Review* 2005:455–512.

———. 2002. Theorizing Connections among Systems of Subordination. *University of Missouri-Kansas City Law Review* 71:227–49.

———. 1999. Separating Equals: Educational Research and the Long Term Consequences of Sex Segregation. *George Washington University Law Review* 67:451–526.

———. 1996. Feminism for Men: Legal Ideology and the Construction of Maleness. *University of California at Los Angeles Law Review* 43:1037–116.

Levit, Nancy, and Robert R. M. Verchick. 2006. *Feminist Legal Theory: A Primer.* New York: New York University Press.

Lewin, Roger. 1992. *Complexity: Life at the Edge of Chaos.* Chicago: University of Chicago Press.

Mayeri, Serena. 2006. The Strange Career of Jane Crow: Sex Segregation and the Transformation of Anti-discrimination Discourse. *Yale Journal of Law and the Humanities* 18:187–272.

McGinley, Ann C. 2010. *Ricci v. DeStefano*: A Masculinities Theory Analysis. *Harvard Journal of Gender and Law* 33:581–623.

———. 2008. Creating Masculine Identities: Bullying and Harassment "Because of Sex." *University of Colorado Law Review* 79:1151–1241.

Men, Masculinities and Gender Relations in Development: Seminars 1998–2000, http://www.brad.ac.uk/acad/bcid/gender/mandmweb/mainpage.html.

Messerschmidt, James W. 2001. Masculinities, Crime, and Prison. In *Prison Masculinities,* edited by Don Sabo, Terry A. Kupers, and Willie London. Philadelphia: Temple University Press, 67–72.

Monahan, Molly, and Barbara J. Risman. 2006. Blending into Equality: Family Diversity and Gender Convergence. In *Handbook of Women and Gender Studies,* edited by Kathy Davis, Mary Evans, and Judith Lorber. London: Sage Publications.

National Association for Single Sex Public Education. 2010. Single-Sex Schools / Schools with Single-Sex Classrooms / What's the Difference? http://www.singlesexschools.org/schools-schools.htm (last visited June 13, 2010).

Parker, Wendy. 2008. Desegregating Teachers. *Washington University Law Review* 86:1–52.

Picciotto, Richard, with Daniel Paisner. 2003. *Last Man Down: A Firefighter's Story of Survival and Escape from the World Trade Center.* New York: Berkley Publishing Group.

Pleck, Joseph. 1995. The Gender Role Strain Paradigm: An Update. In *A New Psychology of Men,* edited by Ronald F. Levant and William S. Pollack. New York: Basic Books, 11–32.

Rabiner, David. 2009. ADHD/ADD in Girls. http://www.helpforadd.com/add-in-girls/ (last visited Nov. 15, 2009).

Ricci v. DeStefano, 129 S.Ct. 2658 (2009).

Ruhl, J. B. 1996. The Fitness of Law: Using Complexity Theory to Describe the Evolution of Law and Society and Its Practical Meaning for Democracy. *Vanderbilt Law Review* 49:1407–90.

Salamone, Rosemary. 2003. *Same, Different, Equal: Re-thinking Single-Sex Schooling.* New Haven, CT: Yale University Press.

Saucedo, Leticia M., and Maria Cristina Morales. 2010. Masculinities Narratives and Latino Immigrant Workers: A Case Study of the Las Vegas Residential Construction Trades. *Harvard Journal of Gender and Law* 33:625–59.

Scott, Elizabeth S., and Laurence Steinberg. 2008. *Rethinking Juvenile Justice.* Cambridge, MA: Harvard University Press.

Segal, Lynne. 1990. *Slow Motion: Changing Masculinities, Changing Men.* London: Virago.

Sotomayor Confirmation Hearing, Day 4, Minority Issues Panel (C-SPAN television broadcast July 16, 2009), available at http://www.c-spanarchives.org/program/287762-104.

Spain, Daphne. 1993. Gendered Spaces and Women's Status. *Sociological Theory* 11(2):137–51.

Stoltenberg, John. 1999. *The End of Manhood: Parables on Sex and Selfhood.* London: Routledge.

Sunstein, Cass R. 1996. Congress, Constitutional Moments, and the Cost-Benefit State. *Stanford Law Review* 48:247–309.

Title VII. 2008. Public Law 88-352, 42 U.S.C. sections 2000e-2 to 2000e-17.

Tolson, Andrew. 1977. *The Limits of Masculinity: Male Identity and Women's Liberation.* New York: Taylor and Francis Books, Ltd.

Tracy, Sarah J., and Clifton Scott. 2006. Sexuality, Masculinity, and Taint Management among Firefighters and Correctional Officers: Getting Down and Dirty with "America's Heroes" and the "Scum of Law Enforcement." *Management Communication Quarterly* 20:6–38.

Valdes, Francisco. 1995. Queers, Sissies, Dykes, and Tomboys: Deconstructing the Conflation of "Sex," "Gender," and "Sexual Orientation" in Euro-American Law and Society. *California Law Review* 83:1–343.

Walby, Sylvia. 2009. *Globalization and Inequalities: Complexity and Contested Modernities.* London: Sage.

———. 2007. Complexity Theory, Systems Theory, and Multiple Intersecting Social Inequalities. *Philosophy of the Social Sciences* 37:449–70.

Waldrop, M. Mitchell. 1992. *Complexity: The Emerging Science at the Edge of Order and Chaos.* New York: Simon & Schuster.

Williams, Joan C., and Stephanie Bornstein. 2008. The Evolution of "FReD": Family Responsibilities Discrimination and Developments in the Law of Stereotyping and Implicit Bias. *Hastings Law Journal* 59:1311–58.

Williams, Verna L. 2004. Reform or Retrenchment? Single-Sex Education and the Construction of Race and Gender. *Wisconsin Law Review* 2004:15–79.

Woods, George. Nov. 15, 2009. Isms . . . Gender, Race, Culture (on file with authors).

Yoder, Janice D., and Patricia Aniakudo. 1997. "Outsider within" the Fire House: Subordination and Difference in the Social Interactions of African American Women Firefighters. *Gender & Society* 11:324–41.

Yoder, Janice D., and Lynne L. Berendsen. 2001. "Outsider within" the Firehouse: African American and White Women Firefighters. *Psychology of Women Quarterly* 25(1):27–36.

2

Masculinity by Law

DEVON W. CARBADO

This chapter argues that formal equality frameworks can produce and entrench normative masculinities at the level of both formal legal doctrine and civil rights advocacy. In advancing this claim, I do not mean to suggest that formal equality is per se problematic. Nor is it my claim that, in the context of gender relationships, formal equality always produces undesirable outcomes. I simply mean to mark some of the ways in which formal equality and masculinity interact to produce inequality. As I will show, these interactions are mediated by race. My hope is to expand our understanding of the sites in which masculinity is produced, the varied contexts in which formal equality operates, and the role law and civil rights discourse plays in constructing gender-normative categories. In short, the chapter highlights how legal doctrine and civil rights advocacy help to create and sustain normative masculinity by law.

As a predicate to the argument, definitions of formal equality and normative masculinities are in order. By formal equality I mean approaches to law and civil rights that frame equality in terms of formal sameness in treatment and define inequality in terms of difference[1] (Carbado and Harris 2008; Harris 2001; Crenshaw 1989). With respect to normative masculinities, my starting point is Nancy Dowd, Nancy Levit, and Ann McGinley's formulation in this volume:

> "Masculinities" has multiple meanings. First, it is a structure that gives men as a group power over women as a group. Second, it is a set of practices, designed to maintain group power, that are considered "masculine." Third, it is the engagement in or the "doing" of these masculine practices by men or women. (Dowd, Levit, and McGinley, this volume)

Drawing on this formulation, one might say that masculinity (along with femininity) is part of a sex/gender system. This system helps to produce and naturalize the male/female dichotomy and a set of ideas and norms about how each side of the dichotomy ought to be expressed—at the level of the body (females should have breasts), self-presentation (males should not wear makeup), social role (females should not be firefighters), and sexual orientation (males should not be sexually intimate with other males).

Each of the foregoing domains—the body, self-presentation, social roles, and sexual orientation—functions as a gender-constitutive field, analogous to Pierre Bourdieu's notion of cultural fields, that produce and consolidate gender normativities.[2] My expression of "normativity" in the plural is intended tentatively to suggest that there are multiple gender normativities, not one, a point to which I will return and interrogate in the conclusion. For now, even when I use the term gender normativity or non-normativity (the plural is discursively clumsy), the reader should be thinking in the plural.

While the precise valence of gender normativity shifts from context to context (compare the gender normativity of the National Hockey League to that of Corporate America), whiteness is always a part of the background, as are the following two alignments: [male/masculine/man] and [female/feminine/woman]. Animating these alignments is the notion that males are supposed to be masculine; that is what makes a male a man. Females are supposed to be feminine; that is what makes a female a woman. Consequently, female masculinities (embodied by masculine women) generally are non-normative, as are male femininities (embodied by effeminate men).[3] This disciplining and disciplinary arrangement operates across the body, self-presentation, social role, and sexual orientation quite literally to make up gender-normative identities.

Race mediates all of this. The normative woman is not only appropriately feminine; she is also white. To put the point the way Kimberlé Crenshaw might, the intersectional experiences of white women dominate our understanding of gender. This is precisely why, historically, black women have been able neither to invoke their particular experiences as black women to ground their discrimination claims nor have those experiences stand in for the experiences of white women (Crenshaw 1989). Against the backdrop of white normativity, white women are "natural" women.

And white men are "natural" men. That is to say, the normative man is not only appropriately masculine, he is also white. He is the norm. Our reference. We are all defined with him in mind. We are all the same as or different from him. The intersectional identity of white normatively masculine men defines what it means to be a man. Against the naturalization of white manhood, black men have been constructed as "failed" men, men whose bodies (and bodily desires) control their minds; men who might more appropriately be referred to as "boys"; men with a "surplus" masculinity that must be quite literally policed. The disciplining and disciplinary nature of the [male/masculine/man] and [female/feminine/woman] alignments cannot be fully understood without engaging the foregoing racial dynamics.

The chapter is organized as follows. I first discuss a case in which a casino fires one of its white female bartenders because she refused to comply with the casino's grooming policy. I show how the court's decision against the plaintiff relied upon a formal equality framework that instantiated normative masculinity. In ruling in favor of Harrah's Casino, the court quite literally permitted that company to make up Jespersen as a white woman. Jespersen lost her case because she resisted that gender conformity.

Next, I move from legal doctrine to civil rights advocacy, focusing first on gay rights advocacy against Don't Ask, Don't Tell. Rather than repudiating the kind of gender conformity the *Jespersen* court legitimized, gay rights advocates adopted a "mainstreaming strategy," whose purpose was to demonstrate that LGBT people are, to borrow from Andrew Sullivan, "virtually normal," which is to say, white and gender normative (Sullivan 1996).

While Don't Ask, Don't Tell is a dead letter and marriage equality now constitutes the epicenter of most gay rights civil rights engagements, for at least a decade, this policy was *the* site for gay rights advocacy. Like the *Jespersen* court, gay rights advocates employed formal equality arguments that traded on white normative masculinities. This is precisely what Michael Warner identifies as "the trouble with normal"—or the mainstreaming of gay rights advocacy—it acquiesces in and reproduces normative gender identities (1999).

To illustrate that the reliance on gender normativity is racialized and a more general phenomenon within civil rights advocacy, I then highlight one of the strategies the American Civil Liberties Union (ACLU) mobilized to challenge racial profiling—presenting "respectable" images of black and Latino men to the American public as icons of racial victimization. Because these men do not evidence the hyper-*physical* masculinity stereotypically associated with men of color, they could function as sympathetic racial victims.[4]

Cumulatively, the foregoing three cases illustrate the interaction between normative masculinity and race at the level of legal doctrine and civil rights advocacy. Jespersen lost her case because, against the backdrop of gender-normative standards, her refusal to wear makeup rendered her female like a man (not a white woman).[5] Gay rights proponents traded on these same normative standards to "win" the hearts and minds of the American mainstream. Their hope was to persuade the American public that gays were "just like everybody else" and therefore should not be excluded from military service (Carbado 2000). This required them to highlight images of gay men who were "virtually normal"—which is to say, white and relatively masculine. Men who were gay like a man. The ACLU, too, framed its advocacy against racial profiling in terms of white normative masculinity. Because hyper-physical masculinity is perceived to be both an expression and cause of black male criminality, the ACLU contestation of racial profiling figured images of men who did not fit this *non*-normative masculine profile.

Female like a Man (Not a Woman)

In August 2000, Darlene Jespersen, a successful and well-liked bartender who had worked at Harrah's Casino in Reno for more than two decades, found herself out of a job. Harrah's fired Jespersen because she refused to comply with the company's grooming policy. Instituted in February 2000 as a part of Harrah's Beverage Department Image Transformation Program, the policy mandated that Harrah's female employees wear makeup. Jespersen refused to do so. Harrah's then terminated her employment and Jespersen responded with a sex discrimination lawsuit (Carbado, Gulati, and Ramachandran 2006; George, Gulati, and McGinley 2011).

Jespersen rested part of her legal argument on a case that was decided some 20 years earlier, *Price Waterhouse v. Hopkins* (1989). In that case, the accounting firm Price Waterhouse denied Ann Hopkins, who was white, partnership. The record revealed that one partner explicitly informed Hopkins that she was too "masculine" and another informed her that, to improve her chances the following year, she should "walk more femininely, talk more femininely, dress more femininely, wear make-up, have her hair styled, and wear jewelry" (ibid. 235). The Court found in Hopkins's favor based on an anti-stereotyping and gender non-conformity theory: employers cannot require females to be feminine and males to be masculine.

Jespersen argued that *Price Waterhouse* applied to her case (*Jespersen v. Harrah's Operating Co., Inc.*, 2006). Her claim, in effect, was that via its grooming policy, Harrah's Casino was asking Jespersen to "dress more feminine, wear makeup [and] have her hair styled." Harrah's was forcing her to align her sex (female) with a normative gender alignment (femininity) (Case 1995; Valdes 1995). The court rejected this argument and Jespersen lost her case (*Jespersen* 2006). The question is why? The short answer is that the Ninth Circuit, the highest court to hear the case, adopted a formal equality approach that legitimized the normative masculinity and femininity Harrah's grooming policy instantiated.

To appreciate the court's formal equality approach, one has to understand the legal doctrine the court employed to adjudicate the case: the "equal burdens" test, a test that discursively reflects a formal equality orientation. Courts apply the equal burdens test to determine whether a company's grooming policy constitutes sex discrimination. If the policy burdens one sex more than the other, a court will conclude that the policy discriminates on the basis of sex. (Note that *Price Waterhouse* was not a grooming case per se, in that the firm did not promulgate a generally applicable set of grooming requirements.) The problem for Jespersen was not just that the "equal burdens" test is facially formalistic (focusing our attention on whether the sexes are being treated the same) but that the court was overly formalistic in its application of the test.

In concluding that Harrah's grooming policy equally burdened men and women, the court reasoned that the policy regulated men's and women's hairstyles, men's and women's clothing, men's and women's shoes, men's and women's fingernails, and men's and women's faces (*Jespersen* 2006). This formal equality approach obscured the fact that Harrah's grooming policy was quite literally producing normative masculinity and femininity and instantiating impermissible sex stereotyping. Harrah's promulgated its policy to ensure that men look and act like men (masculine) and women look and act like women (feminine) (Franke 1995). Women must wear makeup ("face powder, blush, and mascara" and "lip color must be worn at all times") (*Jespersen* 2006, 1107). Men are prohibited from doing so. Women may wear colored nail polish. "No colored polish is allowed" for men (ibid.). Men are not permitted to have ponytails. Women's hair must be "teased, curled, or styled" (ibid.). Men's hair "must not extend below top of shirt collar" (ibid.).

The foregoing differential grooming standards align with our normative assumptions about how men and women should make themselves up. Conventionally, we expect women, not men, to wear makeup. Conventionally, we expect men, not women, to have short hair. Conventionally, we expect women, not men, to wear colored nail polish. These conventions about self-presentation align with a normative gender imperative that women are and should be feminine and that men are and should be masculine. Understood in this way, Harrah's grooming policy was preventing Jespersen from being female like a man.

That Harrah's might have been concerned about female masculinities—and specifically with respect to Jespersen—is a reasonable conclusion in light of how Jespersen embodied her gender. Consider the image of Jespersen in figure 2.1.

Harrah's insistence that Jespersen in particular abide by the grooming policy has to be considered against the backdrop of this image. Harrah's might have concluded that its grooming policy was not going to overly feminize Jespersen; it

Figure 2.1

was simply going to render her make-up (her overall embodiment) more like a woman. Nothing in the policy required her to wear body-revealing clothing. Indeed, her uniform, particularly in the context of Vegas where cocktail waitresses are typically scantily dressed, is somewhat gender-bending. At the very least, Harrah's managers might have thought, Jespersen had to be intelligible as a woman. Its makeup and grooming requirements could help to accomplish exactly that. All of this suggests that, had Jespersen been more conventionally feminine, her refusal to wear makeup might not have triggered litigation. The problem was her "Ask Pat"[6] appearance against which Harrah's grooming policy was a corrective. Whether thinking along the foregoing lines actually motivated Harrah's decision-making is unclear. Nevertheless, it is not unreasonable to think that Jespersen's particular self-presentation—her particular female masculinity—was a subtext in the case—and not just for Harrah's but for the court as well.

And, indeed, the court's reasoning does hint that the particularities of Jespersen's self-presentation informed the decision. One reason the court found the grooming policy to be permissible was that it did not render Jespersen vulnerable to sexual harassment (*Jespersen* 2006). That is to say, from the court's perspective, it mattered that Harrah's was not overly effeminizing Jespersen as a sex object, and against the backdrop of the image shown in figure 2.1, could not have succeeded in doing so if they tried.

Another way to think about how Jespersen's female masculinity worked as a subtext in the case is to imagine a scenario in which the partners at a major law firm—Sullivan & Cromwell, let's say—fired Brian, a male litigator, for showing up to court obviously made up—mascara, nail polish, red lipstick, etc. Assume that this litigator brings a case alleging sex discrimination. Would he win? Probably not, notwithstanding that this case more squarely approximates *Price Waterhouse* in the sense that, unlike *Jespersen*, it does not involve a formal grooming policy (Carbado and Gulati forthcoming).

Judge Richard Posner, the legendary appellate judge, has pretty much said that plaintiffs in such a case would lose. According to Posner, anti-discrimination law does not create a right for "male workers to wear nail polish and dresses and speak in falsetto and mince about in high heels" (*Hamm v. Weyauwega Milk Products, Inc.* 2003, 1067). Note how explicitly Posner trades on normative masculinity. Posner, among many other judges, would not be persuaded by the claim that Brian was the victim of impermissible sex stereotyping. He would insist that Sullivan & Cromwell fired Brian because he failed to abide by the most basic norms of professional self-presentation. Brian, he might add, does not have a right to make himself up (like a woman). That Brian would lose his case helps to explain why Jespersen lost hers.

That the *Jespersen* court did not apply a gender-nonconformity or anti-sex-stereotyping theory does not mean that Harrah's victory was secured. As suggested earlier, the court could have applied the "equal burdens" test less formalistically to find in Jespersen's favor. More particularly, the court could have drawn upon the gendered history of makeup to conclude that the makeup requirements were rooted in a sex-gender system that disadvantages women (Carbado, Gulati, and Ramachandran 2006). By the mid-twentieth-century, makeup became a necessary part of being a woman, a social technology for gender conformity. At the same time, this technology helped to legitimize women's entrance in the workplace, particularly during World

War II. As women increasingly participated in formerly male spheres—politics, economic activities, and the labor market—makeup served to appease an anxiety concerning this intrusion and integration. Makeup signified that gender integration would not mean the disruption of gender hierarchy. While some employers were troubled by the use of makeup on the job (for both safety and cultural reasons), others welcomed it (Black 2004, 34).

The grooming policy in *Jespersen* is best understood in light of the history of makeup. The "*un*equal burden" of makeup is less about the monetary or preparation costs (though neither is trivial) and more about the hierarchical gender roles makeup historically effectuated and maintained. Whether women who "freely" choose to wear makeup reinscribe that hierarchy is open to debate. But when a company mandates that women wear makeup, and prohibits men from doing so, it is enforcing normative gender roles whose distributional consequences have been decidedly unequal (Green 2005). To put all of this slightly differently, while Harrah's grooming policy imposed impermissible sex-stereotyping burdens on both women and men—quite literally making up the former as feminine and the latter as masculine—the history of makeup as a kind of gender palliative suggests that the policy *un*equally burdens women (even as the policy also burdened men). In legitimizing this unequal burden, the Ninth Circuit left Harrah's free to make Jespersen female like a woman.

Gay Like a Man (Not a Woman)

While Harrah's grooming policy required Darlene Jespersen to be female like a woman, not a man, gay rights advocates have required their gay civil rights icons to be gay like a man, not a woman. This strategy shaped gay rights opposition to the Don't Ask, Don't Tell policy, an opposition that relied heavily on comparisons between race and sexual orientation (Carbado 2000).

To challenge Don't Ask, Don't Tell, gay rights proponents analogized the rhetoric the military deployed to exclude (out) gays and lesbians from the military service to the rhetoric the military deployed to exclude African Americans (Eskridge 1993). They reasoned that because we repudiated the latter, we should also repudiate the former. This analogizing of rhetoric was the predicate for a formal equality analogy about discrimination—namely, the exclusion of African Americans from the military is like the exclusion of (out) gays and lesbians. The analogy set up an equivalency between race-based and sexual orientation-based military exclusion that obscured important civil rights history, elided the existence of black gays and lesbians, and produced a civil rights discourse that traded on white normative masculinity (Halley 2000). I elaborate below.

According to David Smith, the spokesperson for the gay and lesbian coalition group Campaign for Military Service, the language the military employed to exclude blacks from military service is like the language the military employed to exclude gays and lesbians. Smith's argument has additional force if we examine two texts: a Department of Defense Directive (Defense Directive) justifying the military's discrimination against gays and lesbians, and a 1942 statement from the Secretary of the Navy (Navy Statement) supporting racial segregation in the armed forces. The Defense Directive reads, in part:

> The presence in the military environment of persons who engage in homosexual conduct or who, by their statements, demonstrate a propensity to engage in homosexual conduct, seriously impairs the accomplishment of military mission. The presence of such members adversely affects the ability of the armed forces to maintain discipline, good order and morale; to foster mutual trust and confidence among service members; to insure the integrity of the system of rank and command; to facilitate assignment and worldwide deployment of service members who frequently must live and work in close conditions affording minimal privacy; to recruit and retain members of the armed forces; to maintain the public acceptability of military service. (Shilts 1993, 378–79)

Now consider the Navy Statement, which in relevant part reads:

> Men on board ships live in particularly close association; in their messes, one man sits beside another; their hammocks or bunks are close together; in their tasks such as those of gun crew, they form a closely knit, highly coordinated team. How many white men would choose, of their own accord, that their closest associates in sleeping quarters, at mess, and in gun crews should be of another race? (Butler 1993, 16–17)

These texts suggest that at different historical moments in America the armed forces have employed military necessity arguments to justify both racial segregation in and the exclusion of (out) gays and lesbians from the military. Blackness and homosexuality threaten military discipline, organization, morale, and readiness. This discursive analogy then became the basis for a comparison about discrimination: Gay exclusion from the military is like black exclusion from the military. However, this formal *in*equality claim obscures the history of Jim Crow, even as it draws on that history as a moral resource.

Consider again the following language from the Navy Statement: "Men on board ships live in particularly close association; in their messes, one man sits beside another; their hammocks or bunks are close together" (Butler 1993, 16). On its face, and read outside of its historical context, this language seems to be more about (homo)sexual anxiety than racial anxiety. The language invites us to think about "cruising"—that is to say (and in this context), the "gay gaze" (Eskridge 1997; Kendall 1997; Thomas 1993). The notion would be that heterosexual military men are worried about being the object of gay desire, for such objectification threatens their notion of manhood (Karst 1991). Read outside of its political and historical context, then, the language from the Navy Statement can be interpreted to be about the relationship among homosexual orientation, manhood, and military social norms—the extent to which homosexual presence threatens heterosexual manhood and heterosexist military culture (Karst 1991; Shilts 1993; Rolison and Nakayama 1994).

But the statement also explicitly speaks of "white men" and men "of another race," querying, rhetorically, whether the former "would choose, of their own accord" to share sleeping quarters with the latter. We know the answer. This explicit invocation of race in the navy document invites an engagement of the specific historical context in which the navy produced the statement. Gay rights proponents did not perform that engagement. Instead, their strategy was to replace the racial signifiers in 1940s military documents with sexual orientation signifiers. Under this approach, the text in the 1942 Navy Statement that reads: "How many *white* men would choose, of their own accord, that their closest associates in sleeping quarters, at mess, and in gun crews should be of another *race*?" becomes: "How many *heterosexual* men would choose, of their own accord, that their closest associates in sleeping quarters, at mess, and in gun crews should be of another *sexual orientation*?" (Reza 1993).

This strategy of replacing race with sexual orientation displaced black civil rights history, even as gay rights proponents were drawing on that history for moral authority. Replacing race with sexual orientation obscures that the Navy Statement was written in the context of Jim Crow. As I discuss more fully below, the pro-segregation military officials who promulgated this document might have been worried about black (presumptively heterosexual) men cruising white (presumptively heterosexual) men. But heterosexuality was so thoroughly embedded in military culture, so naturalized a default, that the concern, presumably, was not consciously about the gay gaze as such or gay bodies as such, though bodies and sexuality as they intersected with race certainly mattered, a point to which I will return presently. Instead, the Navy Statement reflects the then-pervasive notion of the black body as contaminated and contaminating and the perception of black men as inferior and failed men in two contradictory senses.

On the one hand, the notion was that black men were infantile, happy-go-lucky, and effeminate; they were men for whom "boy" is a more appropriate designation. On the other, black men were perceived to be hyper-masculine and sexually aggressive, men for whom "buck" is a more appropriate designation. Instead of reading the Navy Statement abstractly, we should read it against the backdrop of this boy/buck racial dialectic, a racial dialectic that situates black men both between and beyond the social markers of male and man.

This is not to say that sexual orientation and sexuality more generally are irrelevant to this analysis. On the contrary, under the logic of the boy/buck racial dialectic, black men threatened to "turn" or de-masculinize white military men in at least the following two ways: (1) by effeminization (via sexual violence or engendering in white men an infantilized manboyhood); or (2) by corrupting the sexual morality of white men (via same-sex intimacy or other acts of perceived sexual immorality). Thus, when, for example, Georgia Congressman Stephen Pace argued, in a letter to the Secretary of the Navy, against racial integration of the armed forces on the ground that "white boys [would be] forced to sleep with . . . negroes" (Bianco 1996, 61), it is not enough—and indeed is misleading—to say simply that Pace's statement reflects a homophobic panic (as distinct from a racial panic).

Nor is it enough to assert that the military's concern about black and white men *interracially* sleeping together (in terms of sharing the same dormitories) is just like the military's concern about gay and straight men sleeping together (in terms of sexual intimacy or simply sharing the same sleeping quarters). Framing the analogy along either of the preceding axes disaggregates race from sexuality and de-historicizes the context in which Congressman Pace articulated his black racial phobia. More fundamentally, such analogizing obscures that laws barring blacks from military service were crucial sites not merely for regulating race but for constituting race and racial power. In other words, the exclusion of blacks from the military *constituted* blacks and whites as cognizable and oppositional social categories within a regime of racial hierarchy.

All of this is to say that the Navy Statement and Pace's concerns about "white boys [and] negroes" should be understood contextually with reference to the racial dynamics I set out above. As I have already suggested, and want to repeat here, those dynamics were unequivocally invested with sexuality. The Navy Statement and Pace's comments were deeply bound up with and reflected profound anxieties about a quintessential and racially sexualized Jim Crow boundary—the"amalgamation of the races." Concerns about this boundary were not exhausted by the perceived effects that black male presence in, or racial penetration of, the military would have on white men in terms of either sexual intimacy or infantalization. The exclusion of black men shored up the intersectionally constituted and racially masculinist Jim Crow order. Vesting any power in black men—including the power to (tres) pass across a white masculine colorline (the military)—undermined the anti-racial amalgamation imperative that underwrote the entire Jim Crow edifice.

Motivating this imperative was the sense that racial amalgamation always already portended one of the most transgressive acts of racial integration: *heterosexual* intimacy between black men and white women. A black man could become "strange fruit"—the victim of a lynch mob—upon the mere allegation that he crossed that gendered colorline. In the context of Jim Crow, white women constituted a rigorously policed racial and gendered territory. Excluding black men from military service helped to preserve the racial integrity of her borders and at the same time kept both black men and white women in their respective racial and gendered places. Understood in this way, racial segregation in the armed forces helped to manage a racially inflected *heterosexualized* panic that was an important part of the broader disciplinary apparatus of Jim Crow. It is precisely this panic that explains the over-policing of *consensual* black male heterosexuality across the colorline and the under-policing of *unconsensual* white male heterosexuality across that line—which is to say, rape. Simply comparing language in military documents, and substituting identity categories, to advance a formal inequality argument erases this intersectional history, a history within which racism is sexualized.

And yet it would be inaccurate to say that gay rights proponents completely ignored black civil rights history. Indeed, part of the currency of the race analogy is that it trades on the moral authority of the civil rights movement. But the analogy does so without actually engaging the racial conditions under which African Americans were fighting for reform. On the contrary, the gay rights advocacy against Don't Ask, Don't Tell selectively incorporated African American history—and African Americans—to advance an argument about sexual orientation per se (read: presumptively white gays and lesbians of today) and race per se (read: presumptively black heterosexuals of the Jim Crow era). Underwriting the advocacy was the notion that, in an historical sense, gays are like African Americans (because gay experiences with military exclusion is like black exclusion from the military); in a contemporary sense, gays are "just like everybody else" (the white normative heterosexuals in contemporary society).

This strategy should disturb us. It exploits and displaces black civil rights history and trades on white privilege. Unfortunately, the strategy appears to acquire a new rhetorical form: "Gay is the New Black." Whether this expression will ultimately become a gay rights slogan is hard to say (Carbado and Robinson 2011). At the very least, the "Gay is the New Black" frame is an emerging discourse in which gay is not simply *like* black; *it is* black. Under this revised articulation, blackness as we know it is disappeared.

The selective employment of African American identity and experiences helps to explain why black gay men were largely invisible in the gay rights discourse as victims of Don't Ask, Don't Tell and why normatively masculine white men were visible. The "just like everybody else" refrain created a discursive field from which the "but for" gay male victim could grow. This figure is "just like" other white normatively masculine men, "but for" the fact of his sexual orientation. This gay male icon is gay like a man (Hutchinson 1997; Robinson 2009).

Black men could not perform this "gay like a man" role. This might not be obvious. One could surmise that the perceived masculinity "surplus" of black identity would cure the perceived masculinity "deficits" of gay identity. Under this view, blackness could help to normalize—and even mainstream—what it means to be gay. This is not, however, how blackness functions. Its surplus masculinity cannot be sufficiently contained to perform this work. Black men are perceived to be too masculine, in other words, to be authentically gay in the first place.

As Russell Robinson has argued, discourses about black men reify this inauthenticity (2009). While black men are presumed to be on the Down Low (DL)—which implies a desire to live a straight life while secretly and pathologically having sex with men—white men are presumed to be in the closet, which implies being forced to claim straightness against the desire for open and normal relationships with other men. The DL engenders condemnation; the closet, sympathy. Whereas DL men are perceived to be villains, closeted men are constructed as victims. The DL "phenomenon" is pathologized and thus described as an "unnatural" part of the gay experience. The closet, in contrast, is "normalized" and thus described as a "natural" part of being gay. DL men are perceived to be hyper-physically masculine. Closeted men are perceived to be "straight acting." All of this situates black men outside of white gay normativity and thus outside of the "gay like a man" frame.

There is another racial explanation for the absence of black men in the "gay like a man" role white gay men exclusively performed—the image of the "wishy-washy" effeminate black gay man. Marlon Riggs wrote eloquently about this particular iconography. "Snap-swish-and-dish divas have truly arrived," wrote Riggs, "giving Beauty Shop drama at center stage, performing the read-and-snap two-step as they sashay across the movie screen, entertaining us in the castles of our homes" (1999). Riggs' point is that images of black effeminate gay men have been commodified and voyeuristically included in our culture—but always as a non-normative identity. To put the point the way Riggs does, "Negro faggotry is the rage! Black gay men are not" (ibid.).

The intersection of race, masculinity, and sexuality helps to explain why gay rights advocates focused on the white, and not black, casualties of Don't Ask, Don't Tell, despite the fact that African Americans have been disproportionately affected by the policy. Too masculine to be gay and too feminine to be men, black gay men cannot be gay like a man. Thus, while Perry Watkins, a black army sergeant, established an important milestone when he became the first openly gay serviceman to challenge successfully Don't Ask, Don't Tell (*Watkins v. U.S. Army* 1989), gay rights advocates largely marginalized him in their campaign.

As Tom Stoddard, the important gay activist lawyer who directed the Campaign for Military Service, said, "there was a public relations problem with Perry Watkins" (Carbado 2000, 1510). This "public relations problem" was intersectional—a function of Watkins' race, masculinity, and sexuality. The fact that Watkins often performed in drag at military events rendered him a "Snap Queen," a figure clearly outside of the gay mainstream and certainly not "virtually normal."

But even had Watkins embodied a more conventional gender identity, the "gay like a man" role likely would have been unavailable to him. The normalization of white gay identity, and the perceived surplus of black masculinity, would have forever defeated the boy-next-door appeal gay rights advocates sought of their icons.

Enter Keith Meinhold. He had precisely that boy-next-door appeal. A white Navy petty officer who revealed that he was gay on *ABC World News Tonight*, Meinhold became the "poster child" for the gay rights campaign. He appeared on the cover of *Newsweek* magazine, in full Navy uniform, "virtually equal," to borrow from Urvashi Vaid (1995). The caption accompanying his image asks: How Far Will Clinton Go? (Newsweek 1993).

Presumably, gay rights proponents were hoping that the American public would read Meinhold's story, come to see him as an ordinary man, "but for" his sexual orientation, and conclude that Clinton would not be going too far if he admitted men like Meinhold—men who were gay like men—into the military.

This representational strategy was employed with respect to other white gay men as well. Consider how the media represented Joseph Steffan, a former midshipman who was expelled from the Navy Academy a few weeks before graduation.

> The host is interviewing Joseph Steffan. . . . Raised in the Midwest, Catholic, a choir boy in his local church. Steffan was the kid next door. Clean-cut, an excellent student, exceptional in track, he took as his date for the senior prom the high school's homecoming queen. . . . At the Academy he ranked in the top ten of his class, became battalion commander his senior year, and received the unique honor of twice singing, solo, the national anthem at the Army-Navy game.
>
> The TV monitor shifts to a film of Joe Steffan, standing on a platform as the Army-Navy game is about to begin . . . singing the anthem against the red, white, and blue backdrop. . . . Joseph Steffan . . . is now "out" to the U.S.A. (Katzenstein 1996, 233–34)

Significantly, it is not just Steffan who is "out" here. For, in this context, Steffan, like Meinhold, functions as a representative gay man. He is respectable. He is accomplished. He is an athlete. He is America. He is white. He is masculine. *And* he is also gay. I employ "and" and not "but" here because the theater invites us to conceptualize Steffan's gay identity as incidental, rather than fundamental to, his person—which is to say, his manhood. Steffan's normative masculinity, which his whiteness helped to constitute, rendered him gay like a man.

Black Like a Man

If being gay like a man is palatable to the mainstream American public, being black like a man is not. Because of stereotypes about black hyperphysical masculinity, or surplus masculinity, black men have to appear respectable to function as racial victims. Their masculinity has to be "toned down." This is why the ACLU's campaign against racial profiling relied on images of men with gender normative masculinities, men whose masculinities were not in "excess."

Consider, for example, the image shown in figure 2.2, which was excerpted from an ACLU Pamphlet (Carbado 2002).

The caption above the image asks: "What do these men have in common?" One answer, perhaps the easiest, is that they were both racially profiled. But there is another similarity between these two men that explains their appearance on the cover of an ACLU pamphlet—both men signify a normative, and not a hypermasculine, masculinity.

Both men are "respectable." The visual economy of each image disconfirms stereotypes about race and masculinity. They are not thugs. They are not gangsters. They are not drug dealers. They are not hyper-physically masculine. Their presumed surplus masculinity is nowhere to be seen. Both are ordinary men. Their suits and ties, polished shoes, and manicured faces exude middle-class male respectability. They are "just like" gender-normative white men. Therefore, the police should treat them "just like" gender-normative white men. The fact that they were treated differently, against the backdrop of their normative masculinity, is what renders them sympathetic racial victims. This is how formal equality and masculinity intersected in this advocacy. The ACLU's contestation of racial profiling was predicated on black and Latino men having the same normative masculinity as white, heterosexual middle-aged men (Kimmel 2005). To the extent that this sameness did not exist, the ACLU's story about innocence and racial respectability would not have had any traction.

That the racial respectability of these men turned on their normative masculinity is clear from the text of the pamphlet. Indeed, the text narrates a story about both men within which their normative masculinities are explicit. With respect to Carlos Gonzalez, for example, the text reveals that he "is a junior high math teacher" in the community in which he grew up: South Central Los Angeles. He appears to be a responsible family man—a father who plays with and communicates to his son. His experience with racial profiling "humiliated" him. According to Gonzalez, he was made to endure that humiliation "all because two LAPD officers thought I was a hoodlum or a criminal because of the way I looked" (Carbado 2002, 1037). To the extent that Gonzalez does not appear to "look" hyper-physically masculine—in his suit and tie—the "look" to which he refers is, of course, his race. That is precisely why the police encounter is illegitimate. Had Gonzalez looked hypermasculine, had he evidenced a surplus masculinity, he would have been a less palatable victim. His encounter with the police, and their disciplining of him, would have "made sense."

The message the ACLU hopes to convey with this pamphlet is clear: racial profiling "results in the persecution of innocent people based on their skin

Figure 2.2

color" (Carbado 2002, 1037). The political pragmatism behind this idea is also clear: to the extent that (white) people understand that racial profiling affects innocent blacks or Latinas/os, men who are normatively masculine, men who are neither "gangsters" nor "thugs," they are more likely to condemn racial profiling and the police officers who practice it.

None of this is to suggest that the ACLU's campaign against racial profiling has been unhelpful. On the contrary, the ACLU has played an enormously important role in increasing public awareness about, and helping to fashion legal and political responses to, race-based policing. I simply mean to mark the extent to which their approach implicitly traded on the idea that there are "good" (normatively masculine) and "bad" (hyper-physically masculine) blacks. This puts a question mark in front of all black men and invites law enforcement officials to figure out which of us are "good." In turn, black men have an incentive to reiteratively signal that their masculinity is under control. Doing so mitigates the risk that police officers will perceive them as "bad."

This problem of reiteration—or the ongoing performance of a normative masculinity—helps to explain Harvard Professor Henry Louis Gates' encounter with Sergeant James Crowley, a white, male, 11-year veteran of the force (Sweet et al. 2009) who teaches an anti-racial profiling class in the Cambridge Police Department (New York Post 2009). Crowley catapulted into the public arena after he arrested Dr. Gates outside his own home. Professor Gates and Sergeant Crowley have since disagreed on the actual happenings of the incident. Suffice it to say, their altercation made big news. Even President Obama weighed in: "I think it's fair to say, number one, any of us would be pretty angry; number two, that the Cambridge police acted stupidly in arresting somebody when there was already proof that they were in their own home; and, number three, what I think we know separate and apart from this incident is that there's a long history in this country of African-Americans and Latinos being stopped by law enforcement disproportionately. That's just a fact" (ibid.).

For his part, Gates, in an interview with CNN reporter Soledad O'Brien, was emphatic that "this is not about me, this is about the black man in America. If it can happen to me, it can happen to anyone in the United States" (Chew 2009). Implicit in Gates' claim is the idea that the encounter he experienced wasn't supposed to happen to *him*. He is not, after all, the stereotypical hyper-physical masculine black man. He is middle aged, slight in build, walks with a cane, and wears glasses—and he is a Harvard professor. Black men like Gates, with normative (non-threatening) masculinities, are supposed to be safe. Under this view, what happens to Gates portends what will happen to everyone else. If he is unsafe, all of us are. The reverse is not necessarily true: what happens to everyone else does not portend what will happen to Gates.

Except, of course, that Gates was arrested. The reason relates to surplus compliance. Gates didn't supply it. This was dangerous for him not to do. Against the background assumption that *every* black man has a surplus masculinity and thus the racial potential to be hyper-physically masculine, *every* black man has the existential burden of demonstrating surplus compliance, particularly in the context of police interactions.

According to Officer Crowley, he arrested Gates for disorderly conduct because Gates was engaging in "loud and tumultuous behavior in a public space" (CNN 2009). Crowley described Gates as "combative," even after he gave Gates two warnings, which included showing Gates his set of handcuffs. Crowley insisted that he "really didn't want to" arrest Gates but was eventually "forced" to do so after Gates refused to de-escalate the situation (Thompson and Thompson 2009). Crowley's comments in this respect, which he offered in response to the criticism that he acted excessively, suggests that surplus compliance was at least implicitly on his mind (Kang 2005). Particularly noteworthy here is the fact that Crowley's threat and eventual arrest of Gates occurs *after* Gates had established that he was not engaged in a robbery but was inside of his own home. Even under these circumstances, Crowley expected surplus compliance.

Perhaps Gates should have known this. Part of one's Americanization as a black man, after all, is learning the importance of signaling cooperation in the context of police interactions (Carbado 2005). Our presumed surplus masculinity creates a demand for it. Thus, Dr. Robert L. Johnson and Dr. Steven Simring's strategies for people who are racially profiled:

- Don't display anger—even if justified. Most police officers resent challenges to their authority, and may overreact to any real or perceived affront.
- Don't argue the Fourth Amendment. . . . [A]t the point you are stopped, it is important to maintain control of your emotions and your behavior.
- Don't be sarcastic or condescending to the officer. Always be cooperative and polite.
- Don't lose sight of your goal. The objective in most racial profiling scenarios is to end the encounter as quickly as possible with a minimum risk of potential trauma. Getting stopped for no good reason is inconvenient. But being jacked up against your car and searched is an experience that can stay with you for years. Getting handcuffed and taken into custody escalates the nightmare. (Johnson and Simring 2000, 121–22)

Part of mitigating the "risk of potential trauma" is demonstrating that one is not, and at no point in the encounter will become, hyper-physically masculine and dangerous. One has to demonstrate that one's surplus masculinity is stored away. Parents, family members, and community leaders teach black children how to signal this—when, if at all, to speak; when and how to say

"Sir" (Troutt 2001, 60), "Officer," or "Trooper" (Johnson and Simring 2000, 121); how to refrain from making sudden movements (ibid. 125); and when, if at all, to assert one's rights (ibid. 121; Brown-Russell 1998, 34).

From Crowley's perspective, Gates' masculinity was not under control. By simply questioning authority and asserting his rights, Gates was drawing on his surplus masculinity. He was, as such, potentially dangerous—and not just in the sense of causing physical harm but in the sense of threatening Crowley's own masculinity. To borrow from Frank Rudy Cooper, Crowley could have experienced Gates' assertion of his rights as a "masculinity challenge" (Cooper 2009, 698; Cooper 2010) that he (Crowley) *had to* win. Winning required Crowley to both discipline and contain Gates. This secured Crowley's sense of safety and his sense of masculinity. At the same time, because Gates is not black like a man in his everyday life, because he has a normative masculinity (against the backdrop of the hyper-physical masculine/criminal stereotype), his story could add to the story of other respectable black men who have been the victims of racial profiling.

Of course, Gates' celebrity played an enormously important role vis-à-vis the media attention the episode received. But his status as a racial victim did not require that celebrity. It required racial respectability, of which normative masculinity is a part. To put all of this another way, with respect to the American public at large, one cannot be a racial victim and be black like a man.

Conclusion: White Like a Man

Being white like a man, however, is generally (though not always) normative. This is the point that Michael Kimmel makes when he suggests that "the masculinity that defines white, middle-class, early middle-aged heterosexual men is the masculinity that sets the standards for other men" (Kimmel 2005, 30). It is precisely these "standards" that created the formal equality baseline against which at least some Americans determined the legitimacy of Meinhold's and Steffan's civil rights claims. Because each of them embodied the gender-normative standards of which Kimmel speaks, but did not benefit from enacting those standards in the sense of avoiding military exclusion, they were sympathetic civil rights victims. A similar point can be made about the men on the cover of the ACLU's pamphlet. They, too, became sympathetic civil rights victims because their normative masculinity did not protect them from racial profiling.

Kimmel's point about "standards" brings us back to the *Jespersen* case. With respect to men, Harrah's grooming policy required that:

- Hair must not extend below top of shirt collar. Ponytails are prohibited.
- Hands and fingernails must be clean and nails neatly trimmed at all times. No colored polish is permitted.
- Eye and facial makeup is not permitted.
- Shoes will be solid black leather or leather type with rubber (non-skid) soles.

Now recall the men on the ACLU pamphlet and my descriptions of Steffan and Meinhold. Note that the "identity makeup" these men "wore" for their respective civil rights performances is consistent with the grooming policy Harrah's sets forth for its male employees. In other words, none of these men have hair that "extend[s] below [the] top of [the] shirt." Presumably, each has "clean and . . . neatly trimmed [nails] at all times." None wears "[e]ye and facial makeup." The convergence between the (gender) makeup of these men and the (gender) makeup requirements reflected in Harrah's policy is not accidental. Harrah's policy incorporates the gender-normative masculinity "standards" Kimmel references. These standards are expressed in culture, formulated in institutional policies, instantiated in law, and embedded in civil rights.

And they are racially inflected. Specifically, the standardization of masculinity shapes how race generally—and not just whiteness—is normatively expressed. Which is to say, normatively masculine men are racially respectable. "Race Men," to borrow from Hazel Carby, are historical paragons of racial respectability within the black community. Like the men on the cover of the ACLU pamphlet, their public presence typically figured them in suits and ties (Carby 1998).

There is another way in which masculinity shapes how race is expressed—it confers racial standing or authenticity. Consider, for example, Marlon Riggs' observation that he could not "be a black gay man because, by the tenets of black macho, black gay man is a triple negation" (1999, 307). The "tenets of Black Macho" undermine Riggs' status not simply as a man but as an *African American man*. That is the specific intersectional masculinity his gay identity negates (Crenshaw 1989).

Significantly, the "Black Macho" of which Riggs speaks is normative not in the sense that its gender performance is the same as the gender performance that constitutes the masculinity through which Gates and the men on the cover of the ACLU pamphlet become respectable racial victims. Gates would not be exhibit A for the normative masculinity against which Riggs becomes a "triple negation."[7] Nor would the "white, middle-class, early middle-aged heterosexual" masculinity Kimmel invokes. Being white like a man would not, under the tenets of "Black Macho," enhance Riggs' racial authentic as a *black* man (Carbado 1999).[8] Masculinities are contextually normative. Hegemonic masculinity might not be hegemonic everywhere. In this sense, perhaps it makes sense to conceptualize masculinity in terms of "palatable masculinities." This concept decouples the question of whether a particular expression of masculinity is *generally* normative from the question of whether that masculinity is palatable within a *particular* context. Palatable masculinities can be non-normative and normative masculinities can be unpalatable.

This brings me back to the introduction. There, I suggested that we might think of normative masculinity in the plural, recognizing that there are multiple normative masculinities, not one. My example was the difference between the gender normativity of the National Hockey League and the gender normativity of Corporate America. While the gender norms that constitute these two fields are not completely discontinuous, they are certainly not coextensive. For example, whereas physical aggression is completely acceptable in the context of hockey, it is completely unacceptable in the context of corporate America (members of corporate boards typically don't employ fist fights to settle their disputes).

But, perhaps palatable masculinity is a better way to capture that difference than the claim that both fields have different normative masculinities. There is something to Kimmel's point about the standardization of white, middle-aged heterosexual masculinity. All masculinities come into being in the shadow of, and are often explicitly defined with reference to, that gender-normative baseline. It is the masculinity of power—and thus the masculinity against which all of us are habituated.

Moreover, while white, male, middle-aged, middle-class, heterosexual masculinity certainly has a code of conduct with which it is associated, that masculinity is also a "status masculinity" in the sense of being always already normative-masculine-conferring. In other words, the conduct of a white, middle-class, early middle-aged heterosexual man is normative in part not just because of *what* he is doing (that is to say, his conduct), but because *he* is doing it (that is to say, his status).

One can make a similar point about black masculinity as a "status masculinity"; being a black man is always already *non*-normative-conferring. Thus, we might perceive the conduct of a black man as non-normative not because of *what* he is doing, but because *he* is doing it. Think, again, about the very different public discourses about the DL and the closet, essentially the same social phenomenon. Because our identities are differently situated in terms of the normativity or non-normativity they already confer, calling white, middle-class, early middle-aged heterosexual masculinity both normative and hegemonic might be entirely right, even if this masculinity is not palatable in every context.

As should be apparent already, on the one hand, I am uncomfortable with the term hegemonic masculinity because it seems to obscure or elide important contexts in which a generally non-normative masculinity (e.g., hyperphysical masculinity) is normative (e.g., hockey). On the other hand, I am uncomfortable with referring to a particular masculinity as normative simply because there is *some* context in which that masculinity has currency. Such an approach flattens and obfuscates the power differentials among and between different masculinities, enacting an iteration of the formal equality frameworks against which I have been arguing. My introduction of the term "palatable masculinities" is intended to avoid that problem.

But this might be no answer. Masculinities are not palatable in the same way or to the same extent. Here, too, there are power differentials that the rubric "palatable masculinities" flattens. Still, the availability of this term as a register with which to describe masculinity might help to justify the continued use of the terms "hegemonic masculinity" and "normative masculinity," terms we might employ interchangeably to describe, again borrowing from Kimmel, "the masculinity that defines white, middle-class, early middle-aged heterosexual men." Under this approach, my earlier claim that: "Hegemonic masculinity might not be hegemonic everywhere. Being white like a man is not always normative" would be rearticulated to become: "Hegemonic masculinity might not be *palatable* everywhere. Being white like a man is not always *palatable*." Whether this difference makes a difference, theoretically or normatively, I leave to the reader to decide.

NOTES

1. For a more expansive definition of formal equality and its relationship to colorblindness, see Carbado and Harris (2008).
2. Fields are organized around norms, practices, and discourses that are normalized and taken for granted (Bourdieu 1987).
3. In invoking female masculinity here I do not mean to weigh in on the debate of whether female masculinity has its own history or merely mimics male masculinity (though I am persuaded by Judith Halberstam's work), I merely mean to mark what some would perceive as a misalignment between a person's female identity and her self-presentation (Halberstam 1998).
4. Much masculinities studies literature employs the term hypermasculinity and mobilizes that term to discuss perceptions of working-class men, men of color, and men involved in certain sports, such as boxing or hockey. This obscures the extent to which hypermasculinity operates across a number of domains of social life. Corporate America, for example, is hypermasculine, notwithstanding that it is not characterized by the

kind of physicality society generally attributes to black men. For this reason, I employ hyper-*physical* masculine to describe stereotypes about black men. This approach allows us to interrogate hypermasculinity that does not necessarily have physicality as an entailment.

5. Of course, being too feminized (too much like a woman) can also be disadvantageous. Women are punished if they are too masculine and punished if they are too feminine, thus the notion of the catch-22.

6. Julia Sweeney created the fictional androgynous character *Pat* for the comedy show, *Saturday Night Live*. The comic element of the skits involving Pat derived from the constant and futile efforts on the part of Pat's interlocutors to determine Pat's "true" sex. So successful were these skits that they became the basis for a movie, *It's Pat*, in 1994.

7. Frank Rudy Cooper engages an aspect of this problem via the term "bipolar masculinity," which is intended to distinguish black men who are perceived to be hypermasculine and black men whose masculinity aligns more closely with heterosexual white male standards (Cooper 2006, arguing "popular representations of heterosexual black men are bipolar. Those images alternate between a Bad Black Man who is crime-prone and hypersexual and a Good Black Man who distances himself from blackness and associates with white norms").

8. The relationship between normative masculinity, on the one hand, and race and authenticity, on the other, is the subject of a prior work (Carbado 1999). I mark it here simply to broaden the theoretical terms upon which normative masculinity is understood.

REFERENCES

Bianco, David Ari. 1996. Echoes of Prejudice: The Debates over Race and Sexuality in the Armed Forces. In *Gay Rights, Military Wrongs: Political Perspectives on Lesbians and Gays in the Military*, edited by Craig A. Rimmerman. New York: Routledge, 47–71.

Black, Paula. 2004. *The Beauty Industry: Gender, Culture, Pleasure*. New York: Routledge.

Bourdieu, Pierre. 1987. The Force of Law: Toward a Sociology of the Juridical Field. *Hastings Law Journal* 38:805–53.

Brown-Russell, Kathryn. 1998. *The Color of Crime: Racial Hoaxes, White Fear, Black Protectionism, Police Harassment, and Other Macroaggressions*. New York: New York University Press.

Butler, John Sibley. 1993. Homosexuals and the Military Establishment. *Society* 31(1):13–21.

Carbado, Devon W. 2005. Racial Naturalization. *American Quarterly* 57:633–58.

———. 2002. (E)racing the Fourth Amendment. *University of Michigan Law Review* 100:946–1044.

———. 2000. Black Rights, Gay Rights, Civil Rights. *UCLA Law Review* 47:1467–1519.

———. 1999. *Black Men on Race, Gender, and Sexuality: A Critical Reader*. New York: New York University Press.

Carbado, Devon W., and G. Mitu Gulati. Forthcoming. *Acting White*.

Carbado, Devon W., G. Mitu Gulati, and Gowri Ramachandran. 2006. The Story of *Jespersen v. Harrah's*: Makeup and Women at Work. In *Employment Discrimination Stories*, edited by Joel W. Friedman. New York: Foundation Press, 105–53.

Carbado, Devon W., and Cheryl I. Harris. 2008. The New Racial Preferences. *California Law Review* 96:1139–214.

Carbado, Devon W., and Russell Robinson. 2011. *What's Wrong with Gay Rights?* (unpublished manuscript).

Carby, Hazel V. 1998. *Race Men.* Cambridge, MA: Harvard University Press.

Case, Mary Anne C. 1995. Disaggregating Gender from Sex and Sexual Orientation: The Effeminate Man in the Law and Feminist Jurisprudence. *Yale Law Journal* 105:1–105.

Chew, Cassie M. 2009. Harvard Professor and Filmmaker Henry Louis Gates May Make Documentary about Racial Profiling. *The Examiner,* http://www.examiner.com/x-13622-DC-Indie-Movie-Examiner~y2009m7d22-Filmmaker-Henry-Louis-Gates-may-pursue-legal-action-after-arrest, July 22.

CNN. 2009. Charge against Harvard Professor Dropped. *CNN,* http://www.cnn.com/2009/CRIME/07/21/massachusetts.harvard.professor.arrested/, July 21.

Cooper, Frank Rudy. 2010. Masculinities, Post-Racialism, and the Gates Controversy: The False Equivalence between Officer and Civilian. *Nevada Law Journal* 11:1–43.

———. 2009. "Who's the Man?": Masculinities Studies, *Terry* Stops, and Police Training. *Columbia Journal of Gender and Law* 18(3):671–742.

———. 2006. Against Bipolar Masculinity: Intersectionality, Assimilation, Identity Performance, and Hierarchy. *U.C. Davis Law Review* 39:853–903.

Crenshaw, Kimberlé. 1989. Demarginalizing the Intersection of Race and Sex: A Black Feminist Critique of Antidiscrimination Doctrine, Feminist Theory, and Antiracist Politics. *University of Chicago Legal Forum* 1989:139–67.

Eskridge, William N., Jr. 1997. Privacy Jurisprudence and the Apartheid of the Closet, 1946–1961. *Florida State University Law Review* 24:703–838.

———. 1993. Race and Sexual Orientation in the Military: Ending the Apartheid of the Closet. *Reconstruction* 2:52–57.

Franke, Katherine M. 1995. The Central Mistake of Sex Discrimination Law: The Disaggregation of Sex from Gender. *University of Pennsylvania Law Review* 144:1–99.

George, Tracey E., G. Mitu Gulati, and Ann C. McGinley. 2011. The New Old Legal Realism. *Northwestern Law Review* 105:689–735.

Green, Tristin K. 2005. Work Culture and Discrimination. *California Law Review* 93:623–84.

Halberstam, Judith. 1998. *Female Masculinity.* Durham, NC: Duke University Press.

Halley, Janet. 2000. "Like Race" Arguments. In *What's Left of Theory? New Work on the Politics of Literary Theory,* edited by Judith Butler, John Guillory, and Kendall Thomas. New York: Routledge, 40–74.

Hamm v. Weyauwega Milk Products, Inc., 323 F.3d 1058 (7th Cir. 2003).

Harris, Cheryl I. 2001. Equal Treatment and the Reproduction of Inequality. *Fordham Law Review* 69:1753–83.

Hutchinson, Darren L. 1997. Out Yet Unseen: A Racial Critique of Gay and Lesbian Legal Theory and Political Discourse. *Connecticut Law Review* 29:561–645.

Jespersen v. Harrah's Operating Co., Inc., 444 F.3d 1104 (9th Cir. 2006).

Johnson, Robert L., and Steven Simring. 2000. With Gene Busnar. *The Race Trap: Smart Strategies for Effective Racial Communication in Business and in Life.* New York: HarperBusiness.

Kang, Jerry. 2005. Trojan Horses of Race. *Harvard Law Review* 118:1489–1593.

Karst, Kenneth L. 1991. The Pursuit of Manhood and the Desegregation of the Armed Forces. *UCLA Law Review* 38:499–581.

Katzenstein, Mary Fainsod. 1996. The Spectacle of Life and Death: Feminist and Lesbian/ Gay Politics in the Military. In *Gay Rights, Military Wrongs: Political Perspectives on Lesbians and Gays in the Military,* edited by Craig A. Rimmerman. New York: Routledge, 229–49.

Kendall, Christopher N. 1997. Gay Male Pornography after *Little Sisters Book and Art Emporium*: A Call for Gay Male Cooperation in the Struggle for Sex Equality. *Wisconsin Women's Law Journal* 12:21–82.

Kimmel, Michael S. 2005. Masculinity as Homophobia: Fear, Shame, and Silence in the Construction of Gender Identity. In *The Gender of Desire: Essays on Male Sexuality.* Albany: State University of New York Press, 25–42.

Newsweek. 1993. Gays and the Military. *Newsweek,* February 1. Available at http://www. newsweek.com/1993/01/31/gays-and-the-military.html.

New York Post. 2009. Cop Who Arrested Harvard Professor Teaches Racial Profiling Class. *New York Post,* http://www.nypost.com/p/news/national/item_DKK1pGodAVZl-fiO69pAczL, July 23.

Price Waterhouse v. Hopkins, 490 U.S. 228 (1989).

Reza, H. G. 1993. Blacks' Battle in Military Likened to Gays. *Los Angeles Times,* June 14, A3, A18–19.

Riggs, Marlon T. 1999. Black Macho Revisited: Reflections of a SNAP! Queen. In *Black Men on Race, Gender, and Sexuality: A Critical Reader,* edited by Devon W. Carbado. New York: New York University Press, 306–11.

Robinson, Russell. 2009. Racing the Closet. *Stanford Law Review* 61:1463–1533.

Rolison, Garry L., and Thomas K. Nakayama. 1994. Defensive Discourse: Blacks and Gays in the Military. In *Gays and Lesbians in the Military: Issues, Concerns, and Contrasts,* edited by Wilbur J. Scott and Sandra Carson Stanley. New York: Walter de Gruyter, Inc., 121–35.

Shilts, Randy. 1993. *Conduct Unbecoming: Lesbians and Gays in the U.S. Military: Vietnam to the Persian Gulf.* New York: St. Martin's Press.

Sullivan, Andrew. 1996. *Virtually Normal: An Argument about Homosexuality.* New York: Vintage Books.

Sweet, Laurel J., Marie Szaniszlo, Laura Crimaldi, Jessica Van Sack, and Joe Dwinell. 2009. Officer in Henry Gates Flap Tried to Save Reggie Lewis. *Boston Herald,* July 23. Available at http://www.bostonherald.com/news/regional/ view/20090722cop_who_arrested_henry_gates_im_not_apologizing/ srvc=home&position=0.

Thomas, Kendall. 1993. Shower/Closet. *Assemblage* 20:80–81.

Thompson, Krissah, and Cheryl W. Thompson. 2009. Officer Tells His Side of the Story in Gates Arrest. *Washington Post,* July 24. Available at http://www.washingtonpost.com/ wp-dyn/content/article/2009/07/23/AR2009072301073.html?sid=ST2009072301777.

Troutt, David. 2001. The Race Industry, Brutality and the Law of Mothers. In *Not Guilty: Twelve Black Men Speak Out on Law, Justice and Life,* edited by Jabari Asim. New York: HarperCollins Publishers, 53–63.

Vaid, Urvashi. 1995. *Virtual Equality: The Mainstreaming of Gay and Lesbian Liberation.* New York: Anchor Books.

Valdes, Francisco. 1995. Queers, Sissies, Dykes, and Tomboys: Deconstructing the Conflation of "Sex," "Gender," and "Sexual Orientation" in Euro-American Law and Society. *California Law Review* 83:1–343.

Warner, Michael. 1999. *The Trouble with Normal: Sex, Politics, and the Ethics of Queer Life.* New York: Free Press.

Waters, Mary-Alice. 1986. Introduction. In *Cosmetics, Fashions, and the Exploitation of Women,* edited by Joseph Hansen and Evelyn Reed. New York: Pathfinder Press.

Watkins v. United States Army, 875 F.2d 699 (9th Cir. 1989) (en banc).

3

The Multidimensional Turn: Revisiting Progressive Black Masculinities

ATHENA D. MUTUA

Deepening the Multidimensional Analysis

This chapter revisits the theory of progressive masculinities as described in the collection entitled *Progressive Black Masculinities* published by Routledge in 2006 and in particular the article "Theorizing Progressive Black Masculinities." It does so through the lens of multidimensional theory, suggesting that developing progressive black masculinities is consistent with black men's pursuit of racial justice.

Multidimensional theory is and remains outsider jurisprudence (Matsuda 1989; Valdes 1997). That is, it is a theory, arising specifically in the study of law, that is situated in the experiences of and is predominately developed by those who are outside the intellectual mainstream of even those who do feminist and masculinity scholarship—themselves often outside the mainstream of intellectual production. It consists of two central ideas that are both descriptive and methodological. The first idea is that every individual and group can be seen as not only raced (black, white, or Hispanic, etc.) or gendered (masculine, feminine, transgendered), for example, but is simultaneously raced, gendered, classed, sexually oriented, etc.; and that these persistent social hierarchies of race, class, etc., are materially relevant and mutually interacting and reinforcing (Mutua 2006a). The second idea is that a particular context further informs and shapes the operation and interaction of individuals or groups within these hierarchies. So, for example, it is context that structures which aspects of an individual or hierarchies are foregrounded in a particular situation or analysis; and context almost always consists of influential spatial configurations and/or particular historical nuances. For instance, racial profiling of black men often engages the multidimensional interplay of race and gender in what John Calmore has called the patrol and monitoring of anonymous public space (2006).

The original progressive black masculinities project engaged multidimensional theory, or the multidimensional turn in intersectional theory to assess whether black men lacked access to patriarchal privileges as nationalist scholars asserted, or whether black men were privileged by gender and oppressed by race as certain interpretations of intersectionality theory maintained. Multidimensionality theory suggested that in some contexts black men were privileged by gender in relation to black women, and in other contexts they were oppressed by gendered racism as blackmen—one word—and one multidimensional entity. In this chapter I ground the project more deeply in multidimensionality theory. I do so because I believe the multidimensional turn in intersectionality theory better situates masculine identities and practices within the matrix of socially constructed hierarchies, better explains the synergistic interplay between categories such as gender and race, and better explains the role context plays in that interaction. As such, it is a useful tool in explaining and clarifying the gendered racial dynamics present in such phenomena as racial profiling, as well as in understanding the justifications for the project of progressive black masculinities.

The first part of this chapter defines progressive black masculinities. It also briefly summarizes the arguments that support the concept and which seek to encourage black men's engagement with it. Next the chapter discusses the origins and tenets of the multidimensional turn in intersectionality theory. The third part turns to masculinities and hegemonic masculinity theory, situating the insights about the patriarchal gender system and the ranking of masculinities within a multidimensionality framework. The final section then briefly makes the argument for progressive masculinities, drawing on both multidimensionality and masculinities theory.

Progressive Black Masculinities: Definition
and Summary of Arguments

Progressive black masculinities are the "unique and innovative practices of the masculine self actively engaged in struggles to transform social structures of domination" (Mutua 2006b, xi). The progressive black masculinities project understands domination (or maintaining dominance) as a central goal of the patriarchal order as well as the goal of a number of other oppressive social systems such as race, class, and enforced heterosexuality. It rejects arrangements that depend on the subordination and oppression of others. This is particularly important because, in the case of the patriarchal system, the very definition of a man [of masculinity] is, in part, dependent on the subordination of women.

The project rests on three distinct arguments. The first argument embodies an ethical position. Ethics suggests that if black men believe that racism constrains and limits their own and others' human potential and they oppose this, then to the extent that it can be shown that patriarchy and sexism also constrain and limit the human potential of others, particularly that of black women and other women, then they should also oppose these. In other words, it involves a principled commitment to the well-being of not only men but also women and other people. This argument also rests on a certain amount of hopefulness. Given that black men have fought against racism and oppression (and some against other forms of oppression including gender oppression) on behalf of black communities and themselves, they are accustomed to swimming against the tide and taking others along with them. This suggests that they might be enlisted and successful in fighting against the hurtful practices of masculinity.

The second argument is based on the workings of systems of oppression. Specifically, systems of oppression shape and reinforce one another. The argument then is that to the extent black men are committed to undermining racism and racist structures, their success is hindered by gender domination and hierarchy, among other structures that mutually support and reinforce racism. To get rid of racism, it is likely necessary, at least, to disrupt or cripple other systems of oppression. In other words, black men's complicity with hegemonic and patriarchal systems of masculinities undermines black struggles against racism.

The third argument is that, in addition to racism, other systems of domination also hurt black men. Both masculinities theory and the multidimensional turn in intersectionality theory suggest that gender hierarchy also hurts black men. It does so in three interrelated ways. First, it subjects them to the domination of other men while undermining their efforts to combat racism and transform structures of racial domination. Second, it potentially limits the contours of their own identities. And third, in certain contexts it compounds their vulnerability, in part because gender oppression sometimes compounds the oppression wrought by racial domination.

Given these arguments, the fuller definition of progressive black masculinities encourages action, in concert with others, to disrupt racist structures, but also to disrupt all structures of domination. It also embodies a call for edifying action on behalf of black communities, building on black people's and particularly black men's historical action against racism. Further, it encourages black men to personally eschew racist, sexist, classist, and heterosexist action, among others. And, it begins with the notion that men, themselves, will have to more fully define and construct progressive masculinities through the development of creative and innovative practices and ideas.

The project consequently links two distinct but overlapping *political* projects that have the goal of "eradicating relations of domination that constrain and reduce human potential" (Mutua 2006b, 5). The first project is one of progressive black practice or progressive blackness. This is an anti-racist project meant to intervene and disrupt "the normal functioning of a society built on white supremacist foundations" (ibid. 8) while also edifying and valuing black people and their communities, among others, as part of the global family and as a part of that family that has been historically denigrated. It is also part of a larger antidomination or antisubordination project. The second is a project of progressive masculine practice or performances of progressive masculinities. This project seeks to disrupt the workings and structures of what might be variously known as the patriarchal order, the hegemony of men, the gender hierarchy, and/or male domination. It does so through encouraging men to reorient their concepts and practices away from ideal or hegemonic masculinity, which by definition requires the subordination of women and the denigration and domination of men over women, children and, yes, other subordinate or marginal men. Consequently, these political projects are directed toward two overlapping groups, namely, black people generally on the one hand, and men—and particularly black men— on the other.

The Multidimensional Turn in Intersectionality Theory

Multidimensional theory, or the turn in intersectional theory, is and remains outsider jurisprudence. That is, it is a theory, arising specifically in the study of law (though not remaining there), that is situated in the experiences of groups such as black men. Specifically it arises as a theory within the context and at the intersection of critical race and Latcrit theory on the one hand, and LGBT and queer scholarship produced by people of color on the other, all of which maintain strong feminist traditions within their intellectual communities; and all of which, by definition, have had to struggle with the multiplicity and intersection of persistent social hierarchies such as race, gender, and nation (Mutua 2006a).

Development

Multidimensionality theory is an expansion and development of two key insights about identity. These insights are antiessentialism and intersectionality. While the antiessentialist insight had engendered substantial prior debate in feminist, critical race theory, and other intellectual circles by the 1990s, intersectionality emerged as one of the most important theoretical contributions that critical race theorists and feminists have made in the last couple of decades and has become "the primary analytic tool that [they] deploy for theorizing identity and oppression" (Mutua 2010; Nash 2008, 1).

Antiessentialism stands for the proposition that no single experience or perspective reflects the common experience and interest of the people constituting the group called, for example, African Americans (Mutua 2006a). This is so because that group, like most social groups, consists of people that occupy different classes, are differently gendered and, for instance, differently colored, among other things. Instead, all social groups (be they gendered like women or raced like African Americans) contain internal differences; no groups are monolithic. Similarly, individuals are multifaceted and multidimensional. That is, every individual can be seen as raced, classed, and gendered, among other things, as well as a combination of diverse and contradictory selves (see, e.g., Mutua 2006a; Harris 1990). And finally, antiessentialism suggests that the development and imposition of categories that arise in any of these systems impose a limiting and essentialized identity on a complex and multidimensional person or group. In other words, the categories of white, black, Asian American in the racial system, or women, men or transgendered in the gender hierarchy, or bisexual, homosexual, or heterosexual in the sexuality hierarchy, impose constraints and essentialize identity (Cohen 2010, 517–21).

Intersectionality, a term coined by Kimberlé Crenshaw (1991, 1989) and drawing on black feminist scholarship, proffered and expanded a similar idea; namely, that in the context of black women's experiences, multiple systems of oppression affected them. In other words, black women were not simply oppressed by persistent social hierarchies of race-or-sex; rather, both oppressed them (Crenshaw 1991). Feminists and other scholars almost immediately began to further expand this notion by suggesting that the systems of subordination were mutually relating and reinforcing but also that they interacted synergistically to form uniquely situated groups and situations (Ehrenreich 2002; Kwan 1997).

In the midst of these developments, gay men of color sought to expand intersectional theory both substantively and conceptually (Valdes 2002, 1998; Hutchinson 2001, 1999). Substantively they sought to demonstrate the ways in which heterosexual privilege and heterosexism also constituted a system of subordination that should be studied more closely as well as transformed. In addition, these scholars saw, as others had, that within the interactions of these complex multidimensional hierarchies racial groups were also privileged or stereotyped and stigmatized through gendered, sexualized, and class attributes, or that classes often had gendered, sexualized, and racial attributes, and so forth. So, for example, historically to be black was also to be (seen as) sexually deviant (Collins 2004), or to be Asian was to be (seen as) gendered feminine (Yanagisako 1995).

Conceptually, they clarified, as had other studies (such as whiteness studies) that the systems of race, gender, sexuality, and so on, contained not only subordinate but also privileged locations (or categories). Intersectionality had focused on the way that two or more subordinating locations in different systems of oppression created unique experiences for the groups on which they operated, such that black (race) women (gender) for example appeared to have experiences distinct from black men or white women. However, Hutchinson in particular sought to demonstrate that when a *privileged* location or category (e.g., white) of one system intersected with a *subordinated* location in another system (e.g., women), it also created unique situations and could be either privileging or disadvantaging in particular contexts (white women) (Hutchinson 2001). As such, context mattered and the systems of oppression were complex.

Others also began to further develop multidimensionality theory through the analyses of the experiences of black men, seen not simply through a racial lens, but through a gendered one (Cooper 2006; Mutua 2006b). They were examining what appeared to be an intersection between positions of privilege and subordination; namely, men as a privileged gendered category and racialized humanity as a subordinate category. The interaction in certain contexts such as racial profiling demonstrated that the intersections could not be mechanistically applied. In that context black men were *more* prone to be the subject of racial profiling than were black women, even though black women occupied two subordinated categories whereas black men only occupied one. The analysis turned in part on the interaction of context (often involving spatial configurations) and content of the category, such that what a "man" or "masculine" might mean in public space as opposed to what a "woman" or "feminine" (as vulnerable, non-threatening?) might mean in that same space may be more determinative of the outcome than a simple mechanistic compounding of multiple subordinating positions.

Finally, Valdes stressed that while individuals and groups could be situated in all kinds of ways and could possess a host of different traits and expressions, some traits or expressions were socially and systematically stigmatized or rewarded in a way that rendered them "materially relevant." That is, he stressed that he focused on hierarchal *systems* that materially stratified people based on group-held traits and expressions (Valdes 1997; Mutua 2006a).

Each of these analyses not only began to develop multidimensionality as an expansion of intersectional theory, but perhaps also suggests a significant turn.

Tenets of Multidimensionality

Multidimensional theory therefore has a number of precepts, as I have suggested elsewhere. It:

1. Recognizes that individuals have many dimensions, some of which are embodied human traits such as skin color, sex, ear-lobe length, and eye color; and others, which are expressed, such as being Methodist or Catholic, a cat owner or dog owner, etc.

2. Recognizes that groups also are multidimensional. They are internally diverse such that "African Americans" may be seen as a racial group but consists of people who occupy different classes, are gendered differently (men, women, and transgendered people), and are sexualized differently (heterosexuals, homosexuals, bisexuals). Society has selected one trait or expression around which the group is organized, and the group is essentialized based on that one trait or expression. In fact, groups are multidimensional, not monolithic.

3. Focuses on materially relevant systems that structure and rank groups in a hierarchy based on traits or expressions. These traits have been made materially relevant historically through the allocation and denial of resources (both expressive and material) and other patterned practices. Based on these practices, meanings are constructed about those who bear those traits or expressions. In other words: societies take some dimensions

such as color, sex, or a particular religious belief (but in the United States, not ear-lobe length or owning a cat or dog) and construct meanings (through practices) about the groups that possess them. Societies then allocate or deny both material and status-related resources through systems they develop (based on those traits or expressions) such as racism, sexism, and anti-Semitism, for example, which operate through multiple sites and institutions, including law, education, politics, access to health care, etc. (Mutua 2010, 295).

4. Acknowledges that these hierarchal systems form a matrix of privilege and oppression (Froc 2010; Collins 1990, 222–30) that interact, intersect, and are mutually reinforcing such that for example, in the United States, racism is patriarchal and patriarchy is racist (Mutua 2006a), or as bell hooks suggests, the American society is a white supremacist capitalist patriarchy (hooks 1995). At the same time, these categories are unstable and shift in different contexts, such that in the context of anonymous public space, as noted earlier, black men appear much more subject to racial profiling than black women have been, even though black men could be seen as inhabiting a privileged gender category (i.e., men) and a subordinated racial category (i.e., black) as opposed to black women who occupy two subordinated categories.

5. Posits that context matters. This idea has long been a central tenet of critical race theory but is also centrally important to multidimensional theory (Mutua 2006a, 2010; see also Froc 2010, 25–27). For instance, while the concept of "white supremacy" is infinitely clarifying about the nature of racism in the United States or South Africa, it perhaps tells us little about the nature of racism in the context of China.

In addition, context is not only important as an insight but is important methodologically because it directs attention to the specific hierarchy that is foregrounded in a given situation as well as the particular aspects of the system that may be in play. For example, in an essay that preceded the development of multidimensionality theory, Joan Williams once described an interaction with a colleague as they walked down a lunch line. It in some ways captures the shifting interplay of various social hierarchies, traits, and expressions through the changes in situation and context. She noted that when her colleague talked about his children, his reaction struck her as particularly "male." When the topic switched to birth control, his comments struck her as "shockingly Catholic." When he talked, and perhaps flirted, with the cashier, she noted both tension and camaraderie, which she recognized as a "complex dynamic that she had seen between privileged and working-class blacks." Finally when she and her friend sat down to eat, they talked about scholarship and he reminded her of "just another upper-middle-class academic like herself" (Williams 1991, 306). In other words, though these were simply conversational shifts, determining whether race, gender, or some other trait or hierarchy is salient (by structuring an outlook or a particular outcome) will ultimately depend on analyzing the context.

Masculinities Theory and Hegemonic Masculinity

In the context of multidimensional theory, masculinities are a category or location within the patriarchal gender system and order or hierarchy that privileges and provides "men as a group power over women as a group" (Dowd, Levit, and McGinley, this volume). In this patriarchal gender structure many of the society's structures, institutions, and cultural sites of power are gendered male or privilege men and qualities largely associated with men and dominant normative forms of masculinity. Men to varying degrees often engage a set of practices considered "masculine" in order, in part, to access these places and positions which are both designed to and have the effect of maintaining group power vis-à-vis women, to render men, as a group, dominant. Group domination yields privileges from which all men in general benefit.

At the same time, however, men are not a monolithic group, as antiessentialism theory provides and empirical evidence suggests. Rather, they are differentiated in a multitude of ways and these ways are also ranked such that a hierarchy of men and masculinities exists. Although this ranking occurs in multiple ways and changes over time, two significant strands, particularly in the United States in this historical moment, are evident. To be a real man, to demonstrate manliness, is to not be like women or feminine nor to be gay. To be like women is stereotypically to be weak, passive, and subordinate in relation to masculinity, which is often performed and associated with strength, assertiveness, and domination. To be a real man, to be masculine, thus requires the domination of or at least the denigration of women (and other contrast figures) and feminine practices that reinforce the subordination of women (Cooper 2009; Collins 2006; Kimmel 2004). The admonishment not to be gay is linked to the concept that to be gay is to be like a woman. "In particular, gay men submit to the sexual advances of other men and are penetrated like women; sexual practices that lead heterosexual men to stereotype gay men as sissies, faggots or effeminate men. . . . To many people, homosexuality is the negation of masculinity" (Collins 2006, 83). And, the intersection of masculinity in the gendered system with homosexuality in the sexual system constructs the ranking of men, such that straight men are ranked higher than gay men.

Further, other categories that intersect with masculine identities also function to rank men in a hierarchy. That is, race, class, age, etc., also rank men. For example, Patricia Hill Collins in describing the American order notes that "real men" are not like women, they are not gay, not poor, not boys, and may not be black (Collins 2006). Thus, there exists a hierarchy of men and masculinities in which men are ranked in relation to and at the intersection of a multiplicity of other identity categories that they inhabit and against which they must construct their identities. These intersectional identity categories (white men, black men, poor men) and the performances of the masculine self (not like women or gay, but rather, strong, aggressive, and dominant) interact with a host of social structures and institutions that are gendered male, often rewarding with position and prestige those who come close to the ideal norm in identity and/or action. At the same time this interaction of culture and structure penalizes through limited opportunity, limited freedom, censure, bullying, and violence those who are furthest from that norm, limiting the privileges these men can access as a result of their membership in a group that dominates women. In short, a hierarchy of men suggests that men also dominate over "lesser," subordinate, and other marginal men.

Hegemonic masculinities give clues as to what is valued in society. In any given society, the ways in which social hierarchies are established and exist provide some insight into the ideal types or models of masculinity that become dominant or hegemonic. That is, in society different ideal masculine models fight for hegemony at both the local and society-wide levels. These models signal who is considered a "real man" and the way men should act, behave, or perform manliness. These models are hegemonic because both those who disproportionately benefit from them as well as those who are largely oppressed by the models often sign onto them. In the United States, many scholars have noted that the society-wide hegemonic ideal is not only defined by what he or she is not (not women or feminine, not gay, etc.), but it is also a combined identity of elite, white, Anglo, heterosexual, and male/men status and relations, among others (e.g., Collins 2006; Mutua 2006b). In other words, hegemonic masculinity in the United States, in this moment, is a multidimensional idea that is situated in the highest position of power at the intersection and interplay of persistent social hierarchies, such as race, gender, class, sexuality, as well as perhaps religion, age, etc. Thus, the U.S. hegemonic ideal (rather than an actual person) of a real man in the current historical moment is an elite Anglo white heterosexual male.

Few men can live up to the American ideal of masculinity, a seemingly central feature of masculinity in general whereby men must constantly prove their manhood. But the few who do get close, or appear to represent the ideal, have a tremendous stake in maintaining their dominance generally, and dominance over women, other men, themselves, and their own emotions, in particular. Though most men cannot live up to ideal masculinity, many men can live up to some aspects of it. So, for instance, elite class status provides men with money and thus the power to influence, if not control, institutions and apparatuses of violence so that they appear "strong" even if they are physically "weak." Poor men may emphasize their physical strength as a way of presenting themselves as manly, even as they might be powerless in the workforce and have trouble acting as the "breadwinner" or "provider," another apparent requirement of ideal masculinity. In any case, there exist tremendous incentives (privileges, positions) and pressures (group monitoring, bullying, violence), both culturally and materially, to live up to at least some aspects of ideal-hegemonic-masculinity, even as individual men or subgroups resist other aspects. Such actions contribute both to change and consistency of the ideal and contribute to hegemony (Connell and Messerschmidt 2005) while maintaining the construction of masculinities as dominant and dominating.

Progressive Black Masculinities:
The Argument, Embodying the Theories

Black men occupy an intersectional identity in which race shapes their masculine gendered identities and vice versa. While white racial oppression of black identity, as a subordinated racial category, severely limits black men's human potential, their identities as men, the dominant gender category seems a source of privilege that might compensate them for the liability of being black. In other words, meeting the demands of or performing masculinity appears to allow black men to compensate for the penalties that the white racial oppression of blackness levies on them. To the extent that all men face incentives and penalties that encourage them to live up to hegemonic ideals of masculinity, black men appear to have even greater incentives, including compensatory ones.

However, the social construction of race places severe limitations on the ways that black men's assertion of masculinity may aid them. Further, the intersection of racial subordination with masculinities renders black masculinity a secondary status (within the hierarchy of masculinities) reinforcing that subordination. At the same time, the imperatives of masculinities hurt men generally, because, as masculinities scholars suggest, they limit the contours of their personalities and exact a range of costs (Dowd, Levit, and McGinley, this volume). For black men the limitations may be greater and the costs higher. For instance, the intersection of masculinities with racial subordination may make black men more vulnerable to surveillance and violence. These harms in many ways demonstrate the manner in which social hierarchies are mutually reinforcing. At the same time, adhering to masculine imperatives of domination and denigration exacts an additional cost. It undermines the anti-racist struggle of black men in part because it fractures black communities by alienating some of black men's closest allies, namely, black women and sexual minorities. This imperative also harms black women and black sexual minorities in ways not all that dissimilar from the way that black men claim racism hurts them. It limits women and sexual minorities' human potential; and black men's participation in that harm undermines their own claims for justice and human dignity. Progressive black masculinities thus start here—with an ethical challenge to men to struggle against all the systems of domination that harm black people and others.

The political project of progressive black masculinities therefore grounds the project in part in black men's racial justice sentiments and in their historical engagement in anti-racist and other struggles against domination on behalf of black communities. In this sense, the justification for progressive masculinities is not simply that hegemonic masculinity and the persistent social hierarchy of men and masculinities harms black men, but that black men have a historical practice in fighting for justice on behalf of others, and the cause of justice provides additional incentives for creating, pursuing, and practicing alternative and progressive ways of being men.

I now turn briefly to the arguments in support of the progressive black masculinities project.

Anti-Racist Struggle: Progressive Blackness

Of the two projects that make up the project of progressive masculinities, the anti-racism struggle is central to the project of progressive blackness. Said differently, in the United States, race is a hierarchal system of domination socially constructed on the basis of different types (phenotype) of human bodies (Omi and Winant 1994), and with resources both expressive and material distributed and withheld to mark and exaggerate the difference between groups in both perception and fact (MacKinnon 1987). In other words, as the social construction insight suggests, race is not a biological feature but rather a set of practices and social processes that over time construct a hierarchy based on certain features of different phenotyped human bodies. This was the project of white supremacy, with those seen and categorized as white on top and those seen as black on the bottom with other groups ordered in a hierarchy between the two. While whiteness has been a project of supremacy and domination, blackness historically has been a project and struggle for self-determination and self-definition in the face of oppression and denigration.

White supremacy, therefore, is not just a belief or an ideology but a structural system, much like male supremacy, with white supremacy deeply written into the very systems, institutions, and structures of American society. It was initially constructed through the patterned practices and historical social process of whites colonizing and conquering others, complemented in the United States by whites exterminating the Native American population, enslaving and exploiting the labor and expertise of black people, appropriating Latino land and subordinating them, and initially excluding Asians. This was followed by segregation, legal dictatorship, and the near monopolization and hoarding of the country's resources. Over several hundred years and in the process, the cultural value of whiteness and white supremacy has become so institutionalized that it remains present throughout most of the country's systems, structures, and institutions, including schools, government agencies, neighborhoods, businesses, the health care system, etc., despite the elimination of many of its legal supports but evident in continuing racial disparities and inequities.

The cultural value also has been deeply written into the conscious and unconscious patterns of white people's behavior. It remains so pervasive, as Faegin explains, that a mental frame complete with emotional reactions, readily available negative stereotypes about nonwhites, and rationalizing stories have become a structure in most white people's characters while also impacting people of color (Faegin 2009, 11). Thus, this cultural and institutional value became and remains the hidden norm against which most people are measured such that it operates even in the absence of racist intent as a part of the normal functioning of the economy, the schools, and other institutional structures. So, for example, "good schools" code as "white schools" not because black schools are inherently inferior but because a history of slavery, Jim Crow segregation, government housing policies, and white flight have left "good" schools as "white" schools (Mutua 2006a). Active intervention is required to change and disrupt the normal functioning of a society organized around and on the basis of white power and supremacy. Progressive blackness (while having other cultural meanings and content) becomes one of those interventions.

Black men's commitment to anti-racism and their anti-racist struggle on behalf of black communities engenders hope that black men will engage a politics of progressive black masculine performance and activism.

Progressive Masculinities

THE ETHICAL EXTENSIONS OF ANTI-RACIST STRUGGLE

The progressive black masculinities project attempts to connect black men's commitments to fight against racial domination on behalf of themselves and black communities to a commitment to the communities' constituent parts, to the diversity of justice projects that these constituent groups and others must pursue, and to coalition-building with others similarly affected and committed. In other words, the progressive black masculinities project is an ethical project. It is concerned with the existential well-being of black people and black communities. It thus poses an ethical challenge: If black men believe that racial domination is wrong because it limits the human flourishing of black people, then a principled position requires (1) concern for black people, in all their diversity, or the communities' constituent parts; (2) a concern for other groups subjected to racial domination as well as a stand against other systems of domination that limit the humanity of others within the black community; and (3) coalition-building against domination not only with those within the black community but also those outside of it. These are the ethical extensions of progressive black practice and anti-racist struggle.

The constituent parts or subgroups of the black community include women, men, sexual minorities of color, and children, as well as others. The insight suggests that if the anti-racist struggle is in part about black people, then the anti-racist struggle should also be about the structures of domination that affect black people. And this can be understood in two ways. On the one hand, this insight recognizes in part that racial domination itself is gendered, sexed, classed, etc.; it is multidimensional. For example, racial discrimination acts on black men and black women as differently gendered beings, differently, and it poses different obstacles to poor blacks than it does to middle-class black people. On the other hand, the idea could be understood from the perspective that racism is not the only system of domination that limits the human potential of black people and those within black communities; so do, for example, sexism, classism, heterosexism. This is the intersectional and multidimensional insight.

A commitment to human flourishing and against subordination suggests that people committed to fighting against racism and other systems of subordination should be willing to partner and build coalitions with others who are also similarly committed. So, for example, black men and women fighting against gendered oppression should partner with white, Latino, and Asian American women to work to overcome gender and racial domination.

ADHERENCE TO DOMINANT MASCULINITY
UNDERMINES RACIAL JUSTICE

Black men should reorient their masculine practices toward progressive masculinities not only because it is ethical but also because white supremacy and patriarchy are mutually reinforcing systems that undermine the project of racial justice. They do so, for example, by reinforcing black men's subordinate status in the hierarchy of masculinities and by goading them into actions that alienate potential allies in the racial struggle.

Although the assertion of hegemonic masculinity may appear to compensate for the injustices that whites inflict on black people, the socio-historical construction of race and white supremacy in particular, places limitations on the ways the assertion may aid black men. That is, the content of the category called black as developed over time places limitations on compensatory moves. For instance, to the extent that black men and people in general have been constructed as disproportionately poor vis-à-vis white people, only a few black men will be able to attain the status of "provider" that has historically been a part of the masculine ideal. Said differently, race, gender, and class reinforce black men's secondary and subordinate status in the American hierarchy of masculinities. Rethinking the ideal of a sole provider in the current economic and historical moment might render a whole host of men less stressed and committed to finding ways to be partners (Collins 2006).

Further, these kinds of structural limitations may encourage men to behave in ways that over-emphasize certain aspects of hegemonic masculinity, such as violence and sexual potency, that they can access. That is, they may encourage hypermasculinities. In this sense, men who do not have access to money and position may use their physical bodies extremely aggressively as sources of power over and against women, sexual minorities, and other men and children. This move is likely to have multiple negative effects. First, because the patriarchy is racist and white domination is also patriarchal, this action may simply reinforce the stereotype of black men as brutes, again reinforcing their secondary status both in the hierarchy of men and in the racial hierarchy. Second, and perhaps more importantly, it potentially and destructively alienates some of black men's traditional allies, such as black women and black sexual minorities, who also have struggled against racism. The aspiration and attempt at hegemonic masculinity disrupts and fractures black communities undermining solidarity and the anti-racist struggle that depends on these other groups' participation (Kimmel 2006).

BLACK MEN: MASCULINITIES AND GENDERED RACISM

Black men should eschew hegemonic masculinity in their personal lives and define anew progressive masculinities because both the imperatives of masculinities and its intersection with racial subordination or gendered racism hurt black men.

As others have suggested, the imperatives of normative masculinity potentially limit the contours of black men's identities. For example, they are told to be tough, strong, and in control of themselves, their emotions, and those around them. Further, they are counseled to be breadwinners, presidents, warriors, playboys, etc. These instructions belie the full range of human expressions that exist. But, in addition, their performances of masculinity—how they choose to be and act—are heavily monitored and evaluated by other men as well as women to see if they comport to the imperatives of ideal and hegemonic masculinity. These norms and imperatives limit who men are and who they can become. Most men suffer from these limitations in some form or another.

However, these limitations may pose additional costs for black men. For instance, working-class or poor black men may lack the institutional resources that make control of one's environment possible. They have fewer social networks or access to jobs than even poor white men in general. Thus, they may be more easily forced into positions where they act as warriors (soldiers in war), the potential costs of which are extremely high, potentially involving death.

But in addition, the intersection of racial subordination with masculinities may impose other costs, costs which not even black women face. This is so even though black men reap some part of the male dividend, in that those who work tend to make more money than black women (when they can find work), they tend to occupy places of status within black communities, and their issues all too oftenz are given priority vis-à-vis black women both within and without the communities (Carbado 1999). Nevertheless, black men face gendered racism which imposes additional cost on them. For instance, in public space where strangers pass or interact, men are considered dangerous. In that same space, black strangers are also seen as dangerous. But in what Calmore calls anonymous public space, unknown black men, the synergy between racial oppression and gender suspicion is lethal and they are seen as the most dangerous people in this context, in this space. So much so that Calmore refers to them as unwanted traffic (2006). And he argues that these men, particularly if they are young, engender heightened surveillance by the police, who see them as dangerous and criminal and are inclined not only to subject them to heightened surveillance but also to stop, interrogate, and possibly injure them. At the same time, they engender heightened surveillance from other men both like and unlike themselves. All of this attention appears to subject them, even though most are law-abiding, to increased violence by other men.

Progressive black masculinities might bring more trust among black men. More trust may lead to more solidarity for the struggle against racism.

Conclusion: Racial Justice Requires Gender Justice

Multidimensionality is embedded in the justifications and call for progressive masculinities. It suggests that black men, who sit at the intersection of racial subordination and gender privilege, would be aided in their struggle for racial justice, if they also pursued gender justice. It further suggests that black men themselves would also benefit significantly from gender justice.

REFERENCES

Calmore, John O. 2006. Reasonable and Unreasonable Suspects: The Cultural Construction of the Anonymous Black Man in Public Space (Here Be Dragons). In *Progressive Black Masculinities*, edited by Athena D. Mutua. New York: Routledge, 137–54.

Carbado, Devon 1999. *Black Men on Race, Gender, and Sexuality: A Critical Reader*. New York: New York University Press.

Cohen, David S. 2010. Keeping Men "Men" and Women Down: Sex Segregation, Anti-Essentialism, and Masculinity. *Harvard Journal of Law and Gender* 33(2):509–53.

Collins, Patricia Hill. 2006. A Telling Difference: Dominance, Strength, and Black Masculinities. In *Progressive Black Masculinities*, edited by Athena D. Mutua. New York: Routledge, 73–98.

———. 2004. *Black Sexual Politics: African Americans, Gender, and the New Racism*. New York: Routledge.

———. 1990. *Black Feminist Thought: Knowledge, Consciousness and the Politics of Empowerment*. New York: Routledge.

Connell, R. W., and James W. Messerschmidt. 2005. Hegemonic Masculinity: Rethinking the Concept. *Gender & Society* 19:829–59.

Cooper, Frank Rudy. 2009. "Who's the Man?": Masculinities, *Terry* Stops and Police Training. *Columbia Journal of Gender and Law* 18:671–742.

———. 2006. Against Bipolar Black Masculinity: Intersectionality, Assimilation, Identity Performance, and Hierarchy. *U.C. Davis Law Review* 39:853–903.

Crenshaw, Kimberlé. 1991. Mapping the Margins: Intersectionality, Identity Politics, and Violence against Women of Color. *Stanford Law Review* 43:1241–99.

———. 1989. Demarginalizing the Intersection of Race and Sex: A Black Feminist Critique of Antidiscrimination Doctrine, Feminist Theory, and Antiracist Politics. *University of Chicago Legal Forum* 1989:139–67.

Ehrenreich, Nancy. 2002. Subordination and Symbiosis Mechanisms of Mutual Support between Subordinating Systems. *University of Missouri-Kansas City Law Review* 71:251–324.

Faegin, Joe. 2010. *The White Racial Frame: Centuries of Racial Framing and Counter-Framing.* New York: Routledge.

Froc, Kerri A. 2010. Multidimensionality and the Matrix: Identifying Charter Violations in Cases of Complex Subordination. *Canadian Journal of Law and Society* 25(1):21–49.

Harris, Angela P. 1990. Race and Essentialism in Feminist Legal Theory. *Stanford Law Review* 42:581–616.

hooks, bell. 1995. *Killing Rage: Ending Racism.* New York: H. Holt & Co.

Hutchinson, Darren. 2001. Identity Crisis: 'Intersectionality,' 'Multidimensionality,' and the Development of an Adequate Theory of Subordination. *Michigan Journal of Race and Law* 6:285–317.

———. 1999. Ignoring the Sexualization of Race: Heteronormativity, Critical Race Theory, and Anti-racist Politics. *Buffalo Law Review* 47:1–116.

Kimmel, Michael S. 2006. Toward a Pedagogy of the Oppressor. In *Progressive Black Masculinities,* edited by Athena D. Mutua. New York: Routledge, 63–72.

———. 2004. Masculinity as Homophobia. In *Feminism & Masculinities,* edited by Peter F. Murphy. Oxford: Oxford University Press, 182–99.

Kwan, Peter. 1997. Jeffrey Dahmer and the Cosynthesis of Categories. *Hastings Law Journal* 48:1257–92.

MacKinnon, Catharine. 1987. Difference and Dominance: On Sex Discrimination. In *Feminism Unmodified: Discourses on Life and Law.* Cambridge, MA: Harvard University Press, 32–45.

Matsuda, Mari J. 1989. Public Response to Racist Speech: Considering the Victim's Story. *Michigan Law Review* 87: 2320–81.

Mutua, Athena D. 2010. Law, Critical Race Theory and Related Scholarship. In *Handbook Series of Race and Ethnic Studies,* edited by Patricia Hill Collins and John Solomos. Thousand Oaks, CA: Sage, 275–305.

———. 2006a. The Rise, Development and Future Directions of Critical Race Theory and Related Scholarship. *Denver University Law Review* 84:329–94.

———, ed. 2006b. *Progressive Black Masculinities.* New York: Routledge.

Nash, Jennifer C. 2008. re-thinking intersectionality. *feminist review* 89:1–15.

Omi, Michael, and Howard Winant. 1994. *Racial Formation in the United States from the 1960s to the 1990s.* New York: Routledge.

Valdes, Francisco. 2002. Identity Maneuvers in Law and Society: Vignettes of a Euro-American Heteropatriarchy. *University of Missouri Kansas City Law Review* 71:377–98.

———. 1998. Beyond Sexual Orientation in Queer Legal Theory: Majoritarianism, Multidimensionality and Responsibility in Social Justice Scholarship or Legal Scholars as Cultural Warriors. *Denver University Law Review* 75:1409–64.

———. 1997. Under Construction: LatCrit Consciousness, Community, and Theory. *California Law Review* 85(5):1087–1142.

Williams, John. 1991. *Dissolving the Sameness/Difference Debate:* A Post-Modern Path Beyond Essentialism in Feminist and Critical Race Theory. *Drake Law Journal* 2:296-323

Yanagisako, Sylvia. 1995. Transforming Orientalism: Gender, Nationality, and Class in Asian American Studies. In *Naturalizing Power: Essays in Feminist Cultural Analysis,* edited by Sylvia Yanagisako and Carol Delaney. New York: Routledge, 275–98.

4

The King Stay the King: Multidimensional Masculinities and Capitalism in *The Wire*

FRANK RUDY COOPER

The third episode of Home Box Office's (HBO's) critically acclaimed show *The Wire* provides the viewer with a metaphor for the cable police drama's view of life on Baltimore streets during the war on drugs. In a key scene, mid-level drug dealer D'Angelo Barksdale sees his young assistants, "Wallace" and Preston Broadus ("Bodie"), playing checkers with chess pieces (Alvarez 2009).[1] He tries to convince them to play chess by analogizing the game of chess to what inner-city residents call "the game" of drug dealing (ibid. 77). He explains that, just as with individuals in the drug game, each chess piece has a certain role and must move in certain ways. Bodie challenges D'Angelo's statement by noting that a pawn that makes it across the board can become a queen. That does not matter, responds D'Angelo, because only pawns can change roles and pawns "get capped quick. They be out the game early" (ibid.). The key fact is that "the king stay the king" (ibid.). A principal argument of *The Wire* is that in the vast majority of cases, the king stays the king. We might agree, but must ask, who is this king?

We should think of the king as representing hierarchy itself. The king is the whiteness in white supremacy, the masculinity in patriarchy, the straightness in heteronormativity, the economic privilege in capitalism, and so on. The drug game helps illustrate how life is like chess: there are always new pawns seeking to become queens, but even if they do so, they just become enforcers for the preexisting kings. Be they pawns or queens, the subordinate pieces ultimately fail to change the game because they buy into the notion that there should be hierarchy. The individual identity hierarchies of race, gender, sex orientation, class, and so on, reinforce one another in that each assumes the principle that there shall always be hierarchies (Cooper 2006a). That will not change until we find a way to change all of the aspects of the game at once (ibid.).

When it comes to the game of identities, there are several approaches to masculinities studies that we might apply in order to unpack the metaphor of the king staying the king. The predominant approach in law is the "hegemonic masculinities" approach (Cohen 2009; Cooper 2009b; Dowd 2010; A. Harris 2000; McGinley 2004).[2] It would say that the king is the hegemonic, or dominant, man. The hegemonic man is the dominant image of what constitutes the ideal form of masculinity in a given context (Connell 2005; Connell and Messerschmidt 2005). This chapter assumes that a traditional hegemonic masculinities analysis would argue that patriarchy is the prime reason the king stays the king.

Meanwhile, the "multidimensional" masculinities approach that this book advocates notes that any masculinity, be it hegemonic or alternative, is always (1) intertwined with race and other supposedly separate categories of identity and also (2) both experienced and interpreted differently in different contexts (Hutchinson 2000; Mutua 2006; Mutua, this volume; Valdes 1998). Utilizing a "critical race theory" approach (Crenshaw et al. 1995; Cooper 2009a; Delgado & Stefancic 2007; Perea et al. 2007), a multidimensional masculinities theory might note that the war on drugs is not only a war between men, but also simultaneously a war on blacks (Blumenson and Nilsen 2002; Cooper 2002a; Nunn 2002). Still, to understand why the king stays the king in *The Wire's* metaphor, we need to go beyond both hegemonic masculinities' and multidimensional masculinities' usual understandings of the hegemonic man as connoting hierarchies of male over female and white (men) over black (men).

This chapter argues for a richer understanding of the elements of a multidimensional masculinities approach. An underappreciated but important aspect of what constitutes the king is capitalism's hierarchy of the rich over the poor. A critique of capitalism acknowledges that economic exploitation is a foundation of our society that also helps form identities. Analysis of the drug war reveals the ways capitalism both produces a criminal economy that is the Janus face of the "normal" economy and creates a criminal identity that not only is attributed to those whom capitalism exploits but also influences some individuals' senses of self. Thus, masculinities are not only raced, but also classed in the ways they are experienced and interpreted. Utilizing a "ClassCrit" approach (Mutua 2008), this chapter calls for a "materialist multidimensional masculinities." The materialist element adds emphasis on class structures and class identities to the more common multidimensionality analyses of gender and race.

To establish that argument, this chapter proceeds as follows. The first part summarizes why we should "read" *The Wire* and what happens therein. The next part reviews criticisms of and updates a traditional hegemonic masculinities analysis. We go on to discuss what a multidimensional masculinities approach to *The Wire* adds to the analysis. The following section explains what attention to capitalism in *The Wire* adds to the analysis. Finally, the chapter concludes that only a truly multidimensional analysis—one considering class as well as gender, race, and sex orientation—can allow us to truly change the identity game such that the king no longer stays the king.[3]

What Happens in *The Wire*

So, why should we "read" *The Wire* when trying to understand masculinities? First, because it is "surely the best TV show ever broadcast in America" (Weisberg 2006). No less a figure than Barack Obama, the president of the United States, declared it his favorite show (Alvarez 2009). *The Wire's* lasting popularity alone means that it has influenced and continues to influence people's perceptions of the war on drugs and masculinities. Second, and most important, the reason *The Wire* is so well regarded is that it is perceived to be uniquely authentic. Noted sociologists of the inner city William Julius Wilson and Sudhir Venkatesh conclude that, with respect to the cultures of the police, drug dealers, and their surrounding society, *The Wire* is an accurate depiction of life in the inner city during the drug war (Chaddha, Wilson, and Venkatesh 2008). As the editors of an anthology on *The Wire* say, "Its stories scream of verisimilitude" (Marshall and Potter 2009, 8–9). This show is especially attractive to a masculinities theorist because it is a "starkly masculine" battle between mostly male police forces and mostly male drug dealing organizations (Lippman 2009, 55). Both of those groups display distinctly masculine, and even hypermasculine, traits (Cooper 2009b; A. Harris 2000).

In order to provide a shared base of knowledge that is manageable for the reader, the remainder of this part of the chapter briefly summarizes *The*

Wire, especially Season One. In a nutshell, here is what happens in the first season of *The Wire*. Homicide detective Jimmy McNulty attends the murder trial of D'Angelo Barksdale, whom the jury acquits when a key witness recants (Alvarez 2009). Contending that D'Angelo's uncle, Avon Barksdale, leads a drug organization that is responsible for numerous murders, McNulty gets Judge Daniel Phelan to pressure Deputy Commissioner Ervin Burrell and McNulty's boss, Major William Rawls, to investigate Avon. Meanwhile, D'Angelo is demoted from running a housing project tower building to running the "pit" between buildings (ibid. 66). He oversees juveniles Wallace, Bodie, and Malik Carr ("Poot"). Burrell assigns Lieutenant Cedric Daniels to head a special detail investigating Avon's crew, but it is composed of officers other departments wished to cast off. It includes Michael Santangelo from McNulty's unit, Kima Greggs from Daniels's unit, Thomas "Herc" Hauk and Ellis Carver from a Narcotics unit, and Roland "Prez" Pryzbylewski, the son-in-law of politically connected Major Stan Valchek.

In the second episode, Prez, Herc, and Carver go to the projects to show its residents who is in charge, but Prez loses control and pistol whips a youth in the eye. Later in that episode, the detail leads a hasty attempt to bust D'Angelo's crew, but the police break down the wrong door and fail to acquire the main evidentiary prize, the crew's stash of drugs. Showing much greater knowledge of the Barksdale operation, a notorious local stick-up artist, Omar, steals D'Angelo's crew's stash. Later, Wallace and Poot spot Omar's boyfriend Brandon and notify Avon's right-hand man, Stringer Bell, who arranges for Brandon to be tortured, killed, and displayed in the projects.

In a major turn of events, Avon's frontman for his strip club, Orlando, is busted trying to do a drug deal. Orlando agrees to set up one of Avon's henchmen in a drug deal, with Greggs posing as his girlfriend. One of Avon's henchmen shoots Orlando dead and puts Greggs into a coma. In response to Greggs's injury, Burrell orders a major bust of Avon's crew, saying "we must show them who we are!" (*The Wire* 2002, Season One, Episode 11). The season ends with Avon and D'Angelo busted but with Stringer continuing to run the drug operation.

While Season Two provocatively addresses unions, drug dealing at the local level among whites, and the international connections between drug dealing and sex trafficking, Season Three is more important for our purposes because it returns the focus to Avon's drug cartel. With Avon in jail, Stringer runs the cartel, and does so in a very different style. As will be discussed, Stringer models himself after a legitimate businessman, while Avon models himself after a traditional gangster. As a result, the two come into conflict, resulting in Stringer's death and Avon's reincarceration after a brief moment of freedom. Although Season Four's examination of public schools is particularly insightful and Season Five's criticism of the news media is also interesting, this chapter only briefly touches on those seasons. With this admittedly brief framing of the story in mind, the chapter now turns to theoretical concerns.

The Need to Modify "Hegemonic Masculinities"

We can begin our discussion of the hegemonic masculinities approach by defining hegemony. As Antonio Gramsci formulated the idea, it declares that "a social group will try to describe the world in a way that accounts for, but coordinates, the interests of other groups such that they will consent to a structuring of society that promotes the dominant group's interests" (Cooper 2002a, 859). Recognizing hegemony means considering identities to be relational; identities are constituted against one another on "an unequal field of power relations within symbolic, economic, and political structures" (Grosfoguel and Georas 2000, 92). Social groups are each invested with different social capital—"capital of prestige and honor"—and use it to gain relative advantage in competition with other groups (ibid.). According to social theorists Ramón Grosfoguel and Chloe Georas, "The dominant groups of the symbolic, economic, and political fields are the ones with the power to make their social classifications of a society hegemonic" (ibid.).

In this light, it makes sense that some masculinities theorists assume there are attempts to establish a hegemonic masculinity. The hegemonic man is an ideal of manhood that tries to set the norm by which all men will tacitly agree to be judged (Dowd, Levit, and McGinley, this volume). Nonetheless, the idea that there is a hegemonic man or that we should refer to hegemonic masculinity has come under criticism. For instance, Christine Beasley argues we should limit the term to its political meaning—that images of masculinity are propounded as "a political mechanism producing solidarity between different masculinities in a hierarchical order" (2008, 93). Likewise, Jeff Hearn calls for a move from hegemonic masculinities to "the hegemony of men"—the idea that masculinity has allowed men to exercise power over women, as well as subordinated men (2004).

These two critiques do not seem to preclude the possibility that there are both attempts to establish a generally hegemonic masculinity in the United States and also attempts to establish alternatives to that masculinity, either in general or in specific contexts. Critics of the concept of a hegemonic masculinity have argued that there is no one hegemonic masculinity by noting that many masculine norms exist at the same time (Demetriou 2001; Donaldson

1993). That argument aligns with critical race theory's antiessentialism insight, which says that identity groups are often defined based on a lowest common denominator theory that makes certain qualities essential to the group but treats others as mere add-ons (Carbado 1999; Cohen, this volume; Cohen 2010; A. Harris 1990). To define one generally hegemonic masculinity is necessarily to essentialize certain norms as the most important ones. But the masculinities theorist seeks only to recognize the process by which culture essentializes certain qualities as masculine without accepting the hegemonic assertion as defining the truth of masculinity. Thus, the antiessentialist insight is not inconsistent with hegemonic masculinity's assumption that some norms of masculinity are more generally accepted than others (Connell and Messerschmidt 2005). As critical race feminist Angela Harris says, "though one way of doing masculinity may be 'hegemonic' . . . within a friendship network or a social institution, there may be many other ways of being a man that conflict, compete, or form a relationship of interdependence with the hegemonic form" (2000, 783). This chapter thus uses the term hegemonic masculinities, but in more of the political sense that Beasley advocates and while conscious of the risk of forgetting men's collective power over women that Hearn warns of.

Taking the attempt to establish a hegemonic masculinity to be a given, leading masculinities theorist Michael Kimmel defines a central tenet of the hegemonic masculinities approach that would likely be accepted by Beasley and Hearn: that masculinity is fundamentally anxious (Kimmel 2005). Since the means of signaling masculine behavior are governed by cultural norms, men tend to grant others masculine esteem only when they see behaviors that they already associate with masculinity. Manhood is thus a never-ending test of whether one's behaviors measure up to the ideal form of manhood (ibid.). Kimmel identifies rules of the hegemonic form of United States masculinity: (1) denigrate contrast figures, such as women, (2) accrue tokens of success, (3) hold one's emotions in check, and (4) be aggressive (ibid.). Measuring up to those rules is an impossible task, especially given that one could always accrue more tokens of success. Because we are always subject to being "unmasked" as less than manly (ibid.), the need to constantly prove one's masculinity will always lead to anxiety.

As Kimmel's rules suggest, the attempt to prove one's masculinity leads to attempts to distinguish oneself from other, less masculine, figures. The primary contrast figure is women, but in the United States, dominant men also have used racial minorities, Jews, and gay men as contrast figures (ibid.). Further, a man may feel that he appears to be at a disadvantage to other men along some axis of identity. That is, he may feel that he is in "penalty status" because he is not the idealized race, sex orientation, class, and so on (Cooper 2010). He might then compensate for his low status along one axis of identity by subordinating others who are below him along other axes of identity (Pyke 1996; Ehrenreich 2002; Cooper 2002b).

Accounting for the critique of hegemonic masculinity, we are left with the sense that there exist both a hegemonic masculinity in general and also many alternative masculinities that exercise a version of hegemony in specific contexts. For instance, while professional behaviors are generally accepted as the best way to embody masculinity, some cultural contexts, such as beer and truck commercials (Beasley 2008), laud a more working-class hypermasculinity (A. Harris 2000). As Jewel Woods notes,

> Despite the economic trend away from blue-collar jobs, many of the most powerful expressions of masculinity within contemporary American society continue to be associated with blue-collar imagery. . . .
> At the very same time society is becoming less reliant on male brawn, the dominant cultural images of masculinity are largely derived from the "traditional" ideas of maleness. (2008)

Likewise, while whiteness is generally prioritized as most appropriately masculine (Kimmel 2005), black men are often envied in the cultural context (here, a specific topic within popular culture) of sexuality (Dines 2006; A. Harris 2000). The existence of alternative masculinities in some contexts does not disprove the existence of general (though diffuse) hegemonic masculine norms, just that the relationship between hegemonic and alternative masculinities is complicated. The theoretical tool that will best allow us to explore the interactions between the generally hegemonic masculinity and alternative masculinities is critical race theory's multidimensionality theory.

What a Multidimensional Masculinities Approach Adds

Having updated our understanding of the important term, "hegemonic masculinities," we should now consider how multidimensional masculinities theory reveals that race and other aspects of identity are always both imbricated within gender and interpreted in light of the specific cultural context. A scene from The Wire involving a masculinity contest (Cooper 2010; Cooper 2009b) between a white police officer and a black civilian helps demonstrate the utility of multidimensional masculinities theory. In the scene, officers Prez, Herc, and Carver get liquored up (Alvarez 2009). They decide to go to the projects to question people about Avon Barksdale. As they call out questions in front of a building, they encounter a group of black boys from the projects. One boy lounges on their squad car. Prez confronts him. When the boy is disrespectful, Prez pistol whips him with his service revolver. The project's residents protest this behavior by raining down appliances on the officers. Lieutenant Daniels arrives and coaches Prez on how to claim self-defense. It turns out the boy has been blinded in one eye.

Multidimensionality Theory

A full analysis of this scene requires a move from the hegemonic masculinities approach to a multidimensional masculinities approach. Multidimensionality theory is a concept from critical race theory of law (Hutchinson 2000; Mutua 2006; Valdes 1998). It stems from intersectionality theory, which says that people in whom multiple subordinated categories of identity intersect, such as black women, have unique subjective experiences of the world and face unique forms of discrimination (Cooper 2002b; Crenshaw 1991). Multidimensionality theory says that gender, race, class, and other aspects of identity operate simultaneously, inextricably, and in a context-dependent manner (Hutchinson 2000). Gender and race are always co-constituted. For example, a heterosexual black man will have a self identity that differs from that of a gay black man, and gay and straight black men will be treated differently from one another by others (Cooper 2010; Cooper 2006a). Likewise, cultural context matters (Cooper 2006b). For example, heterosexual black men will likely think of themselves differently and be treated differently depending on whether they are in a sports bar or an art gallery (Cooper 2010).[4]

A good example of a multidimensional analysis is critical race theorist Peter Kwan's "cosynthesis" examination of the near-arrest of serial killer Jeffrey Dahmer. Kwan's analysis can be summarized as follows:

> When White police officers were called to the home of White serial killer Jeffrey Dahmer, they construed his bleeding and naked Asian male victim, Konerak Sinthasomphone, as effeminate rather than sinister and dangerous, and chose not to investigate further. If the officers had applied the "sinister and dangerous" stereotype [of Asian men] to Sinthasomphone rather than the "effeminate" stereotype, they might have worried they needed to investigate further and discovered Dahmer's deceit. The reason the officers chose not to investigate was the context: Dahmer's whiteness and maleness granted him authority to depict the relationship as voluntary; the blackness and femaleness of the complaining witnesses deprived

them of authority; and Sinthasomphone's Asian male identity made his opinion irrelevant. (Cooper 2002b, 370; Kwan 1997, 1261–68)

Kwan's example shows that we need to utilize the "multidimensional" insight that cultural context can change the interpretation of the same intersectional identity. Here, the cultural context was the particular mix of privileged and subordinated identities that were in play when the police considered whether to arrest Dahmer.

When applying multidimensionality theory herein, it will be important to recognize that there is both a widely idealized pattern of hegemonic masculinity in the United States and a series of variations thereon that constitute their own distinct, though overlapping, patterns of masculine norms (A. Harris 2000). Of course, what is idealized in a particular cultural context may otherwise be an alternative masculinity, as when the working-class masculinities of firemen are lauded despite the general privileging of professional identities (Chang, this volume; Dowd, Levit, and McGinley, this volume; McGinley 2010). Accordingly, Harris both quotes sociologist Karen Pyke for the proposition that "white heterosexual middle- and upper-class men who occupy order-giving positions . . . produce a hegemonic masculinity that is glorified throughout the culture" (A. Harris 2000, 785 n.31; Pyke 1996, 531) and also recognizes that a certain working-class masculinity exercises a version of hegemony in other contexts (A. Harris 2000). As was suggested earlier, what is hegemonic in one context might not be so in another context.

Alternative Masculinities

Utilizing the multidimensional masculinities theory framework, we might investigate the hegemonic pattern of police officer masculinity as an alternative masculinity. The police officer identity is not generally hegemonic, and yet it is dominant within certain contexts. Working-class masculinities, of which police officer identity is a prime example, are generally subordinated to professional identities (Young 1990). Nonetheless, working-class identities are privileged in some contexts (Beasley 2008; Ehrenreich 2002; A. Harris 2000; Pyke 1996). Likewise, the image of the policeman or firefighter may have cultural power within certain narratives (Chang, this volume; Dowd, Levit, and McGinley, this volume; McGinley 2010), but that does not mean those jobs allow one to amass great power in the form of wealth or substantial influence over national politics. So police officer masculinity is an example of an alternative masculinity that is influential in certain ways and in certain contexts, but not generally normative.

The hegemonic pattern of police officer identity is distinguished from the hegemonic pattern of U.S. masculinity in general by the officer's sense that he must enact a command presence (Cooper 2009b). One has command presence when one takes charge of a situation (ibid.; Newman 2006). The officer projects confidence and decisiveness (Cooper 2009b; Newman 2006). Command presence is also associated with the physical control of suspects. It is justified by the need to control dangerous suspects (Cooper 2009b; Newman 2006). When it is misused, it can amount to police brutality (Cooper 2009b). Seeing the enactment of command presence as the core of the job is a characteristic of policing throughout the country (ibid.; Newman 2006).

Because policemen's self identities are tied up with their ability to enact command presence, they enforce an unwritten rule that civilians must show deference to the badge (Cooper 2010; Cooper 2009b). This rule has its roots in what sociologists Dov Cohen and Joe Vandello call the culture of honor (1998). In a culture of honor, one's reputation for manliness determines how one is treated (ibid.). For instance, herdsmen often cannot keep an eye on every member of their roving flock (ibid.). To discourage poaching, they must have a reputation for punishing anyone who disrespects them (ibid.). Because protecting one's honor is so important, one treats insults as grave threats to one's identity and livelihood (ibid.). Like herders, police officers seem to fear that if they let an instance of disrespect pass, they will be subject to constant challenges (Cooper 2009b; A. Harris 2000). Feeling they might need to impose command presence on a situation at any moment, police officers often feel they must constantly enforce a rule of deference to the badge. As sociologist Steve Herbert notes, "This felt need to assert authority becomes ingrained. Even in situations with minimal danger, officers often conduct pat-down searches or request that citizens position themselves in particular ways" (2006, 101). Officers are often on the lookout for any sign of disrespect of their authority, which they will then punish (Cooper 2009b).

The rule of deference to the badge is linked to masculinity. Criminologist Susan Ehrlich Martin argues that "since a key element of policing—gaining and maintaining control of situations—remains associated with manhood, male officers do gender along with doing dominance" (Martin 1999, 117). The rule of deference to the badge is not only a product of role, but also a product of gender identity. Roles themselves are often gendered. Nurses, for example, are assumed to be female, and police officers are presumed to be male (Cooper 2010; McGinley 2009). Given that policing is thought to require a masculine presence, we should expect that both male and female police officers will sometimes use their role to boost their masculine esteem.

There is another alternative masculinity in Seasons One and Three of *The Wire*, that of the members of the black drug organizations (and civilians who emulate that culture). The young drug dealers and potential future drug dealers are referred to as "corner boys."[5] To illustrate the masculinities of the younger drug dealers, it is helpful to look at the theory of young black men's adoption of a "cool pose" (A. Harris 2000, 784; Majors and Billson 1993). According to this theory, inner-city young black males seek a reputation as nihilistic. As James Braxton Peterson says, the corner boys see their in-school hustle, scamming the teachers and administrators, as preparation for life on the streets (2009). For African American males, masculinity is especially linked to economic success by any means necessary (ibid.). As will be discussed, capitalism and racism combine to create the alienation that leads young men to become drug dealers (ibid.). There is a special emotional trauma associated with becoming a man under conditions of nihilism, which we see in the hopelessness that pervades some inner-city environments (ibid.).

The Clash of Masculinities in The Wire

We learn about the explosiveness of combining the alternative masculinities of police officers and corner boys in the scene where Prez blinds the boy. Prez, Herc, and Carver are a mixed-race group, but their identity at that moment is really police officer "blue." That identity is primed by the belligerence of the youths they face. In a paradigmatic example of punishing disrespect, Prez uses violence in an attempt to express his identity. Likewise, the youths are expressing corner boy masculinity. Their disdain for the police seeks to show they are men, not just boys, who are the equals of the police. As has been noted elsewhere, good cops know how to diffuse these situations (Cooper 2010; Cooper 2009b; D. Harris 2005). Prez cannot do so. Ambivalent about being an officer, Prez defaults to the hypermasculine model of the role, and is unable to diffuse this conflict with the youths. As a result, the combination of these two alternative masculinities is explosive.

This scene also helps demonstrate the multidimensionality principles that categories of identity are (1) co-constituted and (2) context-dependent. Here, the officers' races are co-constituted with their role identity. Carver and Daniels are black, but also "blue," so they support Prez's story. Likewise, the youths are not just boys, but black and underclass. That combination of identities impels them to endanger themselves by challenging the police. Simultaneously, this event is context-driven. Being in the role of police officers seeking information serves as a context factor—a piece of the total multidimensional puzzle that we must consider in order to explain the result—that drives Prez to punish disrespect. Similarly, the location of this confrontation in the ghetto serves as a context factor that not only makes the boys believe they must defend their turf, but also emboldens the police to believe they can get away with lying (A. Harris 2000). In these ways, a multidimensional masculinities approach helps us better understand *The Wire* and the drug war in general.

The Wire's Critique of Capitalism

To make the transitions from a hegemonic masculinities approach, to the multidimensional masculinities approach this book advocates, to the materialist—class-based—multidimensional masculinities approach this chapter calls for, we should look at one more aspect of *The Wire*. Consider a series of scenes where Avon and Stringer clash over the proper approach to the drug business. In the first episode of Season Three, Stringer says, "Sell the shit, make the profit, and later for that gangster bullshit" (Lucasi 2009, 141). Stringer measures the probabilities of becoming the subject of a confession and orders D'Angelo killed even though he is Avon's nephew (*The Wire* 2004, Season Three, Episode Eight). Previously, Avon had resisted Stringer's proposal of a truce with Omar in Season One on grounds that real gangsters do not leave affronts unpunished (Alvarez 2009). On the other hand, Avon would not attack an enemy on a Sunday because of the traditional Sunday truce between ghetto gangsters (Read 2009). Ultimately, Stringer gets Avon jailed and Avon has Stringer killed.

ClassCrit Theory

To fully understand those scenes, we need a multidimensional approach that goes beyond gender and race. A perusal of the masculinities and law literature will confirm that virtually none of its proponents pay significant attention to capitalism. To remedy that omission, we can turn to the emerging ClassCrit movement in law. These scholars argue for a relational understanding of class (Mutua 2008). One's class is both one's level of material wealth and social capital as well as one's sense of self and externally acknowledged prestige. The point of a class critique is to reveal that the wealthy gain their incomes and social capital through the exploitation of individuals from lower strata (ibid.). In the most basic sense, stock holders can gain their dividends only if the company pays its workers less money than their proportionate contribution to the product, yielding profits.

As critical legal scholar Athena Mutua puts it, utilizing sociologist Erik Olin Wright's work, economic power is created for some to the exclusion of others through the structuring of relationships, "whether out of the barrel of a gun, the constrained consent of the population, or otherwise " (Mutua 2008, 902). That constrained consent refers directly to the concept of achieving dominance through the construction of hegemonic norms. For that reason, a ClassCrit approach might be merged with the particular hegemonic masculinities approach this chapter has adopted to form a multidimensional masculinities approach with a materialist focus.

As in the case of hegemonic and alternative masculinities, lifestyles are formed in contradistinction to other lifestyles. Here, for instance, is how philosopher Charles Taylor describes sociologist Pierre Bourdieu's signature concept of the habitus: "Through these modes of deference and presentation, the subtlest notions of social position, of the sources of prestige, and hence of what is valuable and good are encoded" (Taylor 1999, 42). So, as Bourdieu argued, our bodily habits, such as how we hold ourselves and what we eat, reflect our class position (Bourdieu 1984). The connection between wealth levels and lifestyles begins with the fact that our original location in the class structure largely determines what we will do for work, such that "what you *have* determines . . . *the work you have to do*" (Mutua 2008, 903). In fact, in the United States, only about "6.3% of children with parents in the bottom income quintile earn incomes in the top 20% as adults" (Collins et al. 2004, 11). So, being born into a family that has nothing greatly enhances your chances of having a job that does not significantly raise your class status. From our stratified relationships to work—i.e., some of us earn little for our work, some more, and some do not have to work at all—are born the stratified lifestyles known as "underclass," "working-class," "white collar," and so on. While class is structural, "the way in which groups of people understand this structure, discuss it, and are informed by it, is a cultural phenomenon" (Mutua 2008, 905). The remainder of this part of the chapter thus looks at both how capitalism influences the cultural phenomenon known as the drug war and how class influences the self identity of the characters in *The Wire*.

The Economy and the Drug War

According to *The Wire*'s co-creator, David Simon, the problems of the inner city and drug addiction derive from "the fact that these really are the excess people in America, we—our economy doesn't need them. We don't need ten or fifteen percent of our population" (Moyers 2009). Simon suggests that our post-manufacturing economy does not need a portion of the unskilled laborers. He links that obsolescence to the continuation of a futile drug war in the inner city.

In a sense, the drug war itself produces drug dealing. By shrinking the supply of drugs, it drives up the price, thereby making it more appealing to try to become a supplier. Further, advertising encourages the poor to seek a life of conspicuous consumption while the lack of economic opportunities in the inner city makes drug dealing an appealing means of attaining that goal (Peterson 2009). Just as a middle-class suburban white might start a "legitimate" business in order to rise in class, "for D'Angelo, the world of drug trafficking is not some sort of refusal of the norms and ideals of society, crime as some sort of rebellion, but it is an attempt to possess the very dream that has been denied to him" (Read 2009, 127). Although "capitalism does not spread the wealth, just the idea that we could all become wealthy," the idea that one should try to become wealthy unites the wealthy and the under-class, and everyone in between, in the pursuit of money (ibid. 124).

Just as capitalism links drug dealers and "legitimate" business people, capitalism creates the woes of the inner city in general. Margaret Talbot's *New Yorker* article on *The Wire* suggests that Simon agrees with this conclusion. Simon sees the show as "about how contemporary American society and particularly, 'raw, unencumbered capitalism'—devalues human beings" (Talbot 2007, 150). Similarly, in an interview with the PBS television show *Bill Moyers' Journal*, Simon accepts Moyers' characterization of the contemporary United States as an oligarchy. Moyers defines an oligarchy as "government by the few. Or a government in which a small group exercises control for corrupt and selfish purposes" (Moyers 2009). Simon says, "We are a country of democratic ideas and impulses, but it is strained through some very oligarchical structures" (ibid.). Moreover, Simon agrees with Moyers' characterization of Simon's message in *The Wire* as "America's not working for everyday people who have no power. And that's the way the people with power have designed it to work" (ibid.). In the same interview, Simon says *The Wire* is "about the America that got left behind" (ibid.). So, it is fair to say that *The Wire* is about the people without power and how the institutions that are supposed to serve them—schools, the police, politics—fail to do so.

The Multidimensionality of Race and Class

The ravaging of inner cities by drugs, as well as the drug war and its dire consequences for the inner city, can be traced to both the post-industrial neoliberal economy's making these people obsolete and the mainstream culture's race-based disregard for these people. According to Simon, since people in distressed communities know they are not wanted, "they understand that the only viable economic base in their neighborhoods is this multi-billion drug trade" (Moyers 2009). Journalist Bill Moyers thus proposes that the drug trade exists principally to pacify those without economic opportunities (ibid.). Simon agrees and links the drug trade back to race, saying, "And by the way, if it was chewing up white folk, it wouldn't have gone on for as long as it did" (ibid.). Simon thus sees the United States as in a waning phase of social egalitarianism (Amsterdam and Bruner 2000), but permanently so as to inner-city racial minority communities. Stephen Lucasi adds the insight that globalization divides cities into "deserving" and "undeserving" areas (2009, 137), such that blacks, and black men in particular, are harmed more than others (ibid. 136).[6] Simon further implies, and this chapter certainly asserts, that disregard for those deemed economically unnecessary and culturally undeserving is a result of both economic reasoning and a race-based lack of empathy for the drug war's victims.

Kenneth B. Nunn's theory of surplus criminality reinforces the theories of Simon, Moyers, and Lucasi. Nunn says the War on Drugs could easily be called a War on Blacks. He applies Marx's idea that in capitalism there must always be a reserve pool of surplus labor (the unemployed) (Nunn 2002). As the economy expands, it draws workers from the reserve pool of surplus labor. When it retracts, it returns workers to the reserve pool of surplus labor (ibid.). Likewise, says Nunn, the United States has a reserve pool of surplus criminality (the socially marginalized) (ibid.). When crises arise, the mainstream draws on people from the reserve pool of surplus criminality to blame as the criminal element most responsible for the problem (ibid.). When the crisis subsides, these criminals in reserve need no longer be demonized (ibid.). Because of the United States' history of chattel bondage and apartheid, blacks constitute the deepest pool of readily demonizable latent criminals (ibid.).

The Multidimensionality of Race, Class, and Gender in The Wire

Having shown the influence of capitalism on the drug war and capitalism's connection to the race-based nature of the drug war, we can further demonstrate the multidimensionality of race, class, and gender by returning to the scenes that began this part of the chapter. Jason Read's development of the distinction between the "soldier" and the "CEO" is important. He looks at the contrast between drug trade partners Avon and Stringer. Whereas Avon is a soldier who lives by traditional codes of gangsterism, Stringer is a CEO who says, "Sell the shit, make the profit, and later for that gangster bullshit"

(Lucasi 2009, 141). Stringer is thus the economic rational actor who would order killing or refrain from killing depending on whether it is marginally economically profitable. Lucasi's chapter on *The Wire* links Stringer's attitude to globalized neoliberal capitalism: "Stringer's 'nothing but cash' mantra emerges logically from the culture of monetarism—of cash without territory or industry" (2009, 142). Stringer is a pure capitalist. Lucasi cites Simon for the proposition that pure capitalism means being loyal to no one and no code except the goal of accumulating profit (ibid.). In contrast to Stringer, "for Avon, conflict and violence are not subject to calculations that measure cost against benefits, but to a tradition that establishes the rules and conditions of respect" (Read 2009, 128). So Avon would enter conflict to keep "corners" of real estate that are no longer necessary to the drug game (ibid. 129), but would not attack an enemy on a Sunday because of tradition (ibid.).

Note the connection between Avon's code and hegemonic masculinity. Avon's rules "do not serve the ends of profit or even dominance" (ibid. 128). Instead, violence "is constitutive of reputation" (ibid.). This is reminiscent of Cohen and Vandello's description of cultures of honor. As might a sheep herder (or a police officer), Avon feels the need to be violent to deter predators (Cohen and Vandello 1998). When Stringer proposes a truce with Omar in Season One, Avon argues they cannot do that because leaving Omar's disrespect unpunished would embolden others. The hegemony Avon seeks is being "the man" on the inner-city streets. While Avon's behavior is not solely about masculinity (Read 2009), the gangster reputation he seeks certainly is of a type associated with especially masculine men.

Stringer's pure capitalist model is also about reputation (ibid.). Professional masculinity, while sometimes taking a back seat to working-class models in popular culture (Beasley 2008; Chang, this volume; McGinley 2010), is the ultimately more generally prized masculinity (A. Harris 2000). With his reading glasses and more conservative clothing, Stringer cuts a more professional figure than most of the inner-city characters. He also attends college classes as part of his goal of taking the drug organization mainstream. His is thus a more upwardly mobile masculinity than Avon's.

Nonetheless, Stringer is taken advantage of by corrupt state senator Clay Davis and never fully accepted in the bourgeois world. Why? Certainly his crook-to-businessman strategy has reputedly been pulled off by the Irish (think, the Kennedys) and the Italians (think, *The Godfather*). While the class barriers to such a transition are prodigious, *The Wire* suggests more is involved. As a black criminal, Stringer faces further obstacles. Understanding the failure of Stringer's attempt to forge an inner-city but professional masculinity thus requires seeing gender, race, and class as co-constituted and context dependent. It requires a materialist multidimensional masculinities approach.

Conclusion

Stringer is hardly alone among *The Wire's* characters in being unable to move up the ladder. Toward the end of the fifth and final season, Bodie makes a statement that completes *The Wire's* metaphor of the king staying the king: He has never been more than a pawn, for "the game is rigged" (Peterson 2009, 112). If we are to play our way out of the hierarchies *The Wire* identifies, we will need a method for changing the game itself. This chapter does not claim to have discovered that method. But it does assert that whatever else proves true about that method, it will need to account for the multidimensionality of masculinity, including its material dimensions.

NOTES

I thank my research assistant, Armando Ortiz, and reference librarian Diane D'Angelo. Special thanks to Suffolk University Moakley Law Library electronic services and legal reference librarian Rick Buckingham and my co-editor Ann C. McGinley for excellent editing.

1. Descriptions of scenes from *The Wire* are drawn from both watching the show and reading Rafael Alvarez's series guide (Alvarez 2009). For convenience and brevity, citations to the show will be minimal (limited mostly to quotes) and will be to the Alvarez text whenever possible. Cites to the show itself will be identified by Season and Episode, such as "(*The Wire* 2002, Season One, Episode One)".

2. The term "hegemonic masculinity" has come under criticism (Beasley 2008; Coles 2009; Demetriou 2001; Hearn 2004). This chapter refers to hegemonic masculinity, but advocates moving beyond its traditional use.

3. A couple of caveats: This chapter does not purport to conduct a sophisticated analysis of the visual style of *The Wire*, as might a standard television studies piece. Nor should the chapter be understood as suggesting the simplistic notion that because *The Wire* depicts the drug war a certain way, it directly influences its audience to accept its views (LeBesco 2009).

4. This is not to essentialize heterosexual or gay black masculinities, but to recognize tendencies in how people see themselves and others that do seem to exist at this particular cultural moment.

5. Of course girls, such as the character Zenobia, can be "corner boys" (Peterson 2009, 109, 121 n.2).

6. This fits with notorious GOP strategist Lee Atwater's admission: "You're getting so abstract now [that] you're talking about cutting taxes, and all these things you're talking about are totally economic things and a byproduct of them is [that] *blacks get hurt worse than whites*. And subconsciously maybe that is part of it" (Thompson 2006, 254; Cooper 2010).

REFERENCES

Alvarez, Rafael. 2009. *The Wire: Truth Be Told.* New York: Grove Press.

Amsterdam, Anthony G., and Jerome Bruner. 2000. *Minding the Law.* Cambridge, MA: Harvard University Press.

Beasley, Christine. 2008. Rethinking Hegemonic Masculinity in a Globalizing World. *Men and Masculinities* 11:86–103.

Blumenson, Eric D., and Eva S. Nilsen. 2002. How to Construct an Underclass, or How the War on Drugs Became a War on Education. *Journal of Gender, Race & Justice* 6:61–109.

Bourdieu, Pierre. 1984. *Distinction: A Social Critique of the Judgement of Taste.* Translated by Richard Nice. Cambridge, MA: Harvard University Press.

Carbado, Devon W., ed. 1999. *Black Men on Race, Gender, and Sexuality: A Critical Reader.* New York: New York University Press.

Chaddha, Anmol, William Julius Wilson, and Sudhir Venkatesh. 2008. In Defense of *The Wire. Dissent* 55(3):83–86. Available at http://www.dissentmagazine.org/article/?article=1237.

Cohen, David. 2010. Keeping Men Men and Women Down: Sex Segregation, Anti-Essentialism, and Masculinity. *Harvard Journal of Law and Gender* 33:509–54.

———. 2009. No Boy Left Behind?: Single-Sex Education and the Essentialist Myth of Masculinity. *Indiana Law Journal* 84:135–88.

Cohen, Dov, and Joe Vandello. 1998. Meanings of Violence. *Journal of Legal Studies* 27:567–84.

Coles, Tony. 2009. Negotiating the Field of Masculinity: The Production and Reproduction of Multiple Dominant Masculinities. *Men and Masculinities* 12(1):30–44.

Collins, Chuck, Amy Gluckman, Meizhu Lui, Betsy Leondar-Wright, Amy Offner, and Adria Scharf, eds. 2004. *The Wealth Inequality Reader.* Cambridge, MA: Dollars & Sense—Economic Affairs Bureau.

Connell, R. W. 2005. *Masculinities,* 2d ed. Berkeley: University of California Press.

Connell, R. W., and James W. Messerschmidt. 2005. Hegemonic Masculinity: Rethinking the Concept. *Gender and Society* 19(6):829–59.

Cooper, Frank Rudy. 2010. Masculinities, Post-Racialism, and the Gates Controversy: The False Equivalence between Officer and Civilian. *Nevada Law Journal* 11(1):1–43.

———. 2009a. Our First Unisex President?: Black Masculinity and Obama's Feminine Side. *Denver University Law Review* 86:633–61.

———. 2009b. "Who's the Man?": Masculinities Studies, *Terry* Stops, and Police Training. *Columbia Journal of Gender and Law* 18(3):671–742.

———. 2006a. Against Bipolar Black Masculinity: Intersectionality, Assimilation, Identity Performance, and Hierarchy. *U.C. Davis Law Review* 39:853–903.

———. 2006b. The "Seesaw Effect" from Racial Profiling to Depolicing: Toward a Critical Cultural Theory. In *The New Civil Rights Research: A Constitutive Approach,* edited by Benjamin Fleury-Steiner and Laura Beth Nielsen. Burlington, VT: Ashgate, 139–55.

———. 2002a. The Un-balanced Fourth Amendment: A Cultural Study of the Drug War, Racial Profiling and *Arvizu. Villanova Law Review* 47:851–95.

———. 2002b. Understanding "Depolicing": Symbiosis Theory and Critical Cultural Theory. *University of Missouri-Kansas City Law Review* 71:355–76.

Crenshaw, Kimberlé W. 1991. Mapping the Margins: Intersectionality, Identity Politics, and Violence against Women of Color. *Stanford Law Review* 43:1241–99.

Crenshaw, Kimberlé, Neil Gotanda, Gary Peller, and Kendall Thomas, eds. 1995. *Critical Race Theory: The Key Writings That Formed the Movement.* New York: New Press.

Delgado, Richard, and Jean Stefancic, eds. 2000. *Critical Race Theory: The Cutting Edge*, 2nd ed. Philadelphia: Temple University Press.

Demetriou, Demetrakis Z. 2001. Connell's Concept of Hegemonic Masculinity: A Critique. *Theory and Society* 30(3):337–61.

Dines, Gail. 2006. The White Man's Burden: Gonzo Pornography and the Construction of Black Masculinity. *Yale Journal of Law and Feminism* 18:283–97.

Donaldson, Mike. 1993. What Is Hegemonic Masculinity? *Theory and Society* 22:643–57.

Dowd, Nancy E. 2010. *The Man Question: Male Subordination and Privilege*. New York: New York University Press.

Ehrenreich, Nancy. 2002. Subordination and Symbiosis: Mechanisms of Mutual Support between Subordinating Systems. *University of Missouri-Kansas City Law Review* 71:251–79.

Grosfoguel, Ramón, and Chloe S. Georas. 2000. "Coloniality of Power" and Racial Dynamics: Notes toward a Reinterpretation of Latino Caribbeans in New York City. *Identities: Global Studies in Culture and Power* 7:85–125.

Harris, Angela P. 2000. Gender, Violence, Race, and Criminal Justice. *Stanford Law Review* 52:777–807.

———. 1990. Race and Essentialism in Feminist Legal Theory. *Stanford Law Review* 42:581–616.

Harris, David A. 2005. *Good Cops: The Case for Preventive Policing*. New York: New Press.

Hearn, Jeff. 2004. From Hegemonic Masculinity to the Hegemony of Men. *Feminist Theory* 5(1):49–72.

Hutchinson, Darren Lenard. 2000. "Gay Rights" for "Gay Whites"?: Race, Sexual Identity, and Equal Protection Discourse. *Cornell Law Review* 85:1358–91.

Kimmel, Michael. 2005. *The Gender of Desire: Essays on Male Sexuality*. Albany: State University of New York Press.

Kwan, Peter. 1997. Jeffrey Dahmer and the Cosynthesis of Categories. *Hastings Law Journal* 48:1257–92.

LeBesco, Kathleen. 2009. "Gots to Get Got": Social Justice and Audience Response to Mar Little. In *The Wire: Urban Decay and American Television*, edited by Tiffany Potter and C. W. Marshall. New York: Continuum, 217–32.

Lippman, Laura. 2009. The Women of *The Wire* (No, Seriously). In *The Wire: Truth Be Told*. New York: Grove Press, 55–60.

Lucasi, Stephen. 2009. Networks of Affiliation: Familialism and Anticorporatism in Black and White. In *The Wire: Urban Decay and American Television*, edited by Tiffany Potter and C. W. Marshall. New York: Continuum, 135–48.

Majors, Richard, and Janet Mancini Billson. 1993. *Cool Pose: The Dilemmas of Black Manhood in America*. New York: Touchstone.

Marshall, C.W. and Tiffany Potter. 2009. "I Am the American Dream": Modern Urban Tragedy and the Borders of Fiction. In *The Wire: Urban Decay and American Television*, edited by Tiffany Potter and C. W. Marshall. New York: Continuum, 1–14.

Martin, Susan E. 1999. Police Force or Police Service?: Gender and Emotional Labor. *Annals of the American Academy of Political and Social Science* 561:111–26.

McGinley, Ann C. 2010. *Ricci v. DeStefano*: A Masculinities Theory Analysis. *Harvard Journal of Gender and Law* 33:581–623.

———. 2009. Reproducing Gender on Law School Faculties. *Brigham Young University Law Review* 2009:99-155.

———. 2004. Masculinities at Work. *Oregon Law Review* 83:359–433.

Moyers, Bill. 2009. Bill Moyers Journal: Interview with David Simon, April 17. Transcript available at http://www.pbs.org/moyers/journal/04172009/transcript1.html.

Mutua, Athena D. 2008. Introducing ClassCrits: From Class Blindness to a Critical Legal Analysis of Economic Inequality. *Buffalo Law Review* 56:859–913.

———. 2006. Theorizing Progressive Black Masculinities. In *Progressive Black Masculinities*, edited by Athena D. Mutua. New York: Routledge, 3–42.

Newman, Mary. 2006. *Barnes v. City of Cincinnati*: Command Presence, Gender Bias, and Problems of Police Aggression. *Harvard Journal of Law and Gender* 29:485–92.

Nunn, Kenneth B. 2002. Race, Crime and the Pool of Surplus Criminality: Or Why the "War on Drugs" Was a "War on Blacks." *Journal of Gender, Race & Justice* 6:381–445.

Perea, Juan, Richard Delgado, Angela Harris, Jean Stefancic, and Stephanie Wildman. 2007. *Race and Races: Cases and Resources for a Diverse America*, 2d ed. St. Paul, MN: Thomson/West.

Peterson, James Braxton. 2009. *The Wire*: Urban Decay and American Television. In The Wire: *Urban Decay and American Television*, edited by Tiffany Potter and C. W. Marshall. New York: Continuum, 107–21.

Pyke, Karen D. 1996. Class-Based Masculinities: The Interdependence of Gender, Class, and Interpersonal Power. *Gender and Society* 10:527–49.

Read, Jason. 2009. Stringer Bell's Lament: Violence and Legitimacy in Contemporary Capitalism. In The Wire: *Urban Decay and American Television*, edited by Tiffany Potter and C. W. Marshall. New York: Continuum, 122–34.

Talbot, Margaret. 2007. Stealing Life: The Crusader behind "The Wire." *The New Yorker*, October 22, 150–63.

Taylor, Charles. 1999. To Follow a Rule. . . In *Bourdieu: A Critical Reader*, edited by Richard Schusterman. Malden, MA: Blackwell Publishers, 29–44.

Thompson, Mark R. 2006. When God Collides with Race and Class: Working-Class America's Shift to Conservatism. *University of Pittsburgh Law Review* 68:243–66.

Valdes, Francisco. 1998. Afterword—Beyond Sexual Orientation in Queer Legal Theory: Majoritarianism, Multidimensionality, and Responsibility in Social Justice Scholarship or Legal Scholars as Cultural Warriors. *Denver University Law Review* 75:1409–64.

Weisberg, Jacob. 2006. *The Wire* on Fire: Analyzing the Best Show on Television. *Slate*, http://www.slate.com/id/2149566/, September 13.

Woods, Jewel. 2008. Why Guys Have a Man-Crush on Obama; Sure Women Swoon, but Modern Men Seem Weak-Kneed, Too. *Chicago Sun-Times*, July 24.

The Wire. 2004. Created by David Simon. HBO Home Video. DVD.

The Wire. 2002. Created by David Simon. HBO Home Video. DVD.

Young, Iris Marion. 1990. *Justice and the Politics of Difference*. Princeton, NJ: Princeton University Press.

PART II

Telling Stories about (Heroic) Masculinities

5

Rescue Me

ROBERT CHANG

In *Letter to Ma*, Merle Woo writes that when she was a child, she watched as two white cops humiliated her father and how that encounter led her to be embarrassed of her father, whom she began to see as womanly (1984). Reflecting on this experience years later made her realize that Asian American men, simultaneously racialized and emasculated, are victims of both racism and sexism (ibid.). This interplay of racism and sexism affects race and gender dynamics for Asian American men both within Asian American communities and more broadly. In this chapter, I argue that this interplay of race and gender renders the Asian American male firefighter discursively impossible.

The discursive impossibility of the Asian American male firefighter can be seen in popular depictions of firefighters in television shows such as *Rescue Me* (Leary and Tolan 2004), as well as in the absence of such a figure in the iconography of the fallen 9/11 firefighters (Chang 2003). The discursive impossibility of Asian American male firefighters plays out in the real world in their near absence in fire departments, evident but unremedied in recent litigation involving the Fire Department of New York (FDNY) (*United States v. City of New York* 2010b).

When and Where I Enter

Before discussing figurative and literal absences, and the way that these absences are underwritten by the interplay of culture and law, I begin with a brief discussion of my theoretical and political commitments.[1]

I came to race through feminist theory in the early 1990s. This dramatically colors the way that I think about gender and engenders the way that I think about race. As an Asian American man who writes about race and gender, I reject the opening sentence in *Men in Feminism* with which Stephen Heath opens the collection: "Men's relation to feminism is an impossible one" (1987, 1). Instead, I prefer to imagine the possibilities set forth in the collection *Engendering Men* in which the contributors re-theorize male subjectivity and male power through the lens of feminist theory and politics (Boone and Cadden 1990).

In doing so, I try to heed Elaine Showalter's cautionary note about the oppressive possibilities contained in male feminism (1990). In her brilliant essay, "Critical Cross-Dressing: Male Feminists and the Woman of the Year," she examines the film *Tootsie* which stars Dustin Hoffman playing Michael Dorsey, a failing actor whose aspirations to stardom are realized only after he dresses in drag and transforms himself into Dorothy Michaels. As Dorothy Michaels, he becomes a television star and a role model for women (Pollack 1982). Indeed, one film critic, Molly Haskell, "calls Dorothy 'the first genuinely mainstream feminist heroine of our era'" (Showalter 1990, 369–70). Showalter comments that Michael Dorsey's success as Dorothy

> comes primarily, the film suggests, from the masculine power disguised and veiled by the feminine costume. Physical gestures of masculinity provide *Tootsie*'s comic motif of female impersonation. Dorothy Michaels drops her voice to call a taxi, lifts heavy suitcases, and shoves a hefty competitor out of the way. Dorothy's "feminist" speeches too are less a response to the oppression of women than an instinctive situational male reaction to being treated like a woman. The implication is that women must be taught by men how to win their rights.
>
> In this respect, *Tootsie*'s cross-dressing is a way of promoting the notion of masculine power while masking it (Showalter 1990, 371).

Showalter then moves from the film to the recent involvement of certain male critics in feminism, calling this male feminism a form of "critical cross-dressing." She observes:

> If some of them are now learning *our* language, all the better; but there is more than a hint in some recent critical writing that it's time for men to step in and show the girls how to do it, a swaggering tone that reminds me of a recent quip in the *Yale Alumni Magazine* about a member of the class of 1955, Renee Richards: "When better women are made, Yale men will make them." (ibid. 367)

Both examples show the malevolent forms that cross-dressing may engender.

I understand masculinities studies to emerge from feminist theory through this debate over male feminism. To some extent, masculinities studies might be described as creating a more comfortable place for men to engage in feminist and queer methodologies without being situated specifically in either camp (Newton 2002). Though masculinities studies typically takes men as its subject, it should not be confused with the masculinist men's movements of the 1980s and 1990s (Gardiner 2002, ix). Nor is masculinities studies an area limited to men, as this collection and the other leading masculinities studies collections demonstrate (Cooper and McGinley, this volume; Gardiner 2002; Adams and Savran 2002). Judith Gardiner suggests that a major strand of masculinist studies uses "feminist theory to explore some aspect of masculinity" (2002, x). I place my examination of the Asian American male firefighter in this camp.

On the law side, I situate myself as a critical race theorist. Within legal studies, critical race theory interrogates identity as part of the U.S. project of domestic racialization. At times, though, this investigation has been contained and constrained within a black/white racial paradigm and within a national framework that has left "other non-whites" in an uncertain position from which to engage in critique (Gotanda 1985). The developing Asian American jurisprudence and the critical Latina and Latino legal theory movement (LatCrit) have tried to expand the discourse to focus on the treatment and experience of Asian Americans and Latinas and Latinos as necessary to better understand the complicated way that race operates, especially as we move from simple binaries to multigroup conflict and cooperation (Chang and Gotanda 2007).

I follow the lead of feminist legal scholars who ask the "woman question," asking "about the gender implications of a social practice or rule: have women been left out of consideration? If so, in what way; how might that omission be corrected? What difference would it make to do so?" (Bartlett 1990, 837). In asking the Asian American question, my work runs counter to the black/white racial paradigm. This notion of race limits people's understanding and willingness to engage with the history and current state of Asian Americans, as well as with "other non-whites" in the United States. Instead of being interested participants in conversations on race, Asian Americans are seen as interlopers. Yet this status as interloper is precisely why Asian Americans are important in discussions of race—our existence disrupts the comfortable binary of the black/white racial paradigm in which the black racial subject is produced by and through its opposition to the white racial subject, and vice versa. The presence of other racial bodies problematizes this notion of the construction of both black and white racial subjects. Inclusion of Asian Americans operates to denature—de-naturalize—the current paradigm.

The state has had little trouble racializing persons of Asian ancestry. The United States Supreme Court's decisions in *Ozawa v. United States* (1922) and *United States v. Thind* (1923) established with finality the racial bar on naturalization, holding that persons of Asian ancestry could not become naturalized citizens. These cases were followed shortly by the 1924 Immigration Act that consolidated the racial bar on immigration by prohibiting immigration by those ineligible for citizenship (Immigration Act of 1924). This racially neutral language had the effect of excluding people purely on the basis of their Asian ancestry. Yet, despite the ease with which persons of Asian ancestry were racialized by the state, Asian Americans never really became part of the racial topography of America. Nevertheless, in the same way that silences may speak volumes, the enforced invisibility—achieved by exclusion from the political body and through the literal exclusion from the geographic body of the nation-state—may reveal an important structural role persons of Asian ancestry played in the formation of the modern American nation and its racial landscape.

My interrogation of the Asian American male firefighter takes place at the intersection of critical race theory and masculinities studies. My goal in centering the Asian American male firefighter is to disrupt conversations about race and masculinity from which Asian American men find themselves typically excluded. The Asian American is an interloper in the traditional terrain of black/white racial understandings. Similarly, the emasculated, effeminized Asian American male is an intruder in the hypermasculinized firehouse. The policing of masculinity through the training and hazing of new recruits works to make unwelcome the emasculated, effeminized Asian

American male, whose projected uncertain sexuality threatens the stability of the homosocial firehouse.

I begin with cultural representations, starting with the discursive impossibility of the Asian American male firefighter in *Rescue Me*, a television series featuring firefighters in New York City following 9/11. I then shift to struggle over the racial composition of a proposed monument to the fallen 9/11 firefighters. I draw connections between cultural representations and law's failure to see, let alone remedy, the near absence of Asian American men as firefighters and to ask, ultimately, whether we can be heroes, too.

Discursive Impossibility I: *Rescue Me*

Rescue Me is a popular cable television show that centers on the firefighters of FDNY Battalion 15, Engine 99, Ladder Company 62 (Manhattan 62 Truck) and their family and friends. The show takes place in a post-9/11 New York where 9/11 and its aftermath cast a long shadow. This can be seen from the first episode and continues throughout the seasons. For example, Episode 2 of Season 2 opens with the main character, Tommy Gavin, played by one of the show's creators, Dennis Leary, invoking the 60 firefighters from his fire station who perished during 9/11 to try to get out of a parking ticket.

Like most of the FDNY, the firefighters in this fictional firehouse are almost all white and male. The show includes one Latino firefighter, Franco Rivera, played by Daniel Sunjata (who, as an aside, is not Latino). In Season 4, a black firefighter, Bart Johnston, played by Larenz Tate, joins the crew. He insists on being called Shawn. Consistent with the firehouse practice of using adjectives to distinguish between firefighters with the same or similar first names, the other firefighters call him "Black Shawn" to distinguish him from (White) Sean. His race is his distinguishing characteristic. Playing to stereotypes, he was recruited to help Manhattan 62 Truck's basketball team (Shister 2007). There was one female firefighter who had a major recurring role, Laura Miles, played by Diane Farr, who joined toward the end of Season 1 but left at the end of Season 2.

In *Rescue Me*, masculinity is asserted most forcefully through misogyny and homophobia. Misogyny as a dominant theme is evident from the opening scene in the opening episode of the series. Tommy Gavin, the main character, addresses a group of probationary firefighters. The group is nearly all white; we see two brown faces. All men. Tommy says:

> Wanna know how big my balls are? They're as big as two of your heads duct taped together. . . . [The FDNY] is not in the business of making

heroes . . . we're in the business of discovering cowards. [calls the cadets pussies] No room for pussies in the FDNY. I knew 60 men who gave their lives at Ground Zero. Four from my house. (Season 1, Episode 1)

Heroism's opposite is cowardice expressed as a derogatory term for female genitalia. Heroism is also presented as making sex available as a matter of right. A few minutes after the opening scene, Tommy Gavin and Franco Rivera have this exchange at their lockers:

FRANCO: All that pussy I was getting after 9/11. Drying up.
TOMMY: People forget. (Ibid.)

Later, when an emergency alert sounds in the firehouse, we hear an automated woman's voice on the loudspeaker. One of the firefighters comments that they had to make it a woman's voice and lambasts political correctness. Even an automated woman's voice has no legitimate place in the firehouse (ibid.).

This first emergency turns out to be a dud. We find that a black man who was being evicted from his apartment had collected his urine for 24 weeks and then poured it down the stairs. Minorities are present primarily for background color (ibid.).

Women are present as foils in the lives of the firefighters. They require rescuing; they create problems. Laura Miles, the one female firefighter who had a strong presence in Season 2, creates problems for the firehouse when she files a grievance over sexist name-calling and the refusal of Lieutenant Kenny Shea (Lou) to apologize. The result is mandatory sensitivity training for the entire firehouse. We are presented then with a satirized presentation of this sensitivity training, which largely serves merely as an opportunity for racial, sexist, and homophobic name-calling (Season 2, Episode 5).

Homophobia finds its expression throughout the series. The second episode of Season 1 begins with Chief Riley holding a newspaper whose front page screams: "FDNY Vet: I'm Gay; Outs 9/11 Brothers."

CHIEF RILEY: Somebody gotta tell this faggot what's what. No respect. Huh? Widows, families.
LOU: How does he even know they're gay? Does he have sex with all of them? Was there some kind of secret handshake?
CHIEF RILEY: I'm on the job twenty years and I never seen one guy that's a faggot. All of a sudden they're telling me twenty guys that are taking it right up the ass. (Season 1, Episode 2)

Chief Riley's outrage over what he sees as the smearing of 20 of the 343 fallen 9/11 firefighters leads him at the end of this exchange to forbid any in his house from doing anything that might appear "gay." Toward the end of the episode, Chief Riley confronts the firefighter who was the source of the story and beats him into a coma (ibid.).

Chief Riley, initially suspended for his actions, ends up having his suspension lifted after a short trial, during which Chief Riley's gay son Peter, a firefighter with the Boston Fire Department, testifies that his father is completely accepting of his "lifestyle." We know that this is a lie, not just because of Chief Riley's behavior throughout, but also because moments before, outside of the hearing room when Peter says that he wants to drop by to visit his mom, Chief Riley tells him that she does not know he's in town. Peter ends up going back to Boston immediately after the hearing (Season 1, Episode 5).

It seems that nearly every episode is replete with examples of homophobia. One example from Season 2 involves the character Sully, who replaces Tommy in the firehouse when Tommy's personal problems lead him to be reassigned. Sully's gourmet cooking and listening skills make him a hit with the firefighters in Manhattan 62 Truck. He also has a magic touch. Near the beginning of Episode 3 of Season 2, we see Franco's puzzled face as he listens to male grunts and moans of pleasure. He walks into the weight room to find Sully giving a massage to (White) Sean. When Sean tells Franco that he ought to get a massage, the following dialogue ensues:

FRANCO: I only get massages from chicks and only when the massage ain't the main event.
SULLY: Are you saying I'm gay?
FRANCO: No, but there's a first time for everything and rubbing your hands all over another guy is sort of an obvious trigger for setting it off.
SULLY: I don't think so bro. I learned this from a chick I was banging a couple of years ago. She was a professional massage therapist and she taught me everything she knows. (Season 2, Episode 3)

Franco eventually gives in, but with a caveat, insisting, "Your hands stay from the nipples up" (ibid.).

The episode ends with the firefighters putting out a fire and rescuing the denizens of an underground fetishistic sex club. One of those rescued, after his mask is taken off, turns out to be none other than Sully, who admits that he likes to cross dress and have rough sex (ibid.).

Later in the firehouse, Sean freaks out. He had enjoyed the massages from Sully, at one point even saying, "If you were a chick, I'd marry you." He has to shower immediately to (try to) wash off the imprint of Sully's touches in order to secure his own masculinity (ibid.).

The firehouse presents a conflicted site for the production and maintenance of masculinity. Firefighters perform the hypermasculinized activities of putting out fires and rescuing people. Yet in the homosocial world of the firehouse, men do the cooking, cleaning, and caring for each other (McGinley 2010). Anxiety produced by the feminized roles produces a masculinity that is always on the edge and which is secured through the combination of heterosexual promiscuity, misogyny, and homophobia.

One wonders what place Asian American men might have in such a world. The answer, as presented in six seasons of *Rescue Me*, is simple: Asian American male firefighters have no place. Through six seasons of the show, I do not recall any Asian American firefighters. Perhaps that should come as no surprise, given the extremely low number of Asian Americans in the FDNY and in fire departments generally, something I return to later in this chapter.

Discursive Impossibility II: 9/11 Firefighter Iconography

September 11 and its aftermath were marked by moments of inclusion and exclusion. One such moment involved a now famous photograph of three white male firefighters and the controversy over a proposed but now scuttled memorial (Franklin 2002). For the most part, the race of the fallen firefighters did not become an issue until a controversy occurred over a proposed monument that would recognize the firefighters who perished when the World Trade Center Towers came crashing down (Dreher 2002). On 9/11, during the search for survivors, three firemen were photographed raising a

Table 5.1: Demographic Composition, 2001

FDNY	New York City
93% White	35% White
2.7% Black	24.5% Black
3.2% Hispanic	27% Hispanic
	9.8% Asian American
	.2% Native American

flag over the site (Franklin 2002, 64). This image became etched in people's minds. It appeared everywhere and became an important symbol about American courage in the face of tragedy. There was an attack by a foreign enemy. On the site of attack, the flag was raised in the midst of the rubble, proclaiming that America was not yet beaten. Instead of being seen in the rocket's red glare as in our national anthem, the flag was seen above the dust and smoke to give heart to all of America about the resilience of the American will.

The photograph became the basis for a monument that was to be erected at the New York City Fire Department's Brooklyn headquarters (Leo 2002). The men in the photograph are white. The monument was to depict one white, one black, and one Hispanic firefighter. This decision caused an immediate furor (Dreher 2002; Franklin 2002; Leo 2002).

Table 5.2: Demographics before and after lawsuit

1973	2001
5% racial minorities in FDNY	6-7% racial minorities in FDNY
30% racial minorities in NYC	62% racial minorities in NYC

The monument was intended not to honor the individual men who happened to raise the flag. Instead, it was meant to honor all the slain firefighters. It seems that once the decision has been made that the individuals to be depicted in the monument are not in fact modeled on real men, why should their race matter? If the three firemen have a claim, it's not so much that the racial composition has been altered, but that their individual features have been erased.

The furor over the changes is best understood if we consider the way images are deployed to construct history and cultural memory. Constructed history and cultural memory help constitute us as a nation (Sturken 1997). The image and the memorial Nationalism, especially in the aftermath of 9/11, raised the debate to a fever pitch.

The racial composition of the monument might be understood to be an inclusionary gesture. But what would it mean if blacks and Hispanics accepted this symbol? First, who gets excluded by this inclusionary gesture? The organization of the three racialized bodies around the symbol of America represents a vision of who is American. Second, to have one white, one black, and one Hispanic fireman in no way comports with reality. Of the 343 firefighters who died there, an estimated 319 were non-Hispanic whites (Leo 2002). As shown in table 5.1, this 93 percent white figure is actually quite close to the demographic background of the New York City Fire Department, where black firefighters constitute 2.7 percent and Hispanics constitute 3.2 percent of the force (Pitts 2002). It is, however, nowhere near the actual demographic composition of the general population, which consists of 35 percent white, 24.5 percent black, 27 percent Hispanic, 9.8 percent Asian American, and 0.2 percent Native American (New York City Department of City Planning 2010).

To have one white, one black, and one Hispanic fireman might be some-what close to the demographics of the general population. However, it speaks a lie to the largely failed efforts to desegregate the fire department. In a 1973 lawsuit, black and Hispanic plaintiffs won a Section 1981 and 1983 claim based on a violation of the equal protection clause of the Fourteenth Amendment against the New York City Fire Department, and the department was ordered to change its application procedures and examinations (*Vulcan Society* 1973a). At the time, racial minorities constituted 5 percent of the fire department and 30 percent of the general population (*Vulcan Society* 1973b, 1269). Nearly 30 years later, when 9/11 happened, the racial minority composition of the fire department had increased to only somewhere around 6–7 percent in a city that has become even more racially diverse (see table 5.2).

Unasked in the debate about the monument is how the racial composition of the fire department was achieved and maintained. The struggle over the racial composition of the men to be depicted in the monument echoes the struggle over the racial composition of the FDNY. The FDNY looked the way it did in 2001 because race had continued to be a factor in terms of hiring, promotion, and work environment. Also unasked is any question about the absence of Asian American firefighters. The debate about the monument and the attention it brought to the lack of diversity in the FDNY could have led to a shift in hiring practices. Instead, a case decided nearly ten years later in 2010 tries to fulfill the promise of the 1973 case when the Vulcan Society, a group of black firefighters, and the Hispanic Society, a group of Hispanic firefighters, won their discrimination claim against the City of New York. This case, too, would ignore Asian Americans.

Invisible to Law

Lawsuits involving firefighters have recently been in the news. Two reached the Supreme Court in 2009 and 2010 (*Ricci v. DeStefano* 2009; *Lewis v. City of Chicago* 2010), with more possibly on their way (*United States v. City of New York* 2010a; *Briscoe v. City of New Haven* 2010). In public debate and the legal opinions, whites, blacks, Hispanics, and their discrimination claims are explored, while Asian Americans are inconspicuously absent. I say inconspicuous because the absence of Asian Americans comes into view only to those who are looking for it. There is also a gendered absence (McGinley 2010), but that is not the subject of this inquiry.

The first of the recent cases to reach the U.S. Supreme Court is *Ricci v. DeStefano*. In June 2009, the Supreme Court handed down its decision in *Ricci*, a reverse discrimination claim brought against the City of New Haven, Connecticut, by a group of firefighters that included 17 whites and one Hispanic.

The facts arose as follows. In 2003, the New Haven Fire Department had a number of openings for promotion to lieutenant and captain. They administered a test that had a pass rate for African Americans and Hispanics that was far lower than it was for whites. When the city realized this, the city's Civil Service Board, an independent review board, which must vote to certify test results before the promotion process can continue, held hearings and ultimately refused to certify the test results. As a result, promotions were not given based on the test. A group of white firefighters and one Hispanic firefighter, who scored some of the highest results on the tests, filed suit against the city and various officials, claiming both Title VII and Equal Protection violations, as well as a conspiracy to violate their civil rights. After losing on summary judgment, the plaintiffs appealed and eventually ended up in the Supreme Court, with the high court reversing and granting summary judgment for the firefighters.

Missing from the public debate and opinion were Asian Americans. Of the more than 118 test takers in *Ricci*, not one was identified by the District Court as Asian American (*Ricci* 2006, 145). Perhaps this is not surprising given that of the 366 firefighters in the City of New Haven, there is only one Asian American (City of New Haven 2007). The Asian population in New Haven is around 4 percent (U.S. Census Bureau 2006a).

Asian Americans represent approximately 0.7 percent of all firefighters nationwide (Bureau of Labor Statistics 2009), far lower than their overall population numbers, 4.6 percent of the overall U.S. population, would suggest (U.S. Census Bureau 2009). This disparity is meaningful because

[i]t is appropriate to base expected hiring outcomes on local racial demographics because, "absent explanation, it is ordinarily to be expected that nondiscriminatory hiring practices will in time result in a work force more or less representative of the racial and ethnic composition of the population in the community from which employees are hired." (*United States v. City of New York* 2010a, 242 n.11 (quoting *Int'l Bhd. of Teamsters v. United States*, 431 U.S. 324, 340 n.20 (1977))

It remains, of course, to examine if there are other explanations.

The most recent case to reach the U.S. Supreme Court is *Lewis v. City of Chicago* (2010). It involved a challenge by the African-American Fire Fighters League of Chicago (the "League") and a class of African Americans who sued to challenge the hiring practices of the Chicago Fire Department following the administration of an entrance exam in 1995 for entry-level firefighters. The case, filed in September 1998, took five years and four months before a bench trial was held in January 2004, with a ruling in 2005 by Judge Joan Gottschall that the City of Chicago had discriminated against the plaintiffs (*Lewis* 2005). While the case was going on, the number of African Americans in the department declined from 22 percent to 18 percent (Dizikes 2010).

When asked about the decrease in the number of African American firefighters in the Chicago Fire Department, "[d]epartment officials denied that the agency's history had anything to do with current underrepresentation of African Americans. [Department spokesperson] Larry Langford said that, simply put, some people just don't want to become firefighters" (ibid.).

In Chicago, as reported in 2006, Native Americans and Asian Americans were aggregated for reporting purposes and together constituted approximately 1.5 percent of the Chicago Fire Department (Washburn 2006). The 2000 Census tells us that 4.7 percent of the residents of Chicago were Native American and Asian American (U.S. Census Bureau 2006b). If asked about the underrepresentation of Native Americans and Asian Americans, Langford would likely give the same reason that he gave for African American underrepresentation, that some people just don't want to become firefighters.

This response echoes a conclusion reached by Justice Sandra Day O'Connor in examining the constitutionality of a set-aside program for Minority Business Enterprises (MBEs). She found that in a city where the black population was approximately 50 percent, the extremely low percentage (0.67 percent) of contracts awarded to MBEs by the city of Richmond and the extremely low MBE membership in local and state contractors' associations need not be related to discrimination. Instead, the low numbers might just reflect that "Blacks may be disproportionately attracted to industries other than construction" (*City of Richmond v. J.A. Croson Co.* 1989, 503).

Langford and O'Connor's respective responses to the possibility of discrimination in fire departments and the construction industry do not examine the possibility and probability that applicant pools are affected by discrimination, as well as the perception of discrimination. In a society where discrimination remains very real, when individuals see fire departments and the construction trade filled with people who do not look like them, which instead are dominated by whites who have long held access to positions of privilege, it should not come as a surprise that someone's professional aspirations are impacted by what they see. Here, both law and culture play important roles.

Back to New York. In 2009 and 2010, Judge Nicholas Gaurafis made a sweeping set of findings that the City of New York had been guilty of disparate impact discrimination against black and Hispanic applicants and intentional discrimination against black applicants (*United States v. City of New York* 2009, 2010a). Disparate impact exists when an employment practice, neutral on its face, has a disparate impact on a protected group and where the employer is unable to demonstrate that the employment practice is justified as a business necessity. Judge Gaurafis held that the use and scoring of certain written exams had a discriminatory effect on certain minority applicants and failed to test for relevant job skills, and were therefore not justified as a business necessity (*United States v. City of New York* 2009). In a later opinion, he held that the use of such tests, in light of the history of FDNY's hiring practices over a 33 year period following the lapse of the injunction imposed as a result of the successful 1973 discrimination claim brought by individuals who were members of the Vulcan and Hispanic Societies, constituted a pattern or practice of intentional discrimination to exclude Blacks (*United States v. City of New York* 2010a, 263).

Asian Americans are absent from these discussions, except peripherally in an opinion clarifying the remedial scope of Judge Gaurafis's sweeping 2009 and 2010 findings of discrimination:

> The court has not considered or ruled on any evidence regarding other minority candidates. Because compliance relief should be tailored to the City's identified misconduct, the court declines to enforce any particular hiring measures with regard to Asian, Native American, or "other" minority candidates. (*United States v. City of New York* 2010b)

Judge Gaurafis cannot be faulted for not crafting a broader remedy to reach other groups beyond blacks and Hispanics. In order for a court to provide a remedy for an individual or group, that individual or group's claim must be presented appropriately before the court. This problem becomes especially acute for excluded groups when, as a result of litigation, a consent decree is negotiated by the parties whereby the parties agree on a remedial course of action to be taken under the supervision of the court.

The problem for excluded groups can be seen in an example involving the Los Angeles Police Department (LAPD). In the 1990s, the LAPD was under a court order to increase its representation of women, African Americans, and Hispanics. Asian Americans were not included in the consent decree.

However, Asian American civil rights groups that were interested in seeing the LAPD provide opportunities for Asian American applicants, as well as having a diverse police force that might engage in more responsive community policing, were afraid to sue to be included in this consent decree because of the result in *Martin v. Wilks*, in which the Supreme Court recognized a right to challenge as discriminatory a consent decree that orders an employer to hire minorities (1989). Asian Americans feared that if they sought to be included in the consent decree, the entire decree, which benefits other minorities, "could unravel" (U.S. Commission on Civil Rights 1992, 59 n.53).

Once these cases are set in motion, many of which are resolved through consent decrees, problems can arise for groups not included in the litigation or the consent decrees. There are opportunities to formally intervene in these lawsuits if a suitable intervening party can be found (Federal Rules of Civil Procedure 2009). But even when a suitable party exists or is found, the resources necessary to participate in litigation must be found. Even if a suitable party and resources exist, there remains the coalitional politics issue. Will the intervenor be seen as a welcome brother in the struggle to diversify the firehouse? Or will the intervenor be seen as a Johnny-come-lately who walks in late to reap the fruit of the decades-long effort waged by black and Hispanic firefighter groups? Or even worse, as a meddlesome intruder who jeopardizes this decades-long effort? How do we work together when the choice is often presented as a zero-sum game, where more for one group means less for another?

Perhaps those bringing lawsuits, especially when civil rights groups are involved or consulted, ought to consider the interests of those not at the table, and perhaps be encouraged to figure out a way to invite them to the table. Otherwise, as the recent litigation involving municipal fire departments demonstrates, the Asian American firefighter will remain invisible to the law.

Conclusion

I opened by telling the story of Merle Woo, who wrote eloquently about the way that Asian American men are the victims of racism and sexism. She also wrote about how she and her Asian American sisters supported the cause of Asian American men but found that Asian American men often failed to support the cause of Asian American women (Woo 1984). The men seemed blind to the operation of sexism, especially their own sexism, as it affected Asian American women (ibid.). Because the men were themselves victims of sexism, she expected better of them, which made the disappointment all the more bitter.

As we work to fulfill the promises of the civil rights movement and the long struggle to achieve a world where our opportunities are not bounded by the color of our skin, we cannot forget the larger call to justice. The goal is not to just create opportunities for black, Hispanic, and Asian American men to join firehouses and replicate the status quo, where a pathway for men of color to become accepted in the firehouse is to join in this cult of hyper-masculinity through heterosexual conquests, misogyny, and homophobia. Firefighters are heroes, but heroism is no excuse for this kind of behavior. If the price of admission to the firehouse is to engage in this kind of behavior, my hope is that Asian American men, themselves the victims of racism, sexism, and sometimes homophobia, will simply say no.

NOTES

I take my inspiration for this chapter from Paula J. Giddings, *When and Where I Enter: The Impact of Black Women on Race and Sex in America* (1984).

REFERENCES

Adams, Rachel, and David Savran. 2002. *The Masculinity Studies Reader.* Malden, MA: Blackwell.

Bartlett, Katharine T. 1990. Feminist Legal Methods. *Harvard Law Review* 103:829–88.

Boone, Joseph A., and Michael Cadden, eds. 1990. *Engendering Men: The Question of Male Feminist Criticism.* New York: Routledge.

Briscoe v. City of New Haven, 2010 WL 2794212 (D. Conn. 2010).

Bureau of Labor Statistics. 2009. *Employed Persons by Detailed Occupation, Sex, Race, and Hispanic or Latino Ethnicity*, http://www.bls.gov/cps/cpsaat11.pdf.

Chang, Robert S. 2003. (Racial) Profiles in Courage, or Can We Be Heroes, Too? *Albany Law Review* 66:349–71.

Chang, Robert S., and Neil Gotanda. 2007. Afterword: The Race Question in LatCrit Theory and Asian American Jurisprudence. *Nevada Law Journal* 7:1012–29.

City of New Haven. 2007. *State & Local Gov't Info. Report EEO-4.*

City of Richmond v. J. A. Croson Co., 488 U.S. 469 (1989).

Cooper, Frank R., and Ann C. McGinley, eds. 2012. *Masculinities and the Law: A Multidimensional Approach.* New York: New York University Press.

Dizikes, Cynthia. 2010. Black Chicago Firefighters Losing Ground. *Chicago Breaking News Center*, http://www.chicagobreakingnews.com/2010/03/black-chicago-firefighters-losing-ground.html, March 11.

Dreher, Rod. 2002. The Bravest Speak: Firemen on the Flag-Raising Statue That's Raising Racial Ire. *National Review Online*, http://old.nationalreview.com/dreher/dreher011602.shtml, Jan. 16.

Federal Rules of Civil Procedure. 2009. Rule 24.

Franklin, Thomas E. 2002. The After-Life of a Photo That Touched a Nation. *Columbia Journalism Review* 40(6):64–65.

Gardiner, Judith Kegan, ed. 2002. *Masculinities Studies and Feminist Theory: New Directions.* New York: Columbia University Press.

Giddings, Paula J. 1984. *When and Where I Enter: The Impact of Black Women on Race and Sex in America*. New York: William Morrow.

Gotanda, Neil. 1985. "Other Non-Whites" in American Legal History, A Review of *Justice at War*. Review of *Justice at War*, by Peter Irons. *Columbia Law Review* 85:1186–92.

Heath, Stephen. 1987. Male Feminism. In *Men in Feminism*, edited by Alice Jardine and Paul Smith. New York: Routledge, 1–32.

Immigration Act of 1924, ch. 190, 43 Stat. 153 §13(c).

Leary, Denis, and Peter Tolan. 2004. *Rescue Me*. FX Network.

Leo, John. 2002. Color Me Confounded. *U.S. News and World Report*, January 28–February 4, 31.

Lewis v. City of Chicago, 130 S. Ct. 2191 (2010).

Lewis v. City of Chicago, 2005 WL 693618 (N.D. Ill. 2005).

Martin v. Wilks, 490 U.S. 755 (1989).

McGinley, Ann C. 2010. *Ricci v. DeStefano*: A Masculinities Theory Analysis. *Harvard Journal of Gender and Law* 33:581–623.

Newton, Judith. 2002. Masculinities Studies: The Longed for Profeminist Movement for Academic Men? In *Masculinities Studies and Feminist Theory: New Directions*, edited by Judith Kegan Gardiner. New York: Columbia University Press, 176–92.

New York City Department of City Planning. 2010. *Population by Mutually Exclusive Race and Hispanic Origin, New York City and Boroughs, 1990 & 2000*, http://www.nyc.gov/html/dcp/pdf/census/pl3a.pdf.

Ozawa v. United States, 260 U.S. 178 (1922).

Pitts, Leonard. 2002. Politically Correct Version of Sept. 11 Insults Firefighters. *Los Angeles Business Journal*, January 28.

Pollack, Sydney. 1982. *Tootsie*. Columbia Pictures Corporation.

Ricci v. DeStefano, 129 S. Ct. 2658 (2009).

Ricci v. DeStefano, 554 F. Supp. 2d 142 (D. Conn. 2006).

Shister, Gail. 2007. On *Rescue Me*, Rebaptism by Fire. *Philadelphia Inquirer*, June 12. Available at http://www.philly.com/inquirer/columnists/gail_shister/20070612_On_Rescue_Me__rebaptism_by_fire.html.

Showalter, Elaine. 1990. Critical Cross-Dressing: Male Feminists and the Woman of the Year. In *Raritan Reading*, edited by Richard Poirier. New Brunswick, NJ: Rutgers University Press, 364–81.

Sturken, Marita. 1997. *Tangled Memories: The Vietnam War, the AIDS Epidemic, and the Politics of Remembering*. Berkeley: University of California Press.

United States v. City of New York, 683 F. Supp. 2d 225 (E.D. N.Y., 2010a).

United States v. City of New York, 2010 WL 3709350 (E.D. N.Y., 2010b).

United States v. City of New York, 637 F. Supp. 2d 77 (E.D. N.Y., 2009).

United States v. Thind, 261 U.S. 204 (1923).

U.S. Census Bureau. 2009. *State & County QuickFacts, USA*, http://quickfacts.census.gov/qfd/states/00000.html.

U.S. Census Bureau. 2006a. *State & County QuickFacts, New Haven, Conn.*, http://quickfacts.census.gov/qfd/states/09/0952000.html.

U.S. Census Bureau. 2006b. *State & County QuickFacts, Chicago, Ill.*, http://quickfacts.census.gov/qfd/states/17/1714000.html.

U.S. Commission on Civil Rights. 1992. *Civil Rights Issues Facing Asian Americans in the 1990s*. Washington, DC: U.S. Commission on Civil Rights.

Vulcan Society of the New York City Fire Department, Inc. v. Civil Service Commission, 490 F.2d 387 (2d Cir. 1973a).

Vulcan Society of the New York City Fire Department, Inc. v. Civil Service Commission, 360 F. Supp. 1265 (S.D. N.Y. 1973b).

Washburn, Gary. 2006. Most Firefighter Applicants Are White. *Chicago Tribune*, Sept. 26.

Woo, Merle. 1984. Letter to Ma. In *This Bridge Called My Back: Writings by Radical Women of Color*, edited by Cherrie Moraga and Gloria Anzaldua. New York: Kitchen Table: Women of Color Press, 140–47.

6

Manliness's Paradox

JOHN M. KANG

You may be born male, but that doesn't make you manly. Maleness is the random result of biology, but manliness is the work product of vigorous self-fashioning: nature makes you male; to become manly, you must strive. Such is at any rate a familiar story, and one that I will complicate in this Chapter (Gilmore 1990; Goldstein 2006).

What does manliness mean, though? At its heart, it is courage. So tangled is the connection between manliness and courage that male body parts, or at least their vulgarisms, serve as emblems of courage. No less venerable a source than the *Oxford English Dictionary* unabashedly defines "ballsy" as "[c]ourageous, plucky; determined, spirited" (Simpson and Weiner, 913). Female body parts, on the other hand, do not function as honorifics; they're insults. You could pay homage, albeit a barbed one, to a woman's courage by remarking that she has some tough balls, but you could not say idiomatically that a man demonstrated valor by being a brave pussy. For to call a man a pussy is to upbraid him—to verbally un-man him—as a coward. These references, I admit, are bawdy and contemporary, but they are heirs to solemn and ancient etymologies that literally equate the condition of being a man with courage. In Greek, *andreia* signifies man but also courage (Miller 2000, 233). In Hebrew, the "root G-B(V)-R (man) yields GEV(B)URA (courage)" (ibid.). Latin derives "virtus," meaning courage, strength, and forcefulness, from "vir" which means man (ibid.).

This is not to imply that all men behave courageously or that a given man can behave courageously all of the time. Nor do I wish to insinuate that all men endeavor to hold themselves to a standard of valor. I do mean to suggest that, as a matter of cultural principle, failure to comport with courage will tend to render men gender failures. Men are not any more likely than women to possess courage but women, according to societal convention, may be absent valor and still retain their gendered virtues and charms (Miller 2000, 234). If men falter in the face of danger, they are emasculated (ibid.).

Put aside for now whether it is morally just to apply this vaunted standard to men (and its demeaning corollary to women). Observe instead how this standard gives men a breathless choice: either act bravely as your gender requires of you or suffer the consequences of being unmanned. It is vital to understand here that what often motivates a man to behave courageously is the gripping fear—and hence, perhaps a cowardice all its own—that failure to do something that bears the semblance of courage would preempt or undermine his manhood. As such, the line between having, if you will pardon my reversion to vulgarity, tough balls or being a soft pussy is unnervingly thin.

Actually, the metaphor of a line is not especially apt. Better is the idea of paradox: that which passes for manliness in courage is often constituted in part by what conventionally is derided as a feminine vice in cowardice. I explore this paradox in this chapter, offering a dollop of illustrations along the way. Mine is essentially a work of description and I don't have any explicit political axe to grind. If I am pressed to proffer one, I suppose it is to challenge obliquely a well-trod assumption that men enjoy a lavish autonomy denied women. I will suggest that being a man can be, in its own fashion, appallingly oppressive.

The Traditional Account of Manly Courage

That men are supposed to be courageous is a traditional and perhaps boring supposition, but what is curious is how often this view is treated as an axiom of truth, without any explanation, by those in positions of legal authority. Begin with an old and now infamous Supreme Court case, *Bradwell v. Illinois*. Back in 1872, Justice Bradley of the U.S. Supreme Court wrote a concurring opinion, upholding an Illinois law that denied women the right to practice law (*Bradwell v. Illinois* 1872). He stated, "Man is, or should be, woman's protector and defender. The natural and proper timidity and delicacy which belongs to the female sex evidently unfits it for many of the occupations of civil life" (ibid. 141). There is no explanation for why a man is a woman's protector and defender, only that he "is, or should be."

This practice of merely asserting gender differences found expression in another Supreme Court case, this time from 1927. In arguably the most celebrated justification by a judge for free speech, Justice Brandeis announced in *Whitney v. California*: "[The Founding Fathers] valued liberty both as an end and as a means. They believed liberty to be the secret of happiness and courage to be the secret of liberty" (*Whitney v. California* 1927, 375). The quote is harmlessly gender-neutral, but Justice Brandeis subsequently locates courage in the realm of manliness. He states:

> Fear of serious injury cannot alone justify suppression of free speech and assembly. Men feared witches and burnt women. It is the function of speech to free men from the bondage of irrational fears. (ibid. 376)

In Justice Brandeis's imagination, women exist as objects to be acted upon by men, and men are the ones who must summon the courage to save women from the violent fears of men themselves.

Lest you believe such thinking to be a late nineteenth- and early twentieth-century anachronism, read Justice Scalia's dissenting opinion in *United States v. Virginia*. A majority of the justices in *Virginia* struck down as unconstitutional a policy that forbade women from applying to the all-male Virginia Military Institute (VMI). An indignant Justice Scalia argued that the Court had in effect destroyed an institution dedicated to the cultivation of male courage (*United States v. Virginia* 1996, 601). VMI, Justice Scalia wrote, required its first-year cadets to carry at all times a pamphlet titled "The Code of a Gentleman" (ibid.). Among other things, the Code declared:

> The honor of a gentleman demands the inviolability of his word. . . . He is the descendant of the knight, the crusader; he is the defender of the defenseless and the champion of justice . . . or he is not a Gentleman. (ibid. 602) (second ellipsis in original)

To the extent the pamphlet represents a serious commitment, VMI is more than a military academy bent on producing soldiers who will obey orders. It is rather a sanctum where young men learn to fulfill their gendered obligations, as gentlemen who will fight, and if necessary, die. Justice Scalia, however, did not explain why women cadets could not possess this same martial valor.

This absence of explanation is a peculiar accoutrement of some of the most prominent instances of gender discrimination today. In 1992, a House Subcommittee held hearings about the military's exclusion of women soldiers from ground combat, a policy that has never been legally overturned (U.S. Congress 1992). General Merrill McPeak, Chief of Staff of the U.S. Air Force, testified before the subcommittee that he "couldn't think of a logical reason . . . for defending a policy of excluding women from combat assignments" (ibid. 78). That he couldn't think of a logical reason didn't stop the general from stating forcefully that "[c]ombat is about killing people . . . even though logic tells us that women can do that as well as men, I have a very traditional attitude about wives and mothers and daughters being ordered to kill people" (ibid.). Notice how General McPeak self-consciously contrasts "logic" with a "very traditional attitude." The former presumably rests on evidence and reflection, the latter's legitimacy derives mostly from having been accepted, long ago, without question. General McPeak doesn't exactly know why he believes that men, and not women, have—or should be presumed to have—the courage necessary to kill; he just *knows*.

Another person before the subcommittee, General Carl Mundy, Commandant of Marines, echoed General McPeak's objections from tradition. "[W]hen you get right down to it, as General McPeak just said, 'combat' is killing," General Mundy announced (ibid. 79). Combat, General Mundy continued, is sometimes "done with your hands. It is done with a shovel. It is done at close range. It is not good. It is debasing" (ibid.). And "[i]t is something that I would not want to see women involved in and for which I do not believe—and I am grateful that this is my perception—that women are suited to do" (ibid.). Here is the same elliptical argument that had been offered by General McPeak: men have more courage than women to kill, or at least that is what I believe, thank goodness.

These bromides to manly courage mostly serve to massage our intuitions. If we really want to understand manliness as courage, we need a more complicated account. I turn therefore in the next section to the narratives of those who are most expected to exemplify so-called manly courage on a daily basis: soldiers in combat (Goldstein 2006; Miller 2000).

What the Soldiers Believed

Courage is theoretically necessary to endure financial and emotional harm or to accomplish feats inviting such harm, but the courage that passes for manly courage paradigmatically involves physical risk (Goldstein 2006; Miller 2000; Gilmore 1990). Thus, notwithstanding your foolhardiness, you were said to have possessed manly courage when you took up your friend's dare and wrestled an adult alligator in Ft. Lauderdale or when you, affronted by some cutting slight about your manhood, decided to fight that hulking loudmouth at the bar in Key West.

If the quintessential virtue of manliness is physical courage, as I have claimed, then soldiers in combat are best suited to afford testimony about its meaning (Holmes 1985; Goldstein 2006). What they reveal is an uncannily paradoxical view of manliness where courage, the defining male virtue, is often impelled by the feminine vice of cowardice. Let us begin by comparing the shopworn narratives of male valor—delivered by Generals McPeak and Mundy and Justices Scalia and Brandeis—with the words of the soldiers themselves. Few are as good as those of the novelist and Vietnam veteran Tim O'Brien. Drafted into the war, young O'Brien was terrified of the prospect of violent death. He admits:

> [A]t the very center [of my objection to participation in the war], was the raw fact of terror. I did not want to die . . . certainly not then, not there. . . . Driving up Main Street, past the courthouse and the Ben Franklin store, I sometimes felt the fear spreading inside me like weeds. I imagined myself dead. (O'Brien 1990, 44)

Yet O'Brien could not will himself to flee to Canada, an eight-hour drive from his small hometown in Minnesota (ibid.). What held him fast was a fear even greater than death. He says:

> I feared the war, yes, but I also feared exile. I was afraid of walking away from my own life, my friends and my family, my whole history, everything that mattered to me. I feared losing the respect of my parents. I feared the law. I feared ridicule and censure. (ibid. 44–45)

O'Brien continues:

> My hometown was a conservative little spot on the prairie, a place where tradition counted, and it was easy to imagine people sitting around a table down at the old Gobbler Café on Main Street, coffee cups poised, the conversation slowly zeroing in on the young O'Brien kid, how the damned sissy had taken off for Canada. (ibid. 45)

Here was a picture of a young man who was willing to commit conventionally brave deeds, to kill and die, for reasons that were utterly craven. "I would go to the war—I would kill and maybe die—because I was embarrassed not to" (ibid. 59). For O'Brien, "[t]hat old image of myself as a hero, as a man of . . . courage, all that was just a threadbare pipe dream" (ibid. 57).

Because he was too afraid, O'Brien headed to Vietnam and to potential death. Upon arrival, he and his friend Erik, both college graduates, endured the paradox of manly courage. Perhaps tired of the superficial and profane chatter of their fellow draftees, O'Brien and Erik sat behind the barracks and waxed philosophic about the peculiarities of life during war (O'Brien 1999, 47). A suspicious Sergeant Blyton accosted the two. "'A couple of college pussies. . . . Out behind them barracks hiding from everyone and making some love, huh?'" (ibid.). The sergeant confronted Erik:

> You're a pussy, huh? You afraid to be in the war, a goddamn pussy, a goddamn lezzie? You know what we do with pussies, huh? We fuck 'em. In the army we just fuck 'em and straighten 'em out. You two college pussies out there hidin' and sneakin' a little pussy. Maybe I'll just stick you two puss in the same bunk tonight, let you get plenty of pussy so tomorrow you can't piss. (ibid.)

Look at the stunning irony in this passage. On the surface, Sergeant Blyton appears to want to toughen up the college wimps but, upon closer inspection, O'Brien and Erik are in fact being socialized to become magnificent cowards. I have called courage the supreme male virtue, but the sergeant has no interest in introducing his tender draftees into the virtue's sublime rewards. Rather, Sergeant Blyton wishes to bluntly intimidate O'Brien and Erik into abhorring the dread of battle. In other words, he wants for the college boys to fear the hurtful stigma of being a pussy, to fear it so much that they would recoil against *that* fear rather than the fear of violent death.

Once deployed, the fear of showing fear was a partial underwriter for what passed for courage among the members of O'Brien's battalion. He recounts that:

> [The soldiers] carried the soldier's greatest fear, which was the fear of blushing. Men killed, and died, because they were embarrassed not to. It was what had brought them to the war in the first place, nothing positive, no dreams of glory or honor, just to avoid the blush of dishonor. They died so as not to die of embarrassment. (O'Brien 1990, 21)

"It was not courage," O'Brien added, "the object was not valor." (ibid. 22) "Rather, they were too frightened to be cowards" (ibid.).

Sometimes, the soldiers could not maintain the equipoise between their private cowardice and the performative trappings of courage. "Now and then," O'Brien explained of his battalion:

> they squealed or wanted to squeal but couldn't when they twitched and made moaning sounds and covered their heads and said Dear Jesus and flopped around on the earth and fired their weapons blindly and cringed and sobbed and begged for the noise to stop and went wild and made stupid promises to themselves and to God and to their mothers and fathers, hoping not to die. (ibid. 19)

"In different ways," O'Brien added, "it happened to all of them" (ibid.). Afterward, when the firing ended, "they would blink and peek up. They would touch their bodies, feeling shame, then quickly hiding it" (ibid.).

Whereas O'Brien loathed being drafted, Philip Caputo eagerly enlisted in the marines during the Vietnam War. Like O'Brien, however, Caputo also described courage in paradoxical terms that complicated the meaning of manliness. Caputo's drill instructor called him and the other enlistees "scumbags," "shitheads," and, of course, "girls" (Caputo 1977, 9). A standard story is that the harsh drilling was meant to weed out the manly, the brave from the "unsats"—the unsatisfactory—who were weak and lacking courage (ibid.). Yet, paradoxically, the drilling was also meant "to destroy each man's sense of self-worth, to make him feel worthless" (ibid. 10). The only way that a man could feel worthy was by "prov[ing] himself equal to the Corps' exacting standards" (ibid.). Caputo elaborated:

> That awful word—unsat—haunted me. I was more afraid of it than I was of Sergeant McClellan. Nothing he could do could be as bad as having to return home and admit to my family that I had failed. (ibid.)

He continued:

> It was not their criticism I dreaded, but the emasculating affection and understanding they would be sure to show me. I could hear my mother saying, "That's all right, son. You didn't belong in the Marines but here with us. It's good to have you back. Your father needs help with the lawn." (ibid.)

Caputo followed this narrative with a confession that highlighted the underlying cowardice that propels courage. "I was so terrified of being found wanting that I even avoided getting near the candidates who were borderline cases—the 'marginals'" (ibid.).

The same paradoxical relationship where manly courage was crucially underwritten by feminine cowardice prior to combat also manifested itself for Caputo during combat. After passing training, Caputo described his platoon leader who was able to marshal "courage" in his soldiers by terrifying them. William Campbell—Wild Bill to his friends—the platoon leader, had a "conviction, and he was probably right, that discipline in a regular army is ultimately based on fear" (ibid. 29). Specifically, "it was a fear not of military law, but of him" (ibid.). The soldiers "had been convinced that risking the possible consequences of obeying an order was preferable to Wild Bill's wrath, the certain consequence of disobeying it" (ibid.).

A testament to its power, manly courage as paradox found iteration many years before the Vietnam War, by those in the American Civil War. The Princeton historian James McPherson remarks that while Civil War soldiers wrote "much about *courage*," they "wrote even more about cowardice—the mark of dishonor" (1997, 77). So a Civil War veteran penned a novel containing a suggestive scene (ibid.). In the novel, a second lieutenant told a group of women who praised manly courage, "We are as much afraid as you are, only we are more afraid to show it" (ibid.). Real life examples are evocative, too. A South Carolina planter told his daughter: "The honor of our family is involved. . . . A man who will not offer up his life . . . does dishonor to his wife and children" (ibid. 25). An Arkansas farmer informed his wife, "I would feel that my children would be ashamed of me when in after times this war is spoken & I should not have figured in it" (ibid. 24). And at 42 and perhaps beyond the age where he would be physically useful, a Tennessee planter "admonished his wife" that "[n]o man now has a right to stay at home" (ibid.). After his first battle, a private in the Ohio 39th wrote, "I cannot boast of much pluck . . . but I have got my full share of pride and could die before I could disgrace the name I bear" (ibid. 77). A Texas infantryman wrote his wife in 1863 that if he ever showed "the white feather" in battle, "I hope that some friend will immediately shoot me so that the disgrace shall not attach either to my wife or children" (ibid.).

American and British troops in the First and Second World Wars also attested to how courage, or its appearance, was sustained by a potent fear. The American Robert Crisp, who was awarded both the Distinguished Service Order and Military Cross, described his actions as follows:

It was some months and only a few more bullets and shells later that I knew my courage for what it was—a reaction to the shame I felt at being

afraid, a manifestation of an ingrown complex which survived in a reputation for a sort of recklessness which, somehow or other, I had to sustain and exhibit until some more genuine and significant emotion took its
place. (Crisp 1960, 12)

A Captain J.E.H. Neville similarly confessed to his father in January 1917:
"The only thing I'm not certain about is whether I may get the wind up and
show it. I'm afraid of being afraid" (Holmes 1985, 141). Geoffrey Stavert, an
artillery officer in Tunisia from 1942–43, wrote that his "main hope . . . was
not to do anything which would let myself or my family down, and to put
up a good appearance in front of the troops" (ibid. 142). Charles McDonald
confided, "I must not appear afraid. . . . I must give the men confidence in me
despite the fact that they know I'm inexperienced" (ibid.). Raleigh Trevelyan
wrote, after the war:

I remember father saying on embarkation leave that the worst part of battle
was wondering how you were going to behave in front of other people. . . .
I don't think even now I really fear death, or even the process of dying. It
is only the thought of whether or not I shall acquit myself honourably that
obsesses me. (ibid.)

The historian John Ellis observed of his research on soldiers during
World War II that "the fear of showing fear was often more powerful than
the fear of death itself" (1991, 106). And another historian, Richard Holmes,
also remarked of his scholarship about World Wars I and II that "[m]ost
of the soldiers I interviewed acknowledged that they were very frightened
indeed before the battled started, and for many of them the greatest fear
was not of being killed or wounded, but of 'bottling out,' or showing cowardice" (1985, 142).

Conclusion

Not every man cares about being manly, nor does every man who wishes
to be manly believe that he is so, at least not all of the time. But every man
knows that he lives in a world where he is expected to adhere to an ideal of
manliness in which courage is the foremost virtue. I have suggested, however, that there is a paradox that underlies and complicates this expectation.
Men often behave with manifest valor because they are terrified of seeming
afraid. Cowardice, a feminine vice, thus often tends to propel the manly virtue of courage.

NOTES

I am grateful for the comments and encouragement of Ann C. McGinley. Parts of this chapter are derived from John M. Kang, The Burdens of Manliness, 33 *Harvard Journal of Law and Gender* 477 (2010).

REFERENCES

Bradwell v. Illinois, 83 U.S. 130 (1872).

Caputo, Philip. 1977. *A Rumor of War*. New York: Holt, Rinehart and Winston.

Crisp, Robert. 1960. *The Gods Were Neutral*. London: Frederick Muller.

Ellis, John. 1991. *On the Front Lines: The Experience of War through the Eyes of the Allied Soldiers in World War II*. Hoboken, NJ: Wiley.

Gilmore, David D. 1990. *Manhood in the Making: Cultural Conceptions of Masculinity*. New Haven, CT: Yale University Press.

Goldstein, Joshua S. 2006. *War and Gender*. New York: Cambridge University Press.

Holmes, Richard. 1985. *Acts of War: The Behavior of Men in Battle*. New York: Free Press.

McPherson, James M. 1997. *For Cause and Comrades: Why Men Fought in the Civil War*. New York: Oxford University Press.

Miller, William Ian. 2000. *The Mystery of Courage*. Cambridge, MA: Harvard University Press.

O'Brien, Tim. 1999. *If I Die in a Combat Zone: Box Me Up and Ship Me Home*. New York: Broadway Books.

———. 1990. *The Things They Carried*. New York: Broadway Books.

Simpson, John A., and Edmund S. C. Weiner. 1989. *Oxford English Dictionary*. 2d ed. Vol. 1. Oxford: Oxford University Press.

United States v. Virginia, 518 U.S. 515 (1996).

U.S. Congress. House. Committee on Armed Services. 1992. *Gender Discrimination in the Military: Hearings before the Subcommittee on Military Personnel and Compensation and the Defense Policy Panel*. 102d Cong., 2d sess., July 29 and 30.

Whitney v. California, 274 U.S. 357 (1927).

7

Border-Crossing Stories and Masculinities

LETICIA M. SAUCEDO

Narratives in Action: The Construction Worker Project

Immigration law, increasingly restrictive and punitive in its application to border crossers, is believed to have a deep effect on behavioral responses of migrants and on migration patterns into the United States. Policymakers expect that if immigration policy becomes more restrictive, migrants will stop coming (Hanson 2007; Espenshade 1994). Indeed, migration does slow down at times (Hanson 2007; Passel and Cohn 2010). Interestingly, however, the migration pattern does not change much over time (Durand, Massey, and Parrado 1999; Espenshade 1994; Donato, Durand, and Massey 1992). In other words, no matter how restrictive immigration policy becomes, it has thus far failed to stop the circular migration pattern between Mexico and the United States.

In 2008, sociologist M. Cristina Morales and I visited Hidalgo, Mexico, the sending state of many of the workers in residential construction in Las Vegas, Nevada. This trip and the interviews we conducted were part of a larger project involving approximately 100 interviews with male and female workers who discussed with us their work conditions, their migration patterns, and their involvement in organizing or grievance efforts in U.S. workplaces (Saucedo and Morales 2010). In Hidalgo, Mexico, we interviewed 32 male migrants who had worked in the United States and who had returned to their hometowns. Among the topics of conversation with these workers were discussions about their own migration and border-crossing stories. By focusing on their border-crossing stories, this chapter explores the behavioral responses of border-crossing migrants between the United States and Mexico to restrictive immigration measures and to economic and social conditions. The stories explain the migration pattern and the reasons for it, and correspondingly, the reasons that individual immigrants journey across the border.

Border-crossing stories imbue migrants with decidedly masculine characteristics, in keeping with a tradition of mostly male migration to the United States since the implementation of the Bracero Program in the 1940s (Durand, Massey, and Zenteno 2001; Broughton 2008; Ngai 2004). The Bracero Program, the early version of a government-sponsored guest worker program, limited migration to those who could work in traditionally male occupations like farmwork (Ngai 2004). The Bracero Program spawned a set of narratives that characterized northward migration as a masculine activity (Schmidt Camacho 2008). That is still the case now. Today's narratives demonstrate that restricting entry through immigration law does not necessarily stop the immigration flow, or even change individual behavior; instead, migrants perpetuate stories rooted in masculinity that allow them to take and endure increasingly greater risks resulting from border restrictions.

The dynamic between immigration restrictions and migrant masculinities narratives raises important questions about the efficacy of a border policy that emphasizes strong enforcement. Ultimately, the border-crossing narratives illustrate a fundamental miscalculation of restrictive immigration policy, namely that more restrictive immigration laws will change human behavior. Restrictions do not exist in a vacuum and they do not alter human individual behavior in the context of historical, dynamic, collective movement. The paradigm of the rational actor, responding to legal cues, simply does not operate in this context.

The narratives meet at the intersection of immigration and employment, signaling the importance of considering the effects of law in a multidimensional manner, so that the exploitation particular to migrants is more effectively addressed. The stories I review here, and their incorporation of masculinity norms, have powerful implications for policymakers and legal actors. They have a powerful effect on movement across the border, whether or not immigration restrictions are in place.

The Current Border-Crossing Landscape

The 9/11 terrorist attacks brought changes to the legacy of Immigration and Naturalization Service (INS) and introduced security-related rationales for stricter border enforcement (USA PATRIOT Act 2001). The Homeland Security Act of 2002 reorganized immigration agencies, moved them into the newly created Department of Homeland Security (DHS), and created two separate agencies: Immigration and Customs Enforcement (ICE) and the U.S. Citizenship and Immigration Services (USCIS). This change created its own set of immigration restrictions, namely a greater emphasis on border control. The Secure Fence Act of 2006 authorized the construction of a border wall across the southwestern states bordering Mexico. A virtual wall, in the form of an electronic surveillance system, was also authorized by the Act. The federal government is currently experimenting with unmanned aerial vehicles to monitor border activity (Haddal and Gertler 2010).

The calls for increased border enforcement are ever growing. Every day, proponents of border control seek even more restrictive changes to federal immigration enforcement initiatives,[1] or to state law,[2] or even to the Constitution,[3] all in the name of curbing current and future immigration flows from the south.

The history of immigration law demonstrates a constant call for restrictive border policies. In response, in the migrant stories of today, we hear tales of persistence, endurance, risk, and danger, all of which have masculinities underpinnings and all of which animate migrants' self-perceptions as noble, hardworking, heroic actors in the migration stream.

The increasingly restrictive direction of immigration law in the United States has had some effect on the border-crossing experience. It has made it that much more fraught with danger and uncertainty. The narratives provide strong and appealing responses to the economic, political, and social turns in the United States. In very recent times, the specter of mass killings of border crossers, exploitation through human trafficking, and increasingly repressive and militaristic border security on both sides of the border loom large in the imagination of the migrant population (Amnesty International 2010; Ellingwood 2010). The Amnesty report described death as one of the many dangers facing migrants from all over Central and South America. It also documented incidents of kidnapping, threats, and assaults by private parties, as well as incidents of abuse by law enforcement authorities, including extortion and excessive force (Amnesty International 2010).

These dangers are incorporated into the stories of those who either seek to cross into the United States or who have returned to Mexico and are waiting for an opportunity to return to the states.

Masculinities Narratives: Endurance, Persistence, Family Provider, Family Order

The risks of death, trafficking, injury, capture and detention, and illness, and the high monetary and emotional costs of repeated crossing attempts, elicit border-crossing stories unique to the current social and economic conditions on both sides of the border. There are three main narratives that migrants use to describe border crossing and their motivations for it. Each of the narratives emphasizes the masculine character of the individual border crossers and their experiences. I term them the endurance, the family provider, and the family order narratives. The endurance narrative includes in its story a matter-of-fact bravery in enduring the risk and danger involved in border crossing. Persistence required is part of the narrative. The family provider narrative identifies the underlying rationale for border crossing, namely the need to earn money. The family order narrative, in turn, maintains the centrality of the migrant in the family as the head of household and keeper of moral values, discipline, and male authority. This story explains the motivation for circular migration. Migrants perceive they are needed at home to restore order so they make the periodic trek back home to reclaim their role in the household structure and to re-establish proper family relationships despite the risks and costs. Masculinities stories and norms perpetuate the border-crossing pattern, even as crossing becomes more risky and dangerous.

The masculinities narratives we observed are fluid responses to the dynamic conditions that change daily and that continue to make border crossing more or less dangerous, depending on the latest pressures from either the Mexican or the U.S. side of the border. They are the product of men negotiating their own identities despite the obstacles, one of which is the increasingly restrictive nature of immigration law. Other obstacles that the men identified included the economic bust in the United States that caused many of them to lose jobs, and the increasing violence along the border. Because the obstacles themselves change, the narratives are fluid. Often, migrants would start with one set of narratives and blend in elements of one or more of the other narratives as they constructed their stories explaining how they crossed, why they left, and why they returned to Mexico, as well as whether they would make the trek across the border again.

Endurance of Risk and Danger/Persistence

Endurance of risk and danger is a classic, almost essentialist masculine characteristic (Connell 2005). Acting in the face of risk makes one courageous and able to react in masculine ways, according to the theory (Kang 2010). It was a major theme among the workers we interviewed. Over and over again, we heard about how risky and dangerous the journey across the border had become. The narratives portray the migrants as brave, noble, and fearless, all characteristics perceived as necessary for survival abroad. After all, someone who can endure the dangers and risks of the border can make it in the underground world that undocumented migrants inhabit in the United States. And so, the stories incorporate men summoning up the courage to face the dangers, one way or another:

> If you've made the decision to cross, you can do it. It's just a matter of not being afraid and doing your best to cross. Because if you're afraid to go or being afraid to come back then there's no point in coming back. It's when you're indecisive, that something happens there on the border or, something bad happens. But if you're sure that you're going to arrive where you're going, then you'll get there. (Lorenzo)[4]

The descriptions of the dangers make a virtue out of being able to endure the harshness of the crossing:

> The crossing is a bit hard . . . at the same time you take the risk and go. Just as there are bad people, there are also good people. It's things you don't expect, the bad things, but they can happen to anybody. (Julio)

Within the narrative, the migrant takes on heroic qualities simply by accepting the risk:

> The Mexican is so heroic that they don't care if they're dying, or maybe of 10 that are dying, one gets to cross. They think "Well maybe the one who gets to cross will be me. I'll take the risk. I have to cross." (Juan Diego)

The description of the border crosser as Mexican adds a racialized dimension to the already masculine qualities of the migrant. The migrants perceive themselves as bravely enduring the risks of death or injury from lawlessness on the Mexican side of the border and uninhibited by the law enforcement authorities on the U.S. side. Many of the stories incorporate firsthand accounts of facing and standing up to risks and dangers. One particularly poignant story included both the masculinity norm of fearlessness and the noble one of standing up for the morally correct position even in the face of seemingly arbitrary power:

> The first time I left, in July of 2005, Immigration caught me near Las Cruces. So they caught me, not just me—there were a lot of us. And they returned us in their car. We got in their car, and we passed a bridge, and I don't know if they [Immigration] knew or not, but it was downhill and they were going really fast on the bridge. And a person who was in the back of the car where there were two tires, this person was leaning on the tires faced-down, and when the car jumped on the bridge, then he hit himself in the face and was unconscious. So I told Immigration to be careful and to be careful with the person who was hurt. And he told me to shut my mouth. I told him, "No. I won't shut my mouth. I know I'm an illegal immigrant, but what happened to my *paisano*, my friend, my brother, I also have a right to look out for him." There was only foam coming out of his mouth, he couldn't speak anymore. And more immigration officials arrived, about 6 or 7 cars. And the ambulance arrived, but they didn't give him any medication at all. No. They just rubbed him a little and they said, "take him away." And they took us to Santa Rosa, and they held us there. (Raul)

The narratives incorporate stories repeated from others about the specific dangers on the border, as well as stories about the reputations of traffickers and the border patrol on either side. The stories are not meant to counsel others to stay in Mexico. Instead, they offer guidance about what to expect at the border. Interestingly, instead of resulting in cautionary tales against crossing, the experiences of others produce parables designed to help others negotiate the dangers of crossing. One migrant described the danger and how to avoid it:

> The danger begins when one gets to the border. One has to see who, or which coyote they're going to hire to cross because not all of them tell the truth. So the important thing is not to carry a lot of money in your pockets and not to say who is the one who is going to pay over there. It's not good to pay for the crossing on the border but instead to look for a family member in the United States who can lend you the money, but you shouldn't

say who it is, until you're in the United States. Then you can say, "I'm going to call my family so that they can pay you." But before then, you shouldn't say who's going to pay because if not, there are people who say, "I'll cross you over. Tell me who's going to pay." And that person isn't going to cross us over; they're just going to call your family and say, "You know what? I have your relative. We already crossed. Pay me," even though we may still be on this side. That's one of the dangers. (Antonio)

Others warned of thieves and robbers when they retold stories about the misfortunes of others as moral lessons about what crossers should be ready to endure:

So in the Mexican desert there are thieves. They take your good shoes, if you have any, good clothes, jackets. They take your wallet. That's before reaching the border. Once you cross into the U.S. side, if you run into *migra*,[5] well you no longer have anything, not a jacket or a wallet. I know there's a part where there are Mexicans who steal from other Mexicans. (Moises)

Obstacles such as fences, walls, and the desert are some of the expected physical barriers facing migrants. The interviewees see themselves as accepting these dangers as part of the package of crossing the border, even as it becomes more difficult:

They make it harder and harder, more border patrol, more walls, so you think twice about going . . . they began to put fences on the parts of the border where more people crossed, right. That's why one has to look for the entry to be able to go over. But it keeps getting closed off more and more, so those are the obstacles that one thinks about when wanting to go back to the United States. (Mateo)

It's tough to cross. You risk a lot, well, your life, because you have to walk for two nights and rest one day. And there are people who can't take the walking and they faint from not drinking water or for not eating. Or because they don't like to walk far and they get tired and they don't have the resources to cross, and they're left there. You do suffer. . . . It's very difficult. (Mateo)

Other dangers include the risk of being caught and deported by the U.S. Border Patrol, or of being mistreated or detained:

You hear about it, for example, when you know a friend is going over there and all of a sudden he lands there, you find out he is incarcerated for a month, 15 days or a week. And also in the news, they were saying that the government was going to punish the offense of crossing the border with a month in jail. (Ramon)

Some neighbors were caught while trying to cross, and the same thing happened to my brother-in-law. They caught him and they caught him with false documents, so they locked him up and they sent him back here, and he's here now. So you run the risk of being locked up there. (Angel)

The risks themselves were described as increasing and growing more burdensome over time:

We have to walk a lot, right. You risk your life a lot. And so you think about it a lot, right. Before you didn't have to walk a long time, just a short while. Now it's become longer. (Francisco)

The stories of danger and endurance make the rounds in the community. Several migrants described stories they had heard of family members or neighbors who had been captured and detained by immigration authorities in the United States, who inserted microchips under their skin to facilitate surveillance and detection once they tried to cross again. The truth of the stories does not matter as much as the reputation of U.S. immigration authorities as arbitrary, potentially lawless, and all-powerful in their technological superiority. This representation of the dangers bestows upon the migrants who cross a quality of extraordinary bravery.

Some migrants described their ability to endure as arising out of, or intertwined with, necessity and the desire for opportunity, which also frames their identities as family providers:

More than money, it's necessity. That's why the *paisanos* leave. Why? For that same reason. They risk their life. (Ignacio)

Here they pay us 100, or 80 pesos a day. How much is that? It's nothing. It's not enough to support a family. That's why a lot of times we, migrants, risk our lives in the desert to look for a better life. (Paco)

The theme of endurance plays a large role here, as if the men we interviewed understood that their ability to cross depends on that masculine characteristic. The context of a dangerous environment highlights their masculinity.

The theme of persistence, along with its masculine qualities, is also incorporated into the endurance narrative. Persistence is often portrayed as masculine, especially in the stories of entrepreneurial, risk-taking, self-sufficient individuals (Bruni, Gherardi, and Poggio 2005). Rather than characterize being caught at the border as a failure, migrants construct a story in which those who persist can and will eventually cross successfully. The migrant imbued with masculine traits of endurance and persistence utilizes these traits successfully in the labor market after arriving in the United States.

When migrants have to try several times to cross the border, they perceive multiple attempts as evidence of their own stamina, and feel they can handle even the most difficult obstacles to crossing, and later, to finding a job:

> They send you back, but the next day you return, and then they send you back and you cross again because you have to. And no one returns here, well, . . . no one returns without a job, you have to cross. (Julio)

> I never thought, "I couldn't cross. I'm not going to try again." There were only two times, thank God, that they sent me back, and both times I came back and stayed here for about three or four months. And then later I tried again, I was able to cross. (Angel)

The following exchange is typical of the matter-of-factness with which migrants displayed their persistence:

> INTERVIEWER: How many times did you cross? Seven or eight?
> TITO: Yes.
> INTERVIEWER: And did they ever catch you?
> TITO: They got me like . . . three, four times.
> INTERVIEWER: And what happened when they caught you?
> TITO: Well they caught me and deported me back to Mexico. And once on the border, we'd cross again.

Endurance and persistence, at times motivated by necessity or opportunity, are the hallmarks of the successful border crosser, in the eyes of our interviewees.

The Migrant as Family Provider

The family provider or breadwinner narrative is a familiar figure in masculinities studies (Gutmann 2003; Broughton 2008). In the border-crossing stories, the family provider narrative identifies the underlying rationale for movement across the border into the United States. According to the story, migrants move across the border because they feel responsible as heads of household to maintain the family, and provide them opportunities for advancement, despite any perceived risks or danger (Broughton 2008). The family provider story places the migrant at the center of the family and its livelihood, even in—or maybe because of—his absence.

When speaking of their roles as family providers, migrants repeatedly described themselves as responsible for the welfare of their families. This includes providing resources for daily living, for building a house, and for supporting children's educations. Responsibility is a major characteristic of their self-perceptions as well as a motivating force for their continued presence in the United States, whether lawful or not. As one migrant noted:

> I realized that I didn't have what I needed to support my children who were in school. And that was my goal when I left, so that my children would have a better life and to support them so that they could go to school. (Raul)

Typically, migrants describe their reasons for crossing and staying in the United States in terms of family obligation, as the following narrative demonstrates:

> I have family. I have to work, whatever I earn. I have to do it. . . . My intention was to work however I could and to not be without money, to be able to send it here to my family. (Tito)

The migrants emphasized that their responsibilities were not easily ignored. It was as if they were responding to some alternative view of migrants as irresponsible, immoral, or without values for leaving, or for entering the United States without documentation. As one migrant explained his decision:

> I never left thinking, "I'm leaving, and I'm going to forget about everybody." I never thought that. I thought I was going to go and work and do something so that I could come back and build a place to live. (Angel)

Implicit in the family provider narrative is that the movement across the border is for a temporary period. The underlying thread of the narrative is that one cannot be a family provider for long without physically being present with the family.

Sacrifice is part of the family provider masculinities narrative (Broughton 2008). This is a positive masculine attribute that underscores heroic male qualities (Connell 2005). Even those who did not migrate spoke of their migrating relatives as accepting a great sacrifice to cross the border for the family. This aspect of the narrative involves a sense of honor and dignity in their choice to leave their families in order to take care of them: "there aren't any resources here to support a family, so you have to look for something, even if it's far away. You have to try" (Ignacio).

Migrants see themselves as wanting to provide opportunities they did not have (Broughton 2008). They perceived that the family's fate depended on their success and consequently, the theme of sacrifice runs through the stories explaining the decision to cross over:

> More than anything . . . I want to help my children get ahead. I want to help them so that they can go to school, so they won't suffer like I do by having to go to the United States. (Tito)

Sacrifice is typically described as moving away while the rest of the family stays in Mexico. The underlying assumption is that the male migrant would best be able to meet the family's needs by crossing and sending money back home, rather than by staying in the community. This is the case even when it is emotionally difficult to leave, as when a loved one is sick. The following exchange captures the power of the family provider narrative in giving someone permission to leave his family at a time of deep emotional need:

> NICOLAS: I have a son . . . [gets emotional] who didn't talk . . . um, well I would take him to Pachuca to get treatment, and almost a year after he was born I took him over there and he received the treatment and because there wasn't any money, I had to go over there [to the United States].
>
> INTERVIEWER: And you stayed since '98?
>
> NICOLAS: Um, I was there for about a year and a half or two years, and I came back. And I went back because my son didn't get better. I had to go back to pay back everything that we owed.
>
> INTERVIEWER: And would you send money to your family?
>
> NICOLAS: Yes.
>
> INTERVIEWER: How often?
>
> NICOLAS: Every two weeks, or every week when it was needed for my son's treatment. But I did keep my part by sending money to my family.

Sacrifice also involves disregard for the feelings or emotions that accompany separation. The following exchange captures the attitude of putting feelings aside in order to meet obligations to family:

> MANUEL: I was gone for three years because I wanted to build a house, and give my family a better life.
> INTERVIEWER: And you didn't miss your family?
> MANUEL: Yes, well, yes I missed them, but I dealt with it. I had to be far away.

Migrants build solidarity in the act of sacrifice and in moving across the border out of necessity. The sense of participating in a universal movement with the same reasons for crossing as others resonates with migrants:

> Some do it for their families, to offer better opportunities for their family, to maintain something good, and try to give your children the best. Here, we can give them something but not very much. There isn't a lot of money. That's the way it is. Being over there, you can send money and you can make a bit more money. (Ruben)

The family provider narrative also provides the impetus for moving back and forth as the economy and other factors allow. Migrants set their goals for meeting the needs of their family and set out to meet them in their travels. If they do not meet their goals on a first trip, they plan subsequent trips across the border:

> My goal when I left for the first time was to build a home because I was never able to build a house when I worked here. And that was the goal for which I left, to build a house for my family. . . . I didn't have any plans to stay. I wanted to go work and save some money and build a house. . . . I don't know when, but . . . I want to go back because I want to finish my house, it's about 50 percent done and I want to go back to finish my house. (Antonio)

The goals are articulated in terms of both short- and long-term planning, and incorporate aspirations for a better future in Mexico. As one migrant noted:

> My goal was to come back and start a business, and come back one day and have a house and a business. (Paco)

The family provider narrative extends out and expands into a community provider narrative. In addition to meeting obligations to family, migrants in the region see themselves as meeting the needs of their own communities. They contribute to projects that local communities identify or they contribute capital that keeps others—those who cannot leave—employed. Migrants described with pride their involvement in efforts to improve their communities even from afar:

> The [basketball] court you see over there was built on money raised from people over there. (Julio)

Migrants who had resettled in the towns explained their own dependence on private remittances:

> If it weren't for the migrants who send money from there to here, we wouldn't have any work. The migrants send money to build a house, to build a fence or whatever, and our work depends on them. But if they don't send money, then we don't have a job. (Paco)

The family provider narrative is a powerful motivator in keeping the migration flow into the United States active, continuous, and constant. The goal of many of the migrants we interviewed is to be a successful family provider. These are all masculine characteristics, of course, and the trope of the family provider masculinity is familiar in both Latin and North America (Gutmann 2003; Taylor and Behnke 2005). That it was so prevalent and paramount in the stories of migrants is not surprising. The narratives are a powerful counterweight to U.S. public perception of migrants as undesirable forces in our society. Migrants draw strength from this narrative despite anti-immigrant sentiment in the United States.

The Migrant as Keeper of Family Order

One of the most important sets of stories that emerged from our interviews is the narrative that places migrants at the center of family order, even in their absence. This narrative is in keeping with a traditional hegemonic masculinity that affirms male authority, customary family roles, and conservative family values (Broughton 2008). The narratives are expressed when the protagonist faces a choice between work and family (Broughton 2008; Fernández-Kelly 2005).

Their perceived responsibility for family order is a driving force in migrants' narratives explaining circular migration. Migrants perceive that they are responsible for discipline, instilling moral values, and maintaining patriarchal order. It is quite important for migrants to feel they can live up to their responsibility for family order, even as they travel back and forth. It is also important for the migrants to perceive themselves as needed at home at a time when migrants are no longer needed in the U.S. workforce. Over and over again we heard from migrants that they returned to Mexico because their families needed them, rather than because of the economic downturn or because of border restrictions.

The story of family order itself adapts to fit the changing reality of how difficult it is to cross the border into the United States as well as to changes in economic conditions in the United States. Even as restrictions and dangers grew along the border, and as the recession became more severe, migrants in the United States made use of the family order narrative to explain the decision to return to Hidalgo, whether temporarily or permanently. Paramount in the stories of return are the images of children without discipline, a moral compass, or a respect for male authority. The stories made the need to return that much more urgent. While other factors played into the decision to return, family order is always paramount among the reasons given, and often one of the first articulated by the migrants as they recount their stories of return. In fact, the family order narrative becomes essential when the breadwinner identity no longer makes sense because of economic dislocation. It seemed to soften the blow of a lost job or lost economic opportunities as the recession geared up in the United States. The narrative is evident in this migrant's story:

> I came back mostly because of my kids, they need me now that they're small. So I thought, "well, the little I've done, I already did it." I realized that I could share a lot of things with my family, even though I don't have any money. (Angel)

Over and over again, when asked why they returned, migrants alluded to the need to restore order, to re-establish relationships with family, to take care of sick or dying family members, and to restore discipline and traditional family values in their roles as the heads of household:

> I was gone for a long time and my family, my son asked me to come back here with them. I think he needed me and he wanted to see me. That's one of the reasons I decided to come back, so I could be with them. (Manuel)

> Why did I return to Hidalgo? More than anything for my family—to be with them and share with them. I didn't know exactly how long I'd be here and at the same time, once I had been here for three or four months I

realized that my family needed me, just as much as they needed money. (Angel)

I came back because my family was sick. That's why I came back. They didn't fire me, nor was I deported, thank God. I came back because some family members were sick. (Paco)

I worked there for about 6 months and then I came back here because one of my sons got sick. And so I came back and was here for about 2 years and then I went back. (Moises)

They didn't fire me but I had to leave on my own and come back here to my country, my state so that I could devote more time to my family here. (Paco)

I saw that my children had grown and I thought "I'm losing out on my children's childhood." So I decided to stay a while for my children. (Tito)

The specter of the family without order and the father's crucial role in maintaining order was prevalent in the cautionary tales of parents who stayed away too long:

I see that there is some violence in the villages, because of the abandoned children. They begin to steal and drink. They don't do anything and just do things that children shouldn't be doing. Like in the town of El Alberto, nobody goes to school because they have to go to the United States. So there is a lot of violence there because of the kids who are abandoned by their parents. They have to leave them for five, ten years, something like that. And when they [the parents] come back, they are already grown and so they don't educate or guide them. That isn't good. (Julio)

The family order narrative does not preclude any plan to return to the United States:

Yes, more than anything my plan is . . . if there's the opportunity for me to go in about two years, and I could cross fine without any problems, then I'd go to work. I don't know for how long, depends on how long I could stay there. I wouldn't go there to stay. I'd go for a while and then come back. (Angel)

It simply normalizes the circular migration pattern, and makes it more acceptable as a way of life:

> Many of us have come and gone, not for pleasure or for sport, but because of feelings, for the family or a problem that we may have had with the family. We need to leave and enter. (Antonio)

> I see it as normal because almost everyone comes back, they stay a while and then they go back. . . . It's normal because there are those who come for two, three months to see their family and then they go back. (Tito)

The idea that migrants have a responsibility to uphold and foster proper values, a strong family structure, and a sense of discipline and order has profound effects on the circular migration pattern. To the extent that migrants maintain families in Mexico while they work in the United States, the circular migration pattern will continue to be firmly established between Mexico and the United States. The stories evoke a sense of importance and urgency in fulfilling the role of father, husband, son, or brother back in Mexico, allowing migrants to negotiate the tensions between work and family obligations, and the dignity to return when economic conditions worsen in the United States.

The family order narrative operates alongside the other two narratives. At the same time that migrants recounted returning to Mexico to restore family order, they built up the dangers of the border, talked of the need to provide materially for their families, and talked about the prospects of returning to the United States after a period of time in Mexico. The family order narrative feeds into and frames the breadwinner/provider self-perception and into the sacrifice/necessity themes in the risk/danger narrative when convenient or when appropriate. When a migrant had to return to Mexico because he did not have a job, he turned to stories of the need to restore an orderly family structure to explain his return. Neither restrictive immigration policy nor loss of a job was ever mentioned alone as the reason for returning. The family order narrative, one that evokes a masculine take-charge persona, helps bridge the transition back to Mexico. It is key to sustaining the circular migration pattern in spite of the obstacles.

Conclusion: Implications of Border-Crossing Narrative Responses for Immigration Law

The migrants' stories challenge the assumptions behind increasingly restrictive immigration and border enforcement policies. Their direct answers to questions about the effects of restrictive immigration policies on decisions to cross were less revealing than their recounting of why, how, and when they crossed and the obstacles they encountered crossing. We discovered the masculinities narratives running through individual border-crossing stories. The narratives were powerful tools helping migrants face ever-increasing dangers, risks, and restrictions. Rather than respond to immigration restrictions by creating narratives that encouraged staying home, the migrants we interviewed adapted their border-crossing stories with masculinities themes to help them better endure the dangers created by increased restrictions. In other words, increased border restrictions have the opposite behavioral effect than intended, in part because of these masculinities narratives. The narratives also reveal an interesting dynamic in the workplace. The narratives that make migrants protagonists in border crossing stories also make them agents able to endure undesirable workplace conditions (Saucedo and Morales 2010). The same narratives of endurance, persistence, and family provider status cause migrants to accept conditions in the workplace others might not readily accept.

The lessons for immigration law seem fairly obvious. Restrictive border enforcement policies do not dissuade individual migrants from border crossing. Indeed, masculinities narratives help tip the scales in favor of crossing. A more thoughtful approach to immigration enforcement policy must consider the motivations for northward migration and the power of the narratives to facilitate the migration pattern. A focus on legal restrictions works only if the underlying economic and social conditions can actually facilitate compliance. It would be just as masculine, for example, to fulfill the family provider roles without traveling if economic conditions allowed for migrants to stay home. Or, an open border policy would ameliorate the powerful effect of a masculinities narrative that encourages risking the high cost of border crossing, and thus decrease the desire to cross. As the stories here demonstrate, a more holistic, cross-legal, cross-state approach offers more hope of change than the current legalistic immigration restriction regime.

NOTES

1. As an example, President Obama signed the Southwest Border Security Bill in August 2010, which provides for enhanced DHS presence on the U.S.-Mexico border.
2. Arizona's SB 1070 is an example of state efforts to legislate immigration enforcement efforts.
3. For example, there have been calls to reinterpret the Fourteenth Amendment to prohibit birthright citizenship to children of undocumented parents born in the United States (Feere 2010).

4. All of the interviews for this study took place in Hidalgo, Mexico, in August 2008. Interviewees were given pseudonyms to preserve their anonymity. Their "names" appear, where appropriate, at the end of each quote.
5. U.S. Border Patrol.

REFERENCES

Amnesty International. 2010. *Invisible Victims: Migrants on the Move in Mexico.* London: Amnesty International. Available at http://www.amnesty.org/en/library/info/AMR41/014/2010/en.
Arizona S.B. 1070. 2010. 49th Leg., 2d Reg. Sess.
Broughton, Chad. 2008. Migration as Engendered Practice: Mexican Men, Masculinity, and Northward Migration. *Gender and Society* 22(5): 568–89.
Bruni, Attila, Silvia Gherardi, and Barbara Poggio. 2005. *Gender and Entrepreneurship: An Ethnographic Approach.* New York: Routledge.
Connell, R. W. 2005. *Masculinities,* 2d ed. Berkeley: University of California Press.
Donato, Katherine M., Jorge Durand, and Douglas S. Massey. 1992. Stemming the Tide? Assessing the Deterrent Effects of U.S. Immigration and Control. *Demography* 29(2): 139–57.
Durand, Jorge, Douglas S. Massey, and Emilio A. Parrado. 1999. The New Era of Mexican Migration to the United States. *Journal of American History* 86: 518–36.
Durand, Jorge, Douglas S. Massey, and Rene M. Zenteno. 2001. Mexican Immigration to the United States: Continuities and Changes. *Latin American Research Review* 36(1): 107–27.
Ellingwood, Ken. 2010. Mexico Marines Find 72 Bodies at Ranch, Navy Says. *Los Angeles Times,* August 25. Available at http://www.latimes.com/news/nationworld/world/la-fg-mexico-bodies-20100825,0,2229485.story.
Espenshade, Thomas J. 1994. Does the Threat of Border Apprehension Deter Undocumented U.S. Immigration? *Population and Development Review* 20(4): 871–92.
Feere, Jon. 2010. *Birthright Citizenship in the United States: A Global Comparison.* Washington, DC: Center for Immigration Studies.
Fernández-Kelly, Patricia. 2005. Reforming Gender: The Effects of Economic Change on Masculinity and Femininity in Mexico and the U.S. *Women's Studies Review* Fall:69–101.
Gutmann, Matthew C. 2003. Introduction: Discarding Manly Dichotomies in Latin America. In *Changing Men and Masculinities in Latin America,* edited by M. C. Gutmann. Durham, NC: Duke University Press.
Haddal, Chad, and Jeremiah Gertler. 2010. *Homeland Security: Unmanned Aerial Vehicles and Border Surveillance.* Washington, DC: Congressional Research Service. Available at http://www.fas.org/sgp/crs/homesec/RS21698.pdf.
Hanson, Gordon H. 2007. *The Economic Logic of Illegal Immigration.* New York: Council on Foreign Relations.
Homeland Security Act of 2002. Pub. L. No. 107-296, 116 Stat. 2135.
Kang, John M. 2010. The Burdens of Manliness. *Harvard Journal of Law and Gender* 33(2): 477–508.
Ngai, Mae. 2004. *Impossible Subjects: Illegal Aliens and the Making of Modern America.* Princeton, NJ: Princeton University Press.

Passel, Jeffrey S., and D'Vera Cohn. 2010. *U.S. Unauthorized Immigration Flows Are Sharply Down since Mid-Decade*. Washington, DC: Pew Hispanic Center. Available at http://pewhispanic.org/files/reports/126.pdf.

Saucedo, Leticia M., and Maria Cristina Morales. 2010. Masculinities Narratives and Latino Immigrant Workers: A Case Study of the Las Vegas Residential Construction Trades. *Harvard Journal of Law and Gender* 33(2): 625–60.

Schmidt Camacho, Alicia. 2008. *Migrant Imaginaries: Latino Cultural Politics in the U.S.-Mexico Borderlands*. New York: New York University Press.

Secure Fence Act of 2006. Pub. L. No. 109-367, 120 Stat. 2638.

Taylor, Brent A., and Andrew Behnke. 2005. Fathering across the Border: Latino Fathers in Mexico and the U.S. *Fathering* 3(2): 99–120.

USA PATRIOT Act. 2001. Pub. L. No. 107-56, 115 Stat. 272.

PART III

Questioning Segregation in Masculine Spaces

8

Sex Segregation, Masculinities, and Gender-Variant Individuals

DAVID S. COHEN

Dee Farmer was born a man but "underwent estrogen therapy, received silicone breast implants, and submitted to unsuccessful 'black market' testicle-removal surgery" in an effort to become a woman (*Farmer v. Brennan* 1994, 829). When she was convicted of credit card fraud, the Federal Bureau of Prisons assigned her to the general male population, where she wore clothes "in a feminine manner" and projected "feminine characteristics" (ibid.). There, she was brutally raped and beaten (ibid.). Steven Kastl was also born a man and taught at the Maricopa County Community College. After being diagnosed with gender identity disorder, Steven began taking hormones to transition to a woman, legally changed her name to Rebecca, and began living as a woman. However, her employer forbade her from using the women's restroom at the college until she had completed sex reassignment surgery. Nonetheless, Kastl insisted on using the women's restroom and was fired (*Kastl v. Maricopa County Community College District* 2006). Miki Ann DiMarco is an intersex individual with a penis but no testicles who identifies as female. When she was arrested for violating probation, local officials originally housed her with women in the county jail. However, when she was transferred to state prison she was, despite being classified repeatedly as the lowest possible security risk, put in solitary confinement in a men's prison, where she was denied many privileges and could not talk with other inmates (*DiMarco v. Wyoming Department of Corrections* 2004).

As Dee, Rebecca, and Miki Ann learned in these cases and undoubtedly throughout their lives, sex segregation[1] is everywhere. Despite the first statutory and constitutional protections against sex discrimination in American law emerging between four and five decades ago, sex segregation is alive and well. It persists in almost every walk of life: employment, education, criminal justice, the military, restrooms, social organizations, athletics, religion, and more. In this chapter, I use an antiessentialist framework to investigate sex segregation and what it means for masculinities and, in particular, gender-variant individuals,[2] such as transgender, intersex, and gender-nonconforming individuals.

Understanding sex segregation should be a vital part of the study of law and masculinity. In fact, as I argue, current-day sex segregation is one of the central ways that law and society define and construct who is a man and what it means to be a man. When law or society tells people that a place or activity is reserved for men alone, or in the converse, that men are excluded from a particular place or activity, two important messages are sent: one, that there are distinct categories of people based on assumed anatomical differences and that these anatomical distinctions are a legitimate way of organizing and sorting people; and two, that people with the anatomy labeled "male" are supposed to behave in a certain way. As this chapter explores, these messages produce distinct harms for gender-variant individuals.

In looking at sex segregation, masculinities, and gender variance, I focus on two separate theoretical concepts: hegemonic masculinity and the hegemony of men. Ultimately, I argue here that the various forms of sex segregation still existing in the United States help create and perpetuate a particular form of idealized masculinity—what theorists call hegemonic masculinity—that exerts normative power over men to conform. Sex segregation also substantially contributes to the dominance of men over women and nonhegemonically masculine men, a phenomenon that other theorists call the hegemony of men. In both ways, sex segregation contributes to an essentialized view of what it means to be a man—both in the attributes associated with an idealized manhood and in the power ascribed and available to some men over women and other men. As I show, this essentialized view of men and masculinity takes its harshest and most discriminatory toll on gender-variant individuals.[3]

The Stubborn Persistence of Sex Segregation

In 1963, Congress passed the first federal civil rights law covering women, the Equal Pay Act, which required that men and women receive the same pay for the same job (Equal Pay Act). Title VII's prohibition on discrimination in employment based on sex, among other categories, came a year later (Title VII). The 1970s brought Title IX and its prohibition on discrimination based on sex in educational institutions that receive federal funding (Title IX). The Supreme Court also took up the mantle of nondiscrimination based on sex during the 1970s, finally expanding the coverage of the Fourteenth Amendment's Equal Protection Clause in 1976 to prohibit most forms of government discrimination based on sex (*Craig v. Boren* 1976). Thus, over the course of 13 years, women's status under federal law drastically changed, and the elimination of some of the most severe forms of sex discrimination followed.

Yet, almost four decades later, sex segregation is alive and well. In fact, it has persisted in ways that affect most people throughout their lives. In an article that sets the stage for this chapter, I extensively detailed the various forms of sex segregation that continue to exist (Cohen 2011). Here, I will only briefly summarize these forms of sex segregation and the various areas of life that are segregated.

The most obvious form of sex segregation is mandatory sex segregation. Mandatory sex segregation is required by law, such as the exclusion of women from direct ground combat roles in the military or the requirement that only men register for the draft. Within the criminal justice system, prison and jail populations are frequently required by law to be segregated based on sex. State laws also sometimes require transportation, searches, and employment within prisons, jails, and criminal courts to be segregated based on sex. Restrooms, locker rooms, showers, and the like are also regularly required by law to be segregated based on sex. Many states also have laws that require segregation based on sex in the medical context, either segregating those who receive treatment or requiring those who provide treatment to be of the same sex as the patient. Other contexts in which state laws mandate sex segregation include outdoor youth programs, elections, drug and alcohol testing in the private sector, honors, housing, identification card photography, jury sequestration, massage parlors, nudism, schools, and sexual violence programs.

Administrative sex segregation occurs when government-run institutions are not required by law to sex segregate but nonetheless do so in their operating capacity. For instance, government buildings of all types, whether open to the public or not, are likely to have sex-segregated bathrooms and, if within the building's purpose, sex-segregated locker rooms, dressing rooms, or showers, whether for employees or for the public. Correctional facilities also administratively sex segregate, as most separate men and women despite not having a state statute requiring them to do so. Public schools, from elementary and secondary to undergraduate and graduate institutions, also segregate based on sex in bathrooms and locker rooms as well as living arrangements, such as dorms and dorm rooms or fraternity or sorority houses.

Permissive sex segregation is sex segregation that occurs with the explicit permission of the law. Title VII prohibits employment discrimination based on sex but permits employers to sex segregate positions if there "is a bona fide occupational qualification [BFOQ] reasonably necessary to the normal operation of that particular business or enterprise" (42 U.S.C. § 2000e-2(e)(1)). Courts have approved BFOQs in strength-related jobs such as prison guards, privacy-related jobs such as spa, restroom, and health club attendants, and authenticity-related jobs such as acting (Kapczynski 2003; Yuracko 2004). Title IX prohibits sex discrimination in federally funded educational institutions but has several exceptions that permit, in particular contexts and with some limitations, single-sex schools and classes as well as sex-segregated athletics, housing, scholarships, extracurricular activities, and restrooms (Title IX). Various state laws permit sex segregation in health clubs, athletic programs, housing, medical facilities, prisons, and more.

Finally, there is the vast category of voluntary sex segregation, a category that broadly affects people's lives but is mostly outside the realm of the law or government. Private institutions and organizations voluntarily sex segregate in membership, participation, and distribution of honors. These organizations are as numerous as they are diffuse. They include national and local membership organizations. Sports competitions also sex segregate, from the international, to the national, to the local. Religious institutions sex segregate who can ascend to respected positions, where people can worship, or who can attend schools. Performing arts award ceremonies, such as the Academy Awards, also segregate based on sex in who wins awards such as best actor or actress. Finally, there are endless examples of much more micro and informal forms of voluntary sex segregation from groups organized around a particular hobby, interest, or affiliation, such as a gathering of mothers or a men's knitting club, to informal social gatherings, such as a bachelor party or "girls' night out."

Although this list does not paint a picture that is nearly as pervasive and subordinating as race segregation was in this country's history or as sex segregation currently exists in some other countries, it does illustrate that sex segregation continues despite advances in sex discrimination law. And sex segregation continues in almost all walks of life, from requirements imposed by law to everyday choices made by individuals in how to organize their own affairs.

Gender, Antiessentialism, and Masculinities

There are countless theories of gender (Connell 2009). On one extreme is the generally held notion that gender and sex are fixed notions that are inherently linked: men are, or should be, masculine, and women are, or should be, feminine. Under this theory, both sex and gender consist of binaries. Your sex is biologically determined and is either male or female. And, based on which sex you are, your gender is the set of behavioral and psychological characteristics associated with that sex (Connell 2005, 21–27).

At the other end of the spectrum lies the notion that sex and gender are fluid and have no fixed content. According to Judith Butler, there is no preexisting set of characteristics that are masculine or feminine, and what we think of as masculinity or femininity are just the performances of those whom we label as such. To Butler, gender itself also produces the perceived biologically distinct sexes, which in reality are not naturally distinct categories but become so because of gender performance and labels (Butler 1999). Somewhat less extreme is the theory that gender is the constructed social practice that operates on bodies based on their reproductive capacity (Connell 2009). Raewyn Connell puts forth this theory as a way to ground gender in bodies and the way society addresses bodies. She defines gender as the "structure of social relations that centres on the reproductive arena, and the set of practices that bring reproductive distinctions between bodies into social processes" (ibid. 11). Connell's theory shares the social constructivism of Butler's, but insists that bodies and their reproductive capacity are central to thinking about gender.

Antiessentialism is a broad umbrella term that I use to describe these latter two theories about gender, which I believe are the most useful for analyzing sex segregation generally and its effects on masculinity and gender variance more specifically. Essentialism is "the notion that we can identify basic shared characteristics of women (or blacks or gays, etc.) that are essential to the group's experiences and interests" (Cooper 2009, 37). Antiessentialism relies on the observation that there is more variation *within* the societally determined categories "men" and "women" than *between* those two societally determined categories (Hyde 2005). Antiessentialist theory argues that the ordinary binary sex and gender categories fail to take account of this complexity and the multiplicity of human identity and difference, including gender variance. In fact, the existence and imposition of sex and gender categories work to construct identity and difference, rather than merely to reflect difference.

In this sense, antiessentialism is a key component of postmodern and post-structuralist feminist legal theories, closely related theories that recognize the socially constructed nature of identity and difference (Frug 1992; Williams 1990). Applied to legal theory, antiessentialism thus challenges the structures in law and society that create and reinforce identity and difference with respect to sex and gender (Ashe 1987). By confining people to essentialist categories, societal institutions and discourses constrain identity and limit freedom. The value of antiessentialism is that it challenges us to question the structures in law and society that ordinarily seem natural. In this way, antiessentialism is a valuable tool for evaluating sex segregation, as the sex segregation that has survived the feminist legal reforms of the past several decades has been woven into the fabric of society and thus has become less controversial.

Pushing deeper, antiessentialism is a theory not merely about identity but also about challenging the societal forces that impose identity upon people in ways that further hierarchy. Through subtle forms of differentiation in society and law, sex and gender hierarchies are created, perpetuated, and normalized. These essentialist conceptions of gender reinforce not only power differentials between men and women (Higgins 1996), but also power differentials among men. Certain types of men—those who hew to a dominant form of masculinity—are empowered, and others—those who challenge or fail to conform to this dominant masculinity, such as gender-variant individuals—are pressured into conforming or, if they do not, are ostracized or persecuted (Cohen 2009).

Disaggregating the concepts of sex and gender is key to an antiessentialist legal theory (Case 1995; Valdes 1995). Under the essentialist view of sex and gender described above, men are or should be masculine and women are or should be feminine. Biology determines behavior, so the link is required. Gender-variant individuals need to be reformed or ostracized because of their failure to conform to the essentialist ideals. Antiessentialism disentangles the concepts, even going so far as to challenge the idea that there should be any concept of masculinity or femininity (Case 1998). Antiessentialism views characteristics of individuals as just that: individual characteristics which should not be labeled as more appropriate for one sex than the other. Unlike liberal equal treatment theory, which accepts some differences between men and women, antiessentialism calls into question virtually all stereotypes and groupings associated with sex and gender as the product of socially imposed categorization. And it is this socially imposed categorization that results in the furtherance of hierarchy. As argued below, sex segregation is an important and powerful form of this categorization, one that particularly harms gender-variant individuals.

Antiessentialism applied to masculinity results in the concept of masculinities. As Nancy Dowd has described it, "[a]nti-essentialism means exposing affirmative differences among men that challenge dominant definitions of masculinity" (2008, 228). Doing so would be impossible without understanding that there is no such thing as "masculinity" (singular); instead, there are multiple "masculinities" (plural) (Kimmel 1996; Connell 2005). "Multiple masculinities" is the antiessentialist notion that different people experience and live masculinity differently (Connell 1996). Stated otherwise, there is no single masculinity that all men, or even most men, live. As Rob Gilbert and Pam Gilbert write in an analysis of masculinity in Australian schools, "masculinity is diverse, dynamic and changing, and we need to think of multiple masculinities rather than some singular [masculinity]" (1998, 49). These multiple masculinities can be based on the "interplay of gender, class and ethnicity" (Connell 2009, 106–7), as well as other identity factors such as sexual orientation, disability, and national origin. Furthermore, individual men and women can also access and perform different masculinities at different points and sites in their lives, as individual masculine identity is not static over time or within different contexts (Connell and Messerschmidt 2005).

Just because masculinities are varied and culturally contingent does not mean that discussing them means avoiding discussion of men's power. Jeff Hearn has been critical of some masculinities scholarship as being too focused on describing masculinity without paying enough attention to critically assessing how, within a patriarchal society, men and masculinity attain and keep power over women as well as other men (2004). Looking at gender and power is an important part of the antiessentialist project, as essentialist notions of gender reinforce power structures. For masculinities, essentialist notions of who is a man and what is masculinity work to reinforce the dominance of men over women, as well as over men who do not fit within the essentialist notion, such as gender-variant individuals. This understanding of power and masculinity is also an important part of masculinities studies and one that sheds important light on the particular harms faced by gender-variant individuals in a sex-segregated world.

Hegemonic Masculinity

The various forms of sex segregation I have identified are an important part of the construction of hegemonic masculinity in this country, one that is particularly hostile to gender-variant individuals who society labels as men.

Masculinities scholars have argued that there is a contextually contingent idealized masculinity that exerts normative power over men to conform. The theory behind this dominant masculinity, labeled "hegemonic masculinity," was first developed by Connell and has most recently been defined by her as follows: "the configuration of gender practice which embodies the currently accepted answer to the problem of the legitimacy of patriarchy, which guarantees (or is taken to guarantee) the dominant position of men and the subordination of women" (2005, 77). Stated slightly differently, hegemonic masculinity is "the currently most honored way of being a man[. I]t require[s] all other men to position themselves in relation to it, and it ideologically legitimate[s] the global subordination of women to men" (Connell and Messerschmidt 2005, 832).

Unpacking this term makes clear that this concept is rooted in notions of power and is contextual, dynamic, and idealized. Thus, although boys and girls, men and women, live and experience different forms of masculinity within particular contexts, one form of masculinity often exerts the most pressure to conform to it. Hegemonic masculinity is that masculinity and works to subordinate both women and non-hegemonically masculine men (Renold 2005). It subordinates women by definition, as hegemonic masculinity is associated with the characteristics that allow men to subordinate women; it subordinates other men, non-hegemonically masculine men, by labeling their expressions of personhood as inferior to "true" manhood. It is this latter aspect of hegemonic masculinity that has particularly serious consequences for gender-variant individuals.

Theorists have critiqued hegemonic masculinity in various ways, including that it is unclear in its substance (Hearn 2004). However, my working premise is that the notion is nonetheless useful in understanding what conceptions of masculinity exist that exert normative force on people to conform. Though it may be impossible to fully describe such a masculinity because of the wide variety of forces that influence its nature, some understanding of it can come from looking at the forces, such as law, that create and reinforce its hegemony. Sex segregation, with the power or permission of law, in the ways I have identified, is one such force. Particularly following the feminist legal reforms of the past several decades that were supposed to eliminate invidious sex discrimination in our society, the sex segregation that remains is one of the "taken-for-granted ideas and practices" described by Hearn that is "performed with consent [and] without coercion" (2004, 53). In that way, it is one of the important contributors to hegemonic masculinity.

Thus, when law segregates or allows for segregation across all the different areas I have described, we can see some of the ways that law, government institutions, and cultural practices help to associate and maintain the association of particular characteristics with hegemonic masculinity. And, not surprisingly, when law segregates or allows segregation of men, it helps to essentialize masculinity in a way that aligns with characteristics frequently associated with men in a society in which women and non-hegemonically masculine men are subordinated. Although there are certainly other characteristics that sex segregation associates with dominant masculinity, here, I focus on one such characteristic—that men are not feminine (Cohen 2009; Cohen 2010).

Probably the most important aspect of most conceptions of hegemonic masculinity is that masculinity is defined as that which is not feminine, or that which is not associated with girls or women. In an early feminist writing, Nancy Chodorow described how society places immense pressure on boys from an early age "to reject identification with or participation in anything that seems 'feminine'" (1971, 186). Some theorists, like Chodorow, attribute this need for differentiation to the Freudian need of young boys to separate from their mother; others attribute it to the desire to associate with the more dominant part of a patriarchal society rather than the subordinated (Karst 1991); still others attribute it to fear among men to appear to be frail in the eyes of other men (Dowd 2008). Regardless of the origin of this need, most gender theorists acknowledge the simple fact that the dominant societal notion of being masculine means "doing things that cannot and should not be done by women" (Jordan 1995, 75; see also Bird 1996). Ultimately, masculinity requires men to "make it clear—eternally, compulsively, decidedly—that they are not 'like' women" (Kimmel 2008, 4).

Sex segregation in law and society is one of the basic ways that men are differentiated from the feminine and thereby defined by that which is not feminine. This occurs in a variety of the areas of sex segregation described here. For instance, in schools, the recent increase in sex-segregated education for boys has been driven in large part by an essentialist view of masculinity that includes the notion that boys occupy almost completely different worlds than girls (Cohen 2009). In the context of the military, the law keeps what some argue is the most important part of military service from women and leaves that in the hands of men. This is true both in the message this exclusion sends—that, literally, men are full citizens in their military eligibility compared to women, who are limited—and in the effects of this exclusion—that men have more opportunities for leadership than women do because of their ability to participate fully in the military (Karst 1991). All-male social clubs also work to the same effect, as they give men an opportunity to exclude and retreat from the feminine (Rhode 1986; Wecter 1937).

The result of men being separated or retreating from women is that men police each other to avoid exhibiting behaviors that would appear to be feminine. In one study of male-only interactions, a researcher concluded that when men are around other men to the exclusion of women, they believed that "the emotions and behaviors typically associated with women were inappropriate within the male homosocial group" (Bird 1996, 125). Sex-segregated institutions, whether segregated by mandate of law or voluntarily on the part of a private organization, contribute to the hegemonic notion of masculinity that defines being a man as not being feminine.

This aspect of hegemonic masculinity is hardly surprising to gender-variant individuals who have to contend with society's various forms of sex segregation. Two of the examples discussed at the introduction of this chapter are illustrative. Dee Farmer, the man who underwent hormone therapy and "black market" testicle-removal surgery and who wore "feminine clothing" in a men's prison, was beaten and raped for failing to conform to this basic rule of hegemonic masculinity—don't act like a woman (*Farmer* 1994). Rebecca Kastl, the teacher who was transitioning from a man to a woman, was fired for, in the eyes of her employer, being a man who wanted to use the woman's restroom, behavior that crosses the line of men not being like women (*Kastl* 2006).

This key aspect of hegemonic masculinity, that men are not feminine, is particularly problematic for gender-variant individuals. A person whom society, for whatever classification-based reason (Spade 2008), believes to be a man but who lives her life as a woman will encounter these difficulties for exhibiting feminine characteristics. The same is true for a person who identifies as a man but who exhibits feminine characteristics in some aspects of his being. The power of hegemonic masculinity is that it exerts its influence on everyone in telling men that they must not be feminine. The web of sex segregation that continues to exist is an important creator of this aspect of hegemonic masculinity and a powerful site of difficulty for gender-variant individuals.

The Hegemony of Men

Critically evaluating socially constructed notions of identity is one key part of an antiessentialist view of gender. The previous section's focus on hegemonic masculinity, along with its analysis of the harms gender-variant individuals face from such a hegemonic notion of masculinity, falls within this part of the antiessentialist project.

However, the multiplicity of identity is not the only part of antiessentialism; another key part is focusing on equality issues and how power relates to the construction of a seemingly essential identity. In critiquing some of the shortcomings of the concept of hegemonic masculinity, Jeff Hearn has argued that attention should be focused less on that identity concept and more on the way that men, as constructed within society, use power to subordinate women and other men. He calls this an investigation into "the hegemony of men" (2004).

Hearn argues that any critical feminist analysis of men must be concerned about this power that men use to subordinate women and other men. By focusing on hegemonic masculinity, scholars are right to look to the way that men are "a social category formed by the gender system," but should also look at how men are a "dominant collective and individual agents of social practices" (Hearn 2004, 59). Hearn suggests that scholars must study the way that men have differentiated themselves in ways that allow them to exercise power over women, children, and other men. The social structures and systems that perform this function are an important part of the hegemony of men. These social structures and systems might be, as Hearn describes them, men's most "natural(ized), ordinary, normal and most taken-for-granted practices" (2004, 61). These practices, including, as I argue below, various forms of sex segregation, help us understand men's dominance over gender-variant individuals.

Although Hearn sets forth this concept of hegemony of men as mostly an alternative to studying hegemonic masculinity, I find the two useful to discuss in tandem. As the previous section argued, the forms of sex segregation that continue to exist work together to create hegemonic notions of masculinity. In other words, there are common threads that run through the forms of sex segregation that create a powerful message of what it means to be a man. Although there are indeed theoretical problems with the notion of hegemonic masculinity (Connell and Messerschmidt 2005; Beasley 2008), the existence of a patterned ideal, or at least some semblance of such an ideal, and understanding aspects of such an idealized masculinity are important and have concrete implications for gender-variant individuals.

However, as Hearn argues, that is not enough. Understanding this hegemony of men, as described by Hearn, is important as well. By looking to how sex segregation creates opportunities for men to build or maintain power over women and other men, we can see part of the social structures that contribute to, among other things, discrimination and violence against gender-variant individuals. The extent to which these sex-segregated structures are less controversial at this point in time, particularly given that these forms of sex segregation have continued to exist even after the feminist legal reforms of the past several decades, shows that present-day sex segregation is just the type of taken-for-granted practice that Hearn contemplates in his discussion of hegemony (2004). And, to the extent that these practices effectively use power to promote an essentialist view of masculinity, investigating them within the lens of hegemony is an important part of an antiessentialist project.

Hearn's first charge in investigating the hegemony of men is looking to "organizational and institutional ways in which particular men are placed within the social category of men" (2004, 60). By doing so, we can unmask how society creates the category "men" as separate from the category "women." At its most basic level, this is exactly what sex segregation in all its forms does. In particular, when law mandates segregation of men and women, it is making this basic distinction through which people understand that the categorization matters and that deviating from the categorization has consequences. Through the forms of sex segregation described above that weave their ways through our lives, we come to accept the seemingly natural distinction that is created each time we see the word "men" or the word "women." The categories are set up as oppositional and as a legitimate way of thinking about people. The categories are also established as having no gray areas or overlap—a person is either a man or a woman.

Such bifurcation of sex, into the categories of men and women and nothing else, is particularly dangerous for gender-variant individuals in a sex-segregated world. In countless situations, sex-segregated institutions assign a sex to gender-variant individuals. This process is far from uniform, often performed by low-level officials in a snap decision. When a gender-variant individual is classified in a way that does not conform to the individual's self-expression, often the individual faces extreme danger (Spade 2008).

Sex segregation accomplishes this categorization of men throughout men's lives. At an early age, boys encounter the issue when they have to enter a public restroom. If a father accompanies his son, sex segregation poses no problem. However, if a mother accompanies her son, the sex-segregated world of bathrooms poses a problem: does the mother take her son into the women's room or does she send her young son into the men's room unattended (Kogan 2007)? However the mother resolves the issue, the lesson from sex segregation comes through to the son. This lesson of categorization continues throughout life and is what Jacques Lacan calls "urinary segregation" (1977, 151). Urinary segregation, according to Lacan, teaches children and adults that sexual difference is eternal, uncompromising, and based in notions of superiority. Basic human similarity between men and women, in the sense that everyone must eliminate waste and that everyone does so in quite similar ways, becomes a site of constructed difference masquerading as natural (Goffman 1977).

Architectural theorist Joel Sanders expands upon Lacan's theory of language as the differentiator to include the arrangement of space in sex-segregating bathrooms. He argues that sex segregation of the "public bathroom assigns sex and gender identity. The architecture of the public bathroom, where physical walls literally segregate the sexes, naturalizes gender by separating 'men' and 'women' according to the biology of bodily functions" (1996, 17). Not only does this segregation reinforce the opposition of the categories of "men" and "women," it also reinforces the notion that sex is binary without room for gender-variant individuals (Kogan 2009, 1997).

This is exactly the situation encountered by Rebecca Kastl. In the process of transitioning from a man to a woman, she, like everyone else, needed to perform the basic bodily functions of eliminating waste. As she was living her life as a woman during her transition, she wanted to use the women's restroom at work. However, because she was still, in the eyes of her employer, a man, she was fired for her attempts to fit into the binary system of sex-segregated restrooms (*Kastl* 2006). Rebecca's situation is not unique, as restrooms are an everyday site where gender-variant individuals are forced to confront the man/woman binary and constantly risk being "perceived as the wrong person" (Shelley 2008, 78).

Sex-segregated sport produces the same effect from an early age. Children participating in youth sports leagues are often segregated by sex. Even though at early ages children's athletic ability usually does not vary based on sex (Gooren 2008), leagues grouped by sex tell children that sex is a salient characteristic that matters in how children are treated and reaffirm for parents that sex differences are a naturally occurring method of differentiating children (Messner 2002). "The result [is] an apparently 'natural' split based on apparently 'natural' sex differences. What we already believed—that boys and girls are categorically different—became what we saw" (Messner 2002, 23).

The highest level of sport illustrates how these categories are anything but natural when applied to gender-variant individuals. Although the categories are presented as natural to the viewer, who sees the athletes competing within their assigned categories, the Olympics have struggled for decades with how to define who is a man and who is a woman. Until 2000, the International Olympic Committee (IOC) used genetic testing to determine if an athlete was a woman. This test foreclosed transsexuals and some intersex individuals from competing as women, even if the athlete lived her life as a woman or even had sex reassignment surgery. Recently, the IOC has adopted a new policy for transsexuals that allows a person who underwent sex reassignment surgery after puberty to compete as that person's new sex as long as that person has received hormone treatment therapy for two years after surgery and has legally changed his or her sex (Gooren 2008). However, this shift in IOC policy did not prevent the international controversy around Caster Semenya, who was subject to sex verification tests after winning a gold medal in a different international competition in 2009. Speculation that she had an intersex condition led to the controversy, which was just another indication that the seeming categories of men and women, with their natural and diametrically opposed differences, are not so (Knessel 2010). Sport's insistence on sex segregation highlights the difficulties faced by athletes who are suspected of or actually do not conform to gender stereotypes (Buzuvis 2010).

This message comes through in other areas as well. In sex-segregated prisons, prisoners are classified based on what level of security they need and based on their sex, suggesting that sex is an important characteristic that by itself defines people. This sex-segregated system resulted in Miki Ann DiMarco, the intersex individual born with a penis but who lived and identified herself as a woman, being placed in solitary confinement because the prison officials did not know what to do with a person living as a woman in a man's prison. She had to live in isolation despite the fact that she was of the lowest security risk (*DiMarco* 2004). Gender-variant individuals in prisons regularly face these problems of classification (Arkles 2009; Tarzwell 2006; Rosenblum 2000).

In each of these cases, as well as the countless others that gender-variant individuals contend with when trying to fit within society's various forms of sex segregation, these sex-segregated spaces become a primary tool for society to reinforce the binary distinction between men and women, thus marginalizing gender-variant individuals (Kogan 2009). The message delivered, that genitalia matter in classifying and categorizing, is at the heart of most sex segregation.

Particularly troubling for gender-variant individuals is that sex segregation of men also contributes to the development of negative attitudes about and harassment against those who do not conform to the hegemonic masculinity expected of them. Male peer groups actively work to police the boundaries of acceptable behavior for boys and men (Haywood and Mac an Ghaill 1996). This boundary policing occurs more frequently within groups of men and boys than does similar boundary policing within groups of women and girls because men and boys, as the higher status group in society, are more invested in maintaining the group identity. Moreover, males crossing gender boundaries, such as gender-variant individuals, threaten perceptions of ingroup cohesiveness and outgroup inferiority; in other words, if gender-nonconforming males were accepted by their male peer groups, they would call into question the cohesive identity of the group of males and risk making women look less inferior (Leaper 1994). When men display negative and dominating attitudes toward gender-nonconforming males, they also demonstrate to themselves and others that they are not feminine or gay and that they are indeed men and masculine (Curry 1991).

This development of negative and dominating attitudes toward gender-nonconforming males is evident in many sex-segregated settings. With respect to sex-segregated schooling, one of the studies of California's pilot single-sex educational institutions found that boys in the all-boys schools "set the rules of masculinity" by demeaning boys who crossed gender lines with homophobic teasing (Woody 2002). Surveying the research on this issue in the context of sex-segregated schools, Wayne Martino and Bob Meyenn write that "regardless of sexual orientation, those boys who fail to match the expectations of hegemonic heterosexual masculinity are more at risk from the harassing behaviours of other boys as opposed to their female peers" (2002, 313).

Sex-segregated sport is another area in which this gender policing occurs to the detriment of nonconforming men. A study of rugby players found that men on the sex-segregated teams used the same demeaning practices against gender-nonconforming men that they used against women (Schacht 1996). Another study found that gender-nonconforming behavior was policed in all-male locker rooms through derogatory homophobic targeting of individuals who revealed less traditionally masculine sides of their personalities (Messner and Stevens 2007). A study of college men's locker rooms found violent comments and derogatory jokes about gay men to occur "because it helps distance the athletes from being categorized as gay themselves" (Curry 1991, 130).

Sex-segregated bathrooms also provide a space for gender policing and harassment. Men who do not conform to hegemonic masculinity, especially adolescents in schools, are subject to harassment and violence in sex-segregated bathrooms (Browne 2004; Namaste 1996). As the Transgender Law Center has explained:

For many transgender people, finding a safe place to use the bathroom is a daily struggle. Even in cities or towns that are generally considered good places to be transgender (like San Francisco or Los Angeles), many transgender people are harassed, beaten and questioned by authorities in both women's and men's rooms. In a 2002 survey conducted by the San Francisco Human Rights Commission, nearly 50% of respondents reported having been harassed or assaulted in a public bathroom. Because of this, many transgender people avoid public bathrooms altogether and can develop health problems as a result. This not only affects people who think of themselves as transgender, but also many others who express their

gender in a non-stereotypical way but who may not identify as transgender (for instance, a masculine woman or an effeminate man). (Transgender Law Center 2005, 3)

Sex-segregated bathrooms can also be the site for abusive "sex verification" of gender-variant individuals, something that led to the two high-profile murders of Gwen Araujo and Brandon Teena (Bettcher 2007).

Those categorized as men but who do not fit within hegemonic masculinity are also treated poorly in other sex-segregated institutions. In prisons, Dee Farmer's story is illustrative, as she faced brutal violence in a men's
prison because she exhibited feminine characteristics (*Farmer* 1994). Her
story, of course, is not an isolated incident. A comprehensive study summarized and confirmed decades of findings that men who did not exhibit hegemonic masculinity within the prison context were abused or raped (Hensley
et al. 2003). Drug treatment programs and homeless shelters that segregate
based on sex also pose serious risks of punishment or harassment for failure
to fit within the sex binary (Spade 2000).

As with sex segregation's relationship to hegemonic masculinity, sex segregation is a powerful force in furthering the hegemony of men. Other parts
of life have similar effect, as sex segregation is certainly not alone in creating social acceptance of the seemingly natural category "men" or in being
a site for policing gender conformity and punishing those gender-variant
individuals who do not exhibit hegemonic masculinity. But sex segregation's
contribution to these aspects of the hegemony of men must be understood
and addressed as well.

Conclusion

Sex segregation is a powerful force in the lives of gender-variant individuals. In particular, as I have shown in this chapter's discussion of sex segregation and masculinity, sex segregation helps construct hegemonic masculinity
and perpetuate the hegemony of men. Hegemonic masculinity's requirement
that men not be feminine constricts identity in a way that particularly harms
gender-variant individuals. In this sense, institutions such as sex segregation
force everyone, and especially gender-variant individuals, to "do gender" or
"perform gender" in the way that postmodern and antiessentialist gender
theorists have described. Sex segregation also contributes to the hegemony
of men in the sense that it is a taken-for-granted institution that helps to construct and perpetuate the seemingly natural dichotomy between men and
women. It also helps to create environments in which men's relationship to

gender-variant individuals is one of dominance that can lead to discrimination, harassment, and violence.

However, because sex segregation that has survived the feminist reforms of the past half century is now taken for granted, it is rarely questioned despite its link to hegemonic masculinity and the hegemony of men. After all, the cases highlighted in this chapter as well as others involving gender-variant individuals seek solutions for such individuals within the confines of a sex-segregated world and never question the sex segregation in the first place. But gender-variant individuals who live in this world must question the status quo, as the powerful forces of gender policing and identity-based harassment and violence combine to continually make it a struggle for such individuals to fit in a sex-segregated, dichotomy-based world.

NOTES

1. Throughout this chapter, I am using a very strict and particular definition of sex segregation. By using the word "sex," I am referring to segregation that occurs based on a person's perceived status as a man or a woman. "Sex" is a term that refers to perceived biology, not to characteristics, personality, or traits commonly associated with people who share particular genitalia. Thus, "sex" is in contrast to "gender," as is clear when thinking about particular forms of segregation. For instance, people are not required to register for the military draft based on whether they exhibit masculine or feminine characteristics (their "gender") but rather based on their perceived genitalia, their biology (their "sex"). In other words, masculine women are not required to register for the draft; effeminate men are.

   By "segregation," I am referring to complete separation or exclusion by law or other rule. I am not merely referring to a classification in which people are treated differently based on sex. For instance, a law giving a preference for women over men for a particular benefit would be a sex-based classification under constitutional law but is not sex segregation as I am using the term. Moreover, I am not referring to non-rule-based segregation, in which there is no rule that requires separation or exclusion but complete separation or exclusion may result for reasons aside from a rule requiring it. For instance, a high school chess team that happens to have all boys on it but is open to everyone is not sex segregation under this definition.

2. Some of this analysis is adapted from a longer investigation of sex segregation and masculinity generally (Cohen 2010).

3. Although this chapter engages masculinities theory and what it means for gender-variant individuals in the context of sex segregation, there are also implications for women and femininities not discussed here.

REFERENCES

Arkles, Gabriel. 2009. Safety and Solidarity across Gender Lines: Rethinking Segregation of Transgender People in Detention. *Temple Political and Civil Rights Law Review* 18:515–60.

Ashe, Marie. 1987. Mind's Opportunity: Birthing a Poststructuralist Feminist Jurisprudence. *Syracuse Law Review* 38:1129–73.

Beasley, Christine. 2008. Rethinking Hegemonic Masculinity in a Globalizing World. *Men and Masculinities* 11:86–103.

Bettcher, Talia Mae. 2007. Evil Deceivers and Make-Believers: On Transphobic Violence and the Politics of Illusion. *Hypatia* 22:43–65.

Bird, Sharon R. 1996. Welcome to the Men's Club: Homosociality and the Maintenance of Hegemonic Masculinity. *Gender and Society* 10:120–32.

Browne, Kath. 2004. Genderism and the Bathroom Problem: (Re)materialising Sexed Sites, (Re)creating Sexed Bodies. *Gender, Place and Culture* 11:331–46.

Butler, Judith. 1999. *Gender Trouble: Feminism and the Subversion of Identity*, 2d ed. New York: Routledge.

Buzuvis, Erin E. 2010. Transgender Student-Athletes and Sex-Segregated Sport: Developing Policies of Inclusion for Intercollegiate and Interscholastic Athletes. Unpublished manuscript. Available at http://papers.ssrn.com/sol3/papers.cfm?abstract_id=1646059.

Case, Mary Anne. 1998. Unpacking Package Deals: Separate Spheres Are Not the Answer. *Denver University Law Review* 75:1305–20.

———. 1995. Disaggregating Gender from Sex and Sexual Orientation: The Effeminate Man in the Law and Feminist Jurisprudence. *Yale Law Journal* 105:1–105.

Chodorow, Nancy. 1971. Being and Doing: A Cross-Cultural Examination of the Socialization of Males and Females. In *Woman in Sexist Society: Studies in Power and Powerlessness*, edited by Vivian Gornick and Barbara K. Moran. New York: New American Library, 259–91.

Cohen, David S. 2011. The Stubborn Persistence of Sex Segregation. *Columbia Journal of Gender and Law* 20 (forthcoming).

———. 2010. Keeping Men "Men" and Women Down: Sex Segregation, Anti-Essentialism, and Masculinity. *Harvard Journal of Law and Gender* 33:509–53.

———. 2009. No Boy Left Behind? Single-Sex Education and the Essentialist Myth of Masculinity. *Indiana Law Journal* 84:135–88.

Connell, Raewyn. 2009. *Gender: In World Perspective*, 2d ed. Malden, MA: Polity Press.

Connell, R. W. 2005. *Masculinities*, 2d ed. Berkeley: University of California Press.

———. 1996. Teaching the Boys: New Research on Masculinity, and Gender Strategies for Schools. *Teachers College Record* 98:206–35.

Connell, R. W., and James W. Messerschmidt. 2005. Hegemonic Masculinity: Rethinking the Concept. *Gender and Society* 19(6):829–59.

Cooper, Frank R. 2009. Race and Essentialism in Gloria Steinem. *Berkeley Journal of African-American Law & Policy* 11(1):36–48.

Craig v. Boren, 429 U.S. 190 (1976).

Curry, Timothy J. 1991. Fraternal Bonding in the Locker Room: A Profeminist Analysis of Talk about Competition and Women. *Sociology of Sport* 8:119–35.

DiMarco v. Wyoming Department of Corrections, 300 F. Supp. 2d 1183 (D. Wyo. 2004).

Dowd, Nancy E. 2008. Masculinities and Feminist Legal Theory. *Wisconsin Journal of Law, Gender and Society* 23:201–48.

Equal Pay Act, 29 U.S.C. § 206 (2006).

Farmer v. Brennan, 511 U.S. 825 (1994).

Frug, Mary J. 1992. *Postmodern Legal Feminism*. New York: Routledge.

Gilbert, Rob, and Pam Gilbert. 1998. *Masculinity Goes to School*. New York: Routledge.

Goffman, Erving. 1977. The Arrangement between the Sexes. *Theory and Society* 4:301–31.

Gooren, Louis J. 2008. Olympic Sports and Transsexuals. *Asian Journal of Andrology* 10:427–32.

Haywood, Christian, and Máirtín Mac an Ghaill. 1996. Schooling Masculinities. In *Understanding Masculinities: Social Relations and Cultural Arenas*, edited by Máirtín Mac an Ghaill. Philadelphia: Open University Press, 50–60.

Hearn, Jeff. 2004. From Hegemonic Masculinity to the Hegemony of Men. *Feminist Theory* 5:49–72.

Hensley, Christopher, Jeremy Wright, Richard Tewksbury, and Tammy Castle. 2003. The Evolving Nature of Prison Argot and Sexual Hierarchies. *Prison Journal* 83:289–300.

Higgins, Tracy E. 1996. Anti-Essentialism, Relativism, and Human Rights. *Harvard Women's Law Journal* 19:89–126.

Hyde, Janet Shibley. 2005. The Gender Similarities Hypothesis. *American Psychologist* 60:581–92.

Jordan, Ellen. 1995. Fighting Boys and Fantasy Play: The Construction of Masculinity in the Early Years of School. *Gender and Education* 7:69–86.

Kapczynski, Amy. 2003. Same-Sex Privacy and the Limits of Antidiscrimination Law. *Yale Law Journal* 112:1257–93.

Karst, Kenneth L. 1991. The Pursuit of Manhood and the Desegregation of the Armed Forces. *UCLA Law Review* 38:499–581.

Kastl v. Maricopa County Community College District, No. CV-02-1531-PHX-SRB, 2006 WL 2460636 (D. Ariz. 2006).

Kimmel, Michael S. 2008. Introduction. In *The Gendered Society Reader*, 3d ed., edited by Michael S. Kimmel and Amy Aronson. New York: Oxford University Press, 1–6.

Kimmel, Michael. 1996. *Manhood in America: A Cultural History*. New York: Free Press.

Knessel, Anna. 2010. Caster Semenya May Return to Track This Month after IAAF Clearance. *Guardian*, July 6.

Kogan, Terry S. 2009. Transsexuals in Public Restrooms: Law, Cultural Geography and *Etsitty v. Utah Transit Authority. Temple Political and Civil Rights Law Review* 18:673–97.

———. 2007. Sex-Separation in Public Restrooms: Law, Architecture, and Gender. *Michigan Journal of Gender and Law* 14:1–57.

———. 1997. Transsexuals and Critical Gender Theory: The Possibility of a Restroom Labeled "Other." *Hastings Law Journal* 48:1223–55.

Lacan, Jacques. 1977. *Ecrits: A Selection*. Translated by Alan Sheridan. New York: Norton.

Leaper, Campbell. 1994. Exploring the Consequences of Gender Segregation in Social Relationships. In *Childhood Gender Segregation: Causes and Consequences*, edited by Campbell Leaper. San Francisco: Jossey-Bass.

Martino, Wayne, and Bob Meyenn. 2002. "War, Guns and Cool, Tough Things": Interrogating Single-Sex Classes as a Strategy for Engaging Boys in English. *Cambridge Journal of Education* 32:303–24.

Messner, Michael A. 2002. *Taking the Field: Women, Men, and Sports*. Minneapolis: University of Minnesota Press.

Messner, Michael A., and Mark Stevens. 2007. Scoring without Consent: Confronting Male Athletes' Sexual Violence against Women. In *Out of Play: Critical Essays on Gender and Sport*, edited by Michael A. Messner. Albany: State University of New York Press, 107–22.

Namaste, Ki. 1996. Genderbashing: Sexuality, Gender, and the Regulation of Public Space. *Environment and Planning D: Society and Space* 14:221–40.

Renold, Emma. 2005. *Girls, Boys and Junior Sexualities: Exploring Children's Gender and Sexual Relations in the Primary School.* New York: Routledge.

Rhode, Deborah. 1986. Association and Assimilation. *Northwestern University Law Review* 81:106–45.

Rosenblum, Darren. 2000. "Trapped" in Sing Sing: Transgendered Prisoners Caught in Gender Binarism. *Michigan Journal of Gender and Law* 6:499–571.

Sanders, Joel. 1996. Introduction. In *Stud: Architectures of Masculinity*, edited by Joel Sanders. New York: Princeton Architectural Press, 10–25.

Schacht, Steven P. 1996. Misogyny On and Off the "Pitch." *Gender and Society* 10:550–65.

Shelley, Christopher A. 2008. *Transpeople: Repudiation, Trauma, Healing.* Buffalo: University of Toronto Press.

Spade, Dean. 2008. Documenting Gender. *Hastings Law Journal* 59:731–832.

———. 2000. Compliance Is Gendered: Struggling for Gender Self-Determination in a Hostile Economy. In *Transgender Rights*, edited by Paisley Currah, Richard M. Juang, and Shannon Price Minter. Minneapolis: University of Minnesota Press, 217–41.

Tarzwell, Sydney. 2006. The Gender Lines Are Marked with Razor Wire: Addressing State Prison Policies and Practices for the Management of Transgender Prisoners. *Columbia Human Rights Law Review* 38:167–219.

Title IX, 20 U.S.C. §§ 1681-88 (2006).

Title VII, 42 U.S.C. § 2000(e) (2006).

Transgender Law Center. 2005. *Peeing in Peace: A Resource Guide for Transgender Activists and Allies.* San Francisco: Transgender Law Center.

Valdes, Francisco. 1995. Queers, Sissies, Dykes, and Tomboys: Deconstructing the Conflation of "Sex," "Gender," and "Sexual Orientation" in Euro-American Law and Society. *California Law Review* 83:1–377.

Wecter, Dixon. 1937. The Saga of American Society. Quoted in Michael M. Burns, *The Exclusion of Women from Influential Men's Clubs: The Inner Sanctum and the Myth of Full Equality. Harvard Civil Rights-Civil Liberties Law Review* 18:321–407.

Williams, Joan C. 1990. Feminism and Post-Structuralism. *Michigan Law Review* 88:1776–91.

Woody, Elisabeth L. 2002. Constructions of Masculinity in California's Single-Gender Academies. In *Gender in Policy and Practice: Perspectives on Single-Sex and Coeducational Schooling*, edited by Amanda Datnow and Lee Hubbard. New York: RoutledgeFalmer, 280–303.

Yuracko, Kimberly A. 2004. Private Nurses and Playboy Bunnies: Explaining Permissible Sex Discrimination. *California Law Review* 92:147–213.

9

E-race-ing Gender: The Racial Construction of Prison Rape

KIM SHAYO BUCHANAN

In men's jails and prisons as elsewhere, sexual abuse is a form of gender violence. Institutional problems such as overcrowding, inadequate supervision, inappropriate security classification, and lackadaisical investigation contribute to sexual abuse, but prison rape[1] is greatly exacerbated by institutional practices that enforce the most harmful forms of masculinity. Many men's prisons are plagued by homophobia, high rates of physical violence, and an institutional culture that requires inmates to prove their masculinity by fighting (Buchanan 2010; Sabo et al. 2001). Whether the perpetrators of sexual abuse are staff or other prisoners, they tend to target inmates who are less masculine: smaller, weaker, younger, naïve, disabled, effeminate, gay, bisexual or transgendered, or who have been "made gay" by being previously raped (Beck et al. 2010a; Sabo 2001). Thus, a nationwide survey conducted in 2008-09 by the Bureau of Justice Statistics (BJS) revealed that, of all factors associated with prison sexual victimization, prior sexual abuse and non-straight sexual orientation were by far the most powerful predictors that an inmate would be sexually abused (Beck et al. 2010a). Staff and inmate abusers alike target gay, bisexual, and transgender inmates, and those who have been previously abused, for sexual violence (ibid.).

The gendered reality of prison sexual violence is hiding in plain sight. The slang used by both prisoners and staff to describe the victims and perpetrators of sexual violence reveals its gendered nature. The prison rapist is commonly described in hypermasculine terms, as a "jock," "daddy," or "booty bandit." His victim is often described as a "fag," a "queen," or a "punk" who has been "turned out" or "made gay." Thus, in prison as in many hypermasculine institutions in the outside world, same-sex sexual abuse is a practice of gender enforcement that enhances the perpetrator's masculinity while emasculating his target.

But prison rape is rarely addressed, in either popular culture or policy discourse, as a gendered practice. Instead, policymakers, academics, and other commentators persistently, and inaccurately, portray prison sexual abuse as a racial phenomenon. In spite of recent, methodologically rigorous large-scale victimization surveys whose results tend to contradict the stereotype, the conventional understanding remains that prison rape is disproportionately black-on-white (Buchanan 2010).

In the outside world, the myth of the black rapist—the notion of white vulnerability to black men's sexual violence—has long been discredited as a racist trope that has traditionally been deployed to promote institutionalized violence against black men (Wiegman 1995; Duru 2004). In men's prisons, however, this myth remains surprisingly vigorous and influential.

In this chapter, I explore the construction, consequences, and implications of the black-on-white rape myth. How do prisoners, guards, administrators, academics, and other observers come to believe that prison rape is black-on-white when it usually isn't? What is the effect of the black-on-white rape myth on prison law and policy? Why does this stereotype continue to influence prison law and policy when recent studies tend to contradict it? And what does it tell us about our understanding of race and gender in the outside world?

This chapter will proceed in three parts. First, I review the best available empirical data to illuminate the racial dynamics of prison rape. These data do not support the notion that prison rape typically, or disproportionately, involves black prisoners attacking whites. Contrary to stereotype, it is multiracial prisoners, not whites, who report significantly elevated risks of sexual abuse by other inmates that are unexplained by other factors. Moreover, black prisoners report significantly higher rates of sexual abuse by staff than white inmates do. Yet these racial disparities are invisible in policy discourse about race and prison rape.

Second, I review the narrative practices by which prisoners, correctional officials, policymakers, academics, and others come to understand prison rape as typically black-on-white. Accounts from all these sources tend to highlight racial data when they tend to confirm the stereotype—that is, when the victim is white and the perpetrator is black—and ignore racial data that tend to refute it. The black-on-white rape myth seems to broadly influence cultural perceptions about whether and when race is relevant to sexual abuse.

Third, I consider the consequences and implications of the black-on-white rape myth. It seems to influence correctional responses to inmates' individual rape allegations, and gives rise to misguided policy recommendations. Moreover, these stereotype-based policy recommendations tend to deflect policy attention from the institutional and gender dynamics that have been shown to foster sexual violence. Finally, broad cultural acceptance of the black-on-white rape myth reveals assumptions about black and white masculinities that persist in the wider society outside prison.

The Racial Dynamics of Prison Rape

In men's prisons, the data strongly suggest that sexual abuse is not typically black-on-white. Of the six nationwide or statewide, methodologically rigorous victimization surveys that have been conducted in U.S. prisons to date (all conducted between 2006 and 2009),[2] none shows that prison rape typically, or even disproportionately, involves black prisoners assaulting whites (Beck and Harrison 2007, 2008; Beck et al. 2010a, 2010b; Jenness et al. 2007; Wolff et al. 2006, 2008). In every survey that published racial data on overall sexual victimization (by inmates or staff), white inmates reported *the same or lower* overall rates of prison sexual victimization as nonwhite inmates did (Beck and Harrison 2008; Beck et al. 2010a, 2010b; Jenness et al. 2007; Wolff et al. 2006, 2008). For example, in 2007, the BJS found that 2.9 percent of white jail inmates reported any sexual victimization, compared to 3.2 percent of black and Latino inmates and 4.2 percent of multiracial inmates. Other surveys found no significant racial differences in overall rates of sexual victimization reported by black and white inmates (Beck et al. 2010b; Wolff et al. 2006, 2008). None of the six victimization surveys provides any evidence that prison rape is often interracial, or that white inmates are more likely than nonwhites to be sexually abused in prison.[3]

Moreover, the typical prison rapist is not the archetypal burly black prisoner, but a guard or other prison employee. All the surveys found that, in men's prisons and jails, inmates reported higher rates of sexual abuse by staff than by other inmates of any race. (None of these surveys asked for the race of staff abusers.) For example, in the most recent nationwide BJS survey, conducted in 2008–2009, 2.8 percent of prisoners reported sexual abuse by staff, compared to 2.1 percent who reported sexual abuse by other inmates. Likewise, in jails, 2.0 percent of inmates reported sexual abuse by staff, compared to 1.5 percent who reported sexual abuse by other inmates (Beck et al. 2010a).

If the black-on-white prison rape story were true, we would expect victimization surveys to show large racial disparities that consistently pointed to white vulnerability and were not accounted for by other, nonracial factors. Even when we look only at sexual abuse committed by inmates, the survey results do not look like this.

The data on sexual abuse by inmates are mixed. One statewide study found no significant racial differences in sexual abuse by inmates (Wolff et al. 2006, 2008), while another, in California, found that *black* inmates reported the highest rates of sexual victimization (Jenness et al. 2007). The nationwide BJS surveys, by contrast, provide some support for the stereotype of heightened white vulnerability in that white inmates were significantly more likely than their black or Latino counterparts to report sexual abuse *by other prisoners*: in 2008–2009, for example, the BJS found that white (3.0 percent) and multiracial (4.4 percent) prisoners reported significantly higher rates of sexual abuse by other inmates than the 1.3 percent of black, 1.4 percent of Latino, and 2.7 percent of "Other" inmates who reported it (Beck et al. 2010a; see also Beck et al. 2010b; Beck and Harrison 2008). Moreover, a preliminary BJS regression analysis, shown at table 7 of its 2010 report, showed that in prisons (but not in jails), whites' risk of sexual victimization by other inmates remained significantly higher even after controlling for sex, age, weight, marital status, and education (Beck et al. 2010a, 13).

This survey also found that more than 60 percent of male victims described one or more of their inmate assailants as black, compared to 36–39 percent who reported one or more white inmate assailants, and 16–24 percent who described one or more inmate assailants as Latino (Beck et al. 2010a). The BJS provides no information about the racial composition of victim-offender dyads. Because many male victims were assaulted more than once, or by more than one assailant at a time, it is difficult to compare these statistics to the overall prison population, which is 40.1 percent black, 33.1 percent white, 21.1 percent Hispanic, and 5.7 percent "Other" (West 2010). The survey results suggest, though, that black inmates, and to a lesser extent white inmates, may be overrepresented as perpetrators, relative to population.

Nonetheless, the BJS's "final multivariate logistic model," a regression analysis presented at table 12 of its 2010 victimization survey report, found that white inmates' higher reported rates of inmate sexual victimization were wholly accounted for by other, nonracial factors. This regression analysis, unlike the limited analysis presented at table 7, controlled for *all* factors that contribute to inmate vulnerability, including prior sexual abuse, sexual orientation, age, weight, education, marital status, offense, and criminal justice history. It concluded that white prisoners' risk of intimate rape was not significantly different from that of other ethnic groups (Beck et al. 2010a, 18–19). For white, black, Latino, and "Other" prisoners, race did *not* significantly predict the likelihood that other inmates would sexually assault them (ibid.). This result is inconsistent with the notion that black or nonwhite inmates target white inmates for sexual assault.

Meanwhile, all surveys that investigated sexual abuse *by staff* found that black inmates were significantly more likely than whites to say they had been victimized. In 2008–2009, for example, 3.2 percent of black prison inmates reported staff sexual abuse, which was significantly higher than the 2.4 percent of Latino and 2.3 percent of white prison inmates who reported it (Beck et al. 2010a; see also Beck and Harrison 2008; Beck et al. 2010b; Wolff et al. 2008). The BJS's "final" regression analysis found that even after controlling for all other risk factors, black inmates remained significantly more likely than whites to be sexually abused by staff (Beck et al. 2010a, 18). Because staff sexual abuse is considerably more common than sexual abuse by other inmates, and staff members are significantly less likely to victimize whites, all the victimization surveys found that white inmates reported rates of overall sexual abuse that were *the same or lower* than the rates reported by their black counterparts.

The recent survey data do not support the black-on-white account of prison rape. Instead, the surveys reveal two persistent racial disparities that remain statistically significant after controlling for all other factors. One is that multiracial (not white) prisoners may be disproportionately targeted for sexual abuse by other inmates (in prisons; the racial differences in inmate victimization by inmates in jails were not statistically significant). The second is that black and multiracial inmates (in both prisons and jails) seem to be disproportionately targeted for sexual assault by staff. These racial disparities, which warrant further inquiry, have not been acknowledged or explained in academic literature, and they are invisible in policy discourse about prison rape. For example, the National Prison Rape Elimination Commission (NPREC), a major national commission established by the Prison Rape Elimination Act of 2003, heard testimony from prisoners, their advocates, staff, administrators, politicians, and the public between March 2005 and December 2007 and issued a report, with recommended standards for the elimination of prison rape, in June 2009 (National Prison

Rape Elimination Commission 2009a). The committee heard (inaccurate) testimony that prison rape was disproportionately black-on-white, and its recommendations addressed this unsubstantiated concern (Austin 2007; National Prison Rape Elimination Commission 2009b). Nonetheless, in a review of the NPREC transcripts and of its report and recommendations, I have not found any mention of the racial disparities that are better substantiated by the empirical data. No witness or commissioner mentioned, and the NPREC report and recommendations did not address, the vulnerability of multiracial prisoners to other inmates' sexual abuse, nor did the witnesses, report, or standards acknowledge the vulnerability of black or other non-white prisoners to sexual abuse by staff (National Prison Rape Elimination Commission 2009a; National Prison Rape Elimination Commission 2009b; National Prison Rape Elimination Commission 2005–2007).

The victimization survey data do not conclusively refute the black-on-white stereotype (and cannot do so, given the paucity of information provided about perpetrators). But the data do not show the large and consistent racial disparities suggested by the black-on-white account of prison rape. Racial disparities in sexual abuse victimization are inconsistent across studies and analyses. They identify various ethnic groups, including black, multiracial, and white inmates, as facing heightened risks. And where racial disparities are significant at all, the size of racial effects is small compared to the much more powerful predictive effects of prior sexual abuse and nonstraight sexual orientation.

In fact, the individual characteristics that most powerfully predict sexual victimization are gendered, rather than racial. The BJS analysis found that prior sexual abuse and nonstraight sexual orientation are by far the strongest predictors of an inmate's risk of sexual victimization, whether by inmates or by staff (Beck et al. 2010a). As I have shown previously, effeminacy, nonstraight sexual orientation, and prior sexual abuse are often treated by prisoners and staff as failures of masculinity which mark a prisoner as a potential target of sexual abuse (Buchanan 2010). The data indicate that whiteness is not itself an especially important risk factor for sexual victimization, but failed masculinity is.

Black-on-White Prison Rape: Construction of the Myth

Although the data do not support the notion that prison rape is typically black-on-white, many people involved in prisons and their administration—prisoners, correctional officials, policymakers, some judges, and many academics—believe that it is (Buchanan 2010). How do inmates, staff, and other observers come to believe that prison sexual violence is mainly black-on-white—in spite of what they are observing?

Whether inside prison or in the outside world, the myth of black-on-white rape draws on powerful cultural stereotypes that have shaped understandings of black and white masculinities for decades. Black men have long been stereotyped as supermasculine: inhumanly strong, violent, animalistic, hypersexual, and ungovernable (Harris 2000; Wiegman 1995; Duru 2004; Goff et al. 2008). White men are seen (and may see themselves) as effeminate by comparison (Harris 2000; Wiegman 1995; Bederman 1995). The survey data do not contradict these troubling stereotypes as they do the black-on-white myth: to the extent that the BJS found white men facing higher rates of victimization by inmates, it calculates that their vulnerability is shaped by factors other than race. The BJS report did not identify what those factors were, but in general, it found that prior sexual abuse and nonstraight sexual orientation were by far the most powerful predictors of an inmate's risk of sexual victimization.

In prison, popular and academic culture, the presumed vulnerability of white inmates, is explained in terms of racialized masculinity. Many prisoners and guards believe that white inmates are "weak" and "cannot fight as well as black inmates" (Fleisher and Krienert 2006, 103). As one black former prisoner put it, "Young white men from affluent homes are soft and easily intimidated by hardened black criminals," although he offered a more nuanced understanding of their vulnerability: tougher whites, he said, "have no problem, and the weak blacks are victimized; but the white children of affluence are especially marked for servitude" (Johnson and Hampikian 2003, 52).

Other prisoners and correctional officials construe prison rape—which they conflate with interracial dating—as a form of racial revenge. A white inmate claimed that prison rape was "more prevalent" with black prisoners because it "gives them a sense of empowerment over the whitey to take that from him. . . . It's definitely an empowerment thing. It's just like on the streets when you see a black male with a white girl. It's to let the white boys know [they] can get your girls. I've talked to black guys about that in here. They say it's true" (Fleisher and Krienert 2006, 170). Dr. Frank Rundle, a former California prison psychiatrist, declared: "It does happen that blacks often have a preference for white slaves, and that gets into the whole business of racial subjugation and revenge—the same way it does in society. There are a lot of blacks who prefer white women and it has to do sometimes with a conscious kind of revenge" (Rideau and Wikberg 1992, 93).

Prisoners and staff are not alone in the perception that white prisoners' masculinity is especially vulnerable to that of black men. Policymakers often assert that prison rape is "interracial," often without citing any evidence. The Congressional Findings of the Prison Rape Elimination Act of 2003 declare, without citation, that the "frequently interracial character of prison sexual assaults significantly exacerbates interracial tensions" (Prison Rape Elimination Act of 2003, section 2(9)). The generally progressive 2009 recommendations of the National Prison Rape Elimination Commission assert, without evidence, that "being in the racial minority within a given facility characterized by marked racial tension" constitutes a risk factor for sexual victimization (National Prison Rape Elimination Commission 2009b, 29). Nationwide, white inmates constitute less than 35 percent of the male prison population. A plurality is African American, and nearly two-thirds are non-white—black, Latino, mixed, or "Other" (West 2010). Although there is no evidence that prison rape is ordinarily interracial, policymakers focus on the presumed racial dynamics of prison rape at the expense of racial disparities which, unlike the racial rape myth, are substantiated by reliable empirical data. It seems that multiracial prisoners may be vulnerable to inmate rape, and black prisoners remain vulnerable to staff sexual abuse, but policymakers do not acknowledge or address these disparities.

The black-on-white account of prison rape is so entrenched that its factual basis has not yet been challenged in the prison rape literature (but cf. Buchanan 2010). Many contemporary academic commentators uncritically assert, without attribution or by citing 30-year-old sources, that prison rape typically involves black men attacking vulnerable whites.[4] But even before the first large-scale, methodologically rigorous studies were published in 2007, it should have been apparent that the empirical basis of the conventional racial story could not withstand critical scrutiny. Contemporary academics who assert that prison rape is black-on-white rely upon sources published in the late 1960s, 1970s, and early 1980s (particularly Davis 1968; Scacco 1975; Toch 1977; Carroll 1974; Carroll 1977; Lockwood 1980; Nacci and Kane 1984), all of which share conspicuous methodological flaws (Gaes 2008; Gaes and Goldberg 2004). For example, they did not use random probability samples of the surveyed populations (Gaes and Goldberg 2004). The only exception, a federal study conducted in 1982, relied on in-person interviews by "an articulate, black ex-offender" (Nacci and Kane 1984), and its authors provide no data to support their declaration that black assailants outnumber white ones "because they tend to assault in large groups" (ibid.). Another study that is frequently cited today was conducted from 1966 to 1968 by A. J. Davis, a district attorney who estimated the incidence of prison rape based on interviews of non-randomly selected prisoners (Davis 1968). The interviews were conducted by the district attorney, his staff, and police officers. The two most recent studies cited in support of the black-on-white account of prison rape were conducted in 1996 and 2000, and were likewise unreliable: they surveyed a non-random sample of prisoners, obtained response rates of less than 30 percent without comparing survey responders to non-responders, and were conducted by a non-confidential paper and pencil questionnaire, which raises concerns about collusion and lack of independence in filling out the survey (Struckman-Johnson 1996; Struckman-Johnson and Struckman-Johnson 2000; Gaes and Goldberg 2004).

A cursory examination of these and other such studies should reveal that they cannot be relied upon as evidence of the racial dynamics of prison rape in the twenty-first century. The credulity with which these studies' racial findings have been received, and repeated, may reflect their conformity to stereotypical expectations.

By contrast, survey results contradicting the black-on-white stereotype tend to pass unremarked, even by the survey researchers themselves. For example, the results of all the methodologically rigorous large-scale victimization surveys that have been conducted to date tend to contradict the stereotype in several respects, but academics, advocates, and survey researchers have not noted this. The limited data published by the BJS, as well as statewide surveys conducted in 2006 by sociologist Valerie Jenness and economist Nancy Wolff, offer no evidence that white men face heightened overall risk of sexual assault in prison. Rather, the results of these surveys suggest that it is nonwhite prisoners who may face heightened risk of sexual victimization, especially by staff. Although the results of these surveys tend to disconfirm the conventional wisdom about the racial dynamics of prison rape, none of the survey reports challenged the stereotype or analyzed its counter-stereotypical racial findings. Indeed, Wolff, whose own survey found no statistically significant differences in sexual victimization by inmates, nonetheless argued—based on the decades-old non-random studies discussed above—that black prisoners are likely to target whites for rape as a form of "racial vengeance or rage, where the heretofore underclass (people of color) dominate the upper class (whites) and exert this dominance through acts of victimization that are humiliating, shaming, and degrading" (Wolff et al. 2008, 468–69; parentheses in the original).

In formal and informal discussions of prison rape, racial dynamics tend to be highlighted when they confirm the black-on-white racial stereotype, and are nearly invisible when they contradict it. Prisoners whose memoirs discuss inmate vulnerability to prison rape tend to focus more on measures of masculinity than on racial factors. They often describe likely targets as "pretty," "weak," small, young, naïve, or gay (Dennis and Stephens 1998;

Harkleroad 2000; Lumsden 2006; James 2005; Wright 2008). But when they address race at all, inmate authors tend to point out that the attacker is black or the victim is white. For example, in a chapter on inmate rape suggestively titled "The Sexual Jungle," prison writers Wilbert Rideau and Ron Wikberg describe dozens of instances of prison rape (1992). In most of them, they do not mention the race of victim or assailant. But whenever they do mention the race of an assailant, he is black. With one possible exception, whenever they mention the race of a victim, he is white.

A similar narrative practice characterizes judicial opinions. Race is rarely mentioned in Eighth Amendment sexual assault cases, but the rare cases in which race is mentioned point out that the victim was white and the assailant was black. For example, in one 1998 case, the district court judge observed: "Plaintiff, a 5'8" tall, 136 pound white male was 18 years old when he was . . . assigned to share a double cell with inmate Robert Ramey, a thirty-eight-year-old, six-foot one-inch, 290-pound African-American male serving a thirty-three-and-one-half year sentence . . . for forcible sodomy and abduction-with-intent-to-defile a twelve-year-old white male" (*Wilson v. Wright* 1998, 652, 655; see also *Butler v. Dowd* 1992).To these authors, race seems relevant enough to mention when it conforms to the black-on-white stereotype, and goes unmentioned at most other times. This narrative practice leaves a powerful impression that assailants are generally black, and victims are white.

Unfortunately, the BJS's presentation of its statistical data also tends to follow this distinctive narrative pattern. BJS reports tend to draw attention to racial data when they conform to the black-on-white stereotype, and to downplay racial findings when they refute it. For example, in its three most recent reports on sexual abuse that prisoners reported to correctional authorities (Beck and Harrison 2006; Beck et al. 2007; Beck and Guerino 2011), the BJS highlights the race of victims and perpetrators for only those sexual abuse allegations that correctional investigators had found to be "substantiated." "Substantiated" cases represent a very small proportion of sexual abuse allegations that correctional officials hear about (which, because of underreporting, likely represent a tiny proportion of sexual abuse that occurs: see, e.g., National Prison Rape Elimination Commission 2009a; Beck and Harrison 2007; Eigenberg 1989). Of the sexual abuse allegations they do hear about, prison investigators deem more than 80 percent to be either "unsubstantiated" (unproven) or "unfounded" (false) (Beck and Guerino 2011; Beck et al. 2007; Beck and Harrison 2006). In the 2005 and 2006 reports, the BJS published a chart highlighting the racial distribution of "substantiated" cases, that is, the approximately 15 percent of sexual abuse allegations that prison staff believe and may act upon. This chart shows that 72–73 percent of "substantiated" victims are white, and that almost half of their assailants are black. In "substantiated" cases, black perpetrators were more than twice as likely to assault white as black victims (Beck et al. 2007; Beck and Harrison 2006). (The racial results of "substantiated" allegations in 2007–2008, the most recent years available, were essentially similar, but were not presented in chart form (Beck and Guerino 2011).) In none of these reports does the BJS provide any information about the racial distribution of the vast majority of sexual abuse allegations, which correctional investigators deem to be "unsubstantiated" or "unfounded."

Correctional authorities acknowledge that sexual abuse is severely under-reported (Beck and Harrison 2007; National Prison Rape Elimination Commission 2009a). Indeed, "officers are relatively confident that inmates will not report victimization" (Eigenberg 1989, 50). Thus the BJS warns that correctional records of sexual abuse must be viewed with considerable caution (Beck and Harrison 2007). If, however, the results of prison investigations were to be taken at face value, they would suggest that whites (who constitute less than 35 percent of the male prison population) are being sexually assaulted at about four times the rate of nonwhites. None of the victimization surveys provides any evidence that white inmates face such a greatly elevated risk.

The broadly shared cultural pattern of emphasizing racial data that conform to the rape myth and de-emphasizing those that contradict it is replicated in the BJS's most recent survey report, published in August 2010 (Beck et al. 2010a). In the one-page executive summary of this survey, entitled "Highlights," the BJS underlined white prisoners' vulnerability to sexual violence by other inmates, while soft-pedaling its more statistically robust finding that black prisoners were at significantly heightened risk of sexual victimization by staff. The "Highlights" declare that "rates of inmate-on-inmate sexual victimization in prisons and jails were *significantly* higher among inmates who were white or multi-racial compared to blacks" (ibid. 5; emphasis added). Meanwhile, the "Highlights" describe the racial findings with respect to black inmates' disproportionate victimization in muted terms: "After controlling for multiple inmate characteristics, rates of reported staff sexual misconduct were lower among white inmates (compared to black inmates)" (ibid.; parentheses in the original). The language chosen by the BJS to summarize its findings emphasizes white inmates' vulnerability while underplaying that of black inmates. For example, it describes whites' vulnerability as "significant," even though the BJS's "final" statistical analysis shows it not to be, and neglects to describe blacks' vulnerability as "significant" when it is (ibid. table 12 at 18). It characterizes inmate abuse of whites as "victimiza-tion," while describing staff abuse of blacks as "misconduct." Furthermore, although all the BJS's survey data depend on inmate self-reporting, the BJS presents whites' heightened vulnerability as a fact—whites' "rates of inmate-on-inmate sexual victimization . . . were significantly higher"—while treating blacks' heightened vulnerability as an allegation: black inmates "reported" higher rates of sexual abuse by staff. All these descriptive differences tend to reinforce the stereotype of white vulnerability, while downplaying the sur-vey's counterstereotypical findings: that, in the final analysis, whiteness is not a significant risk factor for sexual victimization by other prisoners, but mul-tiracial identity is, and that blackness is a significant risk factor for sexual victimization by staff (ibid. 18, 91).

Official sources, as well as prisoners and academic commentators, tend to emphasize even dubious racial information about prison rape when it tends to confirm the black-on-white stereotype, but tend to underplay even robust racial data when they tend to refute it. There is no reason to believe that this narrative practice is intentional, but it appears that widely held racial stereo-types may influence cultural perceptions of whether and when race matters in rape cases.

Implications of the Black-on-White Rape Myth

The black-on-white rape myth is unsupported by the survey data, but why does it matter? For inmates, it may matter very much: prison guards and investigators acknowledge that they are more likely to believe allega-tions of sexual abuse when the victim is white (Eigenberg 1989; Eigenberg 2000). Since the BJS does not provide a racial breakdown of "unfounded" or "unsubstantiated" allegations—that is, the vast majority of them—the BJS reports do not allow a determination of whether white victims are more likely to report their abuse to prison officials, or prison officials are more likely to believe them, or, most likely, both. A more accurate understanding of the racial dynamics of prison sexual abuse might reveal a need for policy reforms to encourage reporting by non-stereotypical victims, and to address investigators' "unfounding" of non-stereotypical allegations.

From a policy perspective, the stereotype of black-on-white prison rape has several undesirable effects. First, the powerful black-on-white rape myth (or fantasy) eclipses the real racial, gender, and institutional factors that con-tribute to prison sexual abuse. The cultural intuition that stronger, hypersex-ual, violent black men pose a threat to weaker, more intelligent, more civi-lized whites seems to eclipse the racial, gendered, and institutional realities of prison violence that prisoners and guards observe, and statisticians count. We see what we expect to see.

The racial dynamics of sexual abuse, as revealed in victimization surveys, differ substantially from the stereotype. The survey data do not support the notion that white prisoners are the typical victims of prison rape. Multiracial prisoners, on the other hand, may face elevated risk of sexual abuse by other inmates, while black prisoners seem to face a disproportionate risk of sexual abuse by staff. These findings warrant further investigation, but—unlike the black-on-white stereotype—received no attention from NPREC. The black-on-white stereotype tends to foreclose discussion of counterstereotypical racial disparities.

By attributing prison rape to the imagined criminal sexual deviance of black men, the black-on-white rape myth also tends to obscure institutional complicity in the sexual abuse of prisoners. Victimization surveys consistently reveal that correctional staff sexually assault inmates more often than their fellow inmates do. Moreover, policies and practices of institutional governance can create a prison environment that either tolerates or suppresses sexual abuse by staff and inmates. Two recent national commissions have found that sexual abuse (by both staff and prisoners) is more likely in institutions that are ill-designed, overcrowded, and understaffed. (National Prison Rape Elimination Commission 2009a; Commission on Safety and Abuse in America's Prisons 2006). Moreover, correctional officials know that the use of objective, reliable security classification measures, direct supervision of inmates by guards, suppression of physical violence, zero tolerance for sexual violence, mandatory and thorough investigation of every allegation of sexual abuse, the use of modern surveillance technology, and the deployment of internal and independent oversight can greatly reduce sexual abuse in correctional facilities (ibid.; Farbstein and Wener 1989; Beard 2006; Stalder 2006; Horn 2006; Goord 2006).

It is not surprising, then, that the elevated rates of sexual abuse found in some men's prisons are not explained by racial or other demographic characteristics of the inmate population. The most recent BJS analysis found that, in the men's facilities with the highest surveyed rates of sexual violence, inmates reported sexual abuse at more than double the rates that could be predicted based on inmate characteristics (Beck et al. 2010a). It seems likely that these institutions are administered differently—that is, worse—than institutions whose inmate populations are demographically comparable, but which have lower reported rates of sexual victimization.

As I have pointed out previously, prisons with high rates of sexual violence are often administered in accordance with an unacknowledged, gendered mode of institutional governance (Buchanan 2010). Too often, staff and administrators enforce a homophobic institutional culture in which prisoners are expected to prove their masculinity by fighting. It is not uncommon for staff to refuse to protect prisoners against sexual abuse, telling the victim (or potential victim) that he should "be a man" by fighting off his assailants (Buchanan 2010; Human Rights Watch 2001, 153). If he is unable to do so, staff and investigators often refuse to protect the victim or punish the perpetrators, telling the victim that he deserves the abuse because he is, or has been made, "gay" (Buchanan 2010; Just Detention International 2009, 1).

To the extent that institutions enforce this toxic model of masculinity, rather than adopting well-known best practices of institutional governance, the myth of white vulnerability to hypersexual black violence tends to excuse such institutional failure. The racial rape myth attributes prison rape to the criminal sexual deviance of black men, and to the concomitant vulnerability of gentler, more civilized whites. If rape is attributable to the contrasting masculine natures of black and white men, it might seem that there is little (beyond racial segregation) that prison administrators could do to prevent it.

It is hardly surprising, then, that the racial rape myth has given rise to calls for racial segregation in prisons (Scacco 1975; Jacobs 1983; Wolff et al. 2008). In 2008, for example, Wolff called for "practices and policies that minimize [perpetrators'] opportunities" (2008, 469–70) by "separating those with characteristics that make them likely targets from other inmates with predatory characteristics" (ibid. 470). Responsible security classification practices would, of course, require this. But Wolff's racial argument suggests that whites are the "likely targets" who should be separated from the "predators" she characterizes as nonwhite prisoners motivated by "racial vengeance or rage" (ibid. 468–69).

Because best practices of institutional governance require that persons at high risk of being victimized be separated from persons at high risk of being abusive (National Prison Rape Elimination Commission 2009b), it seems likely that correctional authorities who believe, in good faith, that sexual abuse is disproportionately black-on-white will think that racial segregation is an appropriate means to prevent it. In 2005, eight states invoked "the problem of inter-racial rape in prisons" to argue before the United States Supreme Court that racial segregation in prison was not only permissible under the *Turner v. Safley* standard, but was constitutionally required (Brief of the States of Utah et al. 2005).

More subtly, the conventional assumption that prison rape is interracial seems to have influenced the National Prison Rape Elimination Commission to repeatedly exhort prison administrators to investigate what they perceive to be the racial dynamics of prison rape. NPREC rightly recommends data collection, review, and incident analysis with respect to every allegation of sexual assault. However, in light of the absence of quantitative data indicating that race is an important factor affecting sexual abuse, the Standards for the Prevention, Detection, Response and Monitoring of Sexual Abuse that NPREC proposed in 2009 place undue emphasis on racial factors, at the expense of more influential factors such as masculinity, sexual orientation, gender identity, and prior victimization, as well as individual risk factors such as size, weight, and age. Unlike (white) race, all these factors *have* been shown to broadly affect the risk of sexual victimization.

The assessment checklists recommended in the NPREC Standards allow correctional investigators to address any potential factors that they find may affect sexual assault, but they *mandate* a focus on only one: interracial dynamics (National Prison Rape Elimination Commission 2009b). The NPREC Standards call on correctional agencies to review institutions' collected data to "identif[y] problem areas, including any racial dynamics underpinning patterns of sexual abuse" (ibid. 55). They exhort correctional staff to "consider whether incidents were motivated by racial dynamics or any existing racial tensions" at the facility, and require that "officials immediately notify the agency head and begin taking steps to rectify those underlying tensions" (ibid. 53). None of the NPREC data collection recommendations requires that correctional officials consider—or take immediate steps to rectify—any other institutional problems that have been identified as factors contributing to sexual violence, for example: inadequate supervision, inappropriate security classification, overcrowding, high rates of physical violence, homophobia, or an institutional culture in which staff and inmates expect inmates to prove their masculinity by fighting.

Moreover, given that many prison officials are more likely to believe sexual abuse allegations when the victim is white and the assailant is black, it seems likely that officials may perceive that sexual abuse is disproportionately black-on-white within their own institutions, even if BJS statistics indicate that it is not interracial nationwide. NPREC's call for racial data collection based on officials' perception of racial dynamics could generate data that will confirm the stereotype that gave rise to the call in the first place.[5]

The powerful cultural specter—or fantasy—of black-on-white rape seems to inflect perceptions of what is happening in prison, whether the observers are prisoners, staff, administrators, academics, or policymakers. The racial rape myth seems to generate a form of confirmation bias: policymakers, academics, and correctional officials, who ought to know better, have been remarkably credulous of shaky or nonexistent empirical data that tend to confirm their racial preconceptions. Meanwhile, data that raise questions about the stereotype have been largely ignored. For them as for prisoners, judges, and other observers, race seems to be especially salient when sexual abuse is (or seems) black-on-white, yet disappears from public discourse when the facts do not conform to the stereotype.

The myth of black-on-white prison rape reveals the continuing, albeit unacknowledged, power of myths about black and white masculinities in the outside world. The racial retelling of the story of prison rape tends to eclipse the gendered and institutional factors that are known to contribute to prison rape. The chimera of black-on-white prison rape also overshadows better-substantiated racial disparities that have been confirmed and reconfirmed in recent victimization surveys.

Finally, the racial rape myth seems to mask, or even excuse, the gendered institutional practices that foster sexual abuse. Even though prison staff are notorious for telling inmates they must "fight or f—" (Robertson 1995), rape in men's prisons has not, until recently, been recognized as a consequence of institutional enforcement of an especially toxic model of masculinity (Buchanan 2010). Presumably, most Americans would not be satisfied with an explanation of prison rape that repeats what prison officials so frankly tell abused prisoners: that victims deserve to be raped because they are not real men. Yet, despite its shaky empirical foundation, its racist history, and its dehumanizing overtones, the racial rape myth has been advanced and accepted, in public and specialist discourse, meeting far less skepticism than it deserves. Somehow, a gendered practice that would be outrageous if described frankly to the outside world is normalized when a racist trope is used to explain its consequences.

NOTES

This chapter addresses an argument that is elaborated in much more detail in Buchanan (2010).

1. In this chapter, I use "prison rape" as a shorthand for all forms of sexual abuse and victimization in prisons, jails, and other detention facilities. Prison rape or sexual abuse may encompass all forms of forced, coerced, or pressured sex between prisoners, and all sexual contact (whether forced, coerced, pressured, or voluntary) between prisoners and staff.

2. Three of these sexual victimization surveys were conducted nationwide by the Bureau of Justice Statistics: it surveyed jails and prisons nationwide in 2007 and again in 2008–2009, and it surveyed juvenile facilities in 2008–2009, giving rise to four reports: Beck et al. 2010a; Beck and Harrison 2008; Beck and Harrison 2007; and Beck et al. 2010b. The other two were statewide surveys conducted by university-affiliated social scientists, and gave rise to three reports: Jenness et al. 2007 (a statewide survey of

California state prisoners); Wolff et al. 2006 (a statewide survey of state prisoners in an unidentified state); and Wolff et al. 2008 (reporting on the same survey).

3. These findings are inconsistent with the stereotype that white inmates are especially vulnerable to sexual abuse in prison. However, a more comprehensive understanding would require information about the racial dynamics of perpetrator-victim dyads, which is unavailable in the published results of the nationwide surveys. Although Beck and Harrison (2008; 2007) and Beck et al. (2010b) did ask prisoners who said they had been sexually abused by other inmates about the race or ethnicity of their assailants (it did not ask about the race or ethnicity of staff perpetrators), the BJS did not publish the results of this inquiry. The Beck et al. 2010a survey also asked this question, but the report did not provide a breakdown of the race/ethnicity of the assailant by race/ethnicity of the victim. Jenness et al. (2007) found that rape in California prisons was largely intraracial, while Wolff's survey did not ask about the race of the perpetrator (Wolff et al. 2006).

4. Nancy Wolff (Wolff et al. 2006, 836), for example, cited Toch (1977) and Carroll (1974) as authority that "Inmate-on-inmate sexual victimization has an interracial bias, with victims most likely being White and sexual aggressors most likely being black"—even though her own survey had found no statistically significant racial differences in sexual victimization by inmates (Wolff et al. 2006, 844; Wolff et al. 2008, 459). See also, e.g., Fleisher and Krienert 2006, 41–42, 48–49, 51 (citing Lockwood (1980), which reported on a 1974–1975 study, as authority that in "modern decades," prison "sexual aggression often has racial overtones"); Robertson 1999, 18–19 (citing Davis 1968; Carroll 1977; Scacco 1975; and Lockwood (1980) as authority that most victims are white and "African-American inmates disproportionately comprise the population of sexual harassers"); Pinar 2001, 1031–60 (citing numerous sources published between 1964 and 1984 as evidence that black-on-white "[s]exual assault is still feared in prisons today" (ibid. 1031), and that prison rape is black prisoners' means of racial "revenge" (ibid.)); Man and Cronan 2001; O'Donnell 2004; Knowles 1999).

5. As this chapter went to press, the U.S. Attorney General released draft national standards for prison rape prevention which respond to this concern: *National Standards to Prevent, Detect, and Respond to Prison Rape*, 2011.

REFERENCES

Austin, James. 2007. Testimony at the National Prison Rape Elimination Commission hearing on Lockups, Native American Detention Facilities, and Conditions in Texas Penal and Youth Institutions, March 27. Available at http://www.cybercemetery.unt.edu/archive/nprec/20090820155951/http://nprec.us/docs/lockupsintx_austin.pdf.

Beard, Jeffrey A. 2006. Testimony at the National Prison Rape Elimination Commission hearing on Elimination of Prison Rape: The Corrections Perspective, March 23. Available at http://www.cybercemetery.unt.edu/archive/nprec/20090820160531/http://nprec.us/docs/miami_promisingpractices_beard.pdf.

Beck, Allen J., and Paul Guerino. 2011. *Sexual Victimization Reported by Adult Correctional Authorities, 2007–08*. Washington, DC: U.S. Department of Justice, Bureau of Justice Statistics. Available at http://bjs.ojp.usdoj.gov/content/pub/pdf/svraca0708.pdf.

Beck, Allen J., and Paige M. Harrison. 2008. *Sexual Victimization in Local Jails Reported by Inmates, 2007.* Washington, DC: U.S. Department of Justice, Bureau of Justice Statistics. Available at http://bjs.ojp.usdoj.gov/content/pub/pdf/svljri07.pdf.

———. 2007. *Sexual Victimization in State and Federal Prisons Reported by Inmates, 2007* (rev. 2008). Washington, DC: U.S. Department of Justice, Bureau of Justice Statistics.

———. 2006. *Sexual Violence Reported by Correctional Authorities, 2005.* Washington, DC: U.S. Department of Justice, Bureau of Justice Statistics. Available at http://bjs.ojp.usdoj.gov/content/pub/pdf/svrca05.pdf.

Beck, Allen J., Paige M. Harrison, and Devon B. Adams. 2007. *Sexual Violence Reported by Correctional Authorities, 2006.* Washington, DC: U.S. Department of Justice, Bureau of Justice Statistics. Available at http://bjs.ojp.usdoj.gov/content/pub/pdf/svrca06.pdf.

Beck, Allen J., Paige M. Harrison, Marcus Berzofsky, Rachel Caspar, and Christopher Krebs. 2010a. *Sexual Victimization in Prisons and Jails Reported by Inmates, 2008–09.* Washington, DC: U.S. Department of Justice, Bureau of Justice Statistics. Available at http://bjs.ojp.usdoj.gov/content/pub/pdf/svpjri0809.pdf.

Beck, Allen J., Paige M. Harrison, and Paul Guerino. 2010b. *Sexual Victimization in Juvenile Facilities Reported by Youth, 2008–09.* Washington, DC: U.S. Department of Justice, Bureau of Justice Statistics.

Bederman, Gail. 1995. *Manliness and Civilization: A Cultural History of Gender and Race in the United States, 1880–1917.* Chicago: University of Chicago Press.

Brief of the States of Utah, Alabama, Alaska, Delaware, Idaho, Nevada, New Hampshire, and North Dakota as Amici Curiae in Support of Respondent in *Johnson v. California*, 543 U.S. 499 (2005).

Buchanan, Kim S. 2010. Our Prisons, Ourselves: Race, Gender and the Rule of Law. *Yale Law and Policy Review* 29:1–82.

Butler v. Dowd, 979 F.2d 661 (8th Cir. 1992).

Carroll, Leo. 1977. Humanitarian Reform and Biracial Sexual Assault in a Maximum Security Prison. *Urban Life* 5(4):417–37.

———. 1974. *Hacks, Blacks, and Cons: Race Relations in a Maximum Security Prison.* Lexington, MA: Lexington Books.

Commission on Safety and Abuse in America's Prisons. 2006. *Confronting Confinement: A Report of the Commission on Safety and Abuse in America's Prisons.* Available at http://www.prisoncommission.org/pdfs/Confronting_Confinement.pdf.

Davis, A. J. 1968. *Report on Sexual Assaults in the Philadelphia Prison System and Sheriff's Vans.* Philadelphia: District Attorney's Office and Police Department.

Dennis, Don, and Shirley Stephens. 1998. *From the Cell to the Cross.* Abilene, TX: Reflection Publishing.

Duru, N. Jeremi. 2004. The Central Park Five, the Scottsboro Boys, and the Myth of the Bestial Black Man. *Cardozo Law Review* 25:1315–65.

Eigenberg, Helen M. 2000. Correctional Officers and Their Perceptions of Homosexuality, Rape, and Prostitution in Male Prisons. *Prison Journal* 80:415–33.

———. 1989. Male Rape: An Empirical Examination of Correctional Officers' Attitudes toward Rape in Prison. *Prison Journal* 69:39–56.

Farbstein, Jay, and Richard Wener. 1989. *A Comparison of "Direct" and "Indirect" Supervision Correctional Facilities: Final Report.* National Institute of Corrections—Prison Division. Available at nicic.gov/pubs/pre/007807.pdf.

Fleisher, Mark S., and Jessie L. Krienert. 2006. *The Culture of Prison Sexual Violence.* Prepared for the National Institute of Justice. Available at http://www.ncjrs.gov/pdffiles1/nij/grants/216515.pdf.

Gaes, Gerald G. 2008. *Report to the Review Panel on Prison Rape on the Bureau of Justice Statistics Study "Sexual Victimization in Federal and State Prisons Reported by Inmates, 2007."* Available at http://www.ojp.usdoj.gov/reviewpanel/pdfs_mar08/testimony_gaes.pdf.

Gaes, Gerald G., and Andrew L. Goldberg. 2004. *Prison Rape: A Critical Review of the Literature.* Available at http://www.ncjrs.gov/pdffiles1/nij/grants/213365.pdf.

Goff, Philip Atiba, Jennifer L. Eberhardt, Melissa J. Williams, and Matthew Christian Jackson. 2008. Not Yet Human: Implicit Knowledge, Historical Dehumanization, and Contemporary Consequences. *Journal of Personality and Social Psychology* 94:292–306.

Goord, Glenn. 2006. Testimony at the National Prison Rape Elimination Commission Hearing on Elimination of Prison Rape: The Corrections Perspective, March 23. Available at http://www.cybercemetery.unt.edu/archive/nprec/20090820160527/http://nprec.us/docs/miami_promisingpractices_goord.pdf.

Harkleroad, James W. 2000. Control. In *Crime and Punishment: Inside Views,* edited by Robert Johnson and Hans Toch. New York: Henry Holt, 161–63.

Harris, Angela P. 2000. Gender, Violence, Race and Criminal Justice. *Stanford Law Review* 52:777–807.

Horn, Martin F. 2006. Testimony at the National Prison Rape Elimination Commission Hearing on Elimination of Prison Rape: The Corrections Perspective, March 23. Available at http://www.cybercemetery.unt.edu/archive/nprec/20090820160434/http://nprec.us/docs/miami_correctionsoverview_horn.pdf.

Human Rights Watch. 2001. No Escape: Male Rape in U.S. Prisons. Available at http://www.hrw.org/legacy/reports/2001/prison/report.html.

Jacobs, James B. 1983. *New Perspectives on Prisons and Imprisonment.* Ithaca, NY: Cornell University Press.

James, Joy. 2005. *The New Abolitionists: (Neo)slave Narratives and Contemporary Prison Writings.* Albany: State University of New York Press.

Jenness, Valerie, Cheryl L. Maxson, Kristy N. Matsuda, and Jennifer Macy Sumner. 2007. *Violence in California Correctional Facilities: An Empirical Examination of Sexual Assault.* Report submitted to the California Department of Corrections and Rehabilitation. Available at http://ucicorrections.seweb.uci.edu/pdf/FINAL_PREA_REPORT.pdf.

Johnson, Calvin C., Jr., and Greg Hampikian. 2003. *Exit to Freedom.* Athens: University of Georgia Press.

Just Detention International. 2009. *A Call for Change: Protecting the Rights of LGBTQ Detainees,* http://www.justdetention.org/pdf/CFCLGBTQJan09.pdf.

Knowles, Gordon James. 1999. Male Prison Rape: A Search for Causation and Prevention. *Howard Journal of Criminal Justice* 38:267–82.

Lockwood, Daniel. 1980. *Prison Sexual Violence.* New York: Elsevier Science.

Lumsden, Raymond. 2006. *Stronger by the Day: A Gripping Story of Abuse, Neglect, Courage and Redemption.* Dallas, TX: Lighthouse Publishing.

Man, Christopher D., and John P. Cronan. 2001. Forecasting Sexual Abuse in Prison: The Prison Subculture of Masculinity as a Backdrop for "Deliberate Indifference." *Journal of Criminal Law and Criminology* 92:127–86.

Nacci, P. L., and T. R. Kane. 1984. Sex and Sexual Aggression in Federal Prisons. *Federal Probation* 48(1):46–53.

National Prison Rape Elimination Commission. 2009a. *National Prison Rape Elimination Commission Report*. Available at http://www.ncjrs.gov/pdffiles1/226680.pdf.

———. 2009b. *Standards for the Prevention, Detection, Response, and Monitoring of Sexual Abuse in Adult Prisons and Jails*. Available at http://www.ncjrs.gov/pdffiles1/226682.pdf.

———. 2005–2007. Public Hearings. Available at http://www.cybercemetery.unt.edu/archive/nprec/20090820154827/http://nprec.us/home/public_proceedings/.

National Standards to Prevent, Detect, and Respond to Prison Rape. 2011. 76 Fed. Reg. 11,077 (January 24) (amending C.F.R. pt. 115).

O'Donnell, Ian. 2004. Prison Rape in Context. *British Journal of Criminology* 44:241–55.

Pinar, William F. 2001. *The Gender of Racial Politics and Violence in America: Lynching, Prison Rape, and the Crisis of Masculinity*. New York: Peter Lang.

Prison Rape Elimination Act of 2003, Pub. L. 108-79, 117 Stat. 972 (codified as amended at 42 U.S.C. §§ 15601-15609 (2006)).

Rideau, Wilbert, and Ron Wikberg. 1992. *Life Sentences: Rage and Survival Behind Bars*. New York: Times Books.

Robertson, James E. 1999. Cruel and Unusual Punishment in United States Prisons: Sexual Harassment among Male Inmates. *American Criminal Law Review* 36:1–51.

———. 1995. "Fight or F—-" and Constitutional Liberty: An Inmate's Right to Self-Defense When Targeted by Aggressors. *Indiana Law Review* 29:339–63.

Sabo, Don, Terry A. Kupers, and Willie London, eds. 2001. *Prison Masculinities*. Philadelphia: Temple University Press.

Scacco, Anthony M. 1975. *Rape in Prison*. Springfield, IL: Charles C. Thomas.

Stalder, Richard. 2006. Testimony at the National Prison Rape Elimination Commission Hearing on Elimination of Prison Rape: The Corrections Perspective, March 23. Available at http://www.cybercemetery.unt.edu/archive/nprec/20090820160440/http://nprec.us/docs/miami_correctionsoverview_stalder.pdf.

Struckman-Johnson, Cindy. 1996. Sexual Coercion Reported by Men and Women in Prison. *Journal of Sex Research* 33:67–76.

Struckman-Johnson, Cindy, and David Struckman-Johnson. 2000. Sexual Coercion Rates in Seven Midwestern Prison Facilities for Men. *Prison Journal* 80:379–90.

Toch, Hans. 1977. *Living in Prison: The Ecology of Survival*. New York: Free Press.

West, Heather C. 2010. *Prison Inmates at Midyear 2009—Statistical Tables*. Washington, DC: U.S. Department of Justice, Bureau of Justice Statistics. Available at http://bjs.ojp.usdoj.gov/content/pub/pdf/pim09st.pdf.

Wiegman, Robyn. 1995. *American Anatomies: Theorizing Race and Gender*. Durham, NC: Duke University Press.

Wilson v. Wright, 998 F. Supp. 650 (E.D. Va. 1998).

Wolff, Nancy, Cynthia L. Blitz, Jing Shi, Ronet Bachman, and Jane A. Siegel. 2006. Sexual Violence inside Prisons: Rates of Victimization. *Journal of Urban Health* 83:835–48.

Wolff, Nancy, Jing Shi, and Cynthia L. Blitz. 2008. Racial and Ethnic Disparities in Types and Sources of Victimization inside Prison. *Prison Journal* 88:451–72.

Wright, Matthew. 2008. *State Raised: A Deep Look into the World of Prison*. Bloomington, IN: IUniverse.

10

Sport and Masculinity: The Promise and Limits of Title IX

DEBORAH L. BRAKE

Throughout history, sport has been a site where masculinity is learned, performed, and reproduced.[1] In the United States, sports were introduced into schools in response to fears that boys were being feminized by the shift from an agrarian to industrial labor force, leaving boys in the day-to-day care of their mothers. Boys today continue to learn lessons in masculinity from participation in sports. For boys who excel in sports, athletic achievement is a path to a celebrated, traditional masculinity. For boys who lack ability or interest in sport, they risk developing a more marginalized masculinity. So great is the connection between sport and masculinity that some opponents of homosexuality push sports as a "cure" for boys who are, or are perceived to be, gay. In one lawsuit involving a male student's complaints of anti-gay harassment, the principal allegedly told him, "You can learn to like girls. Go out for the football team" (*Schroeder v. Maumee Board of Education* 2003, 871). Through excelling at sports, boys become men and establish their masculine *bona fides.*

The particular masculinity produced through participation in sports is shaped by race, class, and the kind of sport played. The world of men's sports contains layers of privilege and hierarchies of masculinity within it. This hierarchy is costly, in different ways, both to the men who are situated at the top and to the greater numbers of men and women who occupy a more marginalized place in sport.

The entry of girls and women into sports in large numbers—a relatively recent phenomenon that began after Congress enacted Title IX of the Education Amendments of 1972—has complicated the connections between sport and masculinity. The mass participation of girls and women in athletics has the potential to disrupt the masculinizing work of sport. If a girl can be a great athlete, sport may lose its power to turn boys into men. The expanding presence of women athletes has the potential to dilute the hetero-masculine norms associated with sports participation and expand the range of masculinities available to men who participate in sports.

And yet, despite increasing numbers of female athletes, sport remains a primary site for the construction of masculinity. For all its success in opening up athletic opportunities to women, Title IX has not yet succeeded in transforming sport's function as a masculinizing institution. Nor has it destabilized the hierarchy of masculinity within men's sports, or rectified the harms of male sports culture. The law has had somewhat more success in punishing the worst excesses of violence and aggression by male athletes, although this, too, is limited. This chapter considers sport's construction of masculinity and the limits and promise of Title IX in disrupting this process.

Title IX's Feminist Legacy: Expanding Women's Opportunities and Transforming Femininity

Enacted in 1972, Title IX prohibits sex discrimination in educational institutions that receive federal funds, including in athletic programs. Title IX's effect on women's sports has been tremendous. In 1971, the year before the law's enactment, fewer than 300,000 girls nationwide competed in high school sports. Today, girls in high school sports number more than three million (Brake 2010). To put this into perspective, the ratio of girls playing high school sports has gone from one in twenty-seven to nearly one out of every two (ibid.). Sport has gone from being an exceptional and somewhat odd activity for girls to one that is part of normal girlhood and adolescence. The growth of women's sports at the college level is also remarkable. Female intercollegiate athletes have seen their numbers jump from 32,000 in 1971 to over 200,000 today (ibid.). Although it is impossible to pinpoint precisely how much of this growth is directly attributable to Title IX, much evidence suggests that the law has played a significant role in this expansion (Stevenson 2007).

It is hard to overstate the impact of these changes. As more women have become athletes, they have expanded the range of acceptable feminine identities and transformed deeply ingrained understandings about what it means to be a woman. As feminist philosopher Judith Butler explains, women's participation in sport troubles binary understandings of gender and reveals gender to be a performance. The category of woman is itself destabilized as female athletes who were perceived as masculine become accepted as genuine women (Butler 1998).

Sports participation has benefitted girls and women at the individual level as well. Female sports participation has been linked to academic achievement, job success, positive self-esteem, lower incidence of high-risk behaviors such as drug use, smoking, sexual activity and teen pregnancy, and a plethora of health benefits, both mental and physical (Staurowsky et al. 2009; Stevenson 2010). Sport has become a site of empowerment for girls and women, enabling them to develop more positive relationships to their bodies (Bolin and Granskog 2003; Roth and Basow 2004). Although female athletes still contend with negative stereotypes and reckon with the paradox of being both female and athletic in a culture that associates sport with masculinity, there is more room for them to succeed in doing so and to construct positive identities as athletes (Ross and Shinew 2008).

Sport and the Construction of Masculinity

While the greater presence of women in sport has transformed the norms of acceptable femininity for women, it has not similarly expanded the range of masculinities available to men. Sport continues to function as a masculinizing institution, a rite of passage for boys in developing a traditional masculine identity. Sport's production of masculinity reinforces a hierarchy among masculinities in which strength, aggression, and heterosexuality are privileged.

Because it is performed on a public stage and is part of the collection of values that bind people as a community, sport has been identified as one of, if not *the* most significant institution for the reproduction of masculinity. Sport's emphasis on physicality, competition, and winning align it with a particular kind of masculinity, one that starkly differentiates itself from the feminine (Whitson 1990). The objects of differentiation include women and less masculine men. Participants in men's sports construct a masculinity that values strength, discipline, aggression, and loyalty to other men (ibid.). As long as they abide by the norms of their sport and display athletic competence, male athletes are presumed to be heterosexual and clothed with an enviable masculinity (ibid.).

Of course, not all sports masculinize male athletes to the same degree, and not all boys or men are masculinized in precisely the same way through sports participation. The masculinity developed in a football player differs from that of a baseball player, which differs still from that of a golfer or swimmer. The more violent and/or aggressive the sport is, and the less it emphasizes aesthetics, the more masculine it is (Pronger 1990, 19–20). In high school and college sports, the most masculine sports, football and men's basketball, sit at the top of the athletic hierarchy. These two sports draw the largest crowds, receive the largest budgets, have the reputation (if not necessarily the reality) of being profit-makers, require great physical strength and speed, and have high levels of violence and aggression. Men who excel in these sports reap the greatest rewards of the hetero-masculinity that sport constructs.

Race and gender interact in complicated ways in the production of masculinity, and this is true in sport as well. In contrast to other sites where masculinity is developed (such as the workplace, for example), men of color, and black men in particular, have succeeded in developing a celebrated masculinity through sports participation, especially in football and basketball. Through excelling in sports, black boys and men have been able to construct a higher-status masculinity and more varied life paths (Atencio and Wright 2008). And yet, their success is paradoxical because it does not challenge the institutions or structures that situate black men in a position of inequality, nor provide any but a very few with any real economic security through professional sport (Messner 1989).

Black men's success in sport resonates with a deep-seated racial ideology that depicts black men as more physical—and in the West's mind/body dualism, less intellectual—than white men (van Sterkenburg and Knoppers 2004). Race essentialism in sports and the naturalization of a white-black binary permeates discourses about black athletes, although some research suggests that girls are more skeptical than boys of narratives that essentialize black athletes as more "naturally" athletic (Azzarito and Harrison 2008). Black male athletes can excel in sport without challenging this racial ideology, and their success functions to support liberal beliefs in a colorblind meritocracy and to obscure racial injustices in sports and society (Ferber 2007). For example, while black men make up a substantial percentage of the elite athletes in football, basketball, and track, their ranks are thin in other sports. Even within sports, there is tracking by position (Davis 1995; Messner 1989). For example, black football players have encountered resistance when they move into the position of quarterback (Buffington 2005). And despite their large presence as athletes in certain sports, they rarely break into the ranks of coaching or administration (Davis 1999). This racial stratification comports with a racial ideology that permits black men a celebrated masculinity as athletes, but locks them into a physical masculinity grounded in their bodies. The masculinity that comes from coaching men—being a strategic, thinking leader of other men—is less available to African American men. Race discrimination laws, such as Title VII of the Civil Rights Act of 1964, have done little to disrupt the role race plays in constructing the masculine hierarchies in men's sport leadership (ibid.).

By far the most research on race and gender in sports has focused on black male athletes (Davis and Harris 1998). Much less is known about how race interacts with gender in shaping the experiences of, and the construction of masculinity within, other men of color. What information does exist demonstrates the importance of studying race and masculinity in sport with greater particularity. For example, while Latinos, like blacks, have succeeded in breaking into some sports, such as baseball, in large numbers, they too are subject to "stacking," limiting them to playing positions that match up with racial stereotypes. Perceived as being shorter, agile, and quick, Latino baseball players are concentrated in the infield, and are presumed to lack the speed and power necessary for outfield positions (Gonzalez 2001). Even though coaches and managers are mostly recruited from the infield, Latinos are greatly under-represented in these positions, suggesting that their athletic success on the field does not translate into a broader dismantling of racial barriers or racial ideology (ibid.).

Sport studies literature contains even less about Asian men. The virtual absence of information about Asian American men in sport sociology research is itself significant (Coakley 1998). It reflects both the resilience of a binary approach to studying race in sport as a black/white phenomenon and the conflict between stereotypes of Asian men and the dominant masculinity constructed by sport. As Michael Kimmel observes, throughout U.S. history, Asian men have been viewed as "small, soft, and effeminate," serving as "unmanly templates" against which American men are measured (2001, 281). Their low visibility in sport both reflects and reinforces the compromised masculinity of Asian men in U.S. culture.

Class also interacts with race and gender in shaping the masculinity men derive from sports, with certain sports contributing to a more genteel, upper-class masculinity (Messner 1989). Sports typically played in country clubs—spaces which are often racially exclusive and highly class-conscious—develop a more refined "gentlemen's" masculinity. These sports, such as golf, swimming, tennis, and racquetball, do not involve high levels of physical contact or aggression, and have been less welcoming to men of color. In golf, for example, Tiger Woods stands out as the exception to the rule that golf is a white gentlemen's sport. The significance of Woods' success in golf for opening up golf, and other country club sports, to men of color more broadly is diluted by Woods' disavowal of any strong sense of identity as a black man. Woods has referred to himself as "Cablinasian" (for Caucasian, Black, Indian, Asian) and has minimized the significance of his racial background in talking about his legacy in the sport (Billings 2003; Cashmore 2008). The masculinity inculcated by golf and other country club sports remains less available to men of color and men from working-class backgrounds than the very different masculinity constructed by the contact sports.

One window for viewing the distance between the masculinity conferred on male golfers and the masculinity produced by men's contact sports is the recent controversy over Tiger Woods' adultery. The recent hype in reaction to Woods' infidelity—causing him to take a "break" from golf—was likely shaped by the class associations and expectations connected with the sport. As the best golfer in the world, Woods had more to account for when he slipped from grace. The reaction to his affairs, by all accounts voluntary, generated more negative press coverage than allegations of rape, sexual assault, and domestic violence by football and basketball players typically do. In contrast to the negative publicity surrounding Woods' adultery, much of the public reaction to the rape charges brought against NBA star Kobe Bryant rallied around Bryant, painting him as the victim of a promiscuous woman who consented to sex and then cried rape (Anderson 2004; Haddad 2005). Compared to the expectations of unlimited sexual access to women enjoyed by talented football and basketball players, the masculinity inculcated by country club sports is a more refined and cultivated masculinity. The norms of country club masculinity do not, by any means, insist on chastity, but they do prefer that sexual pecadillos be managed discretely. Football and basketball, as more rugged, physical sports with more working-class masculine identities, allow more leeway for flagrant promiscuity. The stars of these sports are expected to have sex with many women, and the women they have sex with are regarded as virtually unrapeable. The most masculine sports construct a kind of hypermasculinity, which confers sexual access to women and privileges above and beyond those conferred on other men.

Despite Title IX's effect of expanding the range of acceptable gender performances by women, the law has not yet significantly changed the masculinizing function of men's sports, nor has it destabilized the hierarchy of masculinities within men's sports. Instead, through its reinforcement of gender as a dividing line in sport and its failure to dislodge the extreme privileging of the most masculine men's sports, Title IX has participated in sport's construction of a dominant hetero-masculinity.

Policing the Gender Line in Sport and Preserving All-Male Enclaves

One of the most significant policy choices Title IX makes is to leave intact the sex-differentiation of athletic teams. Viewed from the perspective of getting more girls and women into sports, there is much to recommend this choice. Because school sports were designed for male bodies, gender-neutral tryouts would likely lead to token representation of female athletes in varsity sports. Such tokenism would reinforce a belief in men's natural athletic superiority and the view that sport is not a place for most women. Those few female athletes who excelled in competition against men would likely be seen as aberrational, unlike normal women. A high level of performance by a few exceptional female athletes would not significantly change cultural norms or challenge the gender binaries that have limited women's participation in sports (Messner 1988). Moreover, sport might become a less empowering place for girls and women without their own teams (Wachs 2003; Landers and Fine 1996; Usher 2005; Hannon and Ratliffe 2007).

Of course, there is no easy answer to the question of whether the law's approach to sex equality in sport should proceed along an assimilationist model, integrating women onto coed teams, or a separatist model, pursuing equality between separate men's and women's sports. The question presents a true dilemma, with a downside either way. A gender-blind assimilationist approach would risk missing out on women's mass participation in sport and the societal changes that have come from making sport a typical part of girls' and women's lives. As shown by the packed stadiums during the women's Final Four, women can play a rousing game of college basketball without men on the court to legitimize their performance. And yet, the current strategy of separation also has downsides, including the risk of reinforcing a second-class status for women's sports and the belief that the top female athletes could never compete with men—a belief that may well be wrong in some cases, but is rarely tested. On balance, however, Title IX makes a respectable choice in prioritizing concrete opportunities for large numbers of women.

And yet, by leaving in place the sex-separate structure of sports, the law reaffirms the salience of sex as a dividing line in sport and preserves the male-only spaces of athletic fields and locker rooms. All-male settings tend to promote a traditional form of masculinity, one that differentiates from and establishes dominance over both women and less masculine men. The absence of women in male-only settings can produce a "hypermasculine ethos" marked by misogyny, belief in male superiority, and homophobia (Levit and Verchick 2006, 102).

To a limited extent, Title IX grants an individual student a right to try out for an athletic team that is offered only to members of the other sex. However, these rights are too narrow to significantly expand men's range of sport opportunities or disrupt the male-only spaces of sport. Under the Title IX regulations, integration rights apply only to students whose access to sport has been limited by sex, and only to sports that are offered exclusively to members of the other sex (Athletics Regulation—Separate Teams 2010). Since female athletes in general have had limited athletic opportunities, the regulation may give them the right to try out for a sport offered only to men. However, the regulation creates an exception for contact sports, defined as sports which involve bodily contact as their purpose or major activity (ibid.). The regulation lists boxing, wrestling, rugby, ice hockey, football, and basketball as contact sports, but the designation may apply to other sports as well. Since most of the sports that a school offers to men but not women are contact sports, Title IX has only rarely been a vehicle for granting women access to male-only teams.

As a result, Title IX has done little to disrupt the male-only enclave of men's sports, thereby missing an opportunity to challenge the culture of men's sports. As David Whitson explains, the presence of women on men's teams could potentially disrupt the process by which men "rehearse their ties as men and reaffirm their differences from women" (1990, 25–26). Since women rarely have enough experience with contact sports to support their own teams, the contact sports exception effectively deprives them of any access to these sports. In doing so, it reaffirms the masculinity of contact sports themselves by signaling their unsuitability for women. It demeans female athleticism as fragile and passive while reaffirming the ultimate masculinity of the most aggressive and dangerous sports by accepting the exclusion of women from these sports.

To some extent, the Equal Protection Clause has eased the impact of the contact sports exception. Since the 1970s, numerous court decisions have relied on the Equal Protection Clause to require schools to permit female athletes to try out for male-only teams in sports not offered to women, even in contact sports (Brake 2010). However, the Equal Protection Clause only applies to state actors, so these precedents are limited to public schools and universities (ibid.). Female athletes at private schools can rely only on Title IX, which applies to any educational institution, public or private, which receives federal funds (including federal student loans). Moreover, the message sent by the contact sports exception goes well beyond its application in particular cases; this message reaffirms that the most masculine of sports are unsuitable for women, and that the men who play these sports are the most masculine of men.

Male students have had even less success using the law to gain access to sports offered only to the other sex, albeit for different reasons. Under Title IX, an athlete has a right to try out for a team offered exclusively to the other sex only if his or her own athletic opportunities have been limited by sex (Athletics Regulation—Separate Teams 2010). Since male athletes have historically been over-represented in school sports programs, this restriction typically leaves male students without a right to try out for sports offered only to women. Cases decided under the Equal Protection Clause take a similar approach, justifying female-only teams based on the important interest in expanding opportunities for girls and women, who still have fewer athletic opportunities. As a result, male students generally do not have a right to try out for teams in sports offered only to women, such as field hockey and volleyball—sports which register as less masculine than the typical menu of sports offered to men (Brake 2010).

In the final analysis, Title IX has not done much to de-gender sports. Most sports retain a gender identity constructed by the gender of their participants and the qualities required to play them (Ross and Shinew 2008; Hardin and Greer 2009). These gender associations are deeply entrenched and widely shared. In one study of black and white boys and girls, all of the students subscribed to gendered perceptions of particular sports, although race and sex influenced how particular sports were gender-typed (for example, black girls in the study were more likely than white girls and all boys to view basketball as gender-neutral rather than more appropriate for boys) (Hannon et al. 2009). Contact sports are the most likely to be gender-typed as masculine (ibid.). Sports that emphasize gracefulness, aesthetics, and accuracy over strength are more likely to be gendered feminine. While the gendering of sports limits both girls' and boys' athletic participation choices, boys are even more reluctant than girls to play sports typed as gender-inappropriate (ibid.).

Title IX has not helped men cross the gender line in sports or gotten them into more feminine sports. Although there is a plausible anti-subordination rationale for this result—preserving limited athletic opportunities for girls and women—it comes with the cost of reinforcing the narrow range of masculinities in men's sports. Male participation in a more diverse range of athletic experiences could serve as a path to developing more fluid gender identities and alternative masculinities in sport (Azzarito and Katzew 2010). By looking at sex equality through a binary lens of male versus female opportunities, Title IX misses an opportunity to broaden the range of masculinities available to male athletes. Men are relegated to more masculine sports and the gender associations of particular sports are reinforced.

The impermeability of the gender line in sport is sealed by the virtual exclusion of women from leadership positions in men's sports. Much attention has been paid to the decline in the percentage of women coaches in women's sports since Title IX was enacted in 1972 (Carpenter and Acosta 2010). Much less concern has been voiced over the near absence of women from the ranks of coaches in men's sports. Less than 3 percent of men's intercollegiate teams are coached by women, a figure that has barely budged in the decades since Title IX was passed (ibid.). Cross-gender coaching occurs much more frequently in women's sports: of the head coaches in women's intercollegiate athletics, 57 percent are men (ibid.). Men even coach women in sports in which they lack varsity experience themselves, such as field hockey and softball. And yet, while men are accepted as leaders in women's sports, the reverse is not true; women are much less likely to be considered capable role models for men's sports (Bracken 2009). This disparity has important consequences. The entrance of women into this realm would disrupt the masculinizing function of sport and likely broaden the range of masculinities sport develops.

In the push for sex equality in sport, the virtual absence of women from jobs coaching male athletes is rarely part of the conversation. Title IX treats the sex of the coach as irrelevant. It does not confer a right to gender diversity among coaches in men's sports, nor a right to same-gender role models in women's sports. Title IX follows employment discrimination law in this regard by requiring only formal equality in the hiring process and not equality of results (Brake 2010).

As a result, there is little room for women in men's sports at any level, from the athletes on up to the coaches and athletic directors. At the same time, there is little room for male athletes to expand the range of masculinities constructed by sport, or to cross the gender line and compete in women's sports. The gender separation of sport leaves intact a structure in which particular sports are gender-typed. This hurts men whose sport offerings are limited to masculine sports, and has a rebound effect on women, who face social penalties when they participate in sports that are cast as too masculine (Ross and Shinew 2008; Hardin and Greer 2009). Although Title IX has gotten women into sport, it has done little to de-gender sport itself.

Follow the Money: Privileging the Most Masculine Sports

Within men's sports there is a hierarchy of masculinities. At the top sit the most masculine sports and the athletes who play them. The privileges conferred by these sports dwarf the status and rewards associated with other men's sports. One of the most visible privileges is the allocation of resources provided to men's sports. A quick review of athletic budgets leaves little question about which sports are the most valued. Football and men's basketball consume by far the greatest share of athletic budgets, leaving all other men's sports to scramble for leftovers. In 2005–2006, the average Division I institution spent more than $7.5 million on football and men's basketball combined—about 88 percent of the total average budget of $8.65 million for all men's sports (DeHass 2008). For perspective, this amount far exceeded what the average Division I institution spent on all women's sports (about $4.5 million) and all other men's sports combined (ibid.).

Title IX purports to require the equal treatment of men's and women's sports. However, limitations in Title IX's legal framework and enforcement make this promise a hollow one, at least when it comes to extending to women a level of treatment equal to that of the most privileged men's sports. For one thing, Title IX does not require equal spending on men's and women's sports. Funding inequality is a factor to consider in measuring compliance, but it does not in and of itself establish a Title IX violation (Athletics Regulation—Equal Opportunity 2010). Instead, compliance is measured by a qualitative comparison of the overall men's and women's programs.

The need for an overall program comparison stems from Title IX's allowance for men and women to play different sports. A sport-specific comparison would provide no way to measure equality when men and women play different sports. However, while the overall program comparison is necessary to accommodate men's and women's different sport interests, it does have a downside. Comparing the level of treatment across men's and women's sports programs overall makes for a messy, information-saturated undertaking. Differences in the equipment, rules, squad sizes, and facilities of different sports make them hard to compare, and the lack of a financial test for parity requires the use of less tangible and more manipulable measures. Moreover, the theory of gender difference underlying the sex-separation of sports makes the different treatment of men's and women's sports seem more acceptable. If men and women are different enough to require separate athletic programs in the first place, the logic goes, why should their teams have the same level of resources and support?

As a result of the messiness of Title IX's overall equal treatment approach and the resistance to its full enforcement, the perks taken for granted in the most-valued men's sports are virtually never extended to any women's sport; nor has the law reined in these extreme expenditures. Football and men's basketball teams receive perks that very few women's teams ever see, including luxury accommodations on nights before home games, high-tech video and digital display equipment in locker rooms, travel by chartered jet, coaching salaries that dwarf even a college president's pay, and money lavished on recruits (universities spend on average twice as much money to recruit male as female athletes) (Brake 2010).

Driving the disparity is the presumption that football and men's basketball deserve their perks because they bring in revenue. The factual basis for the revenue justification has been strongly critiqued elsewhere (Sperber 2000; Zimbalist 2001), but the key point for purposes of this chapter is that, revenue-producing or not, Title IX leaves intact an athletic structure in which the rewards, status, and benefits afforded male athletes in the most masculine sports dwarf those of all other athletes, male and female. Indeed, the very assumption of profitability (however unfounded) only adds to the special status reserved for these male athletes. Most sports programs would fail a profitability test if held to the same accounting standards applied to normal businesses, but the veneer of revenue functions as a value judgment of worthiness, further adding to the celebrity status of the athletes who play these two sports (Brake 2010).

While paying lip-service to equal treatment, Title IX legitimizes a model of sport that spends lavishly on the two most masculine sports, while creating a resources crunch for all other sports, with the result that other (less masculine) men's sports are left scrambling for crumbs and (wrongly) blaming Title IX.

Challenging Hypermasculinity within Men's Sports

Among the privileges bestowed on elite male athletes is a certain status. The masculinity conferred on men by participation in the most-valued sports includes a presumption of heterosexuality and an expectation of unfettered sexual access to women. Their status as elite athletes is often thought to make these men irresistible to women, an assumption that drives the "she was asking for it" public reaction when a celebrated male athlete is accused of sexually assaulting a woman. At its worst, the culture of men's sports contributes to an atmosphere of entitlement in which sex with women is one of the perks of being an athlete. It also sets up a dynamic in which men who do not live up to these norms of masculinity are hazed or harassed. By engaging in demeaning treatment of other men, dominant males reaffirm their own masculinity. The result, to borrow from Angela Harris, is a "hypermasculinity" in which "the strictures against femininity and homosexuality are especially intense and . . . physical strength and aggressiveness are paramount" (2000, 793).

In recent years, Title IX has had some success in checking the most virulent excesses of hypermasculinity in men's sports. These successes show the potential of Title IX to open up more space within men's sports for alternative masculinities, and to punish performances of hypermasculinity that hurt women and marginalized men. However, Title IX's high hurdles for a successful suit make it a limited vehicle for transforming the culture of men's sports in a positive direction. At best, the law may serve as a check on the most extreme forms of masculine aggression in men's sports and prompt educators and administrators to pay more attention to the kinds of masculinities that are being developed and reinforced through male sports participation.

Two recent high-profile cases show the potential for Title IX to intervene when athletic programs encourage or condone expectations of sexual access to women as part of the "perks" to which male athletes are entitled. In one of these cases, the University of Colorado (CU) was charged with collaborating in a football recruiting program that supplied female students to act as "ambassadors" for the male recruits brought to campus (*Simpson v. University of Colorado* 2007). The job of these ambassadors—escorts, really— was to show male recruits "a good time," a thinly veiled euphemism for sex. The lawsuit was brought by two female students who were gang-raped by a group of football players and recruits during one of these recruiting visits. Although the district court granted the university summary judgment on the grounds that it was not responsible for the sexual misconduct of its athletes and visiting recruits, the Tenth Circuit Court of Appeals reversed. The appellate court cited the existence of longstanding concerns about sexual misconduct and abuse of women by male athletes, both in college football generally and at the University of Colorado specifically. The university's failure to adequately supervise its recruiting program or stop the use of female escorts, despite its knowledge of these risks, could establish deliberate indifference, the court concluded.

In a second high-profile case involving extreme hypermasculinity by male athletes, a female student sued the University of Georgia for its role in facilitating a gang-rape involving basketball and football players (*Williams v. Board of Regents of the University System of Georgia* 2007). During the incident, the ringleader, a basketball player, had what the court described as consensual sex with the plaintiff while, unbeknownst to her, a football player was hiding in the closet. When the basketball player gave the cue, the football player emerged from the closet and sexually assaulted the plaintiff. While the assault was taking place, the basketball player called two other athletes (one football player and one basketball player) and told them they were "running a train" on the plaintiff. One of the two (the basketball player) showed up and, with encouragement from the first basketball player, raped the plaintiff. The district court dismissed the complaint for failure to state a claim based on the lack of allegations establishing the university's culpability. The Eleventh Circuit Court of Appeals reversed, citing allegations that university officials had prior notice of sexual assaults and harassment by the basketball player who led the gang-rape before admitting him to the University of Georgia. Allegations that university officials knowingly recruited this player established that they put female students at increased risk of sexual assault. The court also found that the university's response to the gang rape was itself deliberately indifferent: the university waited eight months after receiving the police report before conducting a disciplinary investigation, and ultimately failed to sanction the assailants.

While these are welcome developments, it is too soon to view these cases as heralding a new era for combating misogyny in men's sports. Both cases involved extremely egregious facts showing actual notice of a high risk of sexual assault and a deliberate indifference to these risks on the part of university officials—the strict standard required by Title IX for holding a school liable for sexual harassment by its students (*Davis v. Monroe County Board of Education* 1999). In the *Simpson* case, a high school girl had been sexually assaulted by CU recruits and football players four years before the sexual assault that was the subject of the litigation, and the university ignored explicit warnings from the local district attorney about the use of alcohol and sex in its recruiting program (2007). Moreover, when the CU football coach learned of a sexual assault allegedly committed by one of his players just two months before the events in the *Simpson* case, the coach discouraged the complainant from going forward and closed ranks around the player (ibid.). The facts establishing actual notice and deliberate indifference were also egregious in the *Williams* case. In that case, the university president, basketball coach, and athletic director all knew that the basketball player who orchestrated the gang rape of the plaintiff had numerous disciplinary infractions at prior institutions, including multiple instances of sexual assault and sexual harassment, when they recruited him to play for the University of Georgia (*Williams* 2007, 1289–90). That court expressly emphasized "the extent and limits" of its decision, stating "the facts alleged in this case are extreme" (ibid. 1298–99).

Without evidence of actual notice of prior sexual misconduct by the same assailants or evidence that university officials ignored clear warnings about sexual harassment or abuse in its sports program, lawsuits challenging institutional complicity in male athletes' abuse of women will be difficult to win.

Title IX's high hurdles for establishing liability in such cases, requiring actual notice to an appropriate person with the authority to take corrective action followed by deliberate indifference, make it a limited tool for challenging hypermasculinity in men's sports programs (Scales 2009). Still, the potential to hold schools legally accountable in egregious cases should pressure them to more closely examine their sports programs and the kinds of masculinity they promote.

Title IX has also had some recent success in intervening in male-on-male aggression in men's sports. As masculinity scholars have shown, establishing male dominance over other men is at least as important to the construction of a dominant masculinity as men's relationships to women (Dowd, Levit, and McGinley, this volume). Male posturing for dominant positions in relation to other men is a cornerstone of men's sports culture. Men's locker-room talk valorizes men who live up to the norms of hegemonic masculinity, both in sports and in their relationships with women, while demeaning gender-nonconforming men or men perceived as less masculine (Clayton and Humberstone 2006). The very practice of establishing dominance over other men contributes to the development of a dominant masculinity in the aggressors.

In a 2009 case involving this dynamic, several high school football players made use of an air pump to sexually assault freshman teammates during the school's football camp (*Roe v. Gustine Unified School District* 2009). One of the victims of this and other sexually harassing conduct and homophobic epithets by the same aggressors brought a Title IX lawsuit based on the school's insufficient response. The court found the issues of actual notice and deliberate indifference to be close, but denied the school's motion for summary judgment based on evidence that the football coach was slow to respond because he initially viewed the behavior as childish horseplay. Most significantly, the court rejected the argument that the misconduct was simple hazing and did not amount to discrimination based on sex. The court noted that "the homophobic language used by the perpetrators appears to be part of a larger constellation of sexually-based conduct, which included assaulting Plaintiff with an air hose, exposing their genitalia, and grabbing his bare buttocks in the shower," and concluded that such allegations could conceivably show that "the conduct at issue relates to gender" (ibid. 1027).

This court's ability to comprehend the gendered nature of the football players' harassment contrasts starkly with an earlier judicial refusal to see any connection to gender in a similar acting-out of hypermasculine aggression on a football team. In a 1996 decision, the Tenth Circuit Court of Appeals upheld the dismissal of a Title IX complaint brought by a male high school football player who was sexually harassed by his teammates (*Seamons v. Snow* 1996). As he was coming out of the shower, Brian Seamons was grabbed by five upper-class football players who tied him, naked, to a horizontal towel bar with athletic tape and taped his genitals. To further humiliate him, they brought in a former girlfriend to see him in this condition. The coach viewed the incident as a normal part of athletic culture, since "boys will be boys." When Brian reported the incident to school authorities, the football coach accused him of betraying the team, saying he "should have taken it like a man," and directed Brian to apologize (ibid. 1230). When Brian refused, the coach dismissed Brian from the team; the five assailants went unpunished. In response to Brian's complaints, the school district cancelled the final game of the season, a state playoff game. Brian was threatened and harassed as a result, and the principal suggested he leave the school. Fearing for his safety, Brian transferred to another school.

Despite the deeply gendered nature of these events, the district court dismissed the Title IX complaint for failure to state a claim on the ground that none of this amounted to sex discrimination and the appellate court affirmed. In its decision, the Tenth Circuit minimized the statements that Brian should have taken it "like a man" and "boys will be boys," saying, "the qualities Defendants were promoting, team loyalty and toughness, are not uniquely male" (ibid. 1233). The court also cited the lack of any proof that a female harassment victim would have been treated any better.

Exposure to masculinities literature might have helped the court understand that the events in this case were very much about gender. The football player assailants were furthering their own hypermasculine identities through their sexualized domination of Brian. Brian's masculinity was further marginalized when he reported the attackers, thereby failing to "take it like a man." Traditional masculinity is constructed in more novice male athletes by enduring ritualized bullying and bodily aggression by alpha-male athletes (Light and Kirk 2000). Brian's masculinity was tarnished when he turned in his teammates. The court's comparison of Brian's treatment to that of a similarly situated female student further obscures the gender dynamics in Brian's case. Hypermasculine aggression does not become de-gendered by targeting female as well as male victims. The kind of dominant masculinity performed in Brian's locker room might well have turned against female victims too. For example, a similar kind of hypermasculinity played out at the University of Colorado when a female football player, Katie Hnida, was sexually harassed by her male teammates and then kicked off the team for reporting it (*Simpson* 2007, 1183).

In contrast to the *Seamons* case, the more recent *Roe* decision reflects real progress in judicial understanding of the gender dynamics in men's athletics.

The recognition of male-on-male sexual aggression as a form of sex discrimination has the potential to disrupt the socialization processes in men's sports that construct and elevate a traditional, hegemonic masculinity over alternative masculinities. By policing the outer limits of hypermasculinity in men's sports, whether it targets men or women, Title IX may put pressure on athletic administrators to cultivate locker room cultures with more space for alternative masculinities to flourish.

However, hopes that Title IX will serve as a counterweight to hypermasculinity in men's sports should be tempered by an awareness that, historically, racism has been an integral part of the U.S. legal system's regulation of male sexual violence. Black male athletes who transgress may lose their athletic privileges as "good Blacks," triggering stereotypes of black men as dangerous and naturally aggressive (Ferber 2007, 20). As law professor Ann Scales has noted, African American athletes are disproportionately involved in the high-profile incidents of sexual assaults by athletes, and have been disproportionately singled out in the enforcement of NCAA rules violations (2009). The risk that Title IX will operate as a vehicle for further entrenching racist ideologies about dangerous black men necessitates careful attention to how race influences the regulation of hypermasculinity in sport. And yet, as Scales admonishes, we must resist "divide and conquer" strategies that use racial victimization as a rhetorical strategy for pardoning misogyny and simultaneously work against a racial caste system and a male sports culture that promote violence against women and marginalize men (ibid.).

The Price of Privilege

Masculinities literature instructs that men pay a price for gender privilege, and this is certainly true in sport. Although elite male athletes—especially those in the most masculine sports—have unparalleled perks and advantages, they do not come without cost. Sport sociologists have identified a "toxic jock" identity most present among athletes in the highest-status, highest-contact sports played by male athletes, leading to an over-identification with the role of athlete and greater participation in high-risk behaviors (Miller 2009). The educational costs to elite male athletes are also pronounced. The pressures on student-athletes to win are intense in intercollegiate athletics, especially in the so-called revenue sports. Athletes receive admissions preferences that put a premium on athletic performance, and demands from their coaches are often incompatible with any serious devotion to academics. They must maintain the minimum grade point average required for eligibility, but little or nothing more is expected of them academically. The vast majority of them do not land lucrative careers in professional sports, and many leave college without having acquired much of an education outside of sports (Gohl 2001; Messner 1989). These costs are particularly acute for black male athletes, who are saddled with the double-sided stereotype of athletic superiority and intellectual inferiority, and are particularly vulnerable to "academic neglect" (Duru 2007, 512–13).

Some critics of this status quo call for paying athletes wages to reflect both their market value to the universities that exploit them and their opportunity costs in forgoing other aspects of education. However, paying student-athletes would only legitimize a model of sport based on commodification and educational neglect, and could compound the gender inequality in the present system (since no one seriously advocates paying female athletes for their sports participation). Rather than capitulate to the big business model of sport, we should interrogate a system that puts sports in schools for their educational value but then fails to ensure that the athletes obtain a meaningful education. At the present time, however, neither Title IX nor any other legal reform has managed to reinvigorate an educational model of sports that puts learning first. Male athletes in revenue sports bear the brunt of this system in costs to their education and other (under-developed) aspects of their identities.

And yet, the Title IX culture wars posit a zero-sum game between men and women for dividing an ever-shrinking athletic pie, with the most privileged male athletes determined to preserve their share and the more marginalized male athletes blaming women and Title IX for their own diminishing portion. Instead of examining inequities within men's sports, men blame Title IX when their teams are cut, aligning themselves with higher-status male athletes, despite their divergent interests (Messner and Solomon 2007). This result fits with masculinity theorists' prediction that nonconforming males will acquiesce in the privileging of a dominant masculinity even when they themselves do not benefit from it (Connell 2005). In demonizing Title IX for losses to their programs, men in more marginalized sports fail to consider whether the current system best serves their interests. Despite the vitriolic catcalls lobbed at Title IX whenever men's sports are cut, a number of male athletes have found their lives improved when their sports are demoted to club status, giving them more time for studying and more balance in their lives (Pennington 2008). Framing the issue as men versus women obscures differences in the status and privileges among male athletes, as well as the costs to male athletes from the present structure of sports. Both male and female athletes could benefit from a more equitable model of sport that emphasizes sport's educational value instead of the win-at-all-costs model that prevails today.

Conclusion

Much of the attention paid to Title IX examines its impact on women's opportunities and progress toward equality between male and female athletes. While those matters are important, we need to move beyond comparisons of men and women to consider how sex equality law participates in the construction of masculinity and its potential to disrupt those masculinities that are problematic for women and more marginalized men. In the realm of sport, that work has only just begun.

NOTE

1. I use "sport" to refer to the institution of sport, and "sports" to refer to the collection of athletic activities that it encompasses. Because this chapter addresses sport and masculinity in the context of Title IX, its primary focus is the interscholastic and intercollegiate setting.

REFERENCES

Anderson, Michelle J. 2004. Time to Reform Rape Shield Laws: Kobe Bryant Case Highlights Holes in the Armor. *Criminal Justice* 19(2):14–19.

Atencio, Matthew, and Jan Wright. 2008. "We Be Killin' Them": Hierarchies of Black Masculinity in Urban Basketball Spaces. *Sociology of Sport Journal* 25(2):263–80.

Athletics Regulation—Equal Opportunity. 34 C.F.R. § 106.41(c) (2010).

Athletics Regulation—Separate Teams. 34 C.F.R. § 106.41(b) (2010).

Azzarito, Laura, and Louis Harrison, Jr. 2008. "White Men Can't Jump": Race, Gender and Natural Athleticism. *International Review for the Sociology of Sport* 43(4):347–64.

Azzarito, Laura, and Adriana Katzew. 2010. Performing Identities in Physical Education: (En)gendering Fluid Selves. *Research Quarterly for Exercise and Sport* 81(1):25–37.

Billings, Andrew C. 2003. Portraying Tiger Woods: Characterizations of a "Black" Athlete in a "White" Sport. *Howard Journal of Communications* 14:29–37.

Bolin, Ann, and Jane Granskog. 2003. *Athletic Intruders: Ethnographic Research on Women, Culture, and Exercise.* Albany: State University of New York Press.

Bracken, Nicole. 2009. *Gender Equity in College Coaching and Administration: Perceived Barriers Report.* Indianapolis, IN: National Collegiate Athletic Administration.

Brake, Deborah L. 2010. *Getting in the Game: Title IX and the Women's Sports Revolution.* New York: New York University Press.

Buffington, Daniel. 2005. Contesting Race on Sundays: Making Meaning out of the Rise in the Number of Black Quarterbacks. *Sociology of Sport Journal* 22(1):19–37.

Butler, Judith. 1998. Athletic Genders: Hyperbolic Instance and/or the Overcoming of Sexual Binarism. *Stanford Humanities Review* 6(2), http://www.stanford.edu/group/SHR/6-2/html/butler.html.

Carpenter, Linda Jean, and R. Vivian Acosta. 2010. *Women in Intercollegiate Sport: A Longitudinal, National Study; Thirty-Three Year Update 1977–2010.* Available at http://www.acostacarpenter.org/2010pdf%20combined%20final.pdf.

Cashmore, Ellis. 2008. Tiger Woods and the New Racial Order. *Current Sociology* 56(4):621–34.

Clayton, Ben, and Barbara Humberstone. 2006. Men's Talk: A (Pro)feminist Analysis of Male University Football Players' Discourse. *International Review for the Sociology of Sport* 41(3–4):295–316.

Coakley, Jay. 1998. *Sports in Society: Issues and Controversies.* 6th ed. New York: McGraw Hill.

Connell, R. W. 2005. *Masculinities.* 2d ed. Berkeley: University of California Press.

Davis, Laurel R., and Othello Harris. 1998. Race and Ethnicity in U.S. Sports Media. In *MediaSport,* edited by Lawrence A. Wenner. London: Routledge, 154–69.

Davis, Timothy. 1999. Racism in Athletics: Subtle Yet Persistent. *University of Little Rock Arkansas Law Review* 21:881–900.

———. 1995. The Myth of the Superspade: The Persistence of Racism in College Athletics. *Fordham Urban Law Journal* 22(3):615–98.

Davis v. Monroe County Board of Education, 526 U.S. 629 (1999).

DeHass, Denise. 2008. *2005–2006 NCAA Gender-Equity Report.* Indianapolis, IN: National Collegiate Athletic Association.

Duru, N. Jeremi. 2007. Friday Night "Lite": How De-racialization in the Motion Picture *Friday Night Lights* Disserves the Movement to Eradicate Racial Discrimination from American Sport. *Cardozo Arts & Entertainment Law Journal* 25:485–530.

Ferber, Abby L. 2007. The Construction of Black Masculinity: White Supremacy Now and Then. *Journal of Sport and Social Issues* 31(1):11–24.

Gohl, Sarah E. 2001. A Lesson in English and Gender: Title IX and the Male Student-Athlete. *Duke Law Journal* 50:1123–64.

Gonzalez, Leticia. 2001. The Stacking of Latinos in Major League Baseball: A Forgotten Minority? In *Contemporary Issues in Sociology of Sport,* edited by Merrill Melnick and Andrew Yiannakis. Champaign, IL: Human Kinetics, 187–201.

Haddad, Richard I. 2005. Shield or Sieve? *People v. Bryant* and the Rape Shield Law in High-Profile Cases. *Columbia Journal of Law and Social Problems* 39:185–221.

Hannon, James C., and Thomas Ratliffe. 2007. Opportunities to Participate and Teacher Interactions in Coed versus Single-Gender Physical Education Settings. *Physical Educator* 64(1):11–20.

Hannon, James, Sonya Soohoo, Justine Reel, and Thomas Ratliffe. 2009. Gender Stereotyping and the Influence of Race in Sport among Adolescents. *Research Quarterly for Exercise and Sport* 80(3):676–84.

Hardin, Marie, and Jennifer D. Greer. 2009. The Influence of Gender-Socialization, Media Use and Sports Participation on Perceptions of Gender-Appropriate Sports. *Journal of Sport Behavior* 32(2):207–26.

Harris, Angela P. 2000. Gender, Violence, Race, and Criminal Justice. *Stanford Law Review* 52:777–807.

Kimmel, Michael. 2001. Masculinity as Homophobia: Fear, Shame, and Silence in the Construction of Gender Identity. In *The Masculinities Reader,* edited by Stephen Whitehead and Frank J. Barrett. Cambridge: Polity, 266–287.

Landers, M. A., and Gary Alan Fine. 1996. Learning Life's Lessons in Tee Ball: The Reinforcement of Gender and Status in Kindergarten Sport. *Sociology of Sport Journal* 13:87–93.

Levit, Nancy, and Robert R. M. Verchick. 2006. *Feminist Legal Theory: A Primer.* New York: New York University Press.

Light, Richard, and David Kirk. 2000. High School Rugby, the Body and the Reproduction of Hegemonic Masculinity. *Sport, Education and Society* 5(2):163–76.

Messner, Michael A. 1989. Masculinities and Athletic Careers. *Gender and Society* 3(1):71–88.

———. 1988. Sports and Male Domination: The Female Athlete as Contested Ideological Terrain. *Sociology of Sport Journal* 5(3):197–211.

Messner, Michael A., and Nancy M. Solomon. 2007. Social Justice and Men's Interests: The Case of Title IX. *Journal of Sport and Social Issues* 31(2):162–78.

Miller, Kathleen E. 2009. Sport-Related Identities and the "Toxic Jock." *Journal of Sport Behavior* 32(1):69–91.

Pennington, Bill. 2008. Dropped from Varsity Lineup, but No Longer Grumbling. *New York Times*, December 2.

Pronger, Brian. 1990. *The Arena of Masculinity: Sports, Homosexuality, and the Meaning of Sex.* New York: St. Martin's Press.

Roe v. Gustine Unified School District, 678 F. Supp. 2d 1008 (E.D. Cal. 2009).

Ross, Sally R., and Kimberly J. Shinew. 2008. Perspectives of Women College Athletes on Sport and Gender. *Sex Roles* 58(1-2):40–58.

Roth, Amanda, and Susan A. Basow. 2004. Femininity, Sports, and Feminism. *Journal of Sport and Social Issues* 28(3):245–65.

Scales, Ann. 2009. Student Gladiators and Sexual Assault: A New Analysis of Liability for Injuries Inflicted by College Athletes. *Michigan Journal of Gender & Law* 15(2):205–89.

Schroeder v. Maumee Board of Education, 296 F. Supp. 2d 869 (N.D. Ohio 2003).

Seamons v. Snow, 84 F.3d 1226 (10th Cir. 1996).

Simpson v. University of Colorado, 500 F.3d 1170 (10th Cir. 2007).

Sperber, Murray. 2000. *Beer and Circus: How Big-Time College Sports Is Crippling Undergraduate Education.* New York: Henry Holt.

Staurowsky, Ellen J., Kathleen E. Miller, Sohaila Shakib, Mary Jane De Souza, Gaele Ducher, Noah Gentner, Nancy Theberge, and Nancy I. Williams. 2009. *Her Life Depends on It II: Sport, Physical Activity, and the Health and Well-Being of American Girls and Women.* East Meadow, NY: Women's Sports Foundation.

Stevenson, Betsey. 2010. Beyond the Classroom: Using Title IX to Measure the Return to High School Sports. *Review of Economics and Statistics* 92(2):284–301.

———. 2007. Title IX and the Evolution of High School Sports. *Contemporary Economic Policy* 25(4):486–505.

Title IX of the Education Amendments of 1972, 20 U.S.C. § 1681.

Title VII of the Civil Rights Act of 1964, 42 U.S.C. § 2000e et seq.

Usher, Nikki. 2005. Girls Feeling Like Washouts on Coed Swimming Teams. *Philadelphia Inquirer,* February 11.

Van Sterkenburg, Jacco, and Annelies Knoppers. 2004. Dominant Discourses about Race/Ethnicity and Gender in Sport Practice and Performance. *International Review for the Sociology of Sport* 39(3):301–21.

Wachs, Faye Linda. 2003. "I Was There . . .": Gendered Limitations, Expectations, and Strategic Assumptions in the World of Co-ed Softball. In *Athletic Intruders: Ethnographic Research on Women, Culture, and Exercise,* edited by Anne Bolin and Jane Granskog. Albany: State University of New York Press, 177–200.

Whitson, David. 1990. Sport in the Social Construction of Masculinity. In *Sport, Men and the Gender Order: Critical Feminist Perspectives*, edited by Michael A. Messner and Donald F. Sabo. Champaign, IL: Human Kinetics Books, 19–30.

Williams v. Board of Regents of the University System of Georgia, 477 F.3d 1282 (11th Cir. 2007).

Zimbalist, Andrew. 2001. *Unpaid Professionals: Commercialism and Conflict in Big-Time College Sports*. Princeton, NJ: Princeton University Press.

PART IV

Constructing Masculinities in the Global Context

11

Masculinities and Child Soldiers in Post-Conflict Societies

FIONNUALA NÍ AOLÁIN, NAOMI CAHN, AND DINA HAYNES

A fairly substantial amount of literature has been generated over the years regarding the forms of masculinity that emerge in times of armed conflict and war (Goldstein 2001; Yuval-Davis 1997). This war-focused literature (which links to, among other things, masculinities studies) has drawn from broader theoretical research identifying an organic link between patriarchy, its contemporary manifestations, and various forms of masculinity as they arise within societies and institutions (Connell 2005; Cohen 2009). It builds on, and extends, the more general scholarship that has deepened our under-standing of how masculinities are constructed and differentiated (Chodorow 1994; Connell 1987; Dowd, Levit, and McGinley, this volume). While the war literature has made significant conceptual and practical use of the term "masculinity" to explore the impacts and effects of conflict, the concept has been less applied and understood to be relevant in post-conflict and transi-tional contexts, as societies attempt to move away from conflict. We argue that masculinities theory and its practical implications have been signifi-cantly under-utilized as a lens to explore and address the ending of hostilities in violent societies (Connell 2005; Kimmel 2005). This chapter suggests that with some notable exceptions (Theidon 2009), little attention has been paid to masculinities in conflict-ending contexts. Moreover, throughout the negotiation, reconstruction, mediation, and intervention phases, masculinities studies concepts and theorization have been underutilized and under-applied to the range of post-conflict actions and actors. Bringing masculinities into view in post-conflict settings provides a more thorough means and framework for addressing the complex social and political problems faced by societies seeking to move beyond violence.

Conflicted and post-conflict societies are an ongoing source of international attention and resources. They are sites of extremity and instability in many regions. Their successful transition from violent to peaceful (and typically from illiberal to more liberal forms of governance) has regional and global implications. Understanding the relationship between communal violence, masculinities, and the intergenerational transmission of deeply destructive social behaviors should be fully integrated into social, political, and economic problem solving. Masculinities studies, then, has much to offer the seemingly intractable political, legal, and social problems that accompany violent hostilities.

This chapter proceeds as follows. First we set out the application of relevant theoretical concepts to the conflict, post-conflict, and transitional terrains. We introduce and explore the key concepts of hegemonic and hyper-masculinity, drawing on a feminist approach to masculinities studies. The second part addresses the complex interplay between victim and perpetrator status, and the difficulties for men in acknowledging their own experiences as victimhood. This section offers a more nuanced understanding of male victimhood in violent societies, and the silences and barriers that operate to deny the vulnerability of men. It begins the exploration, continued in the next section, of the effects of conflict on children, including the intergenerational impact. The third part focuses on child soldiers, one of the most visible and vulnerable populations affected by the hypermasculinity of war. It applies theories and constructs from masculinities studies to address the resolution of social, political, and accountability issues that arise from the deployment of child soldiers in armed conflicts. We recognize that the application of masculinities theories does not offer a "one size fits all" solution to every conflict, nor will the issues experienced by and challenging child soldiers be identical across all contexts of violent hostilities. Rather, the knowledge base is one that can widen and deepen our perspectives on child soldiers and allow for creative interventions to support the resolution of a highly complex set of social and cultural issues.

Hegemonic and Hypermasculinities in Conflict Settings

Masculinities theories and feminist analysis have not always worked in tandem, and only relatively recently have feminist scholars sought to address what masculinity studies has to offer feminist theorizing (Dowd 2010). Using the gender lens drawn from various strands of feminist theorizing (Ní Aoláin, Haynes, and Cahn 2011), we start by asking the "man" question, interrogating where and how men are situated in relation to the creation, perpetration, and institutionalization of violence (Dowd 2010). In particular, how are men situated in relation to systematic and structural forms of violence aimed at the destruction of groups, communities, infrastructure, and social functioning? In what ways does hegemonic masculinity work, and how do masculinities operate to benefit even those men who are at the margins of masculinity norms and practice? Are there particular aspects of hegemonic and hypermasculinity that operate in armed conflicts (and their aftermath) that can be differentiated from the forms that appear in comparatively peaceful societies?

We start with the notion of hegemonic masculinity that defines a dominant conception of masculinity as "a man in power, a man with power and a man of power" (Kimmel 2009, 61). Understanding hegemonic masculinity is critical to seeing how the manifestation of manhood in multiple societal settings reinforces the power that some men maintain over women and other men. Hegemonic masculinity affirms such characteristics as "heteronormativity, aggression, activity, sports obsession, competitiveness, stoicism, and not being female or feminine" (Cohen 2009, 144). Hegemonic masculinity is "as much about [men's] relation to other men as it is about relation to women" (Dowd 2008, 233). Somewhat ironically, even within the hierarchies of masculinity, subordinated masculinities can benefit from the social construction of male privilege and values. That hegemonic masculinities are embedded in multiple sites of social interface underscores their pervasive influence upon social interaction between groups of men, within familial and communal settings for men, and between men and women.

Much of the theoretical work exploring masculinities has been undertaken in western liberal societies. Many of the assumptions built into theorizing men and male experiences are grounded in empirical and anecdotal experiences of men living in western democracies, who have at least theoretical access to a range of social and other opportunities and where there is hypothetically greater capacity for social mobility. Important to our comparative application, Western societies are generally not perceived as having abnormal or excessive levels of violence, at least not as measured by conflict violence scales. Accordingly, in societies with fewer opportunities for men and in which access to social and economic capital is highly variable across social and cultural groups, the crossover and application of masculinities theorizing requires some adjustment. In societies where social choice and mobility are far more restricted and cultural assumptions about gender roles and expectations are far more deeply entrenched and immovable, conceptions of manhood may be more rigid and cultural differences as to familial role and communal roles may need to be integrated more fully into the analysis.

Conflict and Hypermasculinity

While some generalizations are accurate concerning the role of masculinities in violent conflicts, the societal context matters. In studying these contexts, masculinity cannot be essentialized based on a view that all men are violent and all women are victims (Abrams 2010; Ní Aoláin et al. 2011). We must also guard against the possibility that apparent challenges to masculinities practices can "[entrench] hegemonic masculinity in other ways by perpetuating gender stereotypes positioning all men as prone to violence and all women as vulnerable to victimization and displacing the men and women that operate outside these binary constructs" (Abrams 2010, 703).

Of particular interest to our analysis is the lens of *hypermasculinity*, "a masculinity in which the strictures against femininity and homosexuality are especially intense and in which physical strength and aggressiveness are paramount" (Harris 2000, 793). Other kinds of masculinities coexist with hypermasculinity, but in situations of conflict, hypermasculinity plays an enlarged and elevated role. Its social traction is intensified when violence is endemic, and other strictures (social, economic, legal) are slackened; and the unloosening of these patterns and hierarchies is particularly fraught in the post-conflict process.

An important reference point across both conflicted and non-conflicted states is the correlation (and in some societies the codependency) of hegemonic and hypermasculinity with the role of the military. In the context of contemporary armed conflicts, the term military includes state military forces but also insurgent groups, secessionist movements, paramilitary organizations, and other non-state military entities. It may also include international military in the form of peacekeepers and hybrid groupings comprised of international and domestic military forces. The military is closely tied to manhood, and, indeed, militaristic actions are supported by an ideology of male toughness (Goldstein 2001; Theidon 2007). Hegemonic masculinity pervades and defines sex roles in the military (Abrams 2010). Men dominate most national and international militaries. A swathe of research provides evidence that the military trains its members to see desirable masculinity as intertwined with violence in an effort to create the appropriate mind-set of soldiers who are prepared to fight aggressively to defend their countries (Baaz and Stern 2009). The military is designed around male images that "tacitly exclude others who contradict their image of the combat, masculine warrior" (Dunivin 1997, 16–17). The military is also clearly identified with institutionalized and highly gendered practices including, until recently, homophobia and the exclusion of women from combat roles in many countries (ibid.). The opposition of military hierarchies in many states to the inclusion of openly gay and lesbian personnel is deeply implicated in the maintenance of ostensibly heterosexual and singularly masculine cultures in the military (Kaplan 2003). By the time conflict ends, men who have acted militarily and the (generally) male political elite are deeply enmeshed in this cultural vision of manhood. As former combatants in Colombia explained to anthropologist Kimberly Theidon, for example, joining a paramilitary group allowed the men "to 'feel like a big man in the streets of their barrios,' to 'go out with the prettiest young women,' and to 'dress well,' privileges they insist would not have been possible if they weren't carrying a gun" (2007, 76). The prevalence of this kind of masculinity poses complex issues for undoing violence, for mainstreaming gender equality, and for remaking societies that have been fractured and deeply divided.

Post-conflict societies present a unique and under-analyzed site of examination for masculinities. One of the main reasons for this lack of attention is the presumption that the post-conflict context is equated to peace and that the absence of war makes moot any analysis of masculinity, which is presumed to have been "tamed" by the end of violent contestation (Ní Aoláin et al. 2011). This presumption is misguided. It fails to account for the many ways that the hypermasculinization inherent in hostilities continues to affect societies and underestimates the ways in which pre-existing conceptions of masculinity influence the transition process. For example, women continue to experience intimate violence in post-conflict societies, and the locales of violence may shift in post-conflict societies such that many violent societies experience significant increases in ordinary criminality as hostilities technically end (Hamber 1998). Moreover, the transition process may attempt to reconstruct the patriarchal legal, social, and cultural institutions that existed pre-conflict (Ní Aoláin et al. 2011). Thus, while armed conflict between combatants may end as a result of a peace treaty or ceasefire agreement, violence may remain a persistent feature of the social and cultural landscape of post-conflict societies.

Understanding what happens post-conflict to men (and women) who have been violent in situations of armed conflict is essential to tracking these patterns of shift and movement in the sites of violence. Masculinities may also be critical to understanding why armed conflict reignites in many theoretically "post"-conflict societies, and why the long-term traction of peace agreements is limited (Collier 2009). Consequently, close attention to the forms and impact of masculinities in the post-conflict milieu is critical for the success of the transition itself.

The post-conflict environment, like the conflict environment, is also "vividly about male power systems, struggles and identity formation" (Handrahan 2004, 433). There may be an enormous flux in the male post-conflict fraternity both on an individual and communal level. Moreover, international organizations and institutions, typically headed by male elites, are arriving to reconfigure the transitioning society. So, men who were in power are losing power, other men (domestic and international) are taking their place, and internationals (generally culturally and politically differentiated other males) are coming into a society to fill a vacuum. In this flux of come and go, the gains and losses made by men as individuals or men as representatives of social, cultural, or political groups are critical to the long-term success of the transition from war to peace. Of particular relevance is what happens to the men who symbolically or practically "lose" the war. In assessing this loss, the tools of masculinities scholarship can evaluate the consequences of these perceived failures on men's own professed self-worth, when value is based upon traits of strength, success, and control in "making" and respecting the man. The ongoing pressure to conform to the idealized version of manhood in a society where social and economic choices are few may be organically linked to the repeat player problem in internal conflicts. This challenge is generally engaged by having the same actors cyclically engaged in violence, then cyclically disarmed and demobilized, only to return to armed combat again. Perpetual cycles of violent conflict intractability may be related to the cultural vision of manhood that props up ongoing reversion to violence, to "securing the win," as much as to other economic and political factors.

One enduring question that emerges from the conflict and masculinities literature is—why do men engage in violence? To begin with, violence, as an aspect of masculinity, is deeply linked to the assertion of social status and the value of self in particular contexts. Violence may literally "make the man" in many societies, and not infrequently the site of the violence is the woman's body. Recent empirical studies investigating why men rape have exposed the fact that soldiers "explicitly link their rationale for rape with their inabilities (or 'failures') to inhabit certain idealized notions of heterosexual manhood"

(Baaz and Stern 2009, 497). Indeed, soldiers pointed to the discord between their embodied experiences and their expectations of themselves as soldiers (men) in the armed forces as a site of frustration, negotiation, and an underlying incitement to sexual violence (ibid.).

While the causes of violence and conflict in a range of societies are complex (Scherrer 2002), a number of cluster causalities are useful to identify. Violence is typically associated with the following: first, economic and social insecurity; second, a lack of legal and political status particularly associated with group or ethnic identity; and third, the lack of opportunity for meaningful self-determination (whether external or internal) within the state. In multiple contexts, engaging in violence is a rational choice for men when few other opportunities may be provided to gain economic security (albeit that participation in violence provides a highly tenuous economic existence or longevity), social status and value within their communities, and security (again albeit tenuous and fragile) for their families and communities.

The existence of such deeply rooted links between the constructions of the masculine self and the social acceptance of "manhood" means that uncoupling the political contexts which bring about the formal end to hostilities from broader social and cultural contexts that produce certain kinds of masculine behaviors and values is complex. The end of violence is not a superficial engagement, but may require deep and difficult entanglement with the masculine construction of self in many societies. In post-conflict societies, where there is no functioning governance or economic structure, such conundrums are compounded by the lack of other opportunities available to men to assert positive masculinities. Such positive masculinities include caretaking and support roles, roles that evidence nurturing capacity, and engaging in a broad range of social and economic activities that in highly gender stratified societies would be gendered female.

Masculinities and the Ending of Conflicts

This question of violence and its ending is central to the post-conflict experience because the cessation of public violence between (generally) male combatants is usually the litmus test for evaluating the success of the transition from war to peace. We take issue with the presumption that the end of *public* violence and the measurement of security based on the safety of *male* combatants should constitute an adequate calculation of peace in any society. Instead, achieving peace requires accounting for, and directly addressing, the causes of violence, a process that requires engaging inter alia with hypermasculinity. Of course, issues of causality are extremely complex, dependent on

variations in social and cultural contexts. Nonetheless, post-conflict literature has begun to explore the strong overlap between the causes of violence
and the emergence of certain forms of masculinity in conflicted societies. If
we fail to address the causalities discussed above within a framework that
integrates gender and masculinities, we may also fail to address the ongoing
realities of how masculinities closely interconnect with post-conflict social,
political, and economic outcomes.

In addition to recognizing the forms and patterns of masculinities emerging in conflict and post-conflict situations, we must also acknowledge the
specific masculinities associated with international intervention and the
cadre of male elites who come into conflict endings exercising multiple roles
and functions. Beyond a more nuanced recognition of these international
masculinities, we also want to address the complex set of role assumptions
for men and women in post-conflict societies. This requires asking the fundamental question of what does it mean "to be a man" in a violent society,
when violence begets status and economic capacity? What happens to such
masculinities when societies transition from violence and move toward
democratic or more liberal forms of political engagement? Which men lose
and gain in such contexts? What happens to women when men experience this role instability? As both Brandon Hamber and Amy Maguire have
explored in post-apartheid South Africa and transitionary Lebanon, respectively, women often bear the brunt of the flux in masculine roles (Hamber
2006; Maguire 2009).

Formal (equality) gains made by women in many post-conflict legislative and constitutional enactments conjoin with the political displacement
of power for many men from the traditional routes provided during armed
conflict to create a complex social and legal terrain. It is upon this territory that women's gains and their intersection with masculinities in flux are
played out. Formal gains for women may, in fact, be nullified or significantly
constrained by the reality of social and community context, in which the
accommodation of men's deeply entrenched social status may outweigh the
enforcement of formal legal norms in practice. Moreover, the social realities
that women confront in highly patriarchal societies are propped up and perpetuated by masculinities in action—limiting the reach of law in subtle and
crosscutting ways.

It is also vital to contextualize the reality of economic fragility faced in
post-conflict zones around the world. Countries emerging from conflict are
some of the poorest on the planet. Consider that, as of 2008, Somalia's Gross
Domestic Product (GDP) per capita was $600; Rwanda's GDP per capita was
$1,000; Burundi's GDP per capita was $400; and Colombia's GDP per capita

was $8,800 (Central Intelligence Agency 2009). They have the highest number of refugee populations (who are predominantly female with child dependents) and internally displaced persons. For example, as of January 2009, Rwanda hosted 55,062 refugees; Somalia hosted 1,842 refugees and 1,277,200 internally displaced persons; Burundi had 21,093 refugees and 100,000 internally displaced persons; and Colombia had 170 refugees and 3 million internally displaced persons (UNHCR 2009). In this context, when one domain of status and economic subsistence is closed off (by the end of violent armed conflict), such societies struggle to replace the dysfunctional economy of war with a functional liberal economy of provision. The tools that for some men provided a means of survival in war are unreliable and may no longer be needed. Men and young boys who are under- or uneducated are at a considerable and material disadvantage in such settings. In this space of economic struggle, Gary Barker and Christine Ricardo illustrate the rise in the parallel economics of criminality and "normal" violence, which allow certain forms of masculinity to endure and provide both status and material gains (2005). They note the particular difficulties of confronting violent masculinities in social settings that have operated to seal off men spatially from women and children. This is further compounded in societies that have deeply stratified gender roles, leaving little room for the expression of positive masculinities in either the public or private sphere. The effects of such stratification are also intensified when one accounts for intergenerational transmission of violent norms, as well as in societies where age stratification is intense, creating intense competition for economic and sexual resources as well as opportunities (ibid. 12).

Male Victimization in Conflict and Post-Conflict Settings

Rather than essentialize men's roles during conflict as characterized by hypermasculinity, it is vital to acknowledge that men and boys may also have been victimized throughout violent conflicts—possibly by abduction, possibly by sexual violence, almost certainly by the violent ritualization that frequently accompanies male initiation into predominantly male military fraternities. A particular taboo is evident in recording or acknowledging the experiences of sexual violence by male combatants and male civilian bystanders.[1]

In this context, scholars have increasingly challenged the tendency to frame some sexual crimes, specifically the crime of sexual enslavement, as one that predominantly describes the experiences of women and enslavement simple (without a gender-based dimension) as only affecting men and boys (Mibenge 2010). In such a limited gender analysis, "men are 'just' slaves whilst their female counterparts are 'just' raped" (ibid. 4) The approach fails to account for the ways in which, in the context of enslavement of boys, sexual vulnerability is ever present and sexual and reproductive ownership limits the ways in which boys' sexual development and maturing is controlled and exploited (ibid.; Bridgewater 2005). Essentialist constructions are clearly overly simplistic and fail to account for the totality of violence and harm experienced by men, women, boys, and girls in conflict contexts.

As Chris Dolan has noted in the context of documenting the rape of men in Northern Uganda, male rape is little discussed (Neumann 2009). Male rape practices in this setting were viewed as an affront to male identity and to the society as a whole and discounted or under-acknowledged in social and political settings. Violent sexual attacks on men were viewed as an attack on the integrity of the community (more so even than the rape of women), but in practice were downplayed in terms of their actual occurrence and little support or social sympathy was forthcoming for victims.[2]

The taboo on addressing male victimization trickles down from the dominance of hegemonic masculinity in which to be a victim is to be relegated to a domesticated and vulnerable status. To be the male victim of sexual violence is to be defined in womanly terms as "soft and weak and incompetent" (MacKinnon 1982, 530). There is some nascent literature that suggests a link between sexual violence of men by men and deeply rooted practices of feminization (UN OCHA 2008). In this telling, sexual violence experienced by men is a direct playing out of wider social (and violent) practices that are generally directed toward women. For many men who experience rape, the result is to undermine their own masculinity in fundamental ways and put in doubt their sexual identity. Based on homophobia, many societies stigmatize the existence of male/male rape because it involves sexual activity between men and is viewed as indicative of homosexuality regardless of the coercion involved (Sivakumaran 2005). Sexual violence experienced by men is, we know, significantly underreported, although empirical proof other than anecdotal evidence is difficult to establish. The statistics of the Peruvian Truth and Reconciliation Commission (TRC) suggest that men may underreport (even as the statistics illustrate that women are the most prevalent victims of sexual violence). Of the 538 cases of sexual violence reported to the TRC, 527 correspond to women and only eleven were attributed to male victims (Duggan, Bailey, and Guillerot 2008). As is generally noted in the context of sexual violence experienced by women, underreporting is rife, and we do not have a deep understanding of the form, dynamics, and scale of sexual violence that men experience in times of conflict. To do so requires not only seeing how hegemonic and hypermasculinities underpin the experience of and response to sexual violence as it affects men, women, and the communities they belong to, but also how it disempowers men and boys from reporting their experiences.

Male victims may feel caught between the hypermasculinization of war and their own feelings of vulnerability and stigma (Gettleman 2009). Facilitating acknowledgment of the experiences of violation by men and boys, ensuring reporting, and advancing healing requires developing programs to aid this population. These programs might include specially trained counselors, targeted educational opportunities for boy soldiers, and specific health care measures. Critical in addressing victimization and powerlessness is identifying ways in which victims, male and female, can benefit from forms of social and economic empowerment and from the development of positive role models that may help them address and move past their victimization.

Child Soldiers and Intergenerational Transmission of Violent Norms

Male and female child soldiers present particular challenges to post-conflict reconciliation, and occupy a unique space by inhabiting the boundaries of being both victims and perpetrators simultaneously (Rosen 2009). Regardless of whether they are subjected to socialization into the military as arms-bearing soldiers, as porters, or camp followers, they provide an important subject for masculinities studies. The deployment of child soldiers has been a historical reality in many societies, yet legal developments recognizing the rights of the child through international treaties such as the Convention on the Rights of the Child (CRC) have transformed international and domestic approaches to the use of children as soldiers and to the imposition of any criminal penalties they might face as a result. The first contemporary legal deterrent to using children as combatants came with Protocol I Additional to the Geneva Conventions of 1977, which makes some advances but does not appear to be an outright prohibition on child combatancy.[3] Despite this and the development of international prohibitions on the use of child soldiers, much legal and cultural work remains to be done in setting generally agreed and enforced international standards on the use of persons under 18 in military contexts (Hamilton and Abu El Haj1997). The difficulties are rife as treaty provisions continue to make a distinction between persons under 15 years of age, for whom the prohibitions are generally robust and absolute, and those between 15 and 18 years old, who can be voluntarily conscripted into military forces.[4] The Optional Protocol to the Convention on the Rights of the Child on the Involvement of Children in Armed Conflicts (Child Soldiers Protocol), which specifically addresses the practice of recruiting and using children as soldiers in armed conflict, bans the use of children under the age of 18 in armed conflicts, although it does permit the voluntary enlistment of 16- and 17-year-olds into armed forces (Optional Protocol 2000). It has not, however, been ratified universally (Coalition to Stop the Use of Child Soldiers 2008; UNICEF 2006). Variable criminal standards across multiple jurisdictions on the age at which a child can be held criminally accountable for various crimes also compound the difficulties in setting coherent and generally agreed standards on minor responsibility in law. Estimates vary as to the numbers of children conscripted into state military forces, militias, and other non-state forces, but may be as high as 300,000 in a given year (Drumbl 2011; E. Kaplan 2005), and they can constitute a significant fighting force. The term "child soldiers" is broadly defined to include all children associated with armed groups, and their roles range from combatants to cooks, porters, or camp followers who are used for sexual services (Fujio 2008; Knudsen 2004). The disarmament of child soldiers must resolve thorny legal, moral, and programmatic questions. They include the following: (1) rehabilitating children who have committed serious and systematic human rights violations; (2) ensuring that such children are accepted by their families and communities when the victims of their crimes may have been family or community members; (3) determining whether child soldiers are eligible for asylum under refugee law or must be barred for having persecuted others; (4) addressing the educational and health needs of boy and girl soldiers in societies with scarce resources; (5) finding ways to address the needs and rights of those victimized by child soldiers; and (6) satisfying the demands for criminal accountability in post-conflict societies. In a broader view, the rehabilitation and reintegration of child soldiers is critical to the long-term stability of violent societies as we increasingly understand the intergenerational effects of armed hostilities over the medium and long term. Children who have absorbed and acted out violent norms pose immense challenges to the sustainability of peace and to the broadest possible realization of stability and security.

One starting point for the application of masculinities studies is the recognition that boys are typically inculcated into cultures whose normative underlay is based on the suppression of emotion. The perceived success of a boy's development (for himself and his family) will be the expression of strength both physical and emotional and the rejection of weakness (judged in similar terms) (Gilmore 1990; Kimmel 2004). The particular weight of responsibility that falls on boys to fulfill masculine and productive expectations from a very early age must be more fully considered in the broader masculinities literature. In societies that experience entrenched and cyclical violence, these pressures are present in concentrated form. When familial and communal structures operate within the dual expectations of the inevitability of violence and of a man's commitment to and support of military action, the pressures for the boy-child and the absorption of hypermasculinity norms comes early and intensely. Moreover, the range of choices offered to or closed off from the boy-child as combatant in waiting should not be underestimated. Here, hegemonic masculinity theory concerning violence as extensions of "normal" masculinity has a particularly deep resonance (Abrams 2010, 714). Moreover, such expectations, reinforced by the normality of hostilities, in turn highlight the need for a man to define his masculinity by defending his family, both in the literal and real senses (Gilmore 1990). These messages are clearly carried across generations. In Northern Ireland, for example, empirical research examining the murderous targeting of Protestant male heads of household in borderland farming communities (a form of ethnic cleansing) illustrates the enormous social pressures on young men (sons left behind) to protect land and family (and equally become the next subject of paramilitary targeting) (Simpson 2009).

The transmission of intergenerational expectations compounds the entrenchment of stratified gender roles, and can nullify any attempts to advance gender equality and the loosening of gendered expectations around caring and parenting for women. The core point is that conflicted societies can mummify highly gendered role expectations for men and for women from early childhood in ways that are quantifiably more intense than in societies not experiencing communal violence. Additionally, in societies experiencing ethnic or religiously driven hostilities, the overlay of "othering" that accompanies the construction of the social and masculine self is profoundly linked to the reproduction of violence through the generations and the valuing and self-identification of the man through violent action. In such contexts, when children engage in violent activities, consent is a highly fraught measurement given the longitudinal socialization to violent norms that may be endemic to upbringing in particular communities.

Child soldiers are a complex group who cannot be essentialized as victims or violent actors (Drumbl 2011). There are numerous factors that influence children to join armed movements voluntarily (or at least without physical coercion), including the poverty in which they live and the lack of opportunities for education or ultimate employment. While not all poor children living in conflict zones become soldiers, it is poverty and conflict that prevent them from attending school or that result in the death of family members who might otherwise provide counsel. One study found that 80 percent of child soldier recruits, compared to 20 percent of a control group of children who had not become soldiers, observed conflict near their homes (Cahn

2006). Serving with an armed force also can be seen as providing various opportunities, including protection and training (Drumbl 2011; Amnesty International 2010). Adolescents who are working or who are in school and doing well are much less likely sources of recruits than unemployed children with no opportunity for school (Cahn 2006). Joining an armed group provides adolescents with the potential for adventure (ibid.). Children may also join to take revenge against other armed groups who have killed family members. Additionally, both boys and girls may join to escape from oppressive home environments, although girls are far more likely than boys to claim that domestic violence or feelings of exploitation were their primary motivation for joining. Once children become associated with armed forces, they undergo efforts to entrench and endorse violence, competitiveness, and destructive capacities; this may become a "proving ground for masculinity" viewed as a "rite of passage, transforming boys into men" (Carreiras 2006, 41). Through participation in conflicts, boys may feel that they have become men, and they may find male role models (Barker and Ricardo 2005).

Child militarization also occurs through coercion, including conscription, abduction, and forced involvement in violent activities, the latter directly aimed at the families and communities they have been taken from. Here, the intended consequences are breaking down familial and social bonds, and destroying the community by the horrific manipulation of its most vulnerable.[5] In order to socialize children into the military, for example, their leaders "deliberately brutalise the children from an early stage, forcing them to commit crimes against their will. . . . Once on the frontlines, the process of brutalisation continues as children are repeatedly obliged to commit abuses, including murder and rape, against civilians and enemy soldiers" (Amnesty International 2003, 6–7). Equally evident are the unique vulnerabilities of young men and male children who have been conscripted into militias, insurgent groups, or paramilitary forces. As the initial indictments from the International Criminal Court illustrate in relation to the harms visited upon child soldiers, acts of sexual violation were intentional and systematic, clearly intended to break bonds between children and their families/communities of origin and force relationships of dependency and shame into the paramilitary organizations (ICC Warrant of Arrest 2006).

Central to the reassertion of normality in many conflicted societies—as a bridge from war to peace—are DDR (disarmament, demobilization, and reintegration) programs. Heavily endorsed and supported by international intervenors (whether states or international institutions), DDR has been the locus for addressing the neutralization as a military threat of the combatant in the post-conflict state. DDR programs and accountability processes have generally failed to account for the emergence of masculinities in violent childhoods, and the "making of the man" in these contexts has long-term effects for the stability and peacefulness of a conflicted society. Demobilization programs that fail to account for the push and pull factors that lead boys into armed conflict cannot hope to effectively contribute to leading a country into sustained peace. The intergenerational transmission of problematic masculinity norms must be more clearly placed in the discourses of transition and peacemaking in order to render post-conflict programs more effective and relevant in securing their stated goal of rendering peace.

Child soldiers may have become adults during the conflict, and will have the same needs as other former combatants for rehabilitation and reintegration. Effective and meaningful DDR would benefit from deconstructing and addressing positively the negative masculinities of militarization processes in which child soldiers have participated. Anyone recruited as a child, however, has also lost educational opportunities and family care and support, issues that must be recognized in any DDR program. Child soldiers who remain children also need services to help them find their families or, where the families cannot be found, make arrangements for foster care (YCare International 2008). Ensuring the integration of children more positively into their families offers some means to redress the complex roles that they must manage in the post-conflict context, helping them manage a transition away from the hypermasculinizing process they have undergone during the conflict and offering positive alternatives. Educational opportunities provided as part of the DDR must recognize the special needs of children whose schooling and emotional development have been so violently disrupted, resocializing them to effectively dismantle individual and collective wartime behavioral patterns and mentalities. Another important and related move is to extend and broaden the categories of combatants for the purposes of DDR programs, ensuring that children who have provided support roles to military or paramilitary forces (as well as those who have been involved in direct hostilities) are included and fully integrated into structured DDR programs. Inclusion in official and appropriately framed DDR programs can, again, help with moving away from a violent mentality instilled by conflict.

Re-socializing former child soldiers requires integrating the information known about the effects of hyper- and other forms of heightened masculinities into the planning and delivery of the DDR programs that are generally constructed and supported by international actors. It means moving the emphasis away from merely handing over guns to neutral arbitrators and instead integrating psychological and reflective counseling into the demilitarization of combatants (Ní Aoláin et al. 2011). Ultimately, and far more difficult, it requires providing other economic and social opportunities for boys and men to express masculinities in ways that are not socially and politically destructive.

A key challenge is developing positive gender roles for young men and women who have been egregiously violent, and who have been equally deeply violated.[6] These multiple contexts of male victimization (made more complex by the victims' parallel roles as perpetrators) require melding into the programmatic structure of DDR programs. In particular, DDR programs need to develop special counseling and training programs addressing the harms experienced directly and more broadly, forcing difficult conversations about men's roles post conflict (United Nations 2006; Bastick 2008). Postconflict programs must be developed and carried out with an awareness and appreciation for the cause and effect of masculinities during war in order to effectuate post-conflict transitional goals in genuinely transformative ways.

Conclusion

While violent masculinities are clearly and inexorably evident in conflicted societies, not all conflicts manifest similar kinds of violence, nor are the patterns of violence consistently duplicated. This suggests that masculinities are not evidenced in the same ways across all conflicts and that limits can be placed on male behavior in war. This insight has relevance for our understanding of how we address the manifestation of masculinities in conflict contexts. Recent empirical work reveals highly relevant variables to the forms and expressions of violence against women in situations of conflict, not only demonstrating the fact of variability but also offering significant insight into the kinds of structural and institutional matters that can dampen certain kinds of violent expression in war, and, in particular, sexual violence against women and men (Wood 2006). Understanding violence and how to transition away from it involves identifying the forms of masculinity that emerge in violent conflicts and what limits can be placed on hypermasculinities or the negative results of hegemonic masculinity in conflict contexts. Factors that limit the experience of harm in war for both men and women include restraining opportunity (namely, ensuring where possible limitation on access to civilians from combatants), creating or lowering incentives to military personnel for certain kinds of violent action, and creating and enforcing a system of effective sanctions which is highly correlated to the effectiveness of military discipline within any military unit or entity (ibid.). These are all relevant frames to think about in addressing the management of inevitable conflict and to lessen violent impact for men and women.

Post-conflict settings require addressing gender in multiple ways, including through close attention to masculinities as part of the high-priority (and funded) measures to end violence. Programs specifically focused on disarming and reintegrating former combatants need to account for masculinities in their mandates and program deliveries. They need to do so in a thoughtful way that integrates scholarly and interdisciplinary insights squarely into the policy arena.

Masculinities discourses and theory have begun to transform scholarly and practical understandings of the methods and means of warfare, as well as to tease out the causalities of war and the means to bring about an end to public communal violence between male combatants. In the context of post-conflict, peacemaking, and transitional discourses, however, attention to masculinities has been much less evident. Our contribution seeks to remedy that gap by bringing the theory and practice of masculinities discourses to bear on these fields, focusing on the particular vulnerability of child soldiers and the victimization of men during conflict. This chapter has sought to rebut the general presumptions that masculinities disappear at the formal ending of hostilities and during the peacemaking phase of conflict. Rather, masculinities are ever present and deeply problematic to ensuring successful outcomes with a sustainable peace. In particular, we suggest that hypermasculinity maintains its presence in post-conflict societies—and is particularly manifest in the experiences of violence in the private sphere for women and the increases in criminality and "ordinary" violence in transitional societies.

Notwithstanding the cultural, legal, and social variations between countries facing post-conflict issues, the core issues around the centrality of gender remain universal. In undertaking this analysis, we are convinced that addressing gender and the differing needs of men and women is not only good policy and practice on its own merits, but that it also meets the first principle of conflicted and post-conflict societies—namely, ensuring that violence ends for all, is not reignited, and that peace is sustainable far into the future.

NOTES

1. It is important, then, to acknowledge the men who have recently come forward in the Congo to attest to having been raped by both rebels and Congolese soldiers alike. The American Bar Association, running a sexual violence legal clinic in Goma, states that more than 10 percent of its rape cases in June 2010 were men who were then cast out by their villages and families, shamed and referred to as "bush wives," the pejorative term used for years to describe women forcibly taken as sex slaves or "wives" of these same soldiers (Gettleman 2009). The experiences of these men were later discounted.

2. In the documentary film *Gender against Men* in which one individual gives evidence about the experience of being raped 20 years earlier, the testimony itself is highly unusual. In the field where the testimony was taken, the speaker was shouted down in a communal setting, as if the community as a whole did not want to "hear" what had been done.

3. Article 77(2) states that: "The Parties to the conflict shall take all feasible measures in order that children who have not attained the age of fifteen years do not take a direct part in hostilities and, in particular, they shall refrain from recruiting them into their armed forces. In recruiting among those persons who have attained the age of fifteen years but who have not attained the age of eighteen years, the Parties to the conflict shall endeavour to give priority to those who are oldest."

4. The European Convention on Human Rights allows for voluntary military service from the age of 16. See also ICCPR standard and jurisprudence. As regards the Geneva Conventions: there are six articles that specifically concern children under the age of 15 in the Fourth Geneva Convention of 1949. Of those articles, half apply to the general child population of a state party while the other half apply to children who fall under the remit of protected persons.

5. Child Soldiers Global Report found at http://www.childsoldiersglobalreport.org/overview-and-benchmarks, which takes a country-by-country assessment of the numbers and experiences of child soldiers.

6. Girls play a multitude of roles in conflicts, and are also socialized into violence (Ní Aoláin et al. 2011).

REFERENCES

Abrams, Jamie R. 2010. The Collateral Consequences of Masculinizing Violence. *William and Mary Journal of Women and the Law* 16:703–52.

Amnesty International. 2010. *Stories from Children Associated with Fighting Forces*, http://www.amnestyusa.org/children/child-soldiers/stories-from-children-associated-with-fighting-forces/page.do?id=1021177.

———. 2003. *Democratic Republic of Congo: Children at War*. Available at http://www.amnesty.org/en/library/info/AFR62/034/2003.

Baaz, Maria Erikkson, and Maria Stern. 2009. Why Do Soldiers Rape? Masculinity, Violence, and Sexuality in the Armed Forces in the Congo (DRC). *International Studies Quarterly* 53:495–518.

Barker, Gary, and Christine Ricardo. 2005. *Young Men and the Construction of Masculinity in Sub-Saharan Africa: Implications for HIV/AIDS, Conflict, and Violence*. Available at http://www.eldis.org/vfile/upload/1/document/0708/DOC21154.pdf.

Bastick, Megan. 2008. Integrating Gender in Post-Conflict Security Sector Reform. Available at http://www.dcaf.ch/publications/kms/details.cfm?lng=en&id=90764&nav1=4.

Bridgewater, Pamela. 2005. Ain't I a Slave: Slavery, Reproductive Abuses and Reparations. *University of California Women's Law Journal* 14:89–161.

Cahn, Naomi R. 2006. Poor Children, Child "Witches" and Child Soldiers. *Ohio State Journal of Criminal Law* 3:413–56.

Carreiras, Helena. 2006. *Gender and the Military: Women in the Armed Forces of Western Democracies*. New York: Routledge.

Central Intelligence Agency. 2009. *The World Factbook*, https://www.cia.gov/
library/publications/the-world-factbook/region/region_afr.html (select a specific country from the drop-down menu; then select economy) (last visited December 1).

Chodorow, Nancy J. 1994. *Femininities, Masculinities, Sexualities: Freud and Beyond*. Lexington: University Press of Kentucky.

Coalition to Stop the Use of Child Soldiers. 2008. *Child Soldiers Global Report 2008*. Available at http://www.child-soldiers.org/library/global-reports.

Cohen, David S. 2009. No Boy Left Behind? Single-Sex Education and the Essentialist Myth
of Masculinity. *Indiana Law Journal* 84:135–88.

Collier, Paul. 2009. *Wars, Guns, and Votes: Democracy in Dangerous Places*. New York:
HarperCollins.

Connell, R. W. 2005. *Masculinities*, 2d ed. Berkeley: University of California Press.

———. 1987. *Gender and Power: Society, the Person, and Sexual Politics*. Stanford, CA: Stanford University Press.

Dowd, Nancy E. 2010. *The Man Question: Male Subordination and Privilege*: New York: New
York University Press.

———. 2008. Masculinities and Feminist Legal Theory. *Wisconsin Journal of Law, Gender
and Society* 23:201–48.

———. 2000. *Redefining Fatherhood*. New York: New York University Press.

Drumbl, Mark. 2011. *Not So Simple: Child Soldiers, Justice, and the International Legal Imagination*. Oxford: Oxford University Press.

Duggan, Colleen, Claudia Paz y Paz Bailey, and Julie Guillerot. 2008. Reparations for Sexual
and Reproductive Violence: Prospects for Achieving Gender Justice in Guatemala and
Peru. *International Journal of Transitional Justice* 2:192–213.

Dunivin, Karin O. 1997. *Military Culture: A Paradigm Shift*, http://www.au.af.mil/au/awc/
awcgate/maxwell/mp10.pdf.

Fujio, Christy C. 2008. Invisible Soldiers: How and Why Post-Conflict Processes Ignore the
Needs of Ex-Combatant Girls. *Journal of Law & Social Challenges* 10:1–21.

Gettleman, Jeffrey. 2010. Symbol of Unhealed Congo: Male Rape Victims, *New York Times*,
Aug. 4, 2010, p. A1.

———. 2009. Symbol of Unhealed Congo: Male Rape Victims, *New York Times*, Aug. 5.
Available at http://www.nytimes.com/2009/08/05/world/africa/05congo.html.

Gilmore, David. 1990. *Manhood in the Making: Cultural Concepts of Masculinity*. New
Haven, CT: Yale University Press.

Goldstein, Joshua S. 2001. *War and Gender: How Gender Shapes the War System and Vice
Versa*. Cambridge: Cambridge University Press.

Hamber, Brandon. 2006. "*We Must Be Careful How We Emancipate Our Women": Shifting
Masculinities in Post-Apartheid South Africa*. Paper presented at the Re-Imagining Wom-
en's Security: A Comparative Study of South Africa, Northern Ireland and Lebanon Round
Table, United Nations University, New York, October 2006. Available at http://www.bran-
donhamber.com/publications/Paper%20Careful%20how%20we%20emancipate.pdf.

———. 1998. "Dr. Jekyll and Mr. Hyde": Problems of Violence Prevention and Reconcilia-
tion in South Africa's Transition to Democracy. In *Violence in South Africa: A Variety of
Perspectives*, edited by Elirea Bornman, René Van Eeden, and M. E. Wentzel. Pretoria,
South Africa: HSRC, 349–69.

Hamilton, Carolyn, and Tabatha Abu El Haj. 1997. Armed Conflict: The Protection of Children under International Law. *International Journal of Children's Rights* 5:1–46.

Handrahan, Lori. 2004. Conflict, Gender, Ethnicity and Post-Conflict Reconstruction. *Security Dialogue* 35:429–55.

Harris, Angela P. 2000. Gender, Violence, Race, and Criminal Justice. *Stanford Law Review.* 52:777–807.

ICC Warrant of Arrest. 2006. *Prosecutor v. Thomas Lubanga Dyilo,* Case No. ICC-01/04-01/06, Feb. 10. Available at http://www.icc-cpi.int/iccdocs/doc/doc191959.pdf.

Kaplan, Danny. 2003. *Brothers and Others in Arms: The Making of Love and War in Israeli Combat Units.* New York: Southern Tier Editions.

Kaplan, Eben. 2005. *Child Soldiers around the World,* http://www.cfr.org/publication/9331/child_soldiers_around_the_world.html.

Kimmel, Michael S. 2009. Masculinity as Homophobia: Fear, Shame, and Silence in the Construction of Gender Identity. In *Sex, Gender, and Sexuality: The New Basics,* edited by Abbey L. Ferber, Kimberly Holcomb, and Tre Wentling. New York: Oxford University Press, 58–70.

———. 2005. *Manhood in America: A Cultural History.* New York: Free Press.

———. 2004. *The Gendered Society.* New York: Oxford University Press.

Knudsen, Christine. 2004. The Problem of Re-acclimating Child Soldiers into Society Assuming Peacekeeping is Successful: Demobilization and Reintegration during an Ongoing Conflict. *Cornell International Law Journal* 37:497–503.

Kron, Josh. 2010. Rape Victims in Congo Raid Now More Than 240. *New York Times.* Sept. 2. Available at http://www.nytimes.com/2010/09/03/world/africa/03congo.html.

MacKinnon, Catherine. 1982. Feminism, Marxism, Method and the State: An Agenda for Theory. *Signs* 7:515–44.

Maguire, Amy. 2009. "Security Starts with the Law": The Role of International Law in the Protection of Women's Security Post-Conflict. In *The Role of International Law in Rebuilding Societies after Conflict: Great Expectations,* edited by Brett Bowden, Hilary Charlesworth, and Jeremy Farrall. Cambridge: Cambridge University Press, 218–43.

Mibenge, Chiseche. 2010. Investigating Outcomes of a Limited Gender Analysis of Enslavement in Post-conflict Justice Processes. *Journal of Peacebuilding and Development* 5:34–46.

Neumann, Daniel (writer). 2009. *Gender against Men.* Kampala, Uganda: Refugee Law Project, DVD.

Ní Aoláin, Fionnuala, Dina Haynes, and Naomi Cahn. 2011. *Beyond the Frontlines: Gender in the Post-Conflict Period.* New York: Oxford University Press.

Optional Protocol to the Convention on the Rights of the Child on the Involvement of Children in Armed Conflict. 2000. G.A. Res. 54/263, Annex I, U.N. GAOR 54th Sess., Supp. No. 49, (Vol. III), U.N. Doc. A/54/49 (Vol. III), at 7.

Protocol I Additional to the Geneva Conventions of 1977, 1125 UNTS 3, 16 ILM 1391 (1977) entered into force Dec. 7, 1978).

Rosen, David M. 2009. Who Is a Child? The Legal Conundrum of Child Soldiers. *Connecticut Journal of International Law* 25:81–118.

Scherrer, Christian P. 2002. *Genocide and Crisis in Central Africa: Conflict Roots, Mass Violence, and Regional War.* Westport, CT: Praeger.

Simpson, Kirk. 2009. *Unionist Voices and the Politics of Remembering the Past in Northern Ireland.* Basingstoke, UK: Palgrave Macmillan.

Sivakumaran, Sandesh. 2005. Male/Male Rape and the "Taint" of Homosexuality. *Human Rights Quarterly* 27:1274–1306.

Theidon, Kimberly. 2009. Reconstructing Masculinities: The Disarmament, Demobilization, and Reintegration of Former Combatants in Colombia. *Human Rights Quarterly* 31:1–34.

——. 2007. Transitional Subjects: The Disarmament, Demobilization and Reintegration of Former Combatants in Colombia. *International Journal of Transitional Justice* 1:66–90.

UNHCR: The UN Refugee Agency. 2009. http://www.unhcr.org (select the specific country under "browse by country" to view the "Statistical Snapshot") (last visited December 1).

UNICEF. 2006. *Convention on the Rights of the Child*, http://www.unicef.org/crc/index_30203.html.

United Nations. 2006. OG 5.10: Women, Gender and DDR. In *Operational Guide to the Integrated Disarmament, Demobilization and Reintegration Standards*. Available at http://unddr.org/iddrs/og/OG_5_10.pdf (last visited December 8, 2010).

UN OCHA. 2008. *Discussion Paper 2: The Nature, Scope and Motivation for Sexual Violence against Men and Boys in Armed Conflict*. Available at http://ochaonline.un.org/OchaL-inkClick.aspx?link=ocha&docId=1092305.

Wood, Elizabeth Jean. 2006. Variation in Sexual Violence during War. *Politics and Society* 34:307–41.

YCare International. 2008. *Overcoming Lost Childhoods: Lessons Learned from the Rehabilitation and Reintegration of Former Child Soldiers in Colombia*, http://www.ycareinternational.org/1375/news-stories/child-soldiers-research-report.html.

Yuval-Davis, Nira. 1997. *Gender and Nation*. London: Sage.

12

Sexuality without Borders: Exploring the Paradoxical Connection between Dancehall and Colonial Law in Jamaica

CAMILLE A. NELSON

It is difficult to connect these different realms, to show the involvements of culture with expanding empires, to make observations
about art that preserve its unique endowments and at the same
time map its affiliations, but, I submit, we must attempt this, and
set the art in the global, earthly context. Territory and possessions
are at stake, geography and power.
Edward Said, *Culture and Imperialism* (1994, 7)

At times it is difficult to conceive of art as doing work. One tends to contem-
plate art as beneficent, existing to entice, enthrall, entertain, and otherwise
bring pleasure to our senses. This is true, but as cultural critic Edward Said
explained, art is also potent. It has the power to construct and disseminate
identitarian norms (Lawrence 1987). The most common interrogation of art
focuses attention on the power of the visual to shape perspectives (Mercer
1994). But the audible aspects of art have received far less attention. This
chapter explores one such art form, reggae music, a subset of which is the site
of considerable controversy.

Recently, critical race theorists and cultural critics have turned their
attention to certain forms of popular American music (Beyer 2000; Bracey
2003; Butler 2009; Chase 1986; Richmond 1998; Smith 2005). Most notably
they have directed their attention to the interrogation of American hip-hop
music (Butler 2009; Folami 2007; Perry 2004). Like the earlier critics of
heavy metal (Goodchild 1986; Lury 1999; Took and Weiss 1994) and rock
and roll (St. Lawrence and Joyner 1991), this generation of scholars has

criticized not only the misogyny and violence in some hip-hop, but also analyzed the caricatured depictions of black life contained in some of the music (Coates 2003; Heaggans 2009; Rutherford 2005; Tribbett-Williams 2000; Weisstuch 2005). Once removed from the American focus on hip-hop, however, scant scholarly attention has been paid to music outside of the United States or to the sociopolitical and cultural relevance of music in an international forum. The relative silence is curious given the role of technology in increasing the transmission and prevalence of music internationally. This project enters this void as a transnational interjection about a particularly influential genre of music.

This chapter focuses upon Jamaican dancehall music [hereinafter "dancehall"], the Jamaican equivalent to hip-hop, and its paradoxical connection to colonial precepts as statutorily embodied in the Offences against the Person Act. Given the proliferation of this type of music not only in Jamaica, but also around the world, attention must be paid to the messages exported as part of a seeming Caribbean culture generally, and a Jamaican identity more specifically. This chapter interrogates national identity construction as transmitted musically and focuses upon one particular identity construction, masculinity. Specifically, it analyzes the ways in which the musical site of dancehall constructs a hyper-heteromasculinity that is bound up in our colonial past. In turn, this manifestation of masculinity is exported via the lucrative and far-reaching musical economy of which Jamaica plays a role out of proportion to its size and population. At the global level, the significance of this manifestation of masculinity is compounded, given that the musical exports from Jamaica often form the extent of what many people know of the small island nation and its people. One thing that many people do not know of is the colonial origins of Jamaica's perceived "cultural homophobia." This chapter centers law in this colonial insinuation of homophobia.

The goals of this chapter are thus twofold. It seeks to problematize the supposed internal Jamaican embrace of homophobic norms by revealing the connections to colonial legal impositions that were used to further the interests of empire. Second, it seeks thereby to challenge the allegations that Jamaica is "the most homophobic place on earth" (Padgett 2006) as self-righteous cultural imperialism that demonizes Jamaica based upon a decontextualized ahistorical reading of Jamaica and its music. One cannot analyze the Jamaican embrace of homophobia as demonstrated in some dancehall without simultaneously interrogating the legal enforcement of the colonial agenda with respect to this small island nation.

The first part of the chapter examines Jamaican laws against sodomy as set forth in the "Unnatural Offences" sections of the Offences against the

Person Act (sections 76, 77) and situates these laws as direct descendants of colonial legislation imposed upon Jamaica under British rule. The second part addresses the power of music and the particular centrality of music in Jamaica. The next part questions whether the nomenclature of "art" is even appropriate to this controversial homophobic dancehall. Additionally, this part elaborates upon the controversial lyrics of some dancehall songs that have been dubbed "murder music." The chapter then explores identity formation with reference to the construction of a national gender identity in Jamaica. This part deals with the indigeneity claim frequently made in response to allegations of Jamaican homophobia; specifically, that homosexuality is alien and imposed by foreign interlopers. The following part addresses some of the political involvements in this discourse of cultural homophobia and reveals the paradoxical bedfellows that politicians and dancehall artists have become. The chapter concludes with calls for the repeal of the sodomy laws as well as for dancehall artists to take a more colonially aware approach to their music.

Remixing Empire: Laws Emergence in Culture

This chapter makes the unabashed presumption that law matters. Law has normative force beyond the precise doctrinal area at issue. Stated thus, this chapter considers law to be not only educative, but also cultural, insofar as its edicts and enforcement signal societal approval and, in the case of homosexuality, opprobrium. Examination of the Jamaican sodomy laws is insightful in this regard. They can be read as telling a story of legal cultural insinuation.

The sodomy laws in Jamaica were colonial impositions. In keeping with their time, they were enacted and enforced to further British interests, not necessarily to promote the interests of the native populations. Paradoxically, these laws have been maintained despite their nefarious origins. These laws are still subject to enforcement and, as will be detailed, have had a profound effect on cultural norms. Betraying the temporal colonial view of homosexuality as abhorrent, the relevant sections of the Offences against the Person Act are tellingly entitled "Unnatural Offences." This nomenclature blatantly situates heterosexuality as the norm by maligning homosexuality as unnatural. Thus section 76 reads as follows:

> Whoever shall be convicted of the abominable crime of buggery, committed either with mankind or with animal, shall be liable to be imprisoned and kept to hard labour for a term not exceeding ten years. (Offence against the Person Act, section 76)

The law conflates anal sex (between men) with sex with animals and punishes both sodomy and bestiality as serious criminal offenses. Interestingly, this same conflation is evident in a recent letter to the editor in the *Jamaican Observer*. In chastising American minister Nancy Wilson for her sexuality, the writer states:

> She might ask us soon to allow a man to marry a pig! Because from a Christian perspective, what would be the difference? Both are an abomination to God, yet homosexuality happens and bestiality too—if one is made legal, so should the other, and the homosexual church can allow for a man to marry a dog—if he finds the companionship of a dog preferable to that of humans. (Monroe 2010, citing a letter to the editor of the *Jamaica Observer* titled "Wilson's homosexual theology ain't right" submitted by J. M. Fletcher)

The singularity of both the legal and the cultural conflation, as expressed above, forces the question from whence did this notion of the equivalence of homosexuality to bestiality come? In the Jamaican context at least, it is possible to posit the substantive legal rule as informing and infusing popular sentiment. This colonially derived law could be conceptualized as the antecedent to the popular anti-homosexual sentiment thought to be prevalent in Jamaica today. The language and spirit of the law treat sex between men as abnormal, unnatural, and freakish and have laid a foundation for an equivalent, and equally disdainful, cultural discourse.

The present Jamaican law continues on by defining attempted unnatural offenses as similarly abominable but a misdemeanor punishable by imprisonment for a term less than seven years, with or without hard labor (Offences against the Person Act, section 77). In finding the requisite "carnal knowledge" upon "proof of penetration only," as opposed to the "emission of seed" (ibid. section 78), the act reveals a curious concern for gender performance. What is to be protected and guarded against is penetration— the vulnerability inherent in penetration seemingly strikes an effeminate chord. In not wanting to appear non-manly and non-masculine, the nation is constructed as non-feminine in order to avoid any connection to feminized notions of weakness (Harris 2000; Stychin 1998). Specifically, the law seems structured to prevent and punish male on male penetration, not similar female on female, or male on female acts. This implicitly references the "threat of the effeminized non-Western state" (Stychin 1998, 12). Without a doubt, non-consensual sex acts—whether with adults or children—are an entirely appropriate subject matter for the law, but there are also identitarian ideals motivating these laws. The concern is as equally steeped in gender as it is in protectionism.

Masculinity, its construction and operation, is the central driving force behind much of this legislation. Section 79 of the Jamaican Offences against the Person Act is explicit in its masculinist focus. There is no room for ambiguity as, unlike the other sections addressing "unnatural offences," it fixes the subject as "any male person." This section, "Outrages on Decency," reads as follows:

> Any male person who, in public or private, commits, or is a party to the commission of, or procures or attempts to procure the commission by any male person of, any act of gross indecency with another male person, shall be guilty of a misdemeanor, and being convicted thereof shall be liable at the discretion of the court to be imprisoned for a term not exceeding two years, with or without hard labour. (Offences against the Person Act, section 79)

In their entirety, these Jamaican laws seek to criminalize non-procreative sex (Alexander 1994). As Professor Jacqui Alexander states, the policing of sex is more than about policing sex (ibid.). For instance, in holding that the Texas anti-sodomy laws were unconstitutional, the majority of the United States Supreme Court stated, "early American sodomy laws were not directed at homosexuals as such but instead sought to prohibit nonprocreative sexual activity more generally" (*Lawrence v. Texas* 2003, 568). Thus, buried within legalese criminalizing certain sexualities are perspectives about nation-building, citizenship, economics, and, of course, gender. Professor Alexander puts it well:

> Embedded here are powerful signifiers about appropriate sexuality, about the kind of sexuality that presumably imperils the nation and about the kind of sexuality that promotes citizenship. Not just (any) *body* can be a citizen any more, for *some* bodies have been marked by the state as non-procreative, in pursuit of sex only for pleasure, a sex that is non-productive of babies and of no economic gain. (Alexander 1994, 6)

This juxtaposition of sexuality and nationhood equates heterosexuality with citizenship. Under this conceptualization homosexuals are non-citizens who imperil the nation (ibid.). Indeed, there is a long colonial history of incentivizing profitable sexuality to ensure wealth creation and nation-building (Nelson 2007). As a construct, the nation therefore embodies intersecting identitarian norms.

In seeking to legitimize themselves post-independence, Jamaicans struck a legislative bargain with their former colonizers. Jamaica replicated colonial sexuality edicts in an attempt to gain global respect. As Alexander notes, "the effects of political economic international processes provoke a legitimation crisis for the state which moves to restore its legitimacy by recouping heterosexuality through legislation" (1994, 7). This bespeaks an independence paradox, as the methodology by which post-colonial legitimation was sought was itself colonial in its origins and object. Specifically, post-independence Jamaica re-enacted the same oppressive legislation that had been imposed upon it pre-independence, and has now refused to repudiate it (Offenses against the Person Act; Luton 2009).

A review of the pre-independence provisions reveals that very little has changed over the course of hundreds of years. While the contemporary criminalization of the "abominable act of buggery" as an unnatural act remains static, the potential penalty has been lessened insofar as the mandatory minimum of a three-year sentence is removed from the provisions. Section 69 of the 1953 Act reads:

> Unnatural Offences
> Whoever shall be convicted of the abominable crime of buggery . . . shall be liable, at the discretion of the Court, to be kept in penal servitude for a term not exceeding ten years, and not less than three years, or to be imprisoned and kept to hard labour for a term not exceeding two years. (Offences against the Person Act 1953, section 69)

The contemporary, post-independence, sodomy legislation is thus virtually identical to the pre-independence colonial legislation of 1953. "By maintaining the logic and essence of these provisions, the post-colonial Jamaican legislators chose to re-inscribe the very same colonial sexual imperatives— that is, sex for procreation is prized and profitable for the building of the nation state" (Nelson 2008, 259). The problematic colonial prerogative is even more evident when one traces the legislative roots further into the past. Note the striking similarity to the buggery provision from the time of King Henry VIII.

> Forasmuch as there is not yet sufficient and condigne punishment appointed and limited by the due course of the laws of the Realm for the detestable and abominable vice of buggery committed with mankind or beast, It may therefore please the King's Highness with the assent of his Lords spiritual and temporal and the Commons the present parliament

assembled that it may be enacted by authority of the same, that the same offence be from henceforth adjudged felony, and such order and form of process therein to be used against the offenders as in cases of felony at the common law. (Moran 1996, 22, quoting An Acte for the Punysshement of the vice of Buggerie, 1533–4. 25 Henry 8, chapter 6)

Perhaps knowledge of this legislative history might serve as a basis upon which to challenge contemporary Jamaican cultural homophobia as indigenous. Rather than homosexuality being alien and homophobia somehow naturally imbedded, these colonial laws would seem to indicate that the sodomy laws themselves are the foreign imposition. However, many Jamaicans cling to the notion of "colonial contamination" (Stychin 1998, 11) "wherein homosexuality is attributed to the white colonizer" (ibid.). This theory "situates homosexuality as a foreign concept and the societal exclusion of homosexuals as organic[ally Jamaican]" (Nelson 2008, 260). The above legislation, however, reveals the fallacy in this position. The foreign imposition is the legal framework, not the sexuality—the colonial contamination is legal. What has to be rooted out, therefore, are the sodomy laws themselves. They are the colonial impositions that have paradoxically come to be thought of as organic and authentic, so much so that they have infected Jamaican culture, including popular musical culture.

Musical Culture—Cultural Music

As with other forms of art, music can be incredibly influential. Just as rap music was referred to as "the Black CNN" (California State University, Sacramento 2004), dancehall is the main cultural conduit in Jamaica. Indeed, "in Jamaica it is virtually cliché to observe that musical performers are the most influential voices among the general population" (Ross 1998, 38). Speaking to the might and persuasiveness of reggae music, Professor Carolyn Cooper has written, "Music is not mere entertainment but ideological weaponry" (2004, 75). This is especially the case given that music has a power to infiltrate and be heard second-hand; this accessibility is not often found with other forms of art. One can come upon and encounter music in a way that one cannot easily access other forms of art. Such musical mobility is increasingly relevant given twenty-first-century technological advancements such as satellite and Internet radio. Thus, in an increasingly small world, music can easily infiltrate beyond class and national boundaries. Music has a potency seldom found in other art forms. This is particularly the case in the small island nation of Jamaica.[1]

Despite having a relatively small population of less than three million residents (Central Intelligence Agency 2010), Jamaica produces a disproportionately large quantity of music. With worldwide sales and distribution garnering billions of dollars annually, the Jamaican music industry is an important part of the national economy (Henry 2006). Worldwide sales of reggae recordings have been valued at about $1.2 billion USD annually; an estimated 25 percent of that, or $300 million USD, flowed to Jamaican musicians and producers, while live performances in Jamaica netted an additional estimated $50 million USD (ibid.). As to the particular power of the Jamaican music industry, one scholar has remarked that it is "now one of Jamaica's most important economic sectors" (Stolzoff 2000, 4). Reggae music provides an economic engine that "provides access to jobs, the opportunity to achieve relatively great success, and a means to sell one's labor and products on the foreign market" (ibid. 8).

The prolific nature of the Jamaican musical heartbeat coupled with technological innovations has meant that Jamaican musical exports are consumed not only by the Jamaican "transnational society" that comprises the Jamaican diaspora. Rather dancehall, even more so than its predecessor genres of reggae, is consumed beyond Jamaican borders (Patterson 2001). However, the messages contained in some dancehall have not played well in some international contexts in which dancehall has entered the mix. Indeed, the homophobia endemic to some dancehall has led to a confrontation with global dimensions. The site of this transnational confrontation is at the confluence of culture, language, gender, class, race, sexuality, and, of course, nationality. Inherently intersectional, the questions posed also beg nuanced contextual thinking in order to generate appropriate solutions. The international response to homophobic dancehall lyrics has not been a thoughtful one. Specifically, the instinct toward boycotts by the North-West is overly broad and mimics colonial tendencies toward punishment rather than dialogue.

Can Hatred Be Art?: How Shall We Interpret Homophobic Lyrics?

But such a claim of North-Western punishment might prove challenging once confronted with the lyrics in issue (Human Rights Watch 2004, appendix). Even those inclined to be fervent free speech proponents might flinch at the explicitly violent homophobia contained in some dancehall.[2] The translations of some popular dancehall songs reproduced below cause one to pause to reflect upon the question of whether the nomenclature of art even applies. For instance, TOK, a group that is composed of four otherwise very talented young men (having been choir members and talent contest winners), sing the following homophobic lyrics:

> From dem a par inna chi chi man car [Once they get together in a gay men's car]
> Blaze di fire mek we bun dem! (Bun dem!) [Blaze the fire, let's burn them! (Burn them!)]
> From dem a drink inna chi chi man bar [Once they drink in a gay bar]
> Blaze di fire mek we dun dem! (Dun dem!) [Blaze the fire, let's burn them! (Kill them!)]....
> Rat tat tat every chi chi man dem haffi get flat die [Rat-tat-tat every gay man will have to die]
> Get flat, mi and my niggas ago mek a pack [Die, me and my comrades will make a pact]
> Chi chi man fi dead and dat's a fact. [Gay men must die and that's a fact.] (Human Rights Watch 2004, 76–77)

The clash between such lyrical violence and assertions of artistry and agency is raw—to deny the artists voice is to invite claims based upon the infringement of free speech, agency, and autonomy, but to allow such vitriol is to invite and incite hatred and violence against Gay Lesbian Bisexual Transgendered (GLBT) communities. Moreover, there is much else for which dancehall could be criticized and condemned by concerned North-Western activists. The music can also be vicious toward women and girls and can be downright vulgar (Cooper 1995; Stolzoff 2000). So of what does this art speak and how shall it be interpreted? Dancehall, like predecessor genres of reggae, cannot be separated from the colonial legacy discussed above—a violent legacy of racism, sexism, and the contested sexualities that are often produced when "isms" collide.

The emergent voices represented in dancehall declare a masculine subject that is contingent upon and derivative of the power of the former colonial lords. Indeed, as was discussed in the first part of this chapter, the homophobic incitement found in some dancehall is related, and legally tethered, to Jamaica's positioning within the British Empire. As the "most potent form of popular culture in Jamaica" (Stolzoff 2000, 1), dancehall has salience for the manner in which Jamaicans attempt to assert independence and sovereignty on the world stage.

Thus situated, dancehall is not simply a noun, but it is also a verb as it defines the maneuver by which "black lower class youth articulate and project a distinct identity in local, national and global contexts" (ibid.). As cultural theorist Andrew Ross has noted, the question of "who governs the reproduction of culture among the educable youth is a concern for any state" (1998, 38–39), but it is particularly relevant for Jamaica given its effective status as a "recolonized state" (ibid.). This is of heightened concern, notes Ross, for Jamaica, a nation with numerous constraints upon the exercise of "its own social, cultural, and economic life [which] has been eroded so radically over the last two decades, as it fell into the Third World 'debt trap' common to so many postcolonial nations" (ibid.). So if nationality is a construct, as we recognize race and gender to be, on what basis have the empowered classes constructed Jamaican citizenship? They have fallen back to the colonial precepts of gender, race, class, and sexuality.

Paradoxically, the hetero-masculinist construction of Jamaica has evolved in a fashion that is directly responsive, in a restitutionary way, to the Jamaican colonial experience. As evinced through the "art" that is homophobic dancehall, one sees glimpses of the colonial past. Such music did not occur in a vacuum. Rather, homophobic dancehall tracks the aforementioned sociolegal cultural legacy. Homophobic dancehall is a manifestation of a contorted colonial history, albeit a connection that has heretofore been unexplored and uncoupled from its legal roots. While this interdisciplinary insight might seem unlikely, it is deserving of discussion, given the power of the law and its cultural seepage. The law has normative force well beyond the statute books and case law. To some people, homophobic dancehall merely bespeaks a genuine Jamaican voice. To others, such claims of indigenous homophobia are contested.

Musical Indigeneity: What Is Authentically Jamaican?

Dancehall artists proclaim a quintessential Jamaican voice and posit an "authentic" Jamaican identity in gendered and sexualized terms. Like all identities, "Jamaicaness" becomes defined in exclusive and oppositional terms—to be Jamaican, according to these artists, is to be a strong, virile, straight man. Noted legal scholar Angela Harris defines hypermasculinity as "a masculinity in which the strictures against femininity and homosexuality are especially intense and in which physical strength and aggressiveness are paramount" (Harris 2000, 793). Expanding from this point, and pushing this definition in a transnational direction, it can be understood that masculinity is an important conduit through which the nation is constructed. Thus, the strictures against femininity and homosexuality take on added fervency during the exercise of post-colonial nation-building.

Furthering this point, Alexander has noted that "citizenship . . . continues to be premised within heterosexuality and principally within heteromasculinity" (1994, 7). In the post-colonial transnational context, the contentious relationship between metropole and subaltern takes on a defiant tone as the colonized seek to exert power in ways that mattered to the former governors—masculinity thus comes to the fore, but ironically on the reified terms of the former colonizer. As such, "nations have been historically constituted in gendered and sexualized terms" (Stychin 1998, 7). Nations have also been constructed in racialized ways and are internationally classed and ordered (Stolzoff 2000, 8). It should not be surprising that these constructs appear not only in the legal texts, as referenced in the first part of the chapter, but also in the lyrics, as cited below.

For instance, these intersecting identity constructs—nation, gender, race, and sexuality—are simultaneously doing work in dancehall artist Sizzla's x-rated song *Nah Apologize:*

> Girls dem sexy, and dem p[u]ssy fat
> Yeah all di girls, di boys dem looking at
> Some bwoy bow down, BOW DOWN DOIN WHAT!
> Nothing in this world could never have mi doin dat
> I dont care if dem ban mi
> Cause mi seh fi bun b[a]ttyman yuh caan wrong mi
> Yo mi nuh born ova England a real African this
> Real real real Rastaman this, BOOM!!!!
> Chorus:
> Rastaman dont apologize to no b[a]ttybwoy
> Yuh diss black people then mi gun a shot yuh bwoy
> Gimme di whole a di girls cause a dem have up di joy
> Inna di Lake of fire mi dash yuh bwoy
> Rrrrrrrr!!!! We apologize to no b[a]ttybwoy
> Diss King Selassie then mi gun will shot yuh bwoy
> Inna di Lake of fire mi dash yuh, AH HOY!!!!
> Gimme di girls because a dem have up di joy
>
> Gwaan like dem smart gwaan like dem crotty
> Shoot dem inna dem head dem too, f[u]c[k]in nasty
> Di gal dem have di p[u]s[s]y and di stiff titty and di cute face
> And di bwoy dem walk pass it
> Damn its di lyrical praise, diss a we mek dem fret

Inna di Biblical days we used to stone dem to death
WHOA! Di sexy girls dem mi sex
a weh mi seh bun b[a]ttyman dont vex, damn![3]

Sizzla, a dancehall artist who also has many spiritual songs, or what might be dubbed "conscious reggae" (Rommen 2006; Lipsitz 1999), excoriates gay men in *Nah Apologize*. He is nonchalant about the possibility of being banned on the airwaves (I don't care if dem ban mi) and, like fellow dancehall artist Elephant Man,[4] Sizzla insists that gay men should be burned (Cause me seh fi bun battyman yuh caan wrong mi) or stoned based on religious grounds (inna de Biblical days we used to stone dem to death).

Betraying the dynamic connection between sexism and homophobia, Sizzla additionally chastises gay men for their lack of appreciation of women as sex objects (Di gal have di pussy and di stiff titty and di cute face, And di bwoy walk pass it). Nodding to pride of race, Sizzla situates himself as authentically black and refuses to apologize for his obvious homophobia in the most violent of terms (Rastaman don't apologize to no battybwoy, Yuh diss black people then mi gun a shot yuh bwoy). According to this logic, homosexuality is cast as white and un-Jamaican—it is situated as the foreign imposition to be eliminated in a post-colonial Jamaica. Implicit in such lyrics are an indigeneity claim that is made more explicitly elsewhere in his lyrics. If one accepts that "the relationship between the national and the global . . . is multidimensional" (Stychin 1998, 6), Sizzla's premise that homosexuality is abnormal and alien is the outgrowth of the hyper-heteromasculinist nation-building exercise.

As Jamaica has sought to extricate itself from its colonial past, it has paradoxically seized upon colonial edicts of appropriate behavior and integrity. Like the law, dancehall has become a cultural regulator of identity boundaries along the lines of race, sexuality, and gender. Certainly in Jamaica, "these are the boundaries around which power coheres" (Alexander 1994, 1). Social theorist Carl Stychin notes that notions of "normalcy" for newly independent nations play out through a post-colonial fixing of gender relations. Specifically, "anything that could be construed as undermining that fixity was construed as the nation's other" (Stychin 1998, 9).

As mentioned above, identity constructs "are contingent upon an oppositional framework," which is exclusive of antagonistic identities (Nelson 2008, 247). In this way, Sizzla's lyrics are in keeping with this irony, situate homosexuality as foreign, specifically English, and further fix himself, and other Rastas, as African, and thus heterosexual. (Yo mi nuh born ova England a real African this; Real real real Rastaman this, BOOM.)

Even more directly, popular dancehall artist Beenie Man sings in one song, "I'm dreaming of a new Jamaica, come to execute all the gays" (Younge 2006). In doing so, he flatly exposes his heterosexual construction of post-colonial Jamaican nationhood. Thus dichotomously defined, homosexuality becomes oppositional to Jamaican masculinity—it becomes a threat to the nation itself. But such an explicit homophobic stance, even if made explicit internationally only through music, was bound to have transnational implications.

Even with Music: The Transnational as Inevitably Political

This musical denunciation has produced a contestation of international import (Mills 2006; Sanneh 2007). Interestingly, the misogyny in dancehall has not met with international condemnation. Only the homophobic lyrics have attracted international attention. Only this, admittedly abhorrent, construction of Jamaican masculinity as hyper-heteromasculine has attracted the attention of activists and agitators alike—their intervention represents a masculinity clash in the global arena. It brings to the fore the international response of condemnation to this Jamaican "nationalist project" (Younge 2006). While the construction of masculinity is situated within a field of competing identity concerns, there has been a national prioritizing of gender, *qua* masculinity, over race, sexuality, and class. As Philip Dayle, the Jamaica legal officer at the International Commission of Jurors, has commented, "In Jamaica nationalism trumps sexual orientation and race trumps sexual orientation. So when faced with nationalism and race together, issues of sexual orientation don't stand a chance" (ibid.).

Seemingly, there can exist no hyphenated gay-Jamaican citizen—that intersection is erased as existing only outside of the national geopolitical space that is Jamaica. Of course politicians have also contributed to this exclusive discourse, labeling the promotion of same-sex equality in Jamaica as foreign meddling about foreign issues. Indeed, the information minister, Senator Burchell Whiteman, stated, "We are certainly not about to respond to any organisation external to this country that may want to dictate to us how and when to deal with the laws of our land" (ibid.). Then Prime Minister P. J. Patterson went further, personalizing the debate by taking offense at the possible relaxing of anti-gay laws by his government. He stated on a live radio program, "My credentials as a life-long heterosexual person are impeccable" (Davis 2001). Present Prime Minister Bruce Golding, while being interviewed on a BBC television program, conceded that gays and lesbians would form no part of his Cabinet, thus effectively excluding GLBT populations from a powerful means of political empowerment (BBC News 2008). It would seem that there is one thing, therefore, that the prime minister of Jamaica, others in his government, Sizzla, TOK, and other dancehall artists have in common. Despite their differences in class, color, and politics, they are bound by their adherence to a nationalist project that is hyper-heteromasculine.

A Conclusion of Colonial Circularity

This dialogue reveals the truism that "'homosexual' difference is indispensable to the creation of the putative heterosexual norm" (Alexander 1994, 6). This is not surprising as, "the social relations of dancehall productions are to a great extent structured by the same social variables found in Jamaica's national economy: massive exploitation, racism, sexism, homophobia, and violence" (Stolzoff 2000, 8). But this chapter argues that dancehall is replicating imposed colonial legal norms of homophobia, or at least further embedding those sentiments.

It goes without saying that the sodomy laws are archaic, a disgrace, and should, therefore, be repealed as repugnant to sexual equality and human rights norms. In many ways, however, that would be the easy bit. Like no other social force in Jamaica, dancehall is a cultural regulator of identity with more reach than the church, the education system, the government, and even the legal system.

One of the central aims of this chapter was to interrogate and respond to this normative homophobia as indigeneity claim. It has attempted to re-source it as part and parcel of the colonial project. Homophobic dancehall music is an unfortunate manifestation of this oppressive past, and this connection to an imposed legal regime must be surfaced. To paraphrase Edward Said, in mapping the affiliations of this musical art form we can perceive its involvement in expanding empires (Said 1994, 7). Having surfaced this connection to the British Empire, the next step will be to see what, if any, effect this revelation might have on these artists, the dancehall musicians who so effectively contribute to the discourse around national identity. It is this chapter's hope that with increased dialogue and greater appreciation of the colonial insinuation of these homophobic norms into Jamaican culture and music, they might be more willing to reject the colonial legal edicts that have also become musically entrenched.

NOTES

Thanks to Rick Buckingham, Frank Rudy Cooper, Diane D'Angelo, and Ann C. McGinley.

1. In Jamaica, a "Dancehall" is any physical space where a sound system is set up to play music for listening and dancing. It need not be enclosed and is often a makeshift

outdoor space cordoned off at night featuring huge loudspeakers and DJs and selectors (not a DJ, as DJs have evolved to be toasters or rappers, but more the player of the music) on a stage. This project focuses on a second usage of the word "Dancehall": a genre of reggae music that has emerged post-roots rock reggae. Dancehall is a faster, more urban, gritty, form of reggae which is often laced with prerecorded rhythm tracks over which the DJ sings or raps in a "roughed-up" voice (Barrow and Dalton 2004; Bradley 2002).

2. For example, the lyrics to Vybz Kartel's *No Dutty Panty* [No Dirty Panties] include:

> If Yah Panty A Black Yuh Pum Pum Fat, If Yuh Panty
> A White Baby Di Pussy Tite, Yuh See If Yuh Cum Here
> Widout Underwear Yuh Ready Fi Suiddung Pan Buddy
> Like Chair, Yuh Panty A Brown Vagina Weigh A Pound
> If A Grey Yuh Nuh Sell Pussy Pre Paid But If Di Panty
> A Blue And Di Croaches A Pink A Infection Di Pussy
> Stink (Baby). (http://www.lyricskeeper.com/vybz_kartel-
> lyrics/225677-no_dutty_panty-lyrics.htm)Similarly, the
> lyrics to a song by Don Youth and Spagga state "Give me
> di naany now; wan di naany now; give me likkle naany,
> cho; why you a gwaan so; in di pum-pum business you
> haffi physically fit; you haffi love di gal make dem feel it."
> Stolzoff's footnotes to this section clarify that "naany is a
> shortened form of punaany, a Jamaican term for vagina that
> is roughly the equivalent of 'pussy' in American vernacular"
> and that "pum-pum is a synonym for punaany." Stolzoff
> calls this a "typical example of . . . romaticiz[ing] rough sex"
> (Stolzoff 2000, 214, 271).

3. *Nah Apologize* lyrics, available at http://www.allthelyrics.com/song/809968/ (last visited Nov. 17, 2010). Loosely translated, the lyrics are:

> The girls, they are sexy and their pussies are fat
> Yes all the girls the boys are looking at
> Some boys bow down [alternatively meaning perform oral
> sex or render themselves subservient)], doing what!
> Nothing in this world could ever make me do that
> I don't care if they ban me
> Because if you burn faggots that's not wrong with me
> Yo, I wasn't born in England, I'm a real African
> I am a real real real Rastaman, boom!
>
> Chorus:
> Rastamen don't apologize to any faggots
> Because if you disrespect black people then I am going to
> shoot you boy
> Give me all the girls because they're the source of joy
> Into the lake of fire is where I will dash you boy
> Rrrrrrr!!! We do not apologize to any faggots
> If you disrespect King Selassie then I will shoot you boy
> Into the lake of fire is where I will dash you ahoy!

Give me all the girls because they're the source of joy

They act like they're smart…
Shoot them in their heads as they are too nasty
The girls have the pussy and the stiff breasts and the cute
faces
Yet these boys walk past it
Damn it's the lyrical praise that it what makes them fret
In the biblical days we used to stone them to death
Whoa! It's the sexy girls who I have sex with
I say burn faggots don't vex damn!

4. Elephant Man's song *Log On* is described as "a dance with foot motion as if squashing a cockroach—the lyrics boast about crushing gay men" (Human Rights Watch 2004, 78–79). See http://www.youtube.com/watch?v=sz8WydzXePI (last visited Nov. 17, 2010).

REFERENCES

Alexander, M. Jacqui. 1994. Not Just (Any)*Body* Can Be a Citizen: The Politics of Law, Sexuality and Postcoloniality in Trinidad and Tobago and the Bahamas. *Feminist Review* 48:5–23.

Barrow, Steve, and Peter Dalton. 2004. *The Rough Guide to Reggae*, 3d ed. London: Rough Guides.

BBC News. 2008. Interview with Bruce Golding. May 20. Available at http://www.youtube.com/watch?v=9cQx-zmHgg8.

Beyer, Jonathan A. 2000. The Second Line: Reconstructing the Jazz Metaphor in Critical Race Theory. *Georgetown Law Journal* 88:537–63.

Bracey, Christopher A. 2003. Adjudication, Antisubordination, and the Jazz Connection. *Alabama Law Review* 54:853–76.

Bradley, Lloyd. 2002. *Reggae: The Story of Jamaican Music*. London: BBC Worldwide.

Butler, Paul. 2009. *Let's Get Free: A Hip-Hop Theory of Justice*. New York: New Press.

———. 2004. Much Respect: Toward a Hip-Hop Theory of Punishment. *Stanford Law Review* 56:983–1016.

California State University, Sacramento. Office of Public Affairs. 2004. Chuck D to Present His "State of the Union." *Sacramento State News*, http://www.csus.edu/news/012004chuckD.stm, Jan. 20.

Central Intelligence Agency. 2010. *The World Factbook: Jamaica*, https://www.cia.gov/library/publications/the-world-factbook/geos/jm.html# (last visited Nov. 16, 2010).

Chase, Anthony. 1986. Toward a Legal Theory of Popular Culture. *Wisconsin Law Review* 1986:527–69.

Coates, Ta-Nehisi. 2003. Keepin' It Unreal: Selling the Myth of Black Male Violence, Long Past Its Expiration Date. *Village Voice*, June 3. Available at http://www.villagevoice.com/2003-06-03/news/keepin-it-unreal/.

Cooper, Carolyn. 2004. *Sound Clash: Jamaican Dancehall Culture at Large*. New York: Palgrave Macmillan.

———. 1995. *Noises in the Blood: Orality, Gender, and the "Vulgar" Body of Jamaican Popular Culture*. Durham, NC: Duke University Press.

Davis, Garwin. 2001. Homophobia Remains High: Gays Remain in Seclusion, Health Officials Worry Homophobia. *The Jamaica Gleaner*, http://www.jamaica-gleaner.com/pages/gay/homophobia.html, July 26.

Folami, Akilah N. 2007. From Habermas to "Get Rich or Die Tryin": Hip Hop, the Telecommunications Act of 1996, and the Black Public Sphere. *Michigan Journal of Race and Law* 12:235–304.

Goodchild, Seth. 1986. Twisted Sister, Washington Wives and the First Amendment: The Movement to Clamp Down on Rock Music. *Entertainment & Sports Law Journal* 2:131–97.

Harris, Angela P. 2000. Gender, Violence, Race, and Criminal Justice. *Stanford Law Review* 52:777–807.

Heaggans, Raphael. 2009. *The 21st Century Hip-Hop Minstrel Show: Are We Continuing the Blackface Tradition?* San Diego, CA: University Readers.

Henry, Roland. 2006. Jamaican Music is a Multi-billion Business, but Tax Avoidance High. *Jamaica Observer*, http://www.jamaicaobserver.com/news/97063_Jamaican-music-is-a-multi-billion-business—but-tax-avoidance-high, Jan. 22.

Human Rights Watch. 2004. *Hated to Death: Homophobia, Violence and Jamaica's HIV/AIDS Epidemic.* Available at http://www.hrw.org/sites/default/files/reports/jamaica1104.pdf.

Lawrence, Charles R., III. 1987. The Id, the Ego, and Equal Protection: Reckoning with Unconscious Racism. *Stanford Law Review* 39:317–88.

Lawrence v. Texas, 539 U.S. 558 (2003).

Lipsitz, George. 1999. World Cities and World Beat: Low-Wage Labor and Transnational Culture. *Pacific Historical Review* 68:213–31.

Lury, Alexis A. 1999. Time to Surrender: A Call for Understanding and the Re-evaluation of Heavy Metal Music within the Contexts of Legal Liability and Women. *Southern California Review of Law and Women's Studies* 9:155–91.

Luton, Daraine. 2009. Buggery Laws Firm—PM Says Life or 15 Years for Same-Sex Offence Breaches. *The Jamaica Gleaner*, http://www.jamaica-gleaner.com/gleaner/20090304/lead/lead1.html, March 4.

Mercer, Kobena. 1994. *Welcome to the Jungle: New Positions in Black Cultural Studies.* New York: Routledge.

Mills, Michael. 2006. Anti-Gay Violence Condoned. *Denver Post*, September 27.

Monroe, Irene. 2010. *Jamaica's Gay Underground Christians*, http://www.irenemonroe.com/2010/03/18/jamaica%e2%80%99s-gay-underground-christians/, March 18.

Moran, Leslie J. 1996. *The Homosexual(ity) of Law.* London: Routledge.

Nelson, Camille A. 2008. Lyrical Assault: Dancehall Versus the Cultural Imperialism of the North-West. *Southern California Interdisciplinary Law Journal* 17:231–78.

———. 2007. American Husbandry: Legal Norms Impacting the Production of (Re)Productivity. *Yale Journal of Law and Feminism* 19:1–48.

Offences against the Person Act (Jamaica). Available at http://www.moj.gov.jm/laws/statutes/Offences%20Against%20the%20Person%20Act.pdf (last visited Nov. 17, 2010).

Offences against the Person Act (Jamaica). 1953. *Laws of Jamaica*, Volume 6.

Padgett, Tim. 2006. The Most Homophobic Place on Earth? *Time*, April 12. Available at http://www.time.com/time/world/article/0,8599,1182991,00.html.

Patterson, Orlando. 2001. The Roots of Conflict in Jamaica. *New York Times*, July 23.

Perry, Imani. 2004. *Prophets of the Hood: Politics and Poetics in Hip Hop.* Durham, NC: Duke University Press.

Richmond, Michael L. 1998. Law and Popular Music: An Étude in Two Movements. *Legal Studies Forum* 22:79–97.

Rommen, Timothy. 2006. Protestant Vibrations? Reggae, Rastafari, and Conscious Evangelicals. *Popular Music* 25:235–63.

Ross, Andrew. 1998. *Real Love: In Pursuit of Cultural Justice.* New York: New York University Press.

Rutherford, Christian D. 2005. "Gangsta" Culture in a Policed State: The Crisis in Legal Ethics Formation amongst Hip-Hop Youth. *National Black Law Journal* 18:305–40.

Said, Edward. 1994. *Culture and Imperialism.* New York: Vintage Books.

Sanneh, Kelefa. 2007. Bring in the Reggae, Hold the Hate. *New York Times,* August 27.

Smith, Abbe. 2005. The Dignity and Humanity of Bruce Springsteen's Criminals. *Widener Law Journal* 14:787–835.

St. Lawrence, Janet S., and Doris J. Joyner. 1991. The Effects of Sexually Violent Rock Music on Males' Acceptance of Violence against Women. *Psychology of Women Quarterly* 15:49–63.

Stolzoff, Norman C. 2000. *Wake the Town and Tell the People: Dancehall Culture in Jamaica.* Durham, NC: Duke University Press.

Stychin, Carl F. 1998. *A Nation by Rights: National Cultures, Sexual Identity Politics, and the Discourse of Rights.* Philadelphia: Temple University Press.

Took, Kevin J., and David S. Weiss. 1994. The Relationship between Heavy Metal and Rap Music and Adolescent Turmoil: Real or Artifact? *Adolescence* 29:613–21.

Tribbett-Williams, Lori A. 2000. Saying Nothing, Talking Loud: Lil' Kim and Foxy Brown, Caricatures of African-American Womanhood. *Southern California Review of Law and Women's Studies* 10:167–207.

Weisstuch, Liza. 2005. Sexism in Rap Sparks Black Magazine to Say, "Enough!" *Christian Science Monitor,* January 12. Available at http://www.csmonitor.com/2005/0112/p11s01-almp.html.

Younge, Gary. 2006. Troubled Island. *The Guardian,* April 27. Available at http://www.guardian.co.uk/world/2006/apr/27/gayrights.comment.

13

Masculinities, Feminism, and the Turkish Headscarf Ban: Revisiting *Şahin v. Turkey*

VALORIE K. VOJDIK

Throughout history, the Islamic veil or headscarf has been a highly contested and politicized symbol, both in Muslim societies and the global political arena. Western colonialists seized upon the Islamic headscarf to symbolize the subordination of women under Islam, justifying colonial occupation as necessary to liberate women from the barbaric oppression of Muslim men. Following the events of 9/11 and the resulting "war on terror," the United States has employed images of Afghani women in dark burqas and face veils to both signify and demonize political Islam. Several European nations, including France, have either banned or considered banning the headscarf in schools, condemning the practice as the symbolic subordination of women that is incompatible with Western notions of gender equality (Scott 2007, 2–4).

The politics of the headscarf have been hotly disputed in Turkey, a secular democracy in which 99 percent of citizens are Muslim. In 1982, Turkey banned women from wearing headscarves for religious purposes in government offices and all universities, both public and private. Leyla Şahin, a female medical student suspended from the Istanbul University for wearing a headscarf, challenged the ban in the European Court of Human Rights (EHCR), alleging that it violated her right to religious freedom and education guaranteed by the European Convention on Human Rights. In 2005, the Grand Chamber of the ECHR rejected her claims, holding that the ban was a necessary and reasonable response to the alleged threat posed by fundamentalist Islam to Turkey's secular democracy (Şahin v. Turkey 2007, 129). The ECHR ignored the gendered nature of the ban, which denies to practicing and covered Muslim women, but not Muslim men, access to a university education. Applying a wide margin of appreciation, the ECHR accepted Turkey's unsupported assertion that the headscarf is a proxy for radical, political Islam and a threat to its secular democracy. Although Leyla Şahin testified that she supported secularism and freely chose to wear the headscarf for religious reasons, the ECHR instead criticized the headscarf as a "powerful external symbol" that appeared to be imposed on women by Islam, a religion that subordinates women (Şahin v. Turkey 2007, 127). The ECHR assumed that Şahin and other covered female students were the passive pawns of radical Islam rather than autonomous or political actors.

Masculinities theory offers a critical lens through which to reconsider the headscarf debate in Turkey. Feminist theorists have argued that women's bodies historically have been used as symbolic sites for struggles over political, national, and other collective identities (Yuval-Davis 1997, 39–67). Masculinities theory provides a useful tool to examine the means through which power is negotiated by and between competing masculinities—at the local, national, and transnational levels (Connell 2005, 71–89). By focusing on the relationships between the headscarf and masculinized power, masculinities theory makes visible the role of the headscarf in constructing relations between men and women, Turkish secular elites and religious leaders, and the West and Islam.

As a regulatory practice, the Turkish headscarf ban employs women's bodies as the site to construct and contest not only local gender relations, but also competing nationalist and global masculinities. As this chapter argues, the headscarf in Turkey constructs boundaries of identity and difference—boundaries between men and women, between Turkish secular elites and political Islamic leaders, and between the global West and transnational Islam. Both secular and Islamist political parties have used the headscarf, and the regulation of women's bodies, to embody competing notions of the Turkish state and national identity (Çinar 2005, 74). As Şahin demonstrates, the struggle between local masculinities in Turkey intersects with the global geopolitical struggle between Western and Islamic masculinities. In upholding the headscarf ban, the ECHR reinvokes Western and Orientalist narratives, constructing the headscarf as a symbol of women's subordination under Islam. Şahin essentializes Islam, condemning Islamic gender relations as incompatible with European notions of gender equality. The discursive use of women's bodies in Şahin, therefore, illustrates the interaction between local struggles over competing masculinities, on the one hand, and global masculinities, on the other hand.

While the political leaders of secularism and Islamism in Turkey are male, women have played an active and constitutive role in the headscarf debate. As Turkish scholar Nilüfer Göle argues, in Turkey, "veiling is the most salient emblem and women the newest actors of contemporary Islamism" (1996, 1). Research suggests that a certain group of women—young, urban, and typically the daughters of migrants from the rural periphery—deliberately embraced the headscarf, challenging the secular elites as a political matter. Many of these women have framed their opposition to the ban within a human rights discourse that demands the individual right to religious expression within Turkey's secular democracy (Onar 2007). Their opposition to the ban disrupts the masculinist construction of the secular elites as the powerful and heroic saviors of women, while simultaneously undercutting the masculinist construction of Islamic political leaders as the protector of women's modesty and honor (Göle 1996, 22). Women's participation in the headscarf debate shifts the semiotics of veiling and challenges the masculinist construction of gender relations in Turkey, even as these Muslim women remain invisible in Şahin and much of the debate over veiling in the West.

Şahin v. Turkey: The Headscarf Ban in the ECHR

In Turkey, approximately 70 percent of Turkish Muslim women cover their heads, a percentage that varies widely depending on region and class. Sura XXIV, Verse 31 of the Qu'ran is read to require Muslim women to "lower their gaze and guard . . . their modesty," and not display or draw attention to "their beauty and ornaments," and "draw their veils over their bosoms and not display their beauty" except to their husbands, fathers, sons, and other specified relatives, slaves, and children (*The Holy Quran* 1987, 904–5). The Qu'ran, however, does not mandate any more specific types of dress. *Fikih*, the books of law, prescribe the manner of veiling, requiring that the hair, head, and neck be covered (called *hijab* in Arabic) and a long cloak or dress be worn loosely over clothes (*jilbab*) (Göle 1996, 93). Islamic scholars and feminists, however, debate whether women must cover their heads and, if so, the specific manner of covering.

The practice of covering is not fixed or universal but varies across time, place, class, and religious interpretations. Veiling appears in different forms, in different places, at different times, and its meanings are both fluid and multiple. Post-9/11, Western media broadcast images of Afghan women in dark *burqas* that completely covered their bodies, face, and even eyes. This particular form of cover was mandated by the Taliban in Afghanistan and is not typical. In Turkey, Muslim women wear multiple forms of cover, ranging from simple headscarves in rural areas to "Islamic high couture" debuted on the catwalk at fashion shows in Istanbul. Only 3 percent of women wear the *carsaf*, a long cloak-type garment worn with a headscarf and a face veil (*niqab*) (Secor 2005, 207–8). Headscarves in Turkey are not typically black but more often brightly colored, in different patterns, designs, and fabrics. While some women also wear the *jilbab*, a loose garment that covers the body, many do not. Younger women in Istanbul can be seen wearing a brightly colored headscarf, stylishly tied close to the head and neck, with tight jeans and high heels or sneakers. In rural areas, many women wear very loose pants and tops with a headscarf tied simply under the chin.

State regulation of veiling also differs widely. While Iran, a Muslim-majority nation, mandates veiling, Turkey, a predominantly Muslim and secular democratic state, bans women from wearing the headscarf in educational institutions and government offices (Zahedi 2007, 88–89, 94–95; Human Rights Watch 2008). The United States generally protects a woman's choice to wear Islamic attire, while France recently banned girls in primary and secondary schools from wearing the headscarf. While the French ban prohibits "conspicuous religious symbols," it was intended primarily to prohibit the Islamic headscarf (Scott 2007, 1–2). Other European nations, including Belgium and Great Britain, recently have banned or considered banning the headscarf or face veil. Many of the state regulations shift over time. In Iran, for example, the Shah Reza in 1932 banned the headscarf as part of his campaign to Westernize the nation. Following the Iranian Revolution in 1979, the government reversed itself and distanced itself from the West, in part by making it a crime for women to appear in public without wearing *hijab* (El Guindi 1999, 174–76).

State regulation of veiling in Turkey similarly has changed over time. The Ottoman Empire, which incorporated Islamic law, issued various decrees requiring veiling and prohibiting certain forms of attire for women that were considered inconsistent with Islam. In 1923, Mustafa Kemal, known as "Atatürk," established the Turkish Republic as a secular democratic state. He instituted a number of reforms that sought to privatize Islam and replace it with Westernized culture. To Atatürk, veiling by Muslim women was "backward" and incompatible with a modern, Western society. While the new republic did not issue a national ban on veiling, Atatürk and his followers ("Kemalists") urged its removal, and many local authorities prohibited the practice (Göle 1996, 73; Çinar 2005, 59, 62–64).

Despite the state's efforts, the headscarf did not disappear, particularly in rural areas. Among rural women who covered, many wore the başörtüsü, a traditional headscarf tied at the neck that loosely covered the head, like many non-Muslim rural women in Greece and Eastern Europe. As rural Muslims began to migrate from the periphery to Istanbul and other urban areas, a growing working and middle class began to emerge in the urban center. Younger women began to appear in public spaces, such as universities, wearing a new form of Islamic cover, called the türban, which was a larger scarf, deliberately arranged to fully cover the hair, neck, and bosom, along with a long, loose-fitting overcoat (Çinar 2005, 78). At the same time, Islamic political parties in Turkey, Iran, and elsewhere were on the rise. Perceiving the türban as a symbol of radical political Islam, Turkey imposed a ban on the wearing of headscarves in universities and public offices in 1982 (ibid. 75, 78–83).

The headscarf ban immediately became a flashpoint for conflict during the mid-1980s between secularists and Islamists in Turkey, particularly in universities, which became the site for the confrontation between Islamists and secular elites. In the mid-1980s, female university students in Istanbul began challenging the ban, arguing that it violated their right to religious freedom. Emerging as new political actors, these young women participated in protests and demonstrations at universities and hunger strikes to persuade state officials to eliminate the ban. In response to the protests, the Higher Education Council twice removed restrictions on wearing the headscarf, in 1989 and 1991. The Turkish Constitutional Court, however, annulled both repeal attempts, holding on March 7, 1989, that secularism was an essential condition for democracy and that, "in a secular regime, religion is shielded from a political role" (Anayasa Mahkemesi 1989, 25). The Court described the act of wearing the headscarf as the "display of a pre-modern image" and a tool of segregation that violated the principles of secularism and threatened the Turkish Republic (Anayasa Mahkemesi 1989; Çinar 2005, 83).

Despite the decision, women and conservative Islamic political parties continued to agitate for repeal of the ban, fueling secular concern that student activism demonstrated the threat of political Islamic parties to Turkey's secular democracy. In 1998, Leyla Şahin, a female medical student, challenged the ban in the ECHR. Şahin was denied access to examinations because she wore a headscarf and later suspended for protesting the headscarf ban. Because she wore a headscarf, Şahin effectively was barred from attending medical school in Turkey. She left to pursue her medical education in Vienna, where she could wear her headscarf while attending medical school. Before the ECHR, Şahin alleged that the ban violated her right to religious freedom under Article 9 of the European Convention on Human Rights (the "Convention") which guarantees a person the freedom to manifest her "religion or belief, in worship, teaching, practice and observance" (Convention for the Protection of Human Rights and Fundamental Freedoms 1950, art. 9, sec. 1). She further argued that the ban violated the right to education guaranteed to all persons under Article 19 of the Convention (ibid., art. 19), as well as Article 8 and Article 2 of Protocol No. 1 to the Convention (Protocol to the Convention for the Protection of Human Rights and Fundamental Freedoms 1952, art. 2, art. 8).

In 2005, the Grand Chamber of the ECHR affirmed the earlier decision of the Chamber of the Court, holding that the Turkish ban on headscarves did not violate the European Convention on Human Rights (*Şahin v. Turkey* 2007, 138). The Grand Chamber conceded that the ban violated Şahin's right to religious expression, but held that the right of religious freedom under Article 9 is not absolute. Instead, Article 9 provides that states may impose "such limitations as are prescribed by law and are necessary in a democratic society in the interests of public safety, for the protection of public order, health or morals, or for the protection of the rights and freedoms of others" (Convention for the Protection of Human Rights and Fundamental Freedoms 1950, art. 9, sec. 2). The ECHR held that, under the limitations clause, a state may restrict the freedom to manifest one's religion or belief where necessary to ensure the protection of the religious beliefs of all citizens. The Grand Chamber also rejected Şahin's argument that the ban violated her right to education guaranteed by Article 2 of the Protocol. While the Court recognized the importance of the right to education, it held that this right is not absolute and is subject to regulation by the State. The Court reasoned that the restriction was foreseeable to those concerned and was enacted through the legitimate aims of protecting the rights and freedoms of others and maintaining public order.

In determining whether the headscarf ban in Turkey was a necessary limitation on the right to religious expression, the ECHR afforded a "margin of appreciation" to the Turkish Republic, deferring to the judgment of Turkish Constitutional Court and state officials as to the alleged threat the headscarf posed to its secular democracy (*Şahin v. Turkey* 2007, 130; see also 126–30). The margin of appreciation arises where questions concerning the relationship between State and religions are at stake under the Convention, on which opinion in a democratic society may reasonably differ widely. In these cases, the ECHR has held that the role of the national decision-making body must be given special importance. In Şahin, the ECHR surveyed the legal regulation of the Islamic headscarf in schools in Europe to determine whether there was a difference of opinion among the nations. No other European nation banned headscarves (or other religious symbols) from universities. The Court specifically noted that France in 2004 adopted legislation banning the Islamic headscarf in primary and secondary schools (ibid. 116). The Court, however, ignored that the French ban did not apply to universities and, as Şahin correctly argued, that no European nation had issued such a ban in higher education.

Rather than conclude that there was not a history of banning religious expression in universities, the ECHR shifted its focus to the broader issue of state regulation of religion. The Court stated that such rules will vary by country according to national traditions and the need to protect the rights and freedoms of others and to maintain public order. In upholding the ban as a necessary limitation on religious freedom, the ECHR emphasized the existence of "extremist political movements" in Turkey, which it described generally as Islamic political groups which "seek to impose their religious symbols and a conception of a society founded on religious precepts" (ibid. 128). Within this context, the Court held that it was understandable that Turkish authorities should ban the headscarf to preserve secularism and to protect the values of pluralism, respect for the rights of others who do not veil, and gender equality.

The ECHR in Şahin also focused on the supposed tension between the right to gender equality and secularism and the Islamic faith. According to the ECHR, the headscarf was an "external symbol" that "appeared to be imposed on women by a religious precept that was hard to reconcile with the principle of gender equality" (ibid. 127). In upholding the ban, the ECHR emphasized that the right of gender equality was a fundamental principle of the European Convention and also guaranteed by the Turkish Constitution. While claiming to advance the right of gender equality, the Grand Chamber ignored the gendered nature of the ban, which denies to practicing and covered Muslim women, but not Muslim men, access to a university education.

The Grand Chamber in Şahin defers to the opinions of the Turkish Constitutional Court and the Republic in conceptualizing Islamic attire as a radical threat to secular democracy. In so doing, the decision does not critically question Turkey's categorization of political Islam as a fundamentalist and radical movement aiming to destroy democracy. By conflating the veil with radical Islam, and assuming that women are political or religious pawns, the ECHR erased Islamic women as active agents and political participants from the debate. Despite the fact that Leyla Şahin supported secularism and wore the headscarf for religious reasons, the ECHR assumed that she and other covered female students were the passive pawns of radical Islam rather than autonomous or political actors. In her dissent to the Grand Chamber opinion, Judge Tulkens observed that the judgment ignored Şahin's argument that she covered "of her own free will" and there was not any evidence that she held fundamentalist views (ibid. 143). Judge Tulkens emphasized that not all women who wear the headscarf are fundamentalists.

Şahin did not end the headscarf debate. In Turkey, the ECHR decision was widely criticized as racist and anti-Muslim. In 2007, the Justice and Development Party ("AKP"), a moderate Islamist political party, won 47 percent of the popular vote in national elections. The AKP sought to challenge the headscarf ban, not as a matter of religion but as a violation of basic rights. With its support, in 2008 the Turkish parliament voted to amend the Turkish Constitution to repeal the ban on headscarves. These amendments were immediately challenged by the secularist party ("CHP"). The Turkish Constitutional Court subsequently voted 9–2 that the constitutional amendments ending the ban were unlawful on the grounds that they violated the constitutional principle of secularism.

Masculinities Theory: Shifting the Frame from Individual Rights to the Masculinities of Identity

Neither the Şahin decision nor the rights-based critique engages sufficiently with the history of the headscarf as a political symbol in Turkey or the role of women's bodies in the struggle for national identity. As feminists have explained, the bodies of women historically have been used as symbolic sites for struggles over ethnic, political, and national identity. Rather than conceptualize the headscarf debate as an issue of individual rights, masculinities theory offers a methodology to understand veiling as a gendered practice that constructs masculinity, the nation, and global relations of power. Seen through the lens of masculinity and feminist theory, the bodies of Turkish women have been symbolic sites for political struggles in Turkey and in the global community. The Turkish headscarf ban functions as a regulatory practice that employs women's bodies as the site to construct and contest competing nationalist masculinities—during the Ottoman Empire, the subsequent creation of the Turkish Republic, and the present struggle between secularists and Islamists.

Like feminist theory, masculinities theory assumes that gender is a social practice constructed by and between men and women as well as within particular social institutions, including the workplace and the state. Men and masculinities are not fixed or unitary but rather multiple and fluid, "across time (history) and space (cultures), within societies, and through life courses and biographies" (Connell, Hearn, and Kimmel 2005, 3). Masculinities theorists have produced ethnographic studies of particular masculinities within specific sociohistorical places, providing a richly textured analysis of process through which gender is constructed (Connell 2005, 71). Theorists such as Connell and Kimmel have demonstrated that men and masculinities are not formed by gender alone but also through social structures including class, ethnicity, racialization, the nation, and globalization (Connell 1995, 75; Kimmel 2005, 414–15). This work reveals the dynamic relationship between masculinities, social institutions, and power.

Masculinities theory provides a critical tool for examining gender in relation to structures of power within the state, the nation, and the world order. According to social scientist R. W. Connell, gender is one means of structuring social practice that necessarily interacts with other social practices such as race, class, nationality, and position within the world order (1995, 75). Masculinities theory provides a complex understanding of the concrete ways in which power is negotiated in society, focusing on the construction of masculinity in particular times and spaces. Like feminist theories, masculinities theory has shifted the focus from individual gender differences to socially constructed gender relations (ibid. 67–76). The methodology has been primarily ethnographic, focusing on the particular processes of construction of masculinity in local sites (Connell 2005, 71).

Moving beyond ethnographic studies of the local, Kimmel and others have focused on the historical and cultural constructions of masculinity and gender within nations and larger societies. Masculinity theorists have asked critical questions about the gendered nature of political struggle between competing groups of men over national identity and state formation. Masculinities theorists have begun to focus on the relationship between local constructions of masculinity and the broader geopolitical order. Kimmel, for example, analyzes the impact of globalization on national and local masculinities (2005, 414). Connell examines the historical relationship between imperialism, colonialism, and globalization on the one hand, and local societies on the other (2005, 72).

The politics of the veil throughout history exemplifies this relationship between globalizing and local masculinities. Feminists have long recognized that gender, and women's bodies in particular, have been used to demarcate the boundaries of collective identities. The female body symbolizes and embodies the nation, serving as the symbolic border guard of national, ethnic, and state collectivities. Women's bodies become the visible marker of ethnic and national difference, and the symbol of national or collective honor. Throughout history, veiling has been used to control women's bodies as a means to construct competing national, ethnic, religious, and political identities. As feminist geographer Anna Secor writes, "veiling is an embodied spatial practice through which women are inserted into relations of power in society" (2005, 204).

Masculinities theory offers a helpful tool to analyze the use of veiling as a regulatory practice as a means to construct collective identities and power in particular social locations. Masculinity historically has been a powerful hegemonic force in constructing nationalism. Both the nation and the military are quintessential sites for the construction and performance of competing masculinities. As Caroline Nagel argues, the politics of the veil in Islamic societies, and the politicization of women's bodies, are examples of the assertion of masculinity and nationalism through the control of women's bodies (2005, 405).

The Ottoman Empire, relying on Islamic law, regulated women's veiling and attire, as well as their presence in the public sphere. Islamic clothing rules historically were based on the differentiation and segregation of the sexes. As Göle argues, "veiling represents femininity, which is hidden from view, while the beard represents a man's masculinity" (1996, 93–94). These rules in turn constructed and preserved the segregation of the sexes within the home and private world, or *mahrem*, as well as the public sphere. The Islamic social system exercises control over women's sexuality and segregation of the sexes, both of which are fundamental aspects of many Islamic masculinities. Within the Islamic social order, veiling maintained the boundaries of separation between the sexes and sought to preserve order in the community.

Western colonial and imperialist powers seized upon the veil as the most visible symbol that marked Islam societies and Muslims as inherently different, backward, and inferior. As Leila Ahmed explains, Islamic practices with respect to women evidenced the essential otherness and inferiority of Islam (1992). Colonialism constructed the narrative of the veil as a means of oppression and degradation of women, a practice that the West decried as symbolizing the barbarism and backwardness of Muslim societies. At the same time, colonial hegemonic masculinity constructed itself as the enlightened and heroic savior of Islamic women, the powerful rescuer of the female victims of the culturally and racially inferior Islamic men. Western and colonial masculinities thus justified the economic and political domination of Muslim societies through the veil, which symbolized the barbaric "Otherness" of Islam societies that must be conquered, both symbolically and literally.

Western colonial masculinities profoundly threatened the honor and power of local Muslim masculinities (Gerami 2005). In response, local Muslim leaders condemned Western criticism of veiling practices, reclaiming the headscarf as a symbol of community honor that required their protection. Women's honor no longer symbolized the honor of a particular clan or tribe; instead it became a symbol of national honor (ibid.). Women's bodies thus became the site for the battle between Western colonialists and Islamic communities and nation-states.

While Turkey was not a part of the colonial world, secularists and Islamists in Turkey have similarly used the female body and the headscarf to construct and embody competing national and political identities (Çinar 2005, 59). Mustafa Kemal Atatürk, called Atatürk, or "father of the nation," led the Turkish National Movement in the Turkish War of Independence, defeated the Allies, and founded the Turkish Republic in 1923. Atatürk came to power as the heroic military leader and renowned father of the Republic. Under his leadership, the new Turkish Republic immediately sought to distance itself from the Ottoman state, invoking the European colonialist argument that blamed Islam for the decline of the empire. As the new leader of the Republic, he sought to transform and Westernize Turkey, both politically and culturally, in order to eliminate stereotypes of Turks as "backward" and "uncivilized" (Onar 2007).

Atatürk adopted policies and laws to remove religion from the public sphere. He eliminated the Ottoman sultanate and the caliphate, placing control over religion in the state. He also replaced the Ottoman Empire's Shari'a law (*seriat* in Turkish) with the Swiss family code, which banned polygamy and gave women equal rights to divorce and custody. Women were granted political rights, which subverted the traditional Ottoman and Islamist gender order (ibid.).

As the father of the new Republic, Atatürk embodied a masculinity that was modern, Western, and secular. As leader of the new Turkish Republic, Atatürk sought to replace the face of Islam with that of the West, transforming Turkey into a modernized nation. Clothing regulations played a key role in his modernizing project. In 1925, Turkey adopted the Hat Law, which banned men from wearing the fez and required male bureaucrats and civil servants instead to wear the (European) hat. In announcing the Hat Law, Atatürk embodied European style, addressing the public wearing a Western suit, tie, and top hat. The abolition of the fez and its replacement with the hat, he explained, was necessary to demonstrate that Turkey was "civilized and advanced" (Çinar 2005, 68–69). The uncovering of women through the elimination of the headscarf was a critical component of his campaign to create the new republic. As Göle succinctly observes, Atatürk sought to replace the face of Islam with the public faces of women who were modern and Western. Under his direction, the new Republic launched a public relations campaign to unveil women. Photographs of women lounging by the sea wearing Western bathing suits were circulated. Turkey conducted its first national beauty pageant in 1929, accompanied by calls from secularist elites for women to show that they met European standards of beauty. Women were urged to participate in pageants, showing off their bodies as part of their "national duty" so that Turkey could be represented at international competitions (Çinar 2005, 70–71). The movement to unveil women was part of the Kemalist campaign to create the "Ideal Woman," no longer oppressed by Ottoman-Islamic rule, but modern, emancipated, and fully visible in the public sphere as citizens (Göle 1996, 14).

The campaign included legal reforms adopted by Atatürk designed to replace Islamic traditional and hierarchal gender relations by adopting Western civil law. As Çinar argues, the unveiling of Muslim women "reset the boundaries of the public and the private, which in turn served the creation and institutionalization of a sense of secular, modern nationhood" (2005, 61). These reforms helped concretely improve the lives of urban elite women in the Turkish center, who not only began to adopt Westernized clothing but also have moved from the private realm of the *mahram* into the public work and political sphere (Göle 1996, 76; Onar 2007, 11).

In response to Atatürk's efforts, conservative Islamist political parties seized upon the headscarf to construct an identity of resistance. As the periphery began to migrate to urban areas, the conservative Islamist Refah Party also deployed women's bodies and the headscarf as the symbolic site of their nationalist project. The headscarf became the banner of the Refah Party and subsequently the symbol of political Islam in Turkey. As Göle observes, political Islam has made itself visible through the re-veiling of women, who serve as "the emblem of politicized Islam" (1996, 83). While the Refah Party ultimately was shut down by the Turkish Constitutional Court, debate over the symbolism of the headscarf continues. The AKP, while committed to secularism, has embraced the headscarf as a political issue, framing it within a human rights discourse that focuses on the rights of women to religious freedom. In response, secularists have continued to portray the headscarf as the embodiment of radical and political Islam, committed to the establishment of an Islamic state and the elimination of Turkish secularism.

Turkish Women and Covering: Negotiating Competing Masculinities

Although masculinities theory has focused primarily on relationships among men, it is critical to consider the role of women within its analysis of the social practice of gender. While secular and Islamic masculinities and political parties have used the headscarf to construct competing claims for national identity and power, women also have been active participants in this debate. The headscarf issue has divided women feminists in Turkey, with "Islamist feminists" and some secular feminists arguing that women have the right to religious freedom and individual choice, and many (but not all) secular feminists arguing that the re-veiling of women is part of a strategy to replace civil law with Shari'a and to mandate veiling as a repudiation of liberal values (Onar 2007, 16).

Western media has largely interpreted Islamic veiling as a symbol of the forced subordination of women who have no meaningful choice but to cover. Post-9/11, the image of the Islamic veil or headscarf has become a symbol of Islamic fundamentalism and radical political Islamism. Islamic covering practices similarly have come to symbolize a system of gender relations that are not merely patriarchal but deviant and incompatible with Western notions of gender equality. Muslim women who cover are not seen as autonomous agents but as oppressed victims. This interpretation, shared by some feminists, recently has been deployed by the EHCR in Şahin and some European governments to justify various bans on veiling.

The assumption that women who veil lack free choice, however, is disputed by many feminists and scholars in Turkey and throughout the Middle East. Research by many Turkish feminist scholars and sociologists suggests that the decision of the young university women to cover reflects a deliberate choice—a choice to embrace political Islam, to express their religious identity, and/or to challenge the secularist ban of religion in the public sphere. Many of the young women who chose to wear the *türban* in the 1980s chose to cover even though their mothers or grandmothers did not. Like Leyla Şahin, these were largely young, urban women whose families had moved from the periphery into the Turkish center. The headscarves that these young women wore (the *türban*) were different from the traditional headscarves worn by their mothers or rural women (Secor 2005, 207; Göle 1996, 90–91).

In *The Forbidden Modern*, Göle discusses her interviews with a diverse range of young women who she concludes have chosen to cover. For many of the university women, the headscarf is a political statement. Many of these women have chosen to cover not because they are perpetuating rural traditions, but because they have consciously chosen to adopt a different form of Islam, one based on the formal study of the Islamic texts. These women have rejected the traditional Turkish understanding of Islam held by their parents. Many (though not all) of these women have embraced *tessetur* as a political symbol and a rejection of secularist political parties in Turkey. (*Tessetur* is a form of dress worn by Muslim women in Turkey.) These young women, Göle argues, are not marginalized members of society but university students, intellectuals, and professionals in urban areas and the political center of Turkey (Göle 1996, 96).

Turkish scholar Yeşim Arat observes that many of these young women were part of the Islamist movement and deliberately chose to cover their heads in universities, which ironically made them even more visible (1998). Disputing that these women were Refah pawns, Arat argues that their decision to confront the secular authorities was an autonomous act of individual political resistance:

> In a polity where religion had traditionally been controlled by the state in the name of secularism, they stood for a criticism of this secular order. Independent of what their private individual reasons for covering the head might have been, they had to assume the responsibility for what they meant in this particular situation. As such, even though they might have acted in solidarity with members of their religious community, they were engaged in an act of individuation and political resistance as they confronted the gaze of the uncovered women who thought of them as different. (Arat 1998, 123)

The politicization of young, educated, and outspoken Turkish women who challenge the regulation of their bodies in the body politic disrupts the dominant and secular masculinity of the Turkish Republic as well as local Islamic masculinities. While Turkish secular elites and many in the West interpret veiling as a means to subordinate and segregate women in the private realm, the emergence of covered women in the public sphere shatters that image. As Göle explains, "the new public visibility of Muslim women, who are outspoken, militant, and educated, brings about a shift in the semiotics of veiling, which has long evoked the traditional, subservient domestic roles of Muslim women" (1996, 21). Through their choice to cover, Leyla Şahin and other young, educated women rejected their role as passive victim of Islamic oppression that has been used to rationalize the compulsory unveiling of women by the secular state. Yet by mobilizing within the political sphere to wear the headscarf, these young women also challenged the

Islamic masculinities that relegate women to a hidden and private *mahrem* (Göle 1996, 22).

Since the 1980s, a variety of styles of covering has emerged, featuring tighter, more form-fitting jackets and stylish raincoats that skim the body rather than hide it completely, smaller and beautifully colored headscarves, and fabrics in a range of beautiful colors, often stylishly coordinated so that the entire outfit matches. Contrary to Western media images of monotonously cloaked women, women who cover mingle freely with uncovered women, symbolizing the acceptance of choice with respect to covering. These newer, fashion-conscious styles of covering arguably do not conform to the requirements of classical Islam, which emphasizes that the purpose of the veil is to preserve modesty and to avoid drawing attention to the female body. As such, they do not represent a throwback to traditional Islam or resistance to modernity or even Westernization, as the Constitutional Court suggested. Instead, the new form of urban covering is decidedly modern—beautiful and self-consciously stylish, incorporating Western and international styles, and based on individual notions of fashion. The Internet is replete with videos of fashion shows from Turkey, Iran, and Saudi Arabia showing tall and lean women, headscarves fashionably tied close to their heads, in high heels and narrow overcoats and tunics walk down the catwalk to distinctively modern, synthesized Middle Eastern club music.

Islamic cover or hijab has become a profitable part of the fashion consumer market in Turkey and globally, marketed over the Internet and through global retail markets. This new version of *hijab* is popularly referred to as "Islamic haute couture" and is neither backward nor traditional. Many Islamic intellectuals have criticized this style of cover, arguing that it transforms the headscarf from a symbol of religious and political identity to a symbol of high fashion in upper-class society (Çinar 2005, 89–90). This internationalized and fashionable form of cover highlights the class and regional differences in covering practices in Turkey. Those women who adopt the more fashionable forms of cover distinguish themselves from the more traditional, rural, or low-income women who wear either the simple headscarf or the outdated long, light-colored raincoat.

Within this context, the act of covering becomes not merely a religious practice or duty, but an individuation of women, many of whom, as Göle argues, unveil and challenge traditional gender identities within Islam and the body politic. The new veiling by young, educated Turkish women appears to reflect the negotiation of their multiple identities as both Islamic and modern, political agents, religious women, and secular consumers in a globalized society. As Nora Onar argues, many of these women have framed the issue of the headscarf ban within Western human rights discourse, shifting the semiotics of the headscarf debate (2007, 4, 16–19; Arat 2001, 43). From a masculinities perspective, these young women can be seen to be actively participating in the construction of gender relations within Turkish society, rejecting the dichotomies between secularism and Islam, East and West, Turkish and cosmopolitan.

Revisiting Şahin: The Headscarf and Global Masculinities

The discursive use of women's bodies in Şahin exemplifies the relationship between local struggles among competing masculinities, and global geopolitical struggles between Islam and the West. The ECHR in Şahin reinvokes Orientalist narratives to justify the regulation of the bodies of Muslim women, limiting Leyla Şahin's right to religious expression to "emancipate" her from her supposed oppression under Islam. The Court frames the Turkish headscarf ban within the anti-Muslim discourse employed by colonialism to justify Western political domination of Islamic societies. In Şahin, the headscarf debate functions as a trope for the contemporary struggle between the West and Islam, between Western hegemonic masculinities and global Islamic masculinities.

The ECHR ignored the multiple meanings of the Islamic headscarf in Turkey, instead accepting Turkey's unsupported assertion that the headscarf symbolized radical political Islam and the subordination of women. While the Court found that the ban violated women's rights to religious expression, it did not require Turkey to prove that the presence of women in headscarves in university classrooms posed an actual or serious threat to its secular democracy. There was no evidence that Şahin's choice to cover caused any disruption or violence or forced any female student to wear the headscarf against her will. Rather than require Turkey to prove that the headscarf ban was necessary and reasonable, the ECHR chose to apply a wide margin of appreciation to the ban, even though no other European nation banned female university students from wearing the headscarf or engaging in other types of religious expression.

The ECHR decision essentializes both Islam and Muslim women like Leyla Şahin, resurrecting Western Orientalist narratives that construct Islam as the dangerous and uncivilized "Other" that oppresses Muslim women. The ECHR justifies the regulation of Muslim women's bodies as a means to emancipate them from Islam, which the ECHR criticized as incompatible with Western principles of gender equality. The Court's criticism of Islam, however, was unsupported by any evidence or analysis. Şahin testified that she freely chose to wear the headscarf because of her religious beliefs, which contradicts the Court's characterization of Islam as oppressing women. The ECHR ignored her uncontradicted testimony, concluding that the headscarf was a "powerful external symbol" that appeared to be imposed upon women by a religion "that was hard to reconcile with the principle of gender equality" (*Şahin v. Turkey* 2007, 127–29). The Court assumed, without evidence, that Şahin and the other university students who chose to wear headscarves were passive pawns of radical Islam, lacking the ability to reason or choose their beliefs.

The decision of the ECHR to defer to Turkey's secular elites effectively insulated the headscarf ban from meaningful review under the Convention, aligning the Turkish secular elites with the West against Islam. In upholding the headscarf ban under European human rights law, the ECHR reproduces colonialist narratives that construct Muslim women as passive victims, Muslim men as their barbaric oppressors, and European geopolitical powers as the heroic agents of women's emancipation. The debates in European nations that have adopted or considered adopting anti-headscarf legislation similarly have essentialized Islam and reinvoked colonialist narratives constructing the headscarf as a symbol of the subordination of women under Islam and the supposed threat posed by radical political Islam. The debates in Europe have occurred in the context of the post-9/11 world, which has been marked by growing anti-Muslim sentiment. While these local struggles are a part of the global struggle in the West over Islam, they also reflect the particular issues faced by nations dealing with an influx of Muslim immigrants at a time when globalization itself threatens to erode national identity.

Supporters of the 2004 ban on schoolgirls' wearing headscarves in France, for example, argued that the headscarf symbolized the subordination of women under Islam and conflicted with French notions of gender equality. In *The Politics of the Veil*, Joan Wallach Scott argues that the French headscarf debate has played out in the context of France's history of colonial domination of Algeria, as well as its difficulties dealing with an immigrant population, many of whom are Muslim and Algerian. The political debate over the Islamic veil reinvoked French colonialist narratives that depicted Islam and Muslims as a separate and inferior race, the barbaric "Other" that required civilization by force, if necessary. In this colonialist masculine narrative, French men are cast as the heroic warriors who rescue women from the oppression of Islam and Algerian Muslim men. Supporters of the ban, however, also include conservative and anti-immigration nationalists who have seized upon the headscarf as the symbolic site of the battle for French identity. As Scott argues, the Popular Front and others seek to preserve what they consider to be the "true" French identity against Muslims and North African immigrants (2007).

As in Turkey, the headscarf debate in France illustrates the dynamic relationship between local and global masculinities. In both nations, the headscarf and the bodies of Muslim women function as the site for the construction of highly contested local and global masculinities. Examining the headscarf debates through the lens of masculinity theory illuminates the reciprocal relationship between the construction of the state and gender relations. In both places, the headscarf constructs boundaries of identity and difference, through both local and global masculinities.

Conclusion

Masculinities theory enriches our understanding of veiling as a gendered practice that constructs masculinity, the nation, and global relations of power. The headscarf in Turkey constructs boundaries of identity and difference—between men and women, Turkish secular elites and political Islamic leaders, and the global West and transnational Islam. Atatürk sought to restructure Turkish gender relations to emancipate women and erase the boundaries between the public and private under Islam. The removal of the headscarf was critical to his goal of creating the Ideal Woman in the new Turkish Republic, one that was Western and modern. The bodies of women were fundamental to the establishment of a new national and Western identity. With the rise of Islamic political parties in the 1980s, male Islamic political leaders likewise used the headscarf as the site to mobilize political support for their political program.

The young Islamic university women who organized politically to challenge the headscarf ban—the Leyla Şahins of the 1980s and 1990s—refused to conform to the gendered expectations of either the secularists or the Islamists. Today, many young women continue to negotiate their religious beliefs with their sense of themselves as women in the public, and global, sphere. These women have participated in the construction of a rights-based discourse rooted in democratic and liberal notions of the individual, defining themselves as autonomous individuals and not merely members of the Islamic *umma*. Their political activism against the ban, and their use of an individual rights discourse, disrupt both secular and Islamic masculinities, and challenge the Orientalist assumptions reflected in the ECHR's analysis in *Şahin*.

REFERENCES

Ahmed, Leila. 1992. *Women and Gender in Islam*. New Haven, CT: Yale University Press.

Anayasa Mahkemesi [Constitutional Court]. 1989. *TC Resmi Gazete* [Official Gazette of Republic of Turkey], 1989, No. 20216. Esas. No. 1989/1 [Basis Number], Karar No. 1989/12 [Decision Number], Decision of March 7.

Arat, Yeşim. 2001. Group-Differentiated Rights and the Liberal Democratic State: Rethinking the Headscarf Controversy in Turkey. *New Perspectives on Turkey* 25:31–46.

——. 1998. Feminists, Islamists, and Political Change in Turkey. *Political Psychology* 19(1):117–31.

Çinar, Alev. 2005. *Modernity, Islam, and Secularism in Turkey*. Minneapolis: University of Minnesota Press.

Connell, R. W. 2005. Globalization, Imperialism, and Masculinities. In *Handbook of Studies on Men and Masculinities*, edited by Michael S. Kimmel, Jeff Hearn, and R. W. Connell. Thousand Oaks, CA: Sage, 71–89.

——. 1995. *Masculinities*. Berkeley: University of California Press.

Connell, R. W., Jeff Hearn, and Michael S. Kimmel. 2005. Introduction to *Handbook of Studies on Men and Masculinities*, edited by Michael S. Kimmel, Jeff Hearn, and R. W. Connell. Thousand Oaks, CA: Sage, 1–17.

Convention for the Protection of Human Rights and Fundamental Freedoms. 1950. *United Nations Treaty Series* 213:221.

El Guindi, Fadwa. 1999. *Veil: Modesty, Privacy, and Resistance*. Oxford, UK: Berg.

Gerami, Shahin. 2005. Islamist Masculinity and Muslim Masculinities. In *Handbook of Studies on Men and Masculinities*, edited by Michael S. Kimmel, Jeff Hearn, and R. W. Connell. Thousand Oaks, CA: Sage, 448–57.

Göle, Nilüfer. 1996. *The Forbidden Modern: Civilization and Veiling*. Ann Arbor: University of Michigan Press.

The Holy Quran. 1987. Translated by Abdullah Yusef Ali. New York: Tahrike Tarsile Qu'ran, Inc.

Human Rights Watch. 2008. Turkey: Constitutional Court Ruling Upholds Headscarf Ban, http://www.hrw.org/en/news/2008/06/05/turkey-constitutional-court-ruling-upholds-headscarf-ban.

Kimmell, Michael S. 2005. Globalization and Its Mal(e)contents: The Gendered Moral and Political Economy of Terrorism. In *Handbook of Studies on Men and Masculinities*, edited by Michael S. Kimmel, Jeff Hearn, and R. W. Connell. Thousand Oaks, CA: Sage, 414–31.

Nagel, Caroline. 2005. Introduction. In *Geographies of Muslim Women: Gender, Religion, and Space*, edited by Ghazi-Walid Falah and Caroline Nagel. New York: Guilford Press, 1–15.

Onar, Nora. 2007. Freedom of Religion v. Secularism?: Universal Rights, Turkish Islamism, and the Headscarf Ban. European & the Mediterrean Convergence, Conflicts & Crisis, Working Paper series, RAMSES Working Paper No. 8/07, 2007. Available at http://www.sant.ox.ac.uk/esc/ramses/onar.pdf.

Protocol to the Convention for the Protection of Human Rights and Fundamental Freedoms. 1952. *United Nations Treaty Series* 213:262.

Şahin v. Turkey. 2007. *European Human Rights Reports* 44:99 (decided November 10, 2005).

Scott, Joan Wallach. 2007. *The Politics of the Veil*. Princeton, NJ: Princeton University Press.

Secor, Anna. 2005. Islamism, Democracy, and the Political Production of the Headscarf Issue in Turkey. In *Geographies of Muslim Women: Gender, Religion, and Space*, edited by Ghazi-Walid Falah and Caroline Nagel. New York: Guilford Press, 203–25.

Yuval-Davis, Nira. 1997. *Gender & Nation*. London: SAGE Publications Ltd.

Zahedi, Ashraf. 2007. Contested Meaning of the Veil and Political Ideologies of Iranian Regimes. *Journal of Middle East Women's Studies* 3(3):75–98.

DEBORAH L. BRAKE is Distinguished Faculty Scholar and Professor of Law at the University of Pittsburgh School of Law. She is the author of *Getting in the Game: Title IX and the Women's Sports Revolution* (NYU Press, 2010).

KIM SHAYO BUCHANAN is Associate Professor of Law at the University of Southern California. Her research addresses race, gender, and the rule of law in men's and women's prisons.

NAOMI CAHN is the John Theodore Fey Research Professor of Law at George Washington University Law School. She is, most recently, co-author of *On the Frontlines: Gender, War, and the Post-Conflict Process* and *Red Families v. Blue Families: Legal Polarization and the Creation of Culture*, and author of *Test Tube Families: Why the Fertility Market Needs Legal Regulation* (NYU Press, 2009).

DEVON W. CARBADO is Professor of Law at the University of California, Los Angeles School of Law. His books include *Black Men on Race, Gender, and Sexuality: A Critical Reader* (NYU Press, 1999) and *Race Law Stories*.

ROBERT CHANG is Professor of Law, Associate Dean for Research and Faculty Development, and is the founding director of the Fred T. Korematsu Center for Law and Equality at Seattle University. He is the author of *Disoriented: Asian Americans, Law, and the Nation-State* (NYU Press, 1999).

DAVID S. COHEN is Associate Professor of Law at the Earle Mack School of Law at Drexel University. His scholarship focuses on gender, masculinity, and sex segregation.

FRANK RUDY COOPER is Professor of Law at Suffolk University Law School in Boston, Massachusetts. His research explores the intersections of race, gender, and class, especially with respect to policing and black masculinities.

NANCY E. DOWD is Professor and David Levin Chair in Family Law, and Director of the Center on Children and Families at the University of Florida Levin College of Law. Her recent publications include *Justice for Kids: Keeping Kids Out of the Juvenile Justice System* (NYU Press, 2011) and *The Man Question: Male Privilege and Subordination* (NYU Press, 2010).

DINA HAYNES is Professor of Law at New England Law School. She is co-author of *On the Frontlines: Gender, War, and the Post-Conflict Process*, and her research focuses on international human rights.

JOHN M. KANG is Professor of Law at St. Thomas University. His research focuses on masculinity and constitutional law.

MICHAEL KIMMEL is SUNY Distinguished Professor in the Sociology Department at Stony Brook University. His books include *The Gendered Society, Manhood in America: A Cultural History,* and *Guyland: The Perilous World Where Boys Become Men.*

NANCY LEVIT holds both a Curator's Professorship and the Edward D. Ellison Professorship at the University of Missouri-Kansas City School of Law. She is co-author of *The Happy Lawyer: Making a Good Life in the Law, Feminist Legal Theory: A Primer* (NYU Press, 2006), and *Jurisprudence— Classical and Contemporary,* and author of *The Gender Line: Men, Women, and the Law* (NYU Press, 1998).

ANN C. MCGINLEY is the William S. Boyd Professor of Law at the William S. Boyd School of Law of the University of Nevada, Las Vegas. A scholar in the area of employment discrimination and disability law, Professor McGinley is co-author of *Disability Law: Cases, Materials, Problems* (5th ed.). Her recent research focuses on masculinities theory and interpretation of employment discrimination law.

ATHENA D. MUTUA is Professor of Law at the University at Buffalo Law School. She is the editor of *Progressive Black Masculinities.*

CAMILLE A. NELSON is Dean and Professor of Law at Suffolk University Law School. Her research addresses the intersection of critical race theory and cultural studies with particular focus on criminal law and procedure, health law, and comparative law.

FIONNUALA NÍ AOLÁIN is concurrently the Dorsey and Whitney Chair in Law at the University of Minnesota Law School and a Professor of Law at the University of Ulster's Transitional Justice Institute in Belfast, Northern Ireland. She is co-author of *On the Frontlines: Gender, War, and the Post-Conflict Process* and author of *Law in Times of Crisis*.

LETICIA M. SAUCEDO is Professor of Law and Director of Clinical Legal Education at the University of California-Davis School of Law. Her research focuses on employment, labor, and immigration law.

VALORIE K. VOJDIK is Professor of Law and Director of Clinical Law Programs at the University of Tennessee College of Law in Knoxville. Her research focuses on the relationship between gender, the law, and social institutions, including the workplace, military, the nation and state, and global relations of power.